Implementing an
## ISO 9000-Based
Quality System

Raymond J. Murphy

**Government Institutes**
Rockville, Maryland

Government Institutes, Inc., 4 Research Place, Suite 200
Rockville, Maryland 20850, USA.
Phone: (301) 921-2300
Fax: (301) 921-0373
Email: giinfo@govinst.com
Internet address: http://www.govinst.com
Government Institutes, Inc., is an ABS Group Company: http://www.abs-group.com/main.htm

Copyright © 1998 by Government Institutes. All rights reserved.

02   01   00   99                5   4   3   2

No part of this work may be reproduced or transmitted in any form or by any means, electronic or mechanical, including photocopying, recording, or any information storage and retrieval system, without permission in writing from the publisher. All requests for permission to reproduce material from this work should be directed to Government Institutes, Inc., 4 Research Place, Rockville, Maryland 20850, USA.

The reader should not rely on this publication to address specific questions that apply to a particular set of facts. The author and publisher make no representation or warranty, express or implied, as to the completeness, correctness or utility of the information in this publication. In addition, the author and publisher assume no liability of any kind whatsoever resulting from the use of or reliance upon the contents of this book.

*Library of Congress Cataloging-in-Publication Data*

Murphy, Raymond J., 1938– .
    Implementing an ISO 9000-based quality system / by Raymond J. Murphy.
        p.       cm.
    Includes bibliographical references.
    ISBN: 0-86587-638-X
    1. ISO 9000 Series Standards. 2. Quality control.    I. Title.
TS156.6.M87         1998
 658.5' 62--dc21
                                           98-35544
                                            CIP

Printed in the United States of America

# TABLE OF CONTENTS

List of Figures and Tables ................................................................................ ix
Preface ................................................................................................................ xiii
Introduction ....................................................................................................... xv

**Chapter 1   Management Commitment**..................................................................1

Management Commitment to Quality ..............................................................1
    Quality Management.....................................................................................2
Empowering Employees through Leadership ..................................................4
Conclusion..........................................................................................................4

**Chapter 2   The ISO 9000 Standards—A Brief History** ....................................5

International Organization for Standardization (ISO).....................................5
    Effects of ISO ...............................................................................................6
    ISO Results ...................................................................................................7
The ISO 9000 Definition of Quality—A Different Look...............................7
    Definition of Quality....................................................................................7
Conclusion..........................................................................................................9

**Chapter 3   Work Process Definition**................................................................. 11

Primary Work Processes.................................................................................. 11
Process Steps—Value Added and Non-Value Added .................................. 12
Primary Work Process Model ........................................................................ 14
Primary Work Process—Controlling Factors ............................................... 16
    Facilities, Equipment, and Allocated Resources..................................... 17
    Training and Knowledge........................................................................... 17
    Procedures and Work Instructions .......................................................... 17
    Performance Standards............................................................................. 17
Management Mindset...................................................................................... 18
    Traditional Management Mindset ............................................................ 18
    Quality and Service Mindset .................................................................... 19
Conclusion........................................................................................................ 19

## Chapter 4  Quality Structure .................................................................................... 21

Quality Systems ................................................................................................... 21
    Terminology and Intent of ISO 9000 ............................................................ 22
Continuous Improvement Steering Committees ................................................. 23
    Steering Committee Guidelines .................................................................... 24
    Continuous Improvement Teams .................................................................. 25
    Sponsor Responsibilities ............................................................................... 27
Quality System Awareness Training ................................................................... 28
Determination of Applicable ISO Standards ....................................................... 29
Conclusion ........................................................................................................... 30

## Chapter 5  Quality System Self Assessment ............................................................ 33

Self-Assessment Guidelines ................................................................................. 33
    Needs Assessment ......................................................................................... 33
Conclusion ........................................................................................................... 34
Needs Assessment Inventory ............................................................................... 35

## Chapter 6  Quality System Implementation Plan Development ............................ 57

Importance of Planning ........................................................................................ 57
Planning Elements ............................................................................................... 57
    Typical Shopping List of ISO 9000 Quality System Plan Elements ........... 58
    Arrangement of Plan Elements ..................................................................... 60

## Chapter 7  The Quality Policy .................................................................................. 61

Importance of the Quality Policy ........................................................................ 61
    Elements of the Quality Policy ..................................................................... 61
Quality Policy Development Steps ...................................................................... 63
    Step 1—Code of Ethics ................................................................................ 63
    Step 2—Mission Statement .......................................................................... 63
    Step 3—Vision Statement ............................................................................ 65
    Step 4—Preparation and Setup .................................................................... 65
    Example of Quality Policy—American Bureau of Shipping ...................... 67
Conclusion ........................................................................................................... 67

## Chapter 8  Quality System Relationship Diagram ................................................. 69

Quality System Manual ....................................................................................... 69
    Conclusion ..................................................................................................... 72

## Chapter 9  Quality System Manual ............................................................................. 73

- Quality System Manual Preparation ..................................................................... 73
  - Assessment.............................................................................................................. 74
  - Distribution and Control ..................................................................................... 74
  - Foundation Material ............................................................................................. 75
  - Quality System Description................................................................................. 77
  - QSM Section Development.................................................................................. 78
  - QSM Sections—Shopping List ........................................................................... 79
  - Cover and Packaging ........................................................................................... 80
  - Standard Page Header ......................................................................................... 81
  - Foreword/Certification ........................................................................................ 81
  - Table of Contents—Cross Reference ................................................................ 82
- Quality System Manuals—Applied Examples....................................................... 83
  - ABS Corporate Quality System Manual—Applied Example ......................... 83
  - Quality System Manual Elements—Applied Example .................................... 85

## Chapter 10  Quality System Procedures .................................................................. 117

- Relationship of Quality System Procedures to Quality System .................... 117
- Quality System Procedures—A Shopping List .................................................. 119
- Developing the Numbering and Indexing System ........................................... 120
- Determine the Standard Formats for Procedures and Work Instructions ... 124
  - Procedure Title Block—Sample Standard Format........................................ 124
  - Work Instruction Title Block—Sample Standard Format ............................ 125
- Development of Procedures and Work Instructions ...................................... 127
  - Procedure Table of Contents ............................................................................ 127
  - Explanation of Each Section of the Contents for the Quality System Procedure ..... 128
- Prepare Remaining Quality System Procedures ............................................... 139
- Conclusion................................................................................................................ 141

## Chapter 11  Primary Work Processes ...................................................................... 143

- Identifying a Primary Work Process................................................................... 143
- Establishing a Primary Work Process ................................................................ 144
  - Step 1—Determine Top Level Functions ....................................................... 144
  - Step 2—List Primary Work Processes............................................................. 146
  - Step 3—Determine Which Processes Require Procedures.......................... 147
  - Step 4—Determine Work Instructions ........................................................... 149
- Conclusion................................................................................................................ 151

## Chapter 12  Training and Knowledge Requirements .......................................... 153

- Training and Knowledge Worksheet.................................................................... 153

Training and Assessment ................................................................................. 155
Training Plan .................................................................................................. 155
On-the-Job Training ........................................................................................ 155
Group Training ............................................................................................... 156
Self-Administered Training ............................................................................. 156
Budget Provisions for Training ....................................................................... 156
Completion of Training Courses ..................................................................... 156
Specific Process Training ................................................................................ 156
Process Training Certification ......................................................................... 157
Conclusion ........................................................................................................... 157

**Chapter 13   Position Description Manual** ................................................................ **159**

Design of Position Descriptions ........................................................................... 159
    Title Matrix .................................................................................................... 160
Organization Charts Manual ................................................................................ 164
Delegation of Authority Manual ........................................................................... 165
    Introduction Section ........................................................................................ 165
    Contents Section ............................................................................................. 165
Conclusion ........................................................................................................... 166

**Chapter 14   Work Process Procedures, Work Instructions, and Check Sheets—Preparation and Assignment** ................................................................ **167**

Work Process Procedures ..................................................................................... 167
Check Sheets ........................................................................................................ 171
    Definition of Check Sheet .............................................................................. 171
    Check Sheets—General .................................................................................. 172
    Criteria for the Use of Check Sheets .............................................................. 173
    Purpose of Check Sheets ................................................................................ 173
    Basis for Determining the Inclusion of a Check Sheet .................................. 173
Preparation and Assignment ................................................................................. 173

**Chapter 15   Controlled Document Issuance** ............................................................... **175**

Conclusion ........................................................................................................... 181

**Chapter 16   Quality System Implementation Instructions** ........................................ **183**

Implementation Handbook .................................................................................... 183
    Module 1—Quality System Implementation Plan ......................................... 184
    Module 2—Quality Policy .............................................................................. 184
    Module 3—Quality Objectives ....................................................................... 185

Module 4—Management Responsibility ...................................................................185
Module 5—Quality System ......................................................................................186
Module 6—Management Review .............................................................................186
Module 7—Organization and Responsibilities .........................................................187
Module 8—Contract Review ....................................................................................187
Module 9—Design Control .......................................................................................188
Module 10—Document and Data Control ................................................................189
Module 11—Purchasing and Supplier Control .........................................................189
Module 12—Control of Customer Supplied Product ...............................................190
Module 13—Product Identification, Status, and Traceability ..................................190
Module 14—Process Control (Work Control) .........................................................191
Module 15—Inspection and Testing .........................................................................192
Module 16—Control of Inspection, Measuring, and Test Equipment .....................192
Module 17—Inspection and Test Status ...................................................................193
Module 18—Control of Nonconforming Product ....................................................193
Module 19—Corrective and Preventive Action .......................................................194
Module 20—Handling, Storage, Packaging, Preservation, and Delivery ................194
Module 21—Control and Retention of Quality Records .........................................195
Module 22—Internal Quality Audits ........................................................................196
Module 23—Training ................................................................................................196
Module 24—Servicing (Customer Servicing) ..........................................................197
Module 25—Statistical Techniques ..........................................................................197
Conclusion ........................................................................................................................197

## Chapter 17  Internal Audits ...............................................................................................199

Auditor Training and Qualifications ................................................................................200
Planning and Conducting and Audit ................................................................................200
Internal Audit Plan ............................................................................................................201
Audit Checklist .................................................................................................................202
    Cover Page ................................................................................................................202
    Instructions Page .......................................................................................................203
    Typical Internal Audit Checklist—Example ............................................................208
    Conclusion Page—Example .....................................................................................208
The Administration of Internal Audits ............................................................................208
    Auditor Meetings ......................................................................................................210
    The Finding Statement ..............................................................................................211
Corrective and Preventive Action ....................................................................................212
Conclusion ........................................................................................................................213

## Chapter 18  Corrective and Preventive Action System ...................................................215

Establishing an Effective System ....................................................................................215
    Purpose of a Continuous Improvement Steering Committee ..................................215

Organization and Responsibilities ................................................................................216
    Continuous Improvement Steering Committee ..............................................216
    Continuous Improvement Teams (CITs) .........................................................216
    Management and Supervisor Responsibilities ................................................216
    Employee Responsibilities ...............................................................................217
    Management System and Quality .....................................................................217
Uses of the Corrective and Preventive Action System ....................................................220
    Corrective and Preventive Action Request (CPARs) .....................................221
    Corrective and Preventive Action System—Definitions ................................224
    Corrective and Preventive Action System—Initiation ...................................225
    Corrective and Preventive Action System—General Description .................225
Conclusion ........................................................................................................................227

## Chapter 19   Beyond ISO 9000 Certification ............................................................229

Journey to Excellence ......................................................................................................229
    Phase 1—Process Management .......................................................................229
    Phase 2—Improve the Processes .....................................................................230
    Phase 3—Management Systems Alignment ...................................................233
    Phase 4—Total Customer Satisfaction ............................................................238
Conclusion ........................................................................................................................238

## Chapter 20   Continuous Improvement .....................................................................241

Tools for Continuous Improvement .................................................................................241
    Process Mapping ..............................................................................................243
    Office Mapping ................................................................................................249
Environment for Continuous Improvement .....................................................................251
How to Be a Part of Continuous Improvement ...............................................................255
Conclusion ........................................................................................................................256

## Chapter 21   Case Study: American Bureau of Shipping (ABS) ............................257

The Mission of ABS .........................................................................................................257
The Mission of ABS Group of Companies .....................................................................257
Background ......................................................................................................................257
The ABS Journey—Overview .........................................................................................258
Foundation of the ABS Journey to Excellence ...............................................................259

**References** ..................................................................................................................265

**About the Author** .......................................................................................................267

# LIST OF FIGURES

Figure I-1–I-4. Implementing an ISO 9000-Based Quality System .............. xvii
Figure 1-1. Quality System Implementation ............................................. 3
Figure 2-1. An Interpretation of ISO 9000 ............................................... 9
Figure 3-1. Quality System Process Steps ............................................... 11
Figure 3-2. Essential and Non-Essential Steps for Producing the Product or Service ............................................................................. 13
Figure 3-3. Primary Work Process ......................................................... 15
Figure 3-4. Controlling Factors of the Primary Work Process ................... 16
Figure 3-5. Comparison of Traditional Mindset with Quality & Service Mindset ............................................................................. 18
Figure 4-1. ISO 9000 Guidelines for Selection and Use ........................... 30
Figure 4-2. Overall Quality System Structure ......................................... 31
Figure 6-1. ISO 9000 Implementation Plan/Overall Schedule. .................. 59
Figure 7-1. Quality Policy Development ................................................. 62
Figure 7-2. Quality System Implementation Plan—Step 1 ........................ 68
Figure 8-1. Quality System Procedure Listing ........................................ 70
Figure 8-2. Quality System Relationship Diagram .................................. 71
Figure 9-1. The Development Process of a Quality System Manual .......... 76
Figure 9-2. Cover and Packaging of Quality Safety Manual ..................... 80
Figure 9-3. Standardized Format for the QSM ....................................... 81
Figure 9-4. Foreword/Certification Content ........................................... 82
Figure 9-5. Cross Referenced Table of Contents .................................... 82
Figure 10-1. Quality System Relationship Diagram Segment ................... 117
Figure 10-2. Logical Manner Approach to the Development of Quality System Procedures ............................................................ 118
Figure 10-3. Numbering and Indexing Method/System .......................... 121
Figure 10-4. Printed Number on Procedure—Sample Format ................. 122
Figure 10-5. Printed Number on Work Instruction—Sample Format ........ 123
Figure 10-6. Printed Number on Quality Records—Sample Format ......... 123
Figure 10-7. Printed Number on Position Descriptions—Sample Format .. 124
Figure 10-8. Procedure Title Block—Sample Format ............................. 125
Figure 10-9. Procedure Title Block for Subsequent Pages ...................... 125
Figure 10-10. Work Instruction Title Block—Sample Standard Format .... 126
Figure 10-11. Work Instruction Title Block for Subsequent Sections ....... 126
Figure 10-12. Procedure and Process Instruction Development Worksheet ... 130

Figure 10-13. Quality System Procedure Development ........................... 140
Figure 10-14. Sample Procedure Planning and Scheduling Document ......... 142
Figure 11-1. Quality System Relationship Diagram ............................... 143
Figure 11-2. Determination of Work Function Names ........................... 145
Figure 11-3. Applied Example—Work Functions ................................. 145
Figure 11-4. Work Function Category Determination ............................ 146
Figure 11-5. Category Determination—Applied Example ....................... 147
Figure 11-6. Procedure Determination ............................................... 148
Figure 11-7. Procedure Determination—Applied Example ..................... 149
Figure 11-8. Procedure and Work Instruction Listing ............................. 150
Figure 11-9. Primary Work Processes Determination ............................. 151
Figure 12-1. Training and Knowledge Determination Worksheet ............... 154
Figure 13-1. Position Description Example ......................................... 161
Figure 13-2. Example of Title Matrix ................................................ 163
Figure 14-1. Quality System Relationship Diagram ............................... 168
Figure 14-2. Assignment and Tracking Matrix for Operating Procedure Development ................................................................. 169
Figure 14-3. Assignment and Tracking Matrix for Work Instruction Development ................................................................. 170
Figure 15-1. A Typical Controlled Document Distribution Matrix for Offices/Departments/Functions ......................................... 176
Figure 15-2. A Typical Controlled Document Distribution Matrix for Individuals ................................................................. 177
Figure 15-3. Typical Master Listing of Controlled Documents ................. 178
Figure 15-4. Signed and Returned Acknowledgment—Applied Example ...... 179
Figure 15-5. Controlled Document Acknowledgment Card ..................... 180
Figure 17-1. Internal Audit Checklist Cover Page ................................. 203
Figure 17-2. Audit Checklist Instructions Page .................................... 204
Figure 17-3. Listing of Internal Audit Categories .................................. 205
Figure 17-4. Typical Internal Audit Checklist Category—Completed .......... 206
Figure 17-5. Example of the Concluding Page of the Internal Audit Report .. 209
Figure 18-1. Method of Addressing Problems in Many Companies ............ 218
Figure 18-2. Correct Method of Bringing Issues to Closure ..................... 218
Figure 18-3. Corrective and Prevention Action Form ............................. 222
Figure 18-4. Simplified Flow Diagram—Applied Example ...................... 226
Figure 19-1. Journey to Excellence ................................................... 231
Figure 19-2. Phase 3—Management Systems and Processes .................... 234
Figure 20-1. Tools for Continuous Improvement (TFCI)—Process Improvement Model ....................................................... 242
Figure 20-2. Process and Office Mapping ........................................... 244

Figure 20-3. Process Map—Correspondence Control ............................ 246
Figure 20-4. Flow Diagram—Correspondence Control .......................... 247
Figure 20-5. TFCI Project Tools ..................................................... 254

# PREFACE

Have you noticed that most of the information published about ISO 9000 is written by those who claim to have the answers for which you have been looking if only you follow their advice or system?

Have you noticed how many ISO 9000 training courses or seminars imply that you will walk away with the ability to implement a Quality System that will meet ISO 9000 requirements, but still leave you disappointed and in need?

You don't need consultants to do the work for you.

You don't need expensive outside training.

You don't need a large internal staff.

You don't need a large amount of time and you don't need to spend a fortune to design, plan, and implement a Quality System that will not only meet the ISO 9000 Standard requirements but will also be a solid foundation for a Total Quality Management System or an anchor for an existing TQM System. What you need, instead, is a very clear commitment from your organization and an equally clear understanding of how to achieve this transformation.

If you are searching for comprehensive step-by-step Quality System development and implementation guidance, coupled with a solid successful application example that will not leave you disappointed, then this book is exactly what you need. This book is:

- A Reference
- A Guide
- A Training Manual
- A Success Story
- A Model

# INTRODUCTION

The format and content of this book is very straightforward, containing no superfluous information. The format was chosen to allow each chapter and each subject within the book to be self-contained. It is a walk through of an ISO 9001-1994 Implementation Process following the map displayed in Figures I-1 through I-4 of this Introduction.

The Quality System, as contained in this book, was implemented within the American Bureau of Shipping (ABS) during a 15-month period, thanks to the commitment of the ABS Chairman and CEO, Frank J. Iarossi, and his entire staff. The ABS Quality System implementation story is told as an application example of the 1994 ISO 9001 Implementation Method detailed in Chapter 21 of this book.

Because the Quality System Implementation Process as presented here is designed to also be the foundation of a Total Quality Management (TQM) and a continuous improvement process, you will see some TQM requirements addressed. An attempt has been made to identify these areas and to site the advantage of so doing.

Quality Systems implementation, although a simple concept, is not easy to achieve. It requires commitment by management and the provision of adequate resources. Initially, it may cause "pain" to the organization and may also cause a predictable set of employee and management reactions until "buy in" is achieved.

These reactions will test senior management's commitment, resolve, and patience. This should be expected and can be overcome rather rapidly. To do so, senior management will have to "walk the talk" and will have to be very consistent in so doing. This is why the implementation of an ISO 9000-based Quality System begins with the decision and commitment of senior management, as discussed in Chapter 1.

Either in advance of this senior management decision, or closely following it, comes the ISO 9000 Quality System Foundation training, as presented in Chapters 2 and 3. This training should include those personnel within the organization who are or will be responsible for the implementation of the system.

Establishment of the organization's quality-related structure and selection of the proper ISO 9000 Standard is covered in Chapter 4, the next logical implementation step.

The internal high level self-assessment of Chapter 5 will provide a baseline for planning the remainder of the Implementation Process, which begins with Chapter 6.

I suggest that the reader complete Chapters 1 through 4 prior to completing the self-assessment contained in Chapter 5. The self-assessment results indicate which chapters of this book apply to the specific organization's needs. This is particularly helpful if a Quality System has already been installed or partially installed.

The remaining chapters cover those Implementation Process steps as shown on the Process Map. It is suggested that the entire map be studied and modified as necessary to be established as your specific organization's Implementation Process Map.

In reading the map, Figures I-1 through I-4 read from the top downward following the arrows. When an arrow flows from the right of an implementation logic box, follow through those steps sequentially before returning to the box and proceeding to the next box.

Chapter references are provided for each box. Here detailed information can be obtained concerning its contents.

So, let's get on with the journey, remembering what Will Rogers said, "Even if you are on the right track, you will get run over if you stand still."

Enjoy!

*Raymond J. Murphy*
*Houston, Texas*

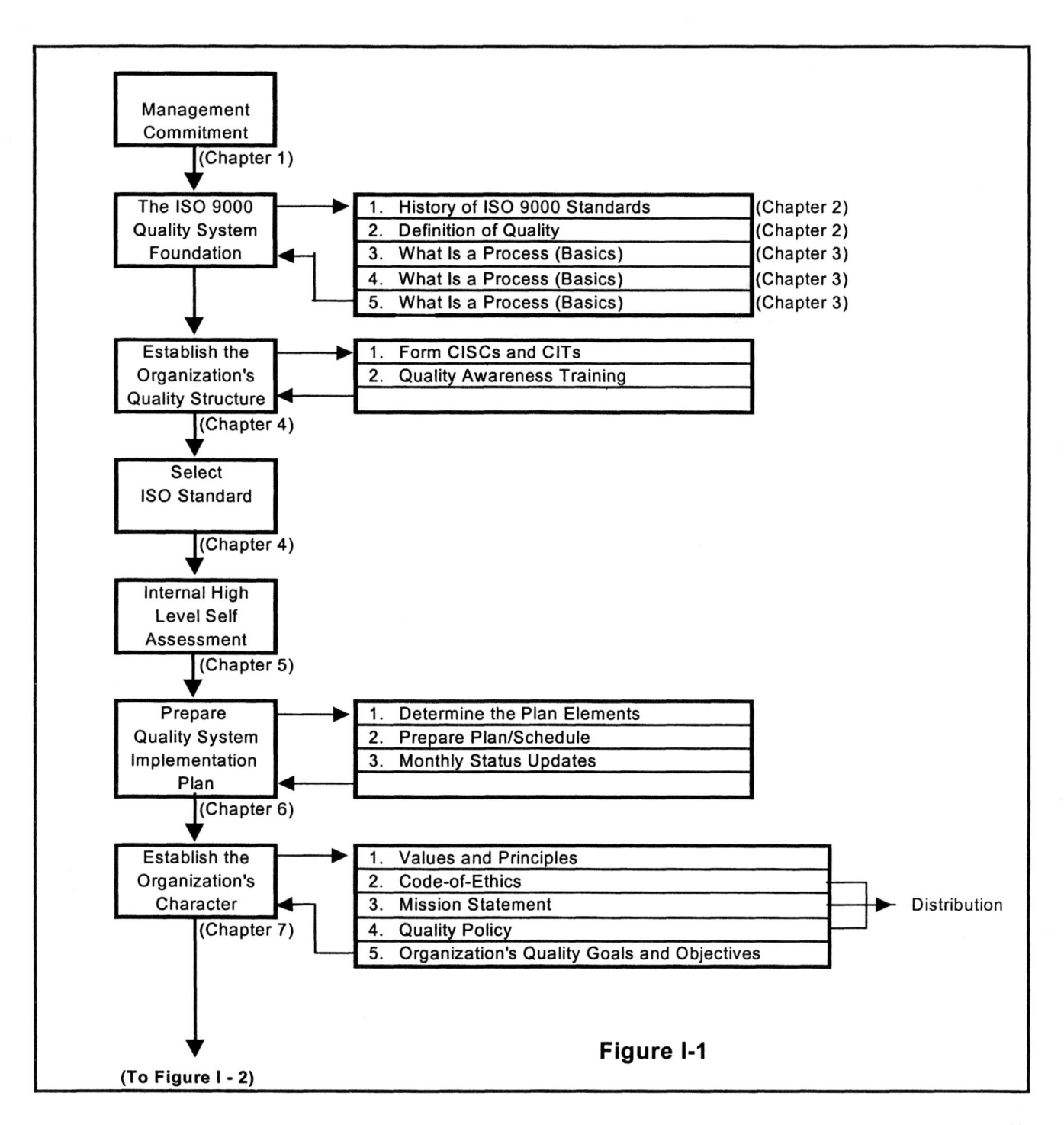

```
┌─────────────────┐
│   Management    │
│   Commitment    │
└────────┬────────┘
      (Chapter 1)
         ↓
┌─────────────────┐      ┌──────────────────────────────────────────────────┐
│  The ISO 9000   │─────→│ 1. History of ISO 9000 Standards    (Chapter 2) │
│  Quality System │      │ 2. Definition of Quality            (Chapter 2) │
│   Foundation    │←─────│ 3. What Is a Process (Basics)       (Chapter 3) │
│                 │      │ 4. What Is a Process (Basics)       (Chapter 3) │
│                 │      │ 5. What Is a Process (Basics)       (Chapter 3) │
└────────┬────────┘      └──────────────────────────────────────────────────┘
         ↓
┌─────────────────┐      ┌─────────────────────────────┐
│  Establish the  │─────→│ 1. Form CISCs and CITs      │
│  Organization's │      │ 2. Quality Awareness Training│
│ Quality Structure│←────│                             │
└────────┬────────┘      └─────────────────────────────┘
      (Chapter 4)
         ↓
┌─────────────────┐
│     Select      │
│  ISO Standard   │
└────────┬────────┘
      (Chapter 4)
         ↓
┌─────────────────┐
│  Internal High  │
│   Level Self    │
│   Assessment    │
└────────┬────────┘
      (Chapter 5)
         ↓
┌─────────────────┐      ┌─────────────────────────────┐
│     Prepare     │─────→│ 1. Determine the Plan Elements│
│ Quality System  │      │ 2. Prepare Plan/Schedule    │
│ Implementation  │      │ 3. Monthly Status Updates   │
│      Plan       │←─────│                             │
└────────┬────────┘      └─────────────────────────────┘
      (Chapter 6)
         ↓
┌─────────────────┐      ┌──────────────────────────────────────────┐
│  Establish the  │─────→│ 1. Values and Principles                 │
│  Organization's │      │ 2. Code-of-Ethics                        │
│    Character    │      │ 3. Mission Statement                     │──→ Distribution
│                 │←─────│ 4. Quality Policy                        │
│                 │      │ 5. Organization's Quality Goals and Objectives│
└────────┬────────┘      └──────────────────────────────────────────┘
      (Chapter 7)
         ↓
                                                    Figure I-1
(To Figure I - 2)
```

**Figure I-1–Figure I-4. Implementing an ISO 9000-Based Quality System**

*xviii / Implementing an ISO 9000-Based Quality System*

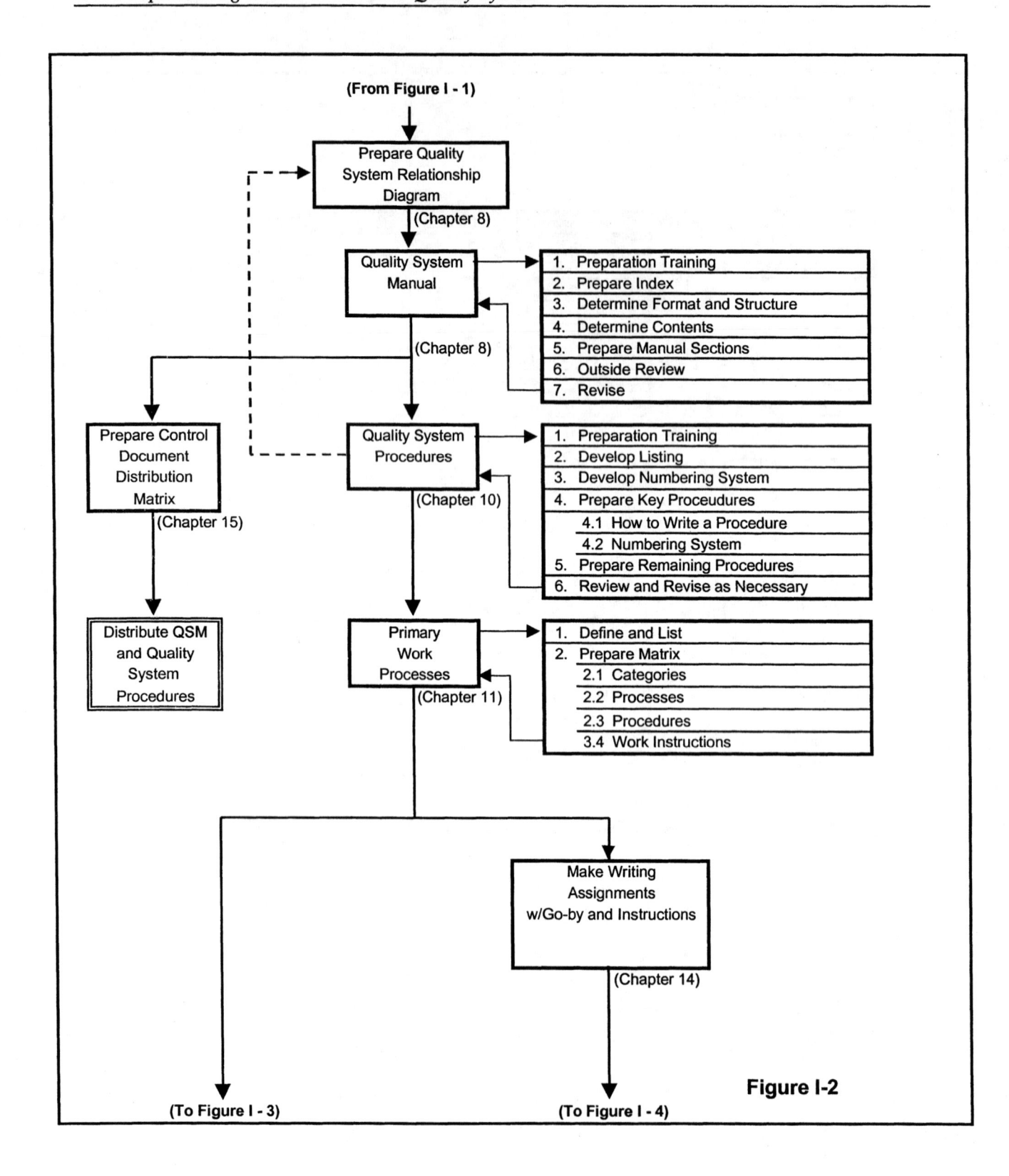

(From Figure I - 1)

↓

**Prepare Quality System Relationship Diagram**
(Chapter 8)

↓

**Quality System Manual** (Chapter 8) →
1. Preparation Training
2. Prepare Index
3. Determine Format and Structure
4. Determine Contents
5. Prepare Manual Sections
6. Outside Review
7. Revise

**Prepare Control Document Distribution Matrix** (Chapter 15)

↓

**Distribute QSM and Quality System Procedures**

**Quality System Procedures** (Chapter 10) →
1. Preparation Training
2. Develop Listing
3. Develop Numbering System
4. Prepare Key Proceudures
    4.1 How to Write a Procedure
    4.2 Numbering System
5. Prepare Remaining Procedures
6. Review and Revise as Necessary

**Primary Work Processes** (Chapter 11) →
1. Define and List
2. Prepare Matrix
    2.1 Categories
    2.2 Processes
    2.3 Procedures
    3.4 Work Instructions

↓

**Make Writing Assignments w/Go-by and Instructions**
(Chapter 14)

(To Figure I - 3)    (To Figure I - 4)

**Figure I-2**

# Flowchart

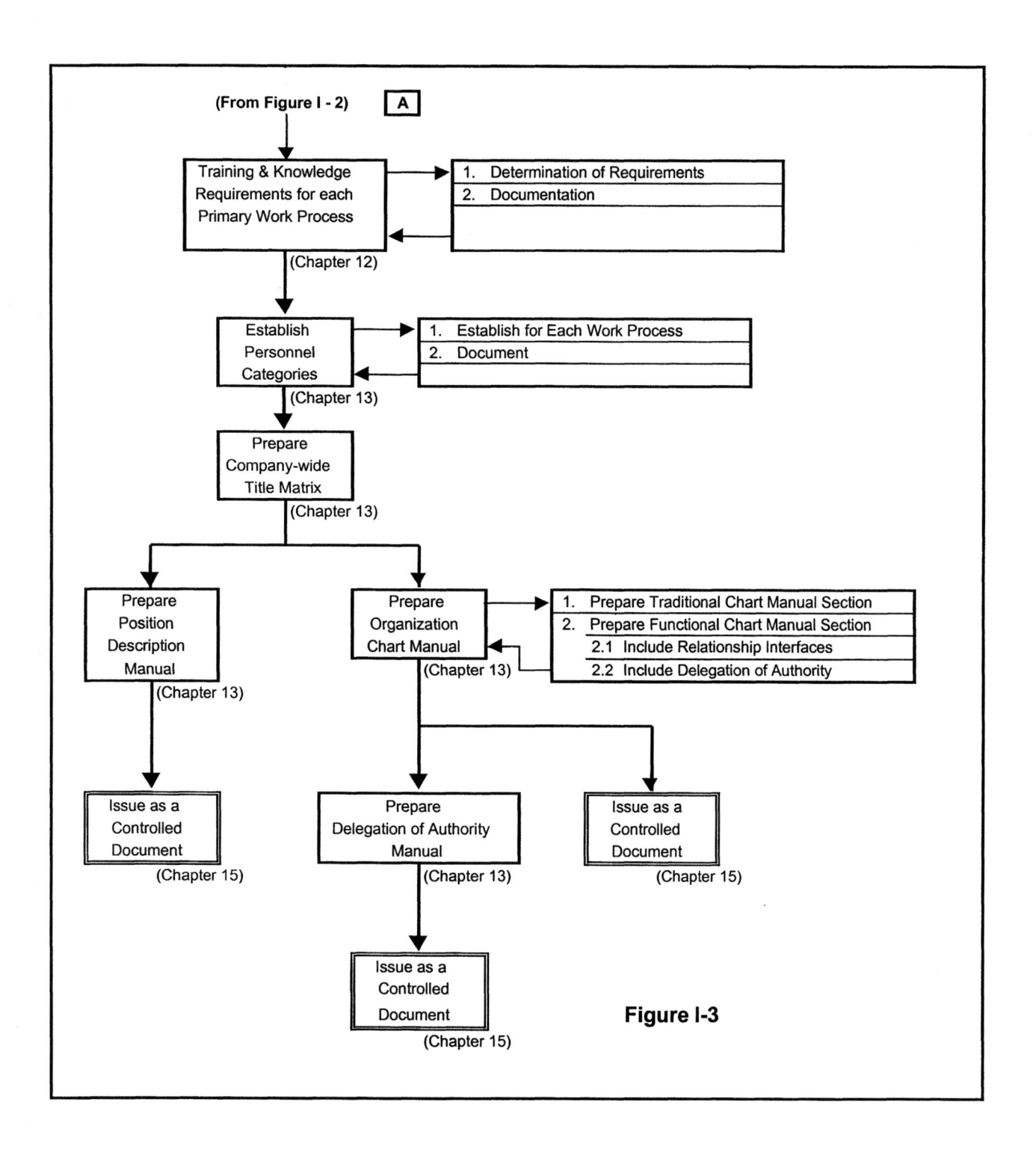

(From Figure I - 2) **A**

**Training & Knowledge Requirements for each Primary Work Process**
1. Determination of Requirements
2. Documentation

(Chapter 12)

**Establish Personnel Categories**
1. Establish for Each Work Process
2. Document

(Chapter 13)

**Prepare Company-wide Title Matrix**

(Chapter 13)

**Prepare Position Description Manual** (Chapter 13)

**Prepare Organization Chart Manual** (Chapter 13)
1. Prepare Traditional Chart Manual Section
2. Prepare Functional Chart Manual Section
   2.1 Include Relationship Interfaces
   2.2 Include Delegation of Authority

**Issue as a Controlled Document** (Chapter 15)

**Prepare Delegation of Authority Manual** (Chapter 13)

**Issue as a Controlled Document** (Chapter 15)

**Issue as a Controlled Document** (Chapter 15)

**Figure I-3**

xx / Implementing an ISO 9000-Based Quality System

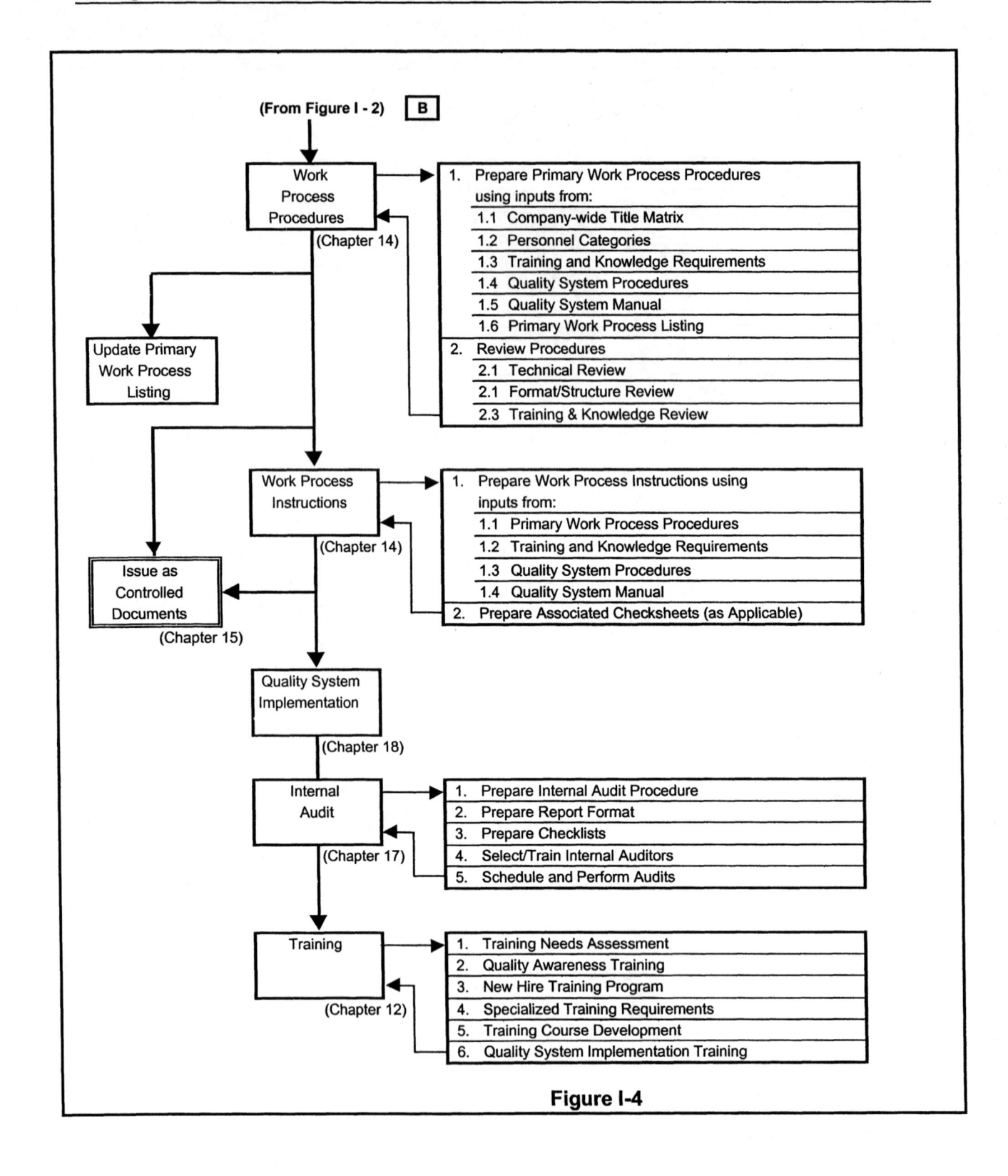

(From Figure I - 2) [B]

**Work Process Procedures** (Chapter 14)

1. Prepare Primary Work Process Procedures using inputs from:
   1.1 Company-wide Title Matrix
   1.2 Personnel Categories
   1.3 Training and Knowledge Requirements
   1.4 Quality System Procedures
   1.5 Quality System Manual
   1.6 Primary Work Process Listing
2. Review Procedures
   2.1 Technical Review
   2.1 Format/Structure Review
   2.3 Training & Knowledge Review

**Update Primary Work Process Listing**

**Work Process Instructions** (Chapter 14)

1. Prepare Work Process Instructions using inputs from:
   1.1 Primary Work Process Procedures
   1.2 Training and Knowledge Requirements
   1.3 Quality System Procedures
   1.4 Quality System Manual
2. Prepare Associated Checksheets (as Applicable)

**Issue as Controlled Documents** (Chapter 15)

**Quality System Implementation** (Chapter 18)

**Internal Audit** (Chapter 17)

1. Prepare Internal Audit Procedure
2. Prepare Report Format
3. Prepare Checklists
4. Select/Train Internal Auditors
5. Schedule and Perform Audits

**Training** (Chapter 12)

1. Training Needs Assessment
2. Quality Awareness Training
3. New Hire Training Program
4. Specialized Training Requirements
5. Training Course Development
6. Quality System Implementation Training

**Figure I-4**

# Chapter 1

# MANAGEMENT COMMITMENT

## MANAGEMENT COMMITMENT TO QUALITY

*Management commitment leads the quality process.* You have heard this said over and over again by almost every quality expert in the world. There have been countless published articles on the subject and numerous books written. Of course, the reason for all this attention is because it is true—and it is vital to the success of any Quality System.

One of the major reasons why Quality Systems fail, whether it is a Total Quality Management (TQM) process or an ISO 9000-based Quality System, is lack of management commitment. The other major reason why TQM processes fail is the lack of implementation of a solid ISO 9000- (or equivalent) based Quality System as the foundation for the TQM process.

In its pure sense, "commitment" describes a deep-seated mental or emotional state that is reflected in consistent patterns of behavior. Commitment leaves no room for compromise.

Because quality also leaves no room for compromise, the "commitment" involved in Total Quality Management and the implementation of an ISO 9000-based Quality System has to be real and honest. It must define a set of values and priorities and a pattern of positive action.

When management becomes committed, in the pure sense, to quality, meaningful change begins. The following shows a sincere commitment of management:

- Implementation of a plan for continuous improvement
- Formation of problem-solving teams to tackle chronic problems. These teams are comprised of a cross-section of various disciplines (corrective action teams or opportunity for improvement teams).
- Use of measurement to indicate problem areas and to control processes
- Dismantling of barriers between departments in order to work together for a common solution

- Perceptive listening to suggestions for improvement from people doing their jobs, and the prompt implementation of those improvements that are accepted by management
- Provisions for the proper tools to all employees so that they may do their best work, the allowance of time to do the job right, and the recognition of quality work
- The commitment of resources to improve processes in all functions of the business

Because only management can make such change happen, management commitment is mandatory. Little or nothing will happen until this is achieved.

## Quality Management

Quality is based on a set of fundamental management concepts that all managers must understand, embrace, and enthusiastically practice. The philosophy is simple: it says that *quality is a key in every organization and must be managed for success in every area of the organization.* In other words:

*Management = planning, organization, control, and measurement*

Therefore, quality cannot be left to chance. Quality must be as carefully and prudently managed as the organization's finances.

There is a difference between managing processes, as described above, and managing people. People do not like to be managed, and quality does not support the managing of people. People want to and should be led.

An interesting message published in the *Wall Street Journal* by United Technologies Corporation in 1984 says it very well:

*Let's get rid of management.*

*People don't want to be managed.*
*They want to be led.*
*Whoever heard of a World manager?*
*World leader, yes.*
       *Educational leader.*
       *Political leader.*
       *Religious leader.*

*Scout leader.*
*Business leader.*
*They lead.*
*They don't manage.*
*The carrot always wins over the stick.*
*Ask your horse.*
*You can lead your horse to water, but you can't manage him to drink.*
*If you want to manage somebody, manage yourself.*
*Do that well and you'll be ready to stop managing and start leading.*

Employee management, leadership, and overall Quality System Implementation might be characterized by a decreasing amount of employee management coupled with a corresponding increase in employee empowerment. This would also correspond to the transition to managing processes and leading people—a Quality System objective.

Are you wondering where this objective is in the ISO 9001 Series Standard? It isn't there. It is simply an unstated necessity for the overall success of a Quality System.

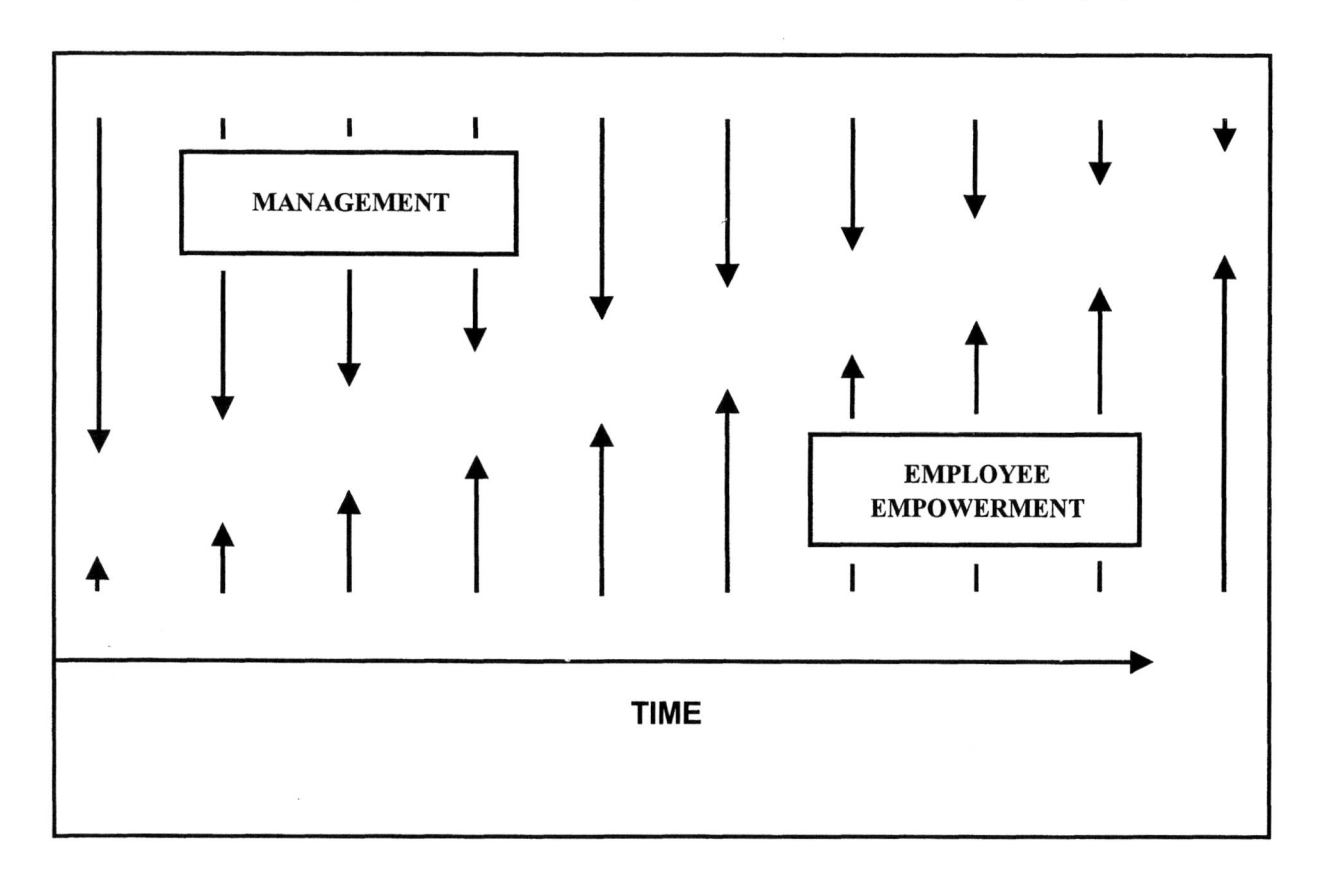

**Figure 1-1. Quality System Implementation**

## EMPOWERING EMPLOYEES THROUGH LEADERSHIP

Every employee should be able to find and solve problems on his or her own, and absorb and create new approaches, new ideas. This is what an effective Quality System does, and it does so through the establishment of a solid system within which the employee can operate. This system is not driven by management-created fear, but by leadership, which is best characterized by:

*A leader is best when people barely know he exists, not so good when people obey and acclaim him, worse when they despise him. But of a good leader who talks little, when his work is done, his aim fulfilled, they will say "we did it ourselves."*

—Cho/Hey

## CONCLUSION

As Tom Peters so aptly states,

*You are either a quality fanatic or you are not in favor of quality.*

Paragraph 4.1 of the ISO 9000 Standard relative to management responsibility includes the following:

- The ultimate responsibility for quality resides with management.
- Management must provide the resources to achieve quality, which includes time, money, and personnel.
- Management must ensure quality policies are understood and implemented.
- Management must define and assign responsibility and authority for quality.
- Management must appoint a quality representative.
- Management must conduct reviews of the Quality System.
- Management must ensure continuing effectiveness of the Quality System to meet objectives.

# Chapter 2

# THE ISO 9000 STANDARDS— A BRIEF HISTORY

## INTERNATIONAL ORGANIZATION FOR STANDARDIZATION (ISO)

The International Organization for Standardization (ISO) is an international organization whose members are the national standards bodies of some 90-plus countries (one from each country). ISO is a nongovernmental organization (NGO) that facilitates the development of global consensus agreements on international standards. The standards are voluntary in nature.

In 1979, the British Standards Institute (BSI) submitted a formal proposal to ISO that a new technical committee should be formed to prepare international standards relating to quality assurance techniques and practices.

The new technical committee was approved and given the number ISO/TC 176, titled Quality Assurance. Twenty (20) member countries became active participants and fourteen (14) countries became observing members. Today there are over 47 participating members and 17 observing members.

The ISO/TC 176 embarked on the idea of making generic Quality Management Standards for worldwide application, using UK BS-5750 Standards and Canadian CSA Z 299 10 Series Standards as the primary base. One could say that BS-5750 and CSA Z 299 were the "mother" and "father" of the ISO 9000 Standards, but only if it is understood that the offspring has now become the "parent."

The first editions of ISO 9000 Standards (ISO 9000 to 9004) were completed in 1986 and published in early 1987, revised and published again in 1994. After issue, the ISO 9000 Standards became the most widespread in the industry, with the most rapid adoption by the international standards community and the greatest sales of any ISO Standard in existence.

*The ISO 9000 concept is that certain generic characteristics of management practice could be usefully standardized, giving mutual benefit to producers and users alike.*

## Effects of ISO

What has happened since the ISO 9000 Standards became available?

1. They have been adopted without change as national standards in almost every country, including all of the European Community (EC), Japan, and the United States.

2. They have the highest worldwide awareness of any standard.

3. Third-party assessment and registration services exist for recognizing conformance to ISO 9000 Standards in most of the more than 70 countries that recognize the ISO Standard.

4. Whether it is true or not, many companies have come to the conclusion that doing business in the integrated market of Europe necessitates being recognized as meeting the requirements of ISO 9000 or better.

5. Many nationally and internationally recognized product certification systems have incorporated the ISO 9000 Standards as a first-phase requirement for approval to use their mark.

6. Very many companies, both large and small, have initiated vigorous company programs to implement the ISO 9000 Standards at their operation sites.

7. Numerous governmental purchasers have made ISO 9000 registration (or its equivalent) a requirement for their large contract suppliers, who have in turn passed the requirement on to their suppliers.

**The ISO 9000 Standards are having a major worldwide impact. Why?**

The ISO 9000 Standards are simply tools to be used to achieve the broad objective of Total Quality Improvement, which is being actively pursued at all levels in today's society.

Businesses in every sector have shifted their emphasis to the quality side of the quality/price equation because they believe that doing so is absolutely necessary to remain competitive in today's global markets. The push for quality and client satisfaction is at an all-time high.

## ISO Results

Remaining competitive in today's global markets is worth repeating. Companies that have successfully implemented an ISO 9000-based Quality System are being pleasantly surprised with reduced costs, reduced products/service cycle times, improved customer relationships, improved employee enthusiasm, innovation, and morale.

It's worth the effort.

**How does the ISO 9000 Quality System accomplish all of this?**

It doesn't. You do!

You do it by simply:

- Writing down what you do
- Doing what you write down
- Providing visible evidence that you are doing that which you have written down
- Identifying errors and opportunities for improving what you do
- Applying corrective action to prevent future errors and to improve what you do.

The ISO 9000-based Quality System provides a formalized and disciplined means of accomplishing this effort. The very positive outputs of the effort happens as a result—and yes, it does take some amount of faith to get through the process until the results begin putting you through.

So let's begin with a very simple definition of "quality."

## THE ISO 9000 DEFINITION OF QUALITY—A DIFFERENT LOOK

### Definition of Quality

The term *quality* has been used and abused in so many ways that it is on the verge of losing all meaning. I personally dislike the term quality and look forward to the day when quality simply becomes the way we do business and live our lives and no longer has to be a standard by which things are measured.

A number of the more popular definitions of quality are associated with various quality gurus:

- Conformance to requirements
   —Philip Crosby
- Fitness for use
   —J. M. Juran
- Exceeding customers' expectations through continuous improvement of processes
   —W. Edwards Deming

For the purposes of ISO 9000:

***Quality is not what we do; it is the way we do things.***

W. Edwards Deming developed the 85-15 Rule:

***85 percent of what goes wrong is the cause of the system; only 15 percent is the cause of the individual.***

Heretofore, management generally focused on who was at fault when an error occurred, finding the guilty party and punishing him or her through reprimand or through negative performance reviews. In reality, a person does not plan to make an error; so why do errors occur?

***A person makes a mistake or error because the system allows that person to do so.***

It is the fault of the system 85 percent of the time and the fault of the person only 15 percent of the time. That is the essence of Deming's 85-15 Rule. Logic then dictates that if we can control the system, control the work processes, we can control the quality.

This gives rise to a very simple approach of how to achieve quality, which is the essence of the ISO 9000 Standard requirements.

***Quality is the result of controlled processes.***

If the process is correct and in control, then the output of that process is more likely to be correct. The ISO 9000 Quality System is, therefore, based on controlling the work processes and the metrics associated with those work processes to ensure that they are in "control."

Process, primary work process, and work process are all terms we must understand in order to fully appreciate the simplistic power of this definition of quality.

***Quality is the way we do things.***

## CONCLUSION

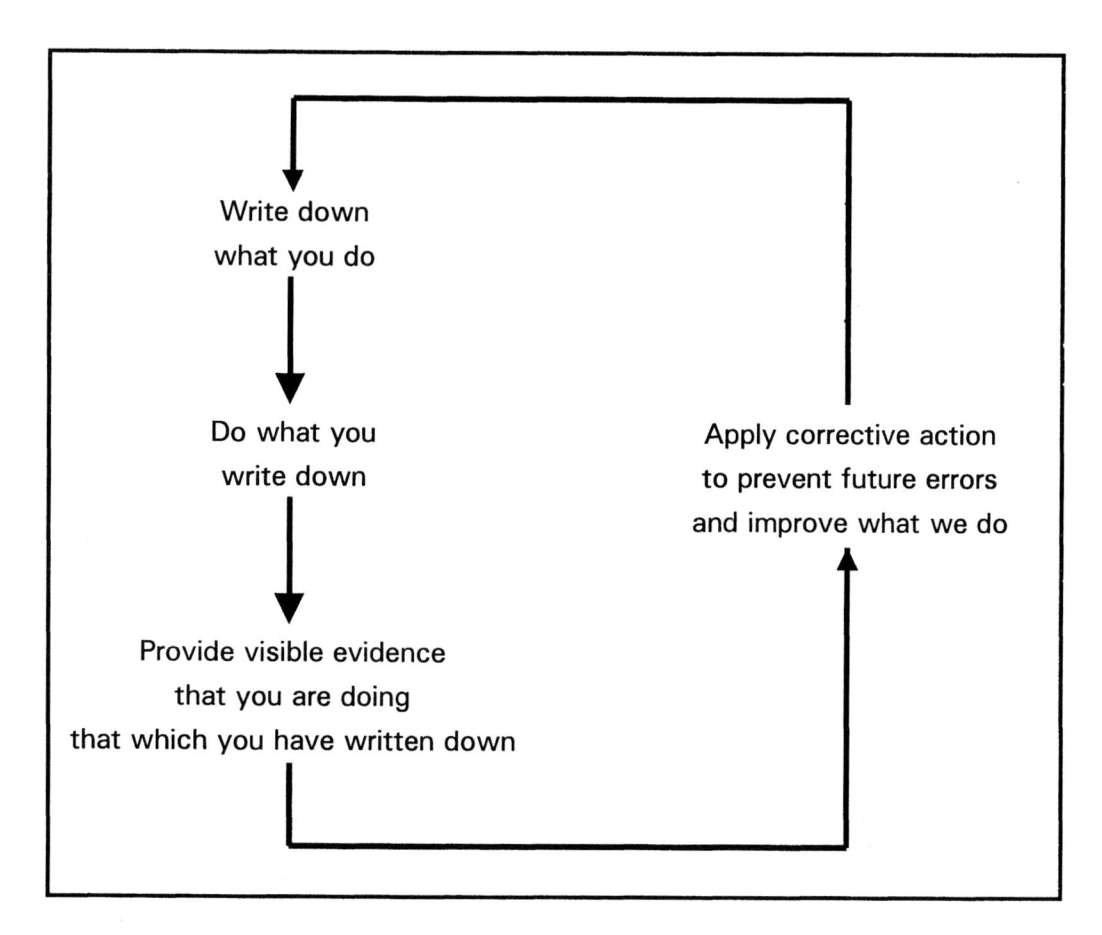

[Flowchart showing a cycle: Write down what you do → Do what you write down → Provide visible evidence that you are doing that which you have written down → Apply corrective action to prevent future errors and improve what we do → (back to start)]

**Figure 2-1. An Interpretation of ISO 9000**

In review:

- Quality is not *what* we do; it is the *way* we do things.
- 85% of what goes wrong is the cause of the system; only 15 % is the cause of the individual (Deming).
- A person makes a mistake or error because the system allows that person to do so.
- Quality is the result of controlled processes.

# Chapter 3
# WORK PROCESS DEFINITION

## PRIMARY WORK PROCESSES

ISO 9000 Quality System implementation begins with an understanding of the organization's Primary Work Processes. In order to implement a Quality System, one must first understand the basics of processes.

*All work is a process—a series of actions that produce a result.*

Each of these series of actions can be represented by a process step, which itself produces an intermediate result or output as shown in Figure 3-1.

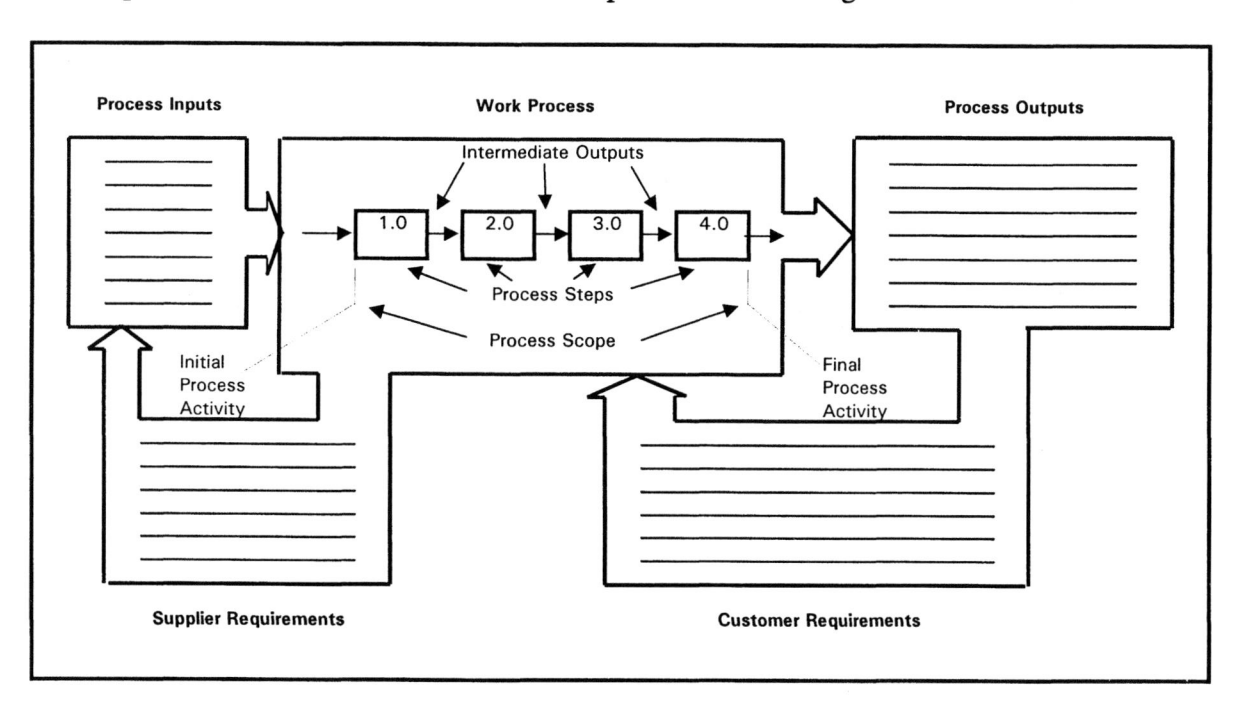

**Figure 3-1. Quality System Process Steps**

The process steps are generally named, numbered, and placed in their respective sequence of occurrence.

The scope of the process is bound by the initial process activity and the final process activity, selection of which is a choice.

Each process has one or more process outputs and one or more process inputs. There may also be process inputs at any of the intermediate stages.

*A process is the work we do to convert process inputs to process outputs.*

Actually, everything we do is a process and can be analyzed using process thinking. Getting dressed, eating, swimming, driving a car, designing a control system, delivering a package, writing a check, auditing a system, and writing a book are all names of processes. Each of these processes is comprised of a sequence of steps producing a result.

Work processes are, of course, those processes we do relative to our work. These may include what are called *Primary Work Processes* (those work processes that deliver products or services directly to an external customer) and *Supporting Work Processes* (those work processes that support the Primary Work Process).

## PROCESS STEPS—VALUE ADDED AND NON-VALUE ADDED

Each Primary Work Process contains both "value added" steps and "non-value added" process steps as shown in Figure 3-2. Value added process steps are those that are essential for producing the product or service output of the Primary Work Process. Non-value added process steps are those steps that are not essential for producing the product or service output of the work process.

One way of looking at this aspect of a Primary Work Process is through the eyes of the customer and asking, "Does this activity or process step add value?" If the answer is "no," then it is a non-value added process step and should be targeted for elimination. In fact, one objective of a good Quality System is to eliminate the non-value added process steps entirely. This is done through challenge questions, such as asking: "Why are we doing this process step?"; "What value does it add to the process?"; "Is it really necessary?"; and "Who does it serve—the customer or management?"

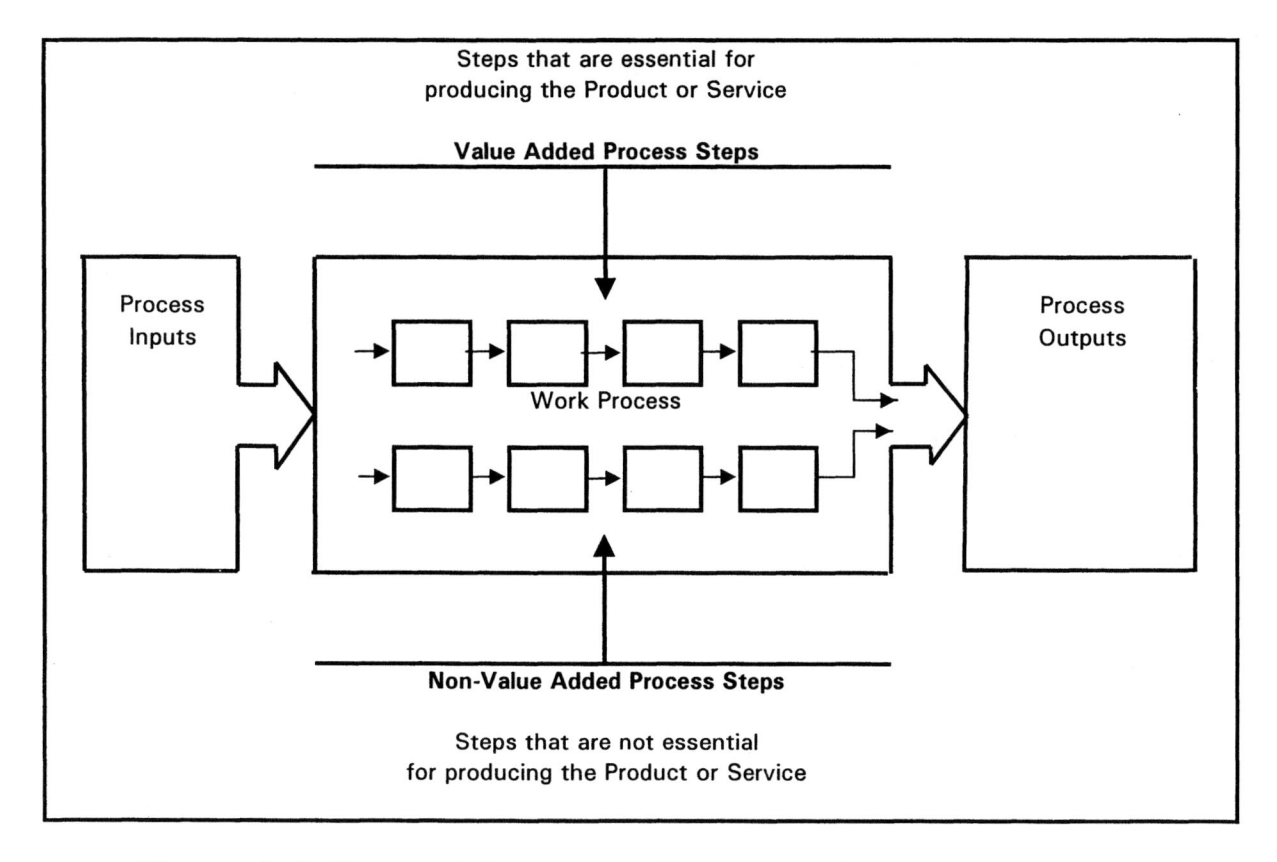

**Figure 3-2. Essential and Non-Essential Steps for Producing the Product or Service**

Another method of looking at the Primary Work Processes in this manner (i.e., through the evaluation of value added process steps) is the definition of waste as offered by Cho/Hey.

*Waste =*
*...anything other than the minimum amount of equipment, materials, parts, space, and worker's time which are absolutely essential to add value to the product or service....*

Viewing the work processes through this definition of waste has both a positive and a negative aspect. In the negative sense, anything short of meeting the value-added requirements of the Primary Work Processes does not meet the quality requirements of the process and therefore must be eliminated. In the positive sense, anything beyond meeting the value added requirements of the Primary Work Processes may exceed the quality requirements of the process but may still be classified as waste because it expends the company resources beyond what is necessary from a process viewpoint. However, there may be marketing or other reasons for those resources; therefore, they must be planned occurrences.

*One key Quality System goal and effort is to eliminate negative waste entirely and unplanned positive waste.*

This can best be accomplished through the complete understanding of the work processes and ISO 9000 Quality System implementation requirements.

## PRIMARY WORK PROCESS MODEL

As stated earlier, Primary Work Processes are those work processes that deliver products or services directly to an external customer (client) and that are generally value added.

The Primary Work Process can be represented in a model consisting of nine (9) elements as shown in Figure 3-3.

1. Work process—as defined above.

2. Process outputs—the deliverable product or service output of the work process.

3. Process customer—the customer(s) to whom the process output is delivered or for whom the work is done.

4. Process output requirements—a description by the customer of the customer expected process outputs.

5. Process inputs—the inputs to the work process that are consumed by the process or that become part of the process output after having had value added.

6. Suppliers—those who provide inputs to the work process.

7. Supplier input requirements—a description by those in the work process of the expected inputs to be provided by the supplier.

8. Process output feedback—feedback to the customer or from the customer relative to the process outputs, satisfaction, complaints, problems, and improvement opportunities.

9. Process input feedback—feedback to the suppliers or from the suppliers relative to the inputs, satisfaction, complaints, problems, and improvement opportunities.

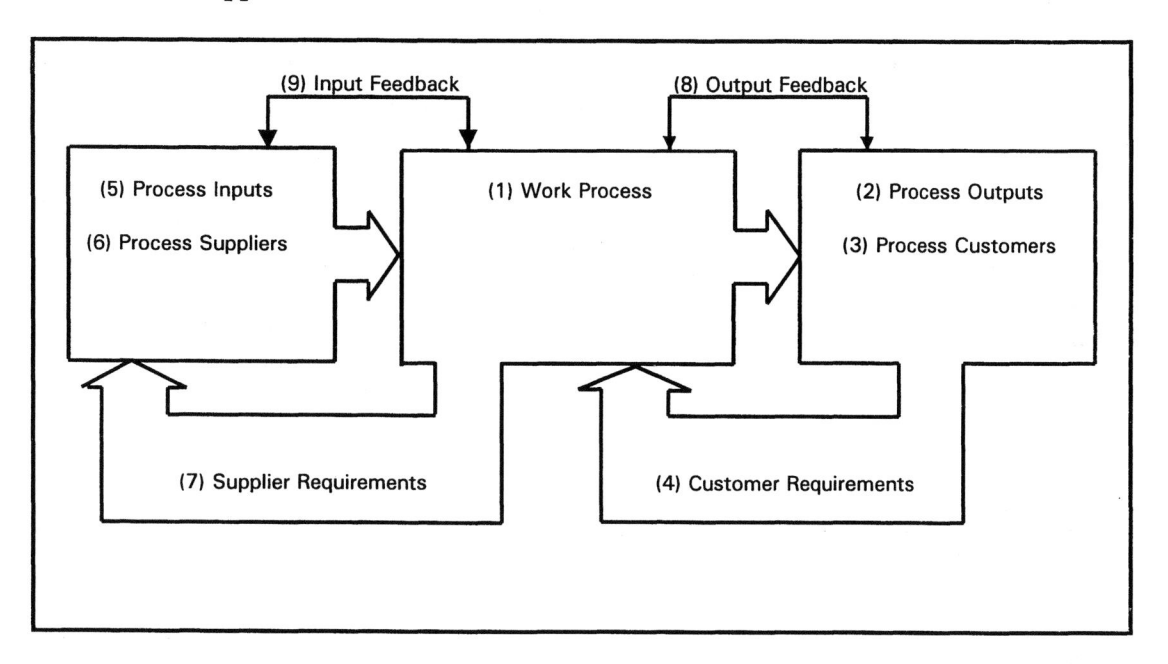

**Figure 3-3. Primary Work Process**

The ISO 9000 Standards view the work processes through the eyes of the customer and the supplier as well as from inside the work processes towards the customer and the supplier.

It is estimated that about 60 percent of customer dissatisfaction and supplier problems are a result of poor communications associated with element numbers (4), (7), (8), and (9) above. These areas are all addressed in the ISO 9001 Standard, paragraphs 4.1, 4.3, 4.4, 4.5, 4.6, 4.7, 4.8, 4.9, 4.10, 4.11, 4.12, 4.13, 4.14, 4.15, 4.16, 4.17, 4.18, and 4.19.

The importance that the ISO 9001 Standard applies to these areas should be obvious. In addition to these communication related areas that directly affect quality, there are a number of other controlling factors of the process that control and affect the quality of the process outputs(s).

## PRIMARY WORK PROCESS—CONTROLLING FACTORS

Work process controlling factors consist of those factors that are controlled by management and that directly affect the quality of the work process output. These controlling factors are not under the control of personnel within the work process. The controlling factors affect the consistency, content, and integrity of the work processes themselves.

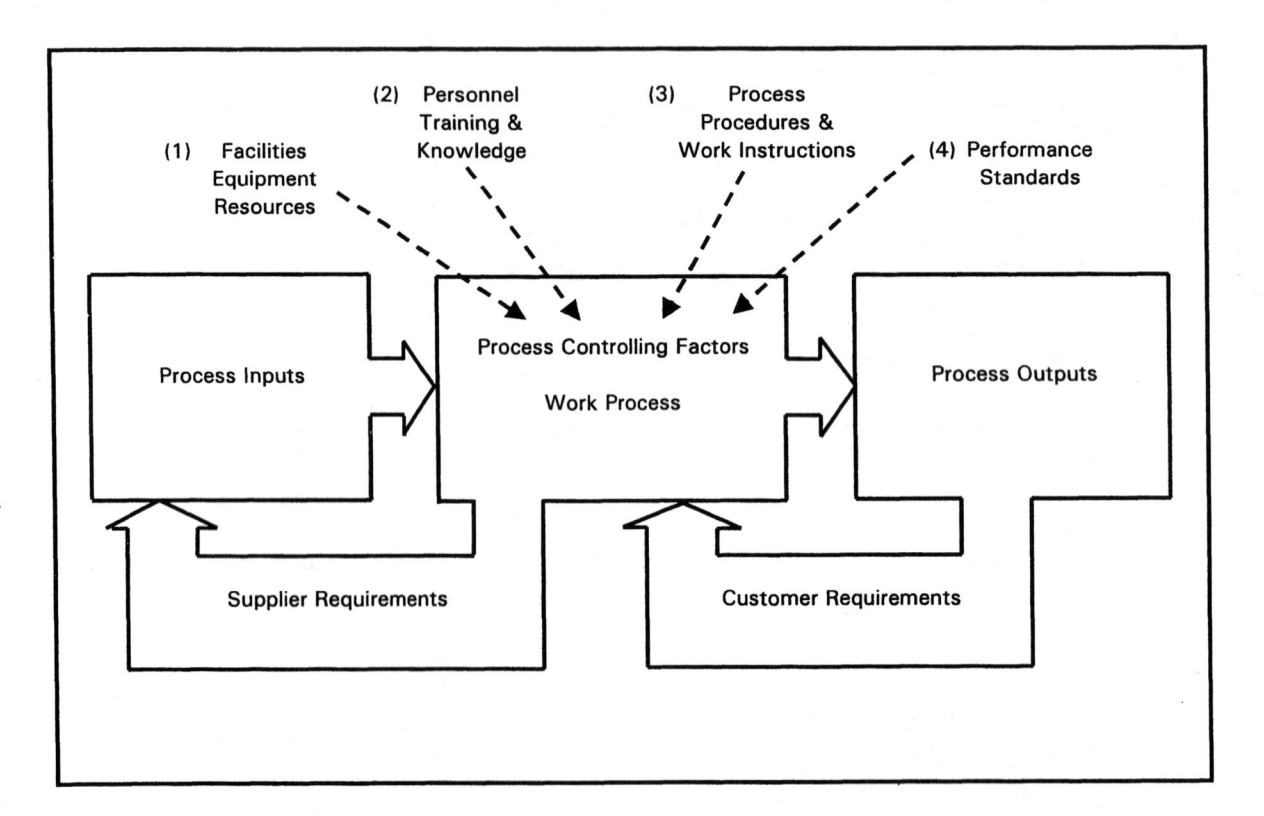

**Figure 3-4. Controlling Factors of the Primary Work Process**

## Facilities, Equipment, and Allocated Resources

Management is responsible for providing proper facilities, equipment, and allocated resources in support of the work process. This responsibility includes the work environment, office equipment, and the process required equipment. The ISO 9000 Standards look at the work processes through the facilities, equipment, and allocated resource requirements.

## Training and Knowledge

Management is responsible for ensuring that the personnel placed into the work process have sufficient knowledge coupled with the necessary training to ensure the quality of the process output. The ISO 9000 Standards look at the work processes through the training and knowledge requirements.

## Procedures and Work Instructions

Management is responsible for ensuring that procedures and work process instructions have been prepared and that all personnel operating within the respective work process have been properly trained in accordance with those procedures and work process instructions. The ISO 9000 Standards look at the work processes through the requirements of the procedures and work process instructions.

## Performance Standards

Management is responsible for ensuring that management does not negatively affect the work process quality through the imposition of unrealistic cost and schedule requirements onto the processes. Management should also avoid setting other negative affecting performance standards as well. The ISO 9000 Standards look at the work processes through the requirements and mindset of management.

There may be other standards that control the Primary Work Process, as well, such as state, federal, local, etc.

# MANAGEMENT MINDSET

## Traditional Management Mindset

The traditional management mindset is represented by a triangle in which the work process, with its associated outputs and inputs, is shown at the base (see Figure 3-3). In this mindset the employees within the processes are generally operating in a "responsive" mode to a management, which carries the responsibility for the processes. As such, most employees serve middle and upper management rather than the customer.

**TRADITIONAL MINDSET**

RESPONSIBLE: Upper Management, Middle Management

RESPONSIVE: PROCESS — Employees — Value Added Process (INPUTS / OUTPUTS)

* The higher up the organization you go, the more important you are.
* Managers are responsible for seeing that everything is done correctly and on time, which places employees in a responsive mode.
* Employees are rewarded for making bosses happy rather than customers.
* Employees are discouraged and sometimes punished for taking initiative or risks necessary to better service the customer.
* As a result, employees feel unable to make a difference.
* The casulty of this mindset is the loss of employee self-esteem.
* Lower level employees are paid less, trained less, rewarded less, told what to do and how to do it more often, and given little flexibility in dealing with customers.

**QUALITY & SERVICE MINDSET**

RESPONSIBLE: Value Added Process — PROCESS — Employees (INPUTS / OUTPUTS)

RESPONSIVE: Middle Management, Upper Management

* Management becomes a service or support organization for its employees, responsive to the needs of the process.
* Customer contact employees are recognized as the most important factor in the providing quality and service.
* Decisions are made based on impact on customers, contact employees, and the process.

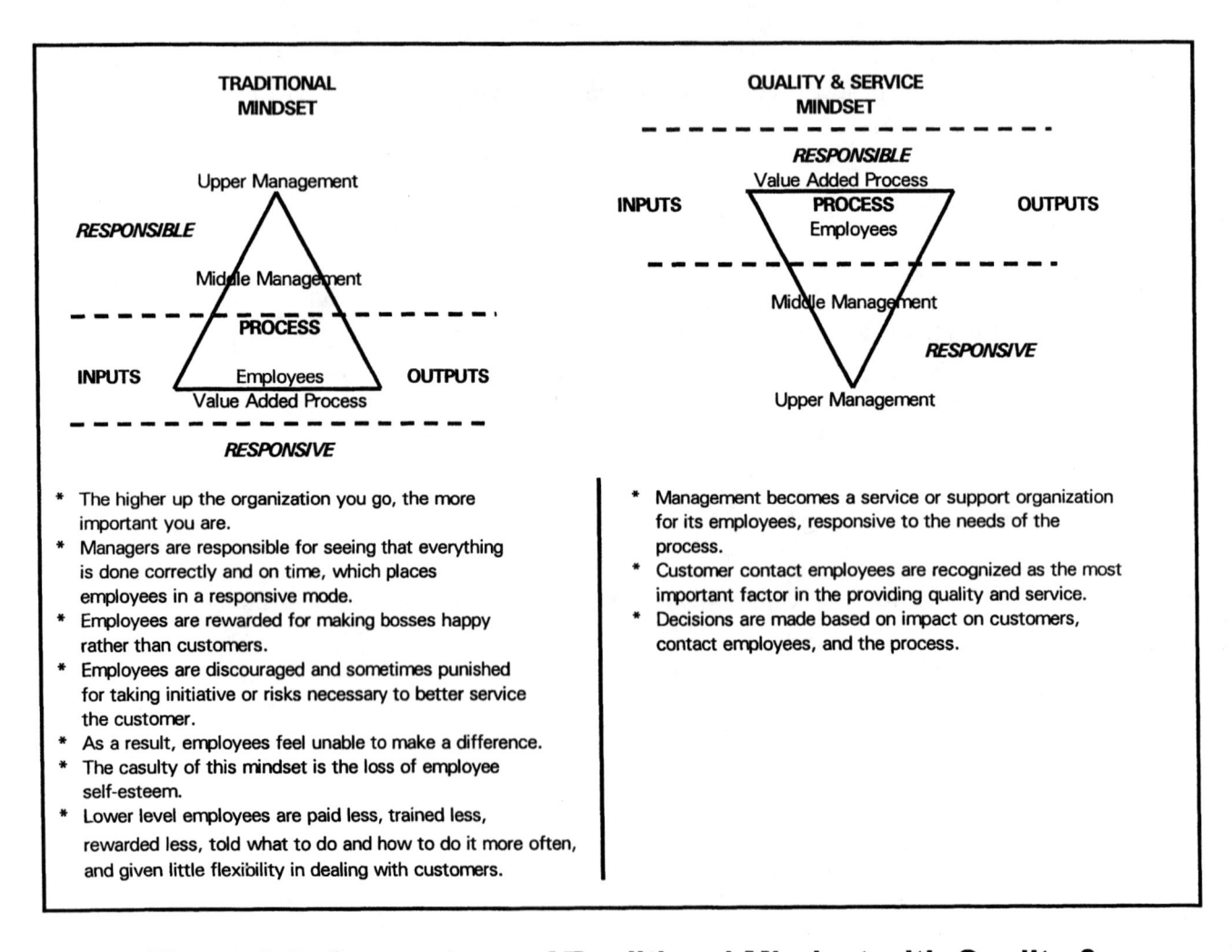

**Figure 3-5. Comparison of Traditional Mindset with Quality & Service Mindset**

There are a number of effects associated with the traditional mindset that negatively affect quality and that are not compatible with an ISO-based Quality System. These effects are listed in Figure 3-5 and should be studied thoroughly.

## Quality and Service Mindset

The correct management mindset of quality and service turns the traditional triangle over, such that the base—containing the work process, with its associated outputs and inputs—is shown at the top. In this mindset, the employees within the processes are responsible for the quality of their work and management is responsive to the needs of the employees and the process. This arrangement matches the Work Process Model, Figure 3-5, where management is responsive to the needs of the process through the controlling factors. This management mindset also allows a significant reduction in non-value added information (such as paper) and significantly improves employee morale.

## CONCLUSION

Management is responsible and should be held accountable for providing proper facilities, equipment, employee training, and employee knowledge of procedures and work process instructions for each Primary Work Process.

Management must not set performance standards that negatively affect the work process.

The ISO 9000 Standards look at the work processes through the process controlling factors.

The quality and service mindset turns the traditional mindset triangle over such that the employee within the process is responsible for the process work quality. Management becomes a service or support organization for its employees, responsive to the needs of employees and the process.

# Chapter 4
# QUALITY STRUCTURE

## QUALITY SYSTEMS

The title page of the ISO 9001 International Standard contains the following definition:

*Quality Systems—the model for quality assurance in design, development, production, installation, and servicing*

As a result, when one uses the terminology "Quality System" it is generally in reference to this ISO model for a Quality Assurance System.

The ISO 9000-Based Quality System requirements focus on control of the Work Processes as stated in Chapter 2.

*Quality is the result of controlled processes.*

The precept is that if the process is controlled, then the output quality of the process is also controlled. The Quality System accomplishes this control by requiring written operating procedures and work instructions for processes that affect quality and by requiring adherence to them.

The ISO 9000 International Standards emphasize prevention and corrective action related to errors (called non-conformances). These non-conformances occur and are found while performing according to the written procedures and work instructions and result in corrective and preventive actions. By having a Quality System, the customer is therefore offered consistent products and services that meet specified requirements. The Quality System, however, does not provide a means for continually improving the processes responsible for producing these products and services.

The Quality System itself is comprised of a Quality System Manual and a limited number of Quality System Procedures. These Quality System Procedures are overarching, in that they set the overall framework for the operating procedures—i.e., service delivery procedures, and work instructions. The content of the operating procedures and work instructions are owned by those responsible for the associated work and must represent adequately "what you do."

If the work performed is not in accordance with the content of the operating procedures, it is not that the Quality System failed, nor that the Quality System does not work. Instead, the failure is evidence that the people are not following the requirements of their own operating procedures. The correction for this might be a change in the associated procedure, more training, or personnel discipline. If a change in the procedure is required, then it involves the Quality System for documentation and re-issue in a controlled manner. The Quality System also gets involved in internal audits of the operations procedures and processes; i.e., are they being followed?

## Terminology and Intent of ISO 9000

Confused? It is easy to become so and takes some getting familiar with the terminology and the intent of the ISO 9000 International Standards in order to minimize the confusion.

*For the purposes of this book, the Quality System is simply that which is defined in the Quality System Manual and the Quality System procedures, coupled with methods for assuring compliance.*

Quality must be integrated into existing management systems and processes and should not be thought of as an additional or separate system. Failure to integrate quality into the existing management systems and processes can—and often does—create an incorrect perception of the relationship between the Quality System and Management System. This incorrect perception is that there are two distinct structures to the organization of the company, one related to the Quality System and one related to the Management System. If one accepts the definition of quality as "the way we do our work," then there really is no difference between the two, and quality is simply integrated into the Management System and structure as "the way we do our work."

Remember that the Quality System does not replace the normal management functions that include resource allocation, decision making, and process improvement, among the numerous other responsibilities.

***The Quality System cannot and does not compensate for poor management.***

It is critical to success that senior management be actively involved in the continuing integration of quality into management systems and processes. It is equally critical to success that senior management be involved in the continuing maintenance of quality relative to management systems and processes. This is most easily accomplished through the formation of a steering committee made up of senior management, which represents all major functions within the company. This steering committee (refer to Figure 4-2) is generally named the Quality Steering Committee (QSC) or Continuous Improvement Steering Committee (CISC), as desired. ABS began with QSCs and changed the name to CISCs after four (4) years to better reflect the changing role of the steering committee from quality to continuous improvement.

## CONTINUOUS IMPROVEMENT STEERING COMMITTEES

The CISC or the QSC, as the case may be, has the responsibility for the overall direction and management of the Quality System and of the integration of quality and maintenance of quality in the organization's management systems and processes. Keep in mind that these are not the same thing—direction and management of the Quality System and integration of quality into management systems.

In regards to the Quality System, as defined above, the CISC (or equivalent) carries the responsibility for successful implementation and continued maintenance of the Quality System, including the following:

- Establish guidelines and priorities for operation of the Quality System.
- Assure that all employees are appropriately trained.
- Address major quality and cycle-time issues.
- Form Corrective Action Teams (CATs) on critical quality matters/issues as deemed necessary.
- Resolve issues forwarded to the CISC from within the organization or from customers.
- Ensure that internal audits are performed and that follow-up actions resulting from those audits are accomplished.
- Review external audit findings and associated follow-up actions.
- Establish an environment of continuous improvement throughout the organization.

The CISC, as is all quality-specific teams, is a consensus group. A consensus group is one in which all participants are equal, regardless of title or position, within the organization. A consensus group arrives at a decision that each member can live with and support—as compared with an autocratic group, where the leader makes the decision, or with a democratic group, where the group votes and the majority vote is accepted as the decision. A consensus group focuses on agreement rather than on disagreement.

## Steering Committee Guidelines

Each steering committee and standing Continuous Improvement Team (CIT), as explained below, should develop a charter and publish a listing of membership.

CISC and CIT meetings must occur on a regular basis with consideration of the following meeting guidelines.

1. Start and finish the meeting on time.

2. Establish and complete the planned agenda.

3. Keep discussions relevant.

4. Do not let the meeting become a staff meeting.

5. Publish meeting minutes within three (3) working days.

6. De-emphasize status or rank.

7. Do not turn the meeting into a problem-solving session; direct problems to the appropriate people or teams for solution.

8. Strive for consensus decisions and stronger commitment to those decisions by all members.

9. Allow only one person to speak at a time; eliminate side conversations.

10. Generate different views and suggestions.

11. Don't criticize.

12. Encourage participation, but don't force it.

13. Critique each meeting as a regular agenda item and apply corrective action at the next meeting.

Each CISC should have an appointed chairperson who is responsible for agenda preparation and for facilitating the meeting.

If there are unit or division CISCs below the top level CISC, they should have a sponsor who resides on the top level CISC. The same is true for CITs or CATs, each having a sponsor residing on the chartering group.

# Continuous Improvement Teams

Continuous Improvement Teams (CITs) manage parts of the Quality System on behalf of the CISC. Each CIT has a sponsor who is a member of the CISC. The sponsor participates in the selection of a chairperson and the CIT membership. Consideration should be given to the following standing (permanent) CITs:

**Communications CIT (C-CIT):** This CIT is responsible for quality awareness and administering the employee quality recognition programs, if there are any. An example of the C-CIT Charter is to:

- Impart an ongoing awareness of the continuous improvement process.
- Encourage participation in the company's continuous improvement process.
- Develop and administer programs that acknowledge participation and achievement in the continuous improvement process.
- Cultivate an environment that encourages two-way communication.
- Nurture a commitment to the company's continuous improvement process.

**Human Resource CIT (HR-CIT):** An example of the HR-CIT Charter is to:

- Provide each employee with a clear understanding of the company's personnel policies, programs, and procedures and the role of the Human Resources Department in its implementation.
- Develop and administer policies, programs, and procedures that meet the needs of employees and their families while being cost effective.
- Provide a support role between management and employees that encourages communication and participation in an open environment.
- Ensure that all policies, programs, and procedures are designed and administered in an equitable manner to all employees in accordance with all local, state, and federal rules and laws.

- Develop and administer a Training and Career Development Plan that will achieve quality and consistency throughout the organization and enhance the level of personnel development of employees.

**Finance CIT (F-CIT):** An example of the F-CIT Charter is to:

- Provide leadership, guidance, direction, education, and monitoring of the continuous improvement system related to financial matters on behalf of the Continuous Improvement Steering Committee or equivalent.
- Assist all employees in determining and tracking work process measurements.

**Information Management Systems CIT (IMS-CIT) or equivalent:** An example of the IMS-CIT Charter is to:

- Encourage within IMS a commitment to quality and continuous improvement in the company's work processes.
- Foster the development of a thorough understanding of the company's Quality System and continuous improvement process among all IMS employees.
- Ensure IMS work processes adhere to the company's Quality System.
- Manage the IMS Corrective and Preventive Action System.

**Work Environment and Safety CIT (WES-CIT):** This CIT is generally more associated with a manufacturing organization and deals with the general work environment and safety, as stated in it's name. The makeup is flexible and the charter is flexible. Some organizations have monthly inspections by the team members with rewards and/or recognition for those areas meeting the developed requirements.

**Customer Satisfaction CIT (CS-CIT):** This CIT deals with a focus on customer satisfaction and the analysis of customer complaints, surveys, etc.

**Operations CIT (OP-CIT):** Depending on the size and complexity of the organization, this CIT would coordinate operations related items and manage the Corrective and Preventive Action System associated with operations. Normally, it is made up of the managers of each the operation departments.

**Training CIT (T-CIT):** This CIT is responsible for the training aspect of the company and is flexible in makeup and charter.

As should be evident, the CITs lend themselves to a TQM process with elements within them that enhance an ISO 9000-based Quality System and in integrating quality into management systems. If the company is implementing an ISO 9000-based Quality System as a part of a Total Quality Management System or process, then it is very important to establish the quality structure that encompasses them both. Although the ISO 9000 Standards do not require the establishment of CISCs, QSCs, or CITs, they do imply that there is a quality structure.

If the quality structure is a multi-unit one, then the establishment of a Quality Council should be a consideration. The Quality Council would have the responsibility for coordination among the various CISCs and to set policy and strategy relative to quality. The Quality Council is usually comprised of the chairpersons of each of the CISCs and selected executive management. The Quality Council would generally meet quarterly.

Of course, any structure within any company is highly dependent upon the size and geographical arrangement of that company and should be adjusted accordingly.

What is presented here may seem quite complex and lend itself for larger organizations more so than it does for the small organizations; however, the functions mentioned within the CISC and CIT charters should be considered independent of who has the responsibility for such.

Bottom line is to keep the quality organizational structure *as simple as possible* but to ensure that the structure meets the needs of the Quality System and its requirements.

## Sponsor Responsibilities

The following are examples of responsibilities that might be assigned to the sponsor of a Continuous Improvement Steering Committee (CISC), Continuous Improvement Team (CIT), or Corrective Action Team (CAT), as the case might be for a given organization.

1. Each CISC, CIT, and CAT will have a sponsor assigned by the originating function who resides on that originating function.

2. The sponsor assists in selection of the team chairperson and team members, as necessary and appropriate.

3. The sponsor assists in the establishment of the team charter, if not already established by the originating function that chartered the team or committee.

4. The sponsor assists in removing any barriers that might interfere with the team's performance of its charter.

5. The sponsor monitors the status of the assigned team or committee and reports that status to the respective originating function that chartered the team or committee.

6. The sponsor of CITs and CATs will not normally attend all meetings.

7. Closeout report presentations are coordinated through the respective sponsor.

8. The sponsor is not to interfere in the CIT or CAT operation except to provide guidance and assistance as necessary.

9. CISC sponsors are normally the highest-ranking individuals of the respective organization represented by the CISC.

## QUALITY SYSTEM AWARENESS TRAINING

Once the Quality System has been established and the Mission Statements, Quality Policy, Quality Goals, and Quality Plan have been developed, it is important to make everyone within the company aware of it. This is generally accomplished through a planned presentation made to all employees. The presentation averages about three hours in duration and may include handouts and an applicable video. The quality awareness presentation should be designed to cover "where we are," "where we are going," "how we are going to get there," and "what is our involvement." The quality awareness material is company specific and should be made a part of the new hire orientation program. The ISO 9000 Standards do not require a quality awareness presentation, but experience shows that it is a necessity to have everyone onboard with a common understanding of the Quality System for the implementation efforts to succeed with a minimum of effort.

A typical quality awareness training index might include:

1. A welcome and an introduction

2. A Mission Statement, including quality policies and goals

3. A definition of quality

4. A definition of Total Quality Management (TQM) (as applicable)

5. A definition of cycle time (as applicable)

6. A presentation of the company's quality structure

7. A description of the company's Quality System

8. A review of "where are we now" and "what comes next"

9. A plan for continuous improvement

10. A video on quality (approximately 25 minutes in length is recommended)

The quality awareness presentation is usually the first exposure of the employee to the Quality System and therefore must be very well conceived and presented, because it sets the stage for success. A senior management representative should participate in each of the sessions.

## DETERMINATION OF APPLICABLE ISO STANDARDS

Almost every ISO 9000 Quality System book published includes a chapter and method for the determination of the applicable ISO Standard for your specific company or organization. It is a very simple process.

ISO 9001, 9002, and 9003 are the Quality System Standards from which to choose. One of these three standards will provide the model for the Quality System being implemented as appropriate for the specific company type.

ISO 9001 is to be used where the company is involved in the design, development, production installation, and servicing of a product of service.

Care must be taken not to dismiss ISO 9001 too quickly, because many service companies do design and develop those services, requiring ISO 9001 compliance.

ISO 9002 is used where there is no design activity.

ISO 9003 is used by companies manufacturing relatively simple products that conform to specified requirements and that can be quality assured by final inspection and test without the need for any special quality control during production.

ISO 9000 and ISO 9004-1 provide general guidance on Quality System requirements and should be consulted to obtain assistance with the understanding of ISO 9001, 9002, and 9003.

The ISO 9000 Standard guidelines for selection and use should be read prior to making the decision as to which standard to use. This standard is easy to read and understand.

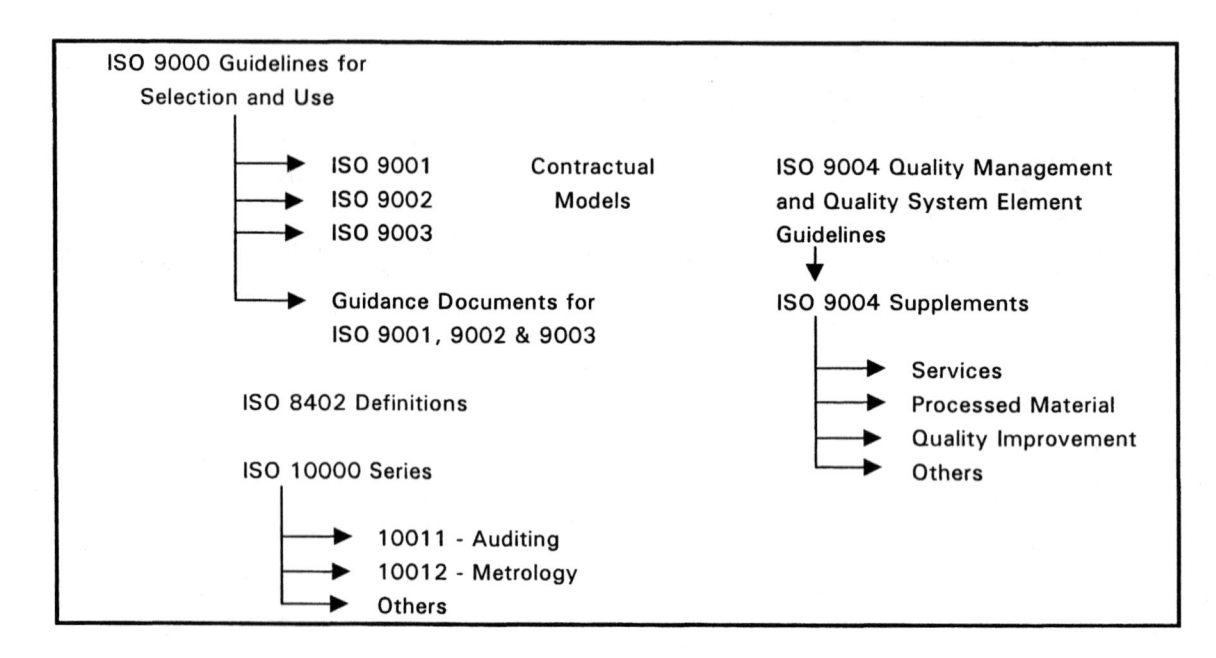

```
ISO 9000 Guidelines for
   Selection and Use
           |
           ├──▶ ISO 9001      Contractual      ISO 9004 Quality Management
           ├──▶ ISO 9002        Models         and Quality System Element
           ├──▶ ISO 9003                       Guidelines
           |                                           ▼
           └──▶ Guidance Documents for         ISO 9004 Supplements
                ISO 9001, 9002 & 9003                  |
                                                       ├──▶ Services
   ISO 8402 Definitions                                ├──▶ Processed Material
                                                       ├──▶ Quality Improvement
   ISO 10000 Series                                    └──▶ Others
           |
           ├──▶ 10011 - Auditing
           ├──▶ 10012 - Metrology
           └──▶ Others
```

**Figure 4-1. ISO 9000 Guidelines for Selection and Use**

## CONCLUSION

In summary, the normal management functions of operations should include, if they do not already:

- Problem identification
- Prioritization

- Prioritization
- Corrective action
- Measurement
- Follow-up
- Verification
- Process improvement
- Continuous improvement

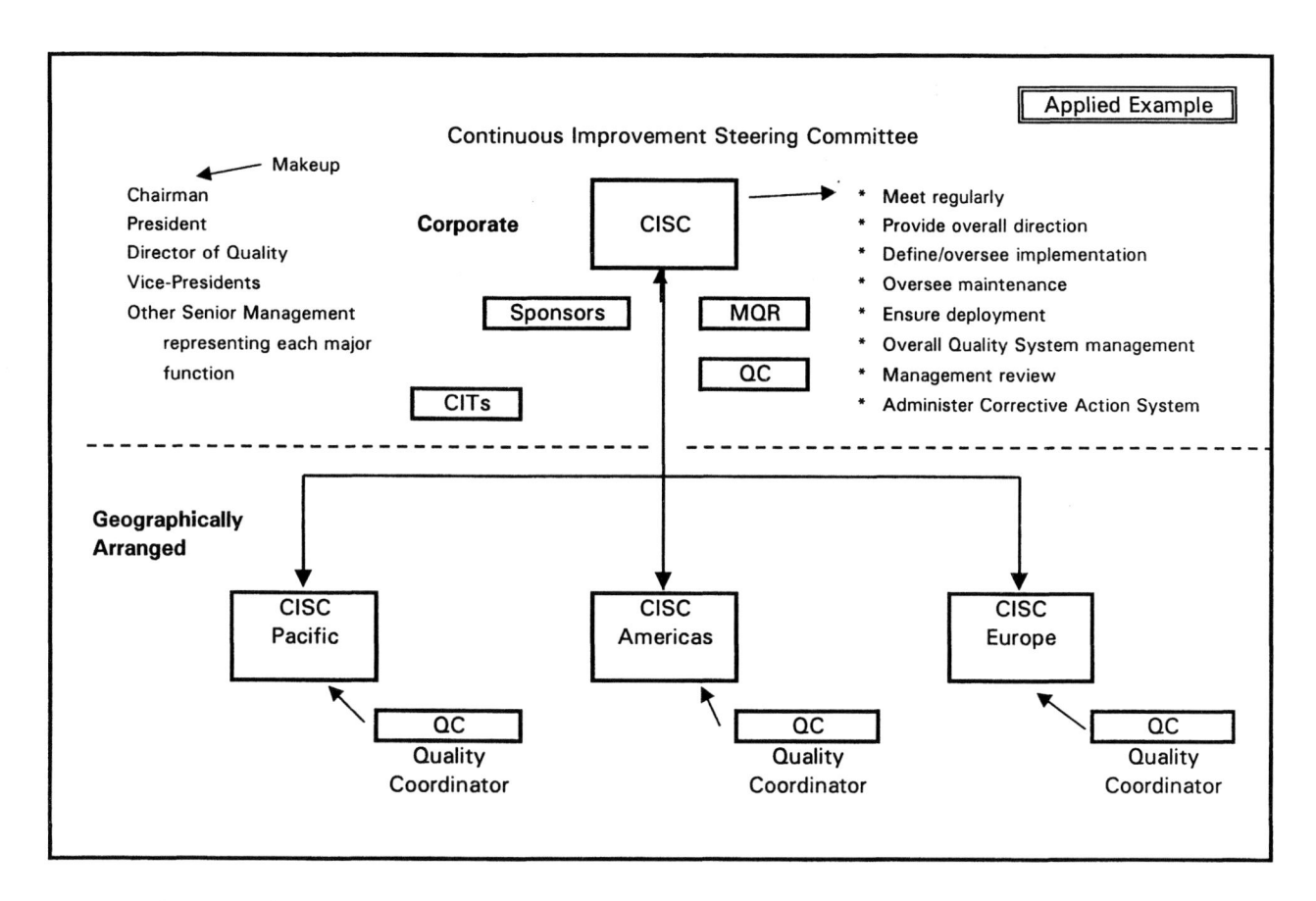

```
                                                              Applied Example
              Continuous Improvement Steering Committee

        Makeup
Chairman                                        *  Meet regularly
President              Corporate      CISC   →  *  Provide overall direction
Director of Quality                             *  Define/oversee implementation
Vice-Presidents                                 *  Oversee maintenance
Other Senior Management     Sponsors    MQR     *  Ensure deployment
  representing each major                       *  Overall Quality System management
  function                              QC      *  Management review
                              CITs              *  Administer Corrective Action System

-------------------------------------------------------------------

Geographically
Arranged

           CISC              CISC              CISC
           Pacific           Americas          Europe

              QC                QC                QC
           Quality           Quality           Quality
          Coordinator       Coordinator       Coordinator
```

**Figure 4-2. Overall Quality System Structure**

The Quality System requires operations to have a method of providing products/services that consistently meet specified requirements. This is accomplished through the requiring of operations procedures/work instructions, training, and resource allocation. The Quality System also requires independent audit of operations for compliance with the respective procedures/work instructions, noting variations as non-conformances.

The Quality System provides overarching procedures that define how to write operations procedures/work instructions, format requirements, and methods for change and their controlled distribution, but not their content.

The formation of steering committee(s) is one method of ensuring continuous involvement of management in the quality improvement process.

# Chapter 5

# QUALITY SYSTEM SELF ASSESSMENT

## SELF-ASSESSMENT GUIDELINES

Some companies and organizations avoid self-assessments because of a feeling of inadequacy or of not really wanting to know the present status of their respective Quality System, or for a number of unexplained reasons. They should not do so!

Self-assessment is an effective tool for establishing a baseline with which to compare later status and a real learning experience that speeds up the implementation process.

Provided in this chapter is a model for self-assessment coupled with a unique method of rating and prioritizing needs. The method may be adapted and customized to assess almost any organizational area or function.

In addition, a complete self-assessment versus the 1994 ISO 9001 Standard is provided, the results of which are cross referenced to the 1994 ISO 9001 Standard.

From this self-assessment, one can determine the company or organization Quality System implementation needs that can be used to develop a Quality System Implementation Plan (see Chapter 6).

## Needs Assessment

The self-assessment is based on a series of questions for each element of the ISO 9001-1994 Standard, which includes two viewpoints, "current implementation status" and perceived importance" of the element. The results are expressed in numerical form and prioritized based on implementation need.

The information can then be converted into a Quality Action Plan relative to the Quality System.

It is suggested that each member of the management team making up the Quality Steering Committee or equivalent quality system structure complete the assessment questionnaire. The results should then be analyzed, averaged, and compiled using the

"Needs Assessment Listing—Ranked by Need" form. The results of this effort can then be used in the development of the Quality System Implementation Plan and in the determination of priorities of effort.

In addition, each specific section of the self-assessment should be individually analyzed to determine the individual element implementation needs or commitment as noted in Columns A and B of the form. Any Column A element of less than 4 indicates an implementation need for that element and any Column B element of less than 4 indicates a lack of commitment or understanding for that elements' importance.

## Conclusion

It is suggested that this self-assessment be completed annually for the first two years of the implementation process. It is also noted that the format may be adapted for other use within the company or organization.

## Needs Assessment Inventory

| In your view, with what success is this being achieved in your company?<br>5 4 3 2 1<br>Column A | 4.1 Management Commitment<br><br>Instructions: Read the assessment question/statement and circle your response in Column A and B; total column A and enter in the marked box.<br>5 4 3 2 1 | In your view, how important is this item?<br>5 4 3 2 1<br>Column B |
|---|---|---|
| 5 4 3 2 1 | 1. Is Senior Management committed to Quality? | 5 4 3 2 1 |
| 5 4 3 2 1 | 2. Has management developed and published a Quality Policy? | 5 4 3 2 1 |
| 5 4 3 2 1 | 3. Do all employees know and understand the Quality Policy? | 5 4 3 2 1 |
| 5 4 3 2 1 | 4. Has management established a Quality Structure within the organization; i.e., Continuous Improvement Steering Committee, Continuous Improvement teams, or equivalent? | 5 4 3 2 1 |
| 5 4 3 2 1 | 5. Is there an organization chart identifying the inter-relation of all personnel who manage, perform, and verify work affecting quality? | 5 4 3 2 1 |
| 5 4 3 2 1 | 6. Is the Company's organizational structure such that it allows for employee involvement in problem identification and problem solving? | 5 4 3 2 1 |
| 5 4 3 2 1 | 7. Is there a Director of Quality or equivalent? | 5 4 3 2 1 |
| 5 4 3 2 1 | 8. Has management developed, published, and distributed a Mission Statement? | 5 4 3 2 1 |
| 5 4 3 2 1 | 9. Does the organization have a published Code-of-Ethics? | 5 4 3 2 1 |
| 5 4 3 2 1 | 10. Have the organization's Quality goals and objectives been established? | 5 4 3 2 1 |
| Any A Item of < 4 reflects a need in that category. | Summation A     Difference<br>[ 50 ] − [ ] = [ ]<br><br>00-10 = Excellent<br>11-20 = Needs Work<br>21-30 = Strong Need<br>31-50 = Very Strong Need | Any B Item of < 4 reflects a need for improved commitment in that category. |

## Needs Assessment Inventory *(continued)*

| In your view, with what success is this being achieved in your company?<br>5  4  3  2  1<br>Column A | 4.2 Quality System<br><br>Instructions: Read the assessment question/statement and circle your response in Column A and B; total column A and enter in the marked box. | In your view, how important is this item?<br>5  4  3  2  1<br>Column B |
|---|---|---|
| 5  4  3  2  1 | 1. Is the Quality System documented and maintained as defined in a Quality Manual? | 5  4  3  2  1 |
| 5  4  3  2  1 | 2. Have documented procedures been prepared and distributed? | 5  4  3  2  1 |
| 5  4  3  2  1 | 3. Have the procedures and the Quality System been effectively implemented? | 5  4  3  2  1 |
| 5  4  3  2  1 | 4. Have "How the requirements for quality will be met" been defined and documented? | 5  4  3  2  1 |
| 5  4  3  2  1 | 5. Are there prepared Quality Plans or equivalent? | 5  4  3  2  1 |
| 5  4  3  2  1 | 6. Have resource needs been assessed, including personnel, equipment, and training? | 5  4  3  2  1 |
| 5  4  3  2  1 | 7. Is there a process in place that provides a continuous forward looking analysis of quality, measurement, and verification requirements? | 5  4  3  2  1 |

Summation A        Difference

**35** − ☐ = ☐

00-07 = Excellent
08-14 = Needs Work
15-22 = Strong Need
23-35 = Very Strong Need

Any A Item of < 4 reflects a need in that category.

Any B Item of < 4 reflects a need for improved commitment in that category.

## Needs Assessment Inventory *(continued)*

| In your view, with what success is this being achieved in your company?<br>5  4  3  2  1<br>Column A | 4.3 Contract Review<br><br>Instructions: Read the assessment question/statement and circle your response in Column A and B; total column A and enter in the marked box. | In your view, how important is this item?<br>5  4  3  2  1<br>Column B |
|---|---|---|
| 5  4  3  2  1 | 1. Have documented procedures for Contract Review and the coordination of associated activities been established and are they maintained? | 5  4  3  2  1 |
|  | 2. Is each accepted tender, order, and contract reviewed to ensure that: |  |
| 5  4  3  2  1 | 2.1 The requirements are adequately defined and documented? | 5  4  3  2  1 |
| 5  4  3  2  1 | 2.2 The differences between tender and accepted order requirements are resolved? | 5  4  3  2  1 |
| 5  4  3  2  1 | 2.3 The capability to meet contract or accepted order requirements exist? | 5  4  3  2  1 |
| 5  4  3  2  1 | 3. Is there a documented procedure for identifying how amendments to a cotnract are made and correctly transferred to concerned functions? | 5  4  3  2  1 |
| 5  4  3  2  1 | 4. Are records of contract reviews maintained? | 5  4  3  2  1 |

Summation A  Difference

$$30 - \boxed{\phantom{00}} = \boxed{\phantom{00}}$$

00-06 = Excellent
07-12 = Needs Work
13-18 = Strong Need
19-30 = Very Strong Need

Any A Item of < 4 reflects a need in that category.

Any B Item of < 4 reflects a need for improved commitment in that category.

## Needs Assessment Inventory *(continued)*

| In your view, with what success is this being achieved in your company? | 4.4 Design Control<br><br>Instructions: Read the assessment question/statement and circle your response in Column A and B; total column A and enter in the marked box. | In your view, how important is this item? |
|---|---|---|
| 5  4  3  2  1<br>Column A | | 5  4  3  2  1<br>Column B |
| 5  4  3  2  1 | 1. Have documented procedures for the verification and control of the design of products or services been established and are they maintained? | 5  4  3  2  1 |
| 5  4  3  2  1 | 2. Are plans for each design and development activity prepared, maintained and utilized? | 5  4  3  2  1 |
| 5  4  3  2  1 | 3. Are interfaces between different groups which input to the design process defined and the necessary information documented, transmitted and regularly reviewed? | 5  4  3  2  1 |
| 5  4  3  2  1 | 4. Are design inputs identified, documented and reviewed? | 5  4  3  2  1 |
| 5  4  3  2  1 | 5. Are formal documented reviews planned and conducted at appropriate stages of design? | 5  4  3  2  1 |
| 5  4  3  2  1 | 6. Are design outputs documented and expressed in terms of requirements that can be verified? | 5  4  3  2  1 |
| 5  4  3  2  1 | 7. Is design verification performed at appropriate stages of the design? | 5  4  3  2  1 |
| 5  4  3  2  1 | 8. Is design validation performed to ensure that the product or service conforms to the defined user needs or requirements? | 5  4  3  2  1 |
| 5  4  3  2  1 | 9. Are all design changes and modificaitons identified, documented, reviewed and approved by authorized personnel before realization? | 5  4  3  2  1 |
| | [ 45 ] − [   ] = [   ] | |
| Any A Item of < 4 reflects a need in that category. | 00-09 = Excellent<br>10-18 = Needs Work<br>19-27 = Strong Need<br>28-45 = Very Strong Need | Any B Item of < 4 reflects a need for improved commitment in that category. |

## Needs Assessment Inventory *(continued)*

| In your view, with what success is this being achieved in your company?<br>5  4  3  2  1<br>Column A | 4.5 Document and Data Control<br><br>Instructions: Read the assessment question/statement and circle your response in Column A and B; total column A and enter in the marked box. | In your view, how important is this item?<br>5  4  3  2  1<br>Column B |
|---|---|---|
| 5  4  3  2  1 | 1. Have documented procedures been established and maintained to control all documents and data for work affecting quality? | 5  4  3  2  1 |
| 5  4  3  2  1 | 2. Are documents and data reviewed and approved for adequacy by authorized personnel prior to issue? | 5  4  3  2  1 |
| 5  4  3  2  1 | 3. Is there a Master List or equivalent Document Control procedure identifying the current revision status of documents? | 5  4  3  2  1 |
|  | 4. Are controls in place to ensure that: |  |
| 5  4  3  2  1 | 4.1 The pertinent issues of appropriate documents are available at all locations where the work is performed? | 5  4  3  2  1 |
| 5  4  3  2  1 | 4.2 Invalid and obsolete documents are promptly removed from all points of issue or use? | 5  4  3  2  1 |
| 5  4  3  2  1 | 4.3 Any obsolete documents retained for legal or knowledge preservation purposes are suitably identified? | 5  4  3  2  1 |
| 5  4  3  2  1 | 5. Are changes to documents reviewed and approved by the same functions/organizations that performed the original review and approval (unless otherwise designated)? | 5  4  3  2  1 |
| Any A Item of < 4 reflects a need in that category. | Summation A    Difference<br>[ 35 ] − [  ]  =  [  ]<br><br>00-07 = Excellent<br>08-14 = Needs Work<br>15-22 = Strong Need<br>23-35 = Very Strong Need | Any B Item of < 4 reflects a need for improved commitment in that category. |

## Needs Assessment Inventory *(continued)*

| In your view, with what success is this being achieved in your company?<br>5  4  3  2  1<br>Column A | 4.6 Purchasing and Supplier Control<br><br>Instructions: Read the assessment question/statement and circle your response in Column A and B; total column A and enter in the marked box. | In your view, how important is this item?<br>5  4  3  2  1<br>Column B |
|---|---|---|
| 5  4  3  2  1 | 1. Have documented procedures been established and maintained to ensure that purchased product or services conform to specified requirements? | 5  4  3  2  1 |
| 5  4  3  2  1 | 2. Are suppliers of product or services evaluated and selected on the basis of their ability to meet specified requirements? | 5  4  3  2  1 |
| 5  4  3  2  1 | 3. Is the type and extent of control exercised over suppliers of product and services defined? | 5  4  3  2  1 |
| 5  4  3  2  1 | 4. Are quality records of acceptable suppliers of product and services established and maintained? | 5  4  3  2  1 |
| 5  4  3  2  1 | 5. Do purchasing documents contain data that clearly describe the product or service? | 5  4  3  2  1 |
| 5  4  3  2  1 | 6. Are purchasing documents reviewed for adequacy of specified requirements prior to release? | 5  4  3  2  1 |
| 5  4  3  2  1 | 7. Do procedures include verification at the suppliers' facilities (if applicable) and customer verification of the supplier product or service (if applicable) | 5  4  3  2  1 |

Summation A       Difference

[ 35 ] − [    ] = [    ]

00-07 = Excellent
08-14 = Needs Work
15-22 = Strong Need
23-35 = Very Strong Need

Any A Item of < 4 reflects a need in that category.

Any B Item of < 4 reflects a need for improved commitment in that category.

## Needs Assessment Inventory *(continued)*

| In your view, with what success is this being achieved in your company?<br>5  4  3  2  1<br>Column A | 4.7 Control of Customer Supplied Product<br><br>Instructions: Read the assessment question/statement and circle your response in Column A and B; total column A and enter in the marked box. | In your view, how important is this item?<br>5  4  3  2  1<br>Column B |
|---|---|---|
| 5  4  3  2  1 | 1. Have documented procedures been established and maintained for verification, storage, and maintenance of customer supplied product that is provided for incorporation or use? | 5  4  3  2  1 |
| 5  4  3  2  1 | 2. Has a means been established for recording and reporting to the customer any customer provided product that is lost, damaged, or otherwise unsuitable for use? | 5  4  3  2  1 |

Summation A        Difference

$$10 - \boxed{\phantom{00}} = \boxed{\phantom{00}}$$

00-02 = Excellent
03-04 = Needs Work
05-06 = Strong Need
07-10 = Very Strong Need

Any A Item of < 4 reflects a need in that category.

Any B Item of < 4 reflects a need for improved commitment in that category.

## Needs Assessment Inventory *(continued)*

| In your view, with what success is this being achieved in your company?<br><br>5  4  3  2  1<br>Column A | 4.8 Product Identification, Status, and Traceability<br><br>Instructions: Read the assessment question/statement and circle your response in Column A and B; total column A and enter in the marked box.<br><br>5  4  3  2  1 | In your view, how important is this item?<br><br>5  4  3  2  1<br>Column B |
|---|---|---|
| 5  4  3  2  1 | 1. Where appropriate, have procedures been established and maintained for identifying the product or service provided by suitable means from receipt through installation? | 5  4  3  2  1 |
| 5  4  3  2  1 | 2. Where traceablity is a specified requirement, have procedures been established, documented, and maintained for unique identification of individual product, service, or batches? | 5  4  3  2  1 |

Summation A — Difference

| 10 | − | | = | |

00-02 = Excellent
03-04 = Needs Work
05-06 = Strong Need
07-10 = Very Strong Need

Any A Item of < 4 reflects a need in that category.

Any B Item of < 4 reflects a need for improved commitment in that category.

## Needs Assessment Inventory *(continued)*

| In your view, with what success is this being achieved in your company?<br>5  4  3  2  1<br>Column A | 4.9 Process Control (Work Control)<br><br>Instructions: Read the assessment question/statement and circle your response in Column A and B; total column A and enter in the marked box. | In your view, how important is this item?<br>5  4  3  2  1<br>Column B |
|---|---|---|
| 5  4  3  2  1 | 1. Have the production, installation, and servicing processes that directly affect quality (Primary Work Processes) been identified and planned? | 5  4  3  2  1 |
| 5  4  3  2  1 | 2. Are there assurances that these Primary Work Processes are carried out under controlled conditions? (Documented procedurees, proper equipment, compliance with standards/codes, monitoring, approvals, stipulated workmanship criteria, suitable equipment maintenance). | 5  4  3  2  1 |
| 5  4  3  2  1 | 3. Are requirements documented and controlled for any qualification of process operations, including equipment and associated personnel? | 5  4  3  2  1 |
| 5  4  3  2  1 | 4. Are records maintained for qualified processes, equipment and personnel? | 5  4  3  2  1 |

Summation A      Difference

$$\boxed{20} - \boxed{\phantom{0}} = \boxed{\phantom{0}}$$

00-04 = Excellent
05-08 = Needs Work
09-12 = Strong Need
13-20 = Very Strong Need

Any A Item of < 4 reflects a need in that category.

Any B Item of < 4 reflects a need for improved commitment in that category.

## Needs Assessment Inventory (continued)

| In your view, with what success is this being achieved in your company?<br>5  4  3  2  1<br>Column A | 4.10 Inspection and Testing<br><br>Instructions: Read the assessment question/statement and circle your response in Column A and B; total column A and enter in the marked box. | In your view, how important is this item?<br>5  4  3  2  1<br>Column B |
|---|---|---|
| 5  4  3  2  1 | 1. Have procedures been established and maintained for inspection and testing activities in order to verify that the specified requirements are met? | 5  4  3  2  1 |
| 5  4  3  2  1 | 2. Are the required inspection and testing documented? | 5  4  3  2  1 |
| 5  4  3  2  1 | 3. Is incoming product inspected or otherwise verified prior to use? | 5  4  3  2  1 |
| 5  4  3  2  1 | 4. Is evidence of conformance of incoming product provided? | 5  4  3  2  1 |
| 5  4  3  2  1 | 5. Is there an incoming "fast track" mechanism with proper controls and procedures (release of incoming product prior to verification)? | 5  4  3  2  1 |
| 5  4  3  2  1 | 6. Is in-process inspection, testing, and monitoring (as applicable) carried out in accordance with documented procedures or by a process specific quality plan. | 5  4  3  2  1 |
| 5  4  3  2  1 | 7. Do the documented procedures or quality plan include hold points until the required inspection, testing, or monitoring (as applicable) are carried out? | 5  4  3  2  1 |
| 5  4  3  2  1 | 8. Do the procedures include positive product recall? | 5  4  3  2  1 |
| 5  4  3  2  1 | 9. Is final product or service inspection and testing carried out in accordance with documented procedures or specific quality plan to complete the evidence of conformance of the finished product or service to specified requirements? | 5  4  3  2  1 |
| 5  4  3  2  1 | 10. Are there documented methods in place to ensure that no product is dispatched until all of the activities specified in the procedure or quality plan have been satisfactorily completed and verified? | 5  4  3  2  1 |
| 5  4  3  2  1 | 11. Are records maintained that provide evidence that the product has been inspected or tested and whether the product has passed or failed? | 5  4  3  2  1 |

Summation A  Difference

[ 55 ] − [   ] = [   ]

Any A Item of < 4 reflects a need in that category.

```
00-11 = Excellent
12-22 = Needs Work
23-33 = Strong Need
34-55 = Very Strong Need
```

Any B Item of < 4 reflects a need for improved commitment in that category.

## Needs Assessment Inventory *(continued)*

| In your view, with what success is this being achieved in your company? | 4.11 Control of Inspection, Measuring, and Test Equipment<br><br>Instructions: Read the assessment question/statement and circle your response in Column A and B; total column A and enter in the marked box. | In your view, how important is this item? |
|---|---|---|
| 5  4  3  2  1<br>Column A | | 5  4  3  2  1<br>Column B |
| 5  4  3  2  1 | 1. Have documented procedures been established and maintained to control, calibrate, and maintain inspection, measuring, and test equipment (including test software) used to demonstrate the conformance to the specified requirements? | 5  4  3  2  1 |
| 5  4  3  2  1 | 2. Has the test software or comparative reference hardware (when used) been checked to ensure that they are capable of verifying the acceptability of the product? | 5  4  3  2  1 |
| 5  4  3  2  1 | 3. Is technical data available for verification that the test software and devices are functionally adequate? | 5  4  3  2  1 |
| 5  4  3  2  1 | 4. Have control procedures been established for inspection, measuring, and test equipment which included:<br>4.1  The requirements for selection? | 5  4  3  2  1 |
| 5  4  3  2  1 | 4.2  The identification of and traceability to a Standard? | 5  4  3  2  1 |
| 5  4  3  2  1 | 4.3  The calibration process employed? | 5  4  3  2  1 |
| 5  4  3  2  1 | 4.4  The maintenance of calibration records? | 5  4  3  2  1 |
| 5  4  3  2  1 | 4.5  The retention of historical data for each piece of equipment or software? | 5  4  3  2  1 |
| 5  4  3  2  1 | 4.6  Insurance of suitable environmental conditions? | 5  4  3  2  1 |
| 5  4  3  2  1 | 4.7  Insurance that the handling, preservation, and storage is such that the accuracy and fitness for use is maintained? | 5  4  3  2  1 |
| 5  4  3  2  1 | 4.8  Insurance that the calibration settings are safeguarded from unauthorized adjustments? | 5  4  3  2  1 |

Summation A  —  Difference

| 55 | − | ☐ | = | ☐ |

00-11 = Excellent
12-22 = Needs Work
23-33 = Strong Need
34-55 = Very Strong Need

Any A Item of < 4 reflects a need in that category.

Any B Item of < 4 reflects a need for improved commitment in that category.

# Needs Assessment Inventory *(continued)*

| In your view, with what success is this being achieved in your company?<br>5  4  3  2  1<br>Column A | **4.12 Inspection and Test Status**<br><br>Instructions: Read the assessment question/statement and circle your response in Column A and B; total column A and enter in the marked box. | In your view, how important is this item?<br>5  4  3  2  1<br>Column B |
|---|---|---|
| 5  4  3  2  1 | 1. Has the inspection and test status of product been identified to indicate the conformance or non-conformance of product with regard to inspection and tests performed? | 5  4  3  2  1 |
| 5  4  3  2  1 | 2. Is the identification of inspection and test status maintained and defined in documented procedures or quality plan? | 5  4  3  2  1 |

Summation A − ☐ = Difference ☐

10

00-02 = Excellent
03-04 = Needs Work
05-06 = Strong Need
07-10 = Very Strong Need

Any A Item of < 4 reflects a need in that category.

Any B Item of < 4 reflects a need for improved commitment in that category.

## Needs Assessment Inventory *(continued)*

| In your view, with what success is this being achieved in your company?<br>5  4  3  2  1<br>Column A | 4.13 Control of Non-conforming Product<br><br>Instructions: Read the assessment question/statement and circle your response in Column A and B; total column A and enter in the marked box. | In your view, how important is this item?<br>5  4  3  2  1<br>Column B |
|---|---|---|
| 5  4  3  2  1 | 1. Are documented procedures established and maintained to ensure that product that does not conform to specified requirements is prevented from unintended use or installation? | 5  4  3  2  1 |
| 5  4  3  2  1 | 2. Does control of non-conforming product provide for identification, documentation, evaluation, segregation (when practical), and disposition of non-conforming product? | 5  4  3  2  1 |
| 5  4  3  2  1 | 3. Has the responsibility for review and authority for the disposition of non-conforming product been defined? | 5  4  3  2  1 |
| 5  4  3  2  1 | 4. Is non-conforming product reviewed in accordance with documented procedures? | 5  4  3  2  1 |
| 5  4  3  2  1 | 5. Is repaired or reworked product re-inspected in accordance with documented procedures or the product quality plan? | 5  4  3  2  1 |

Summation A          Difference

25  −  ☐  =  ☐

00-05 = Excellent
06-10 = Needs Work
11-15 = Strong Need
16-25 = Very Strong Need

Any A Item of < 4 reflects a need in that category.

Any B Item of < 4 reflects a need for improved commitment in that category.

## Needs Assessment Inventory *(continued)*

| In your view, with what success is this being achieved in your company?<br>5  4  3  2  1<br>Column A | 4.14 Corrective and Preventive Action<br><br>Instructions: Read the assessment question/statement and circle your response in Column A and B; total column A and enter in the marked box.<br>5  4  3  2  1 | In your view, how important is this item?<br>5  4  3  2  1<br>Column B |
|---|---|---|
| 5  4  3  2  1 | 1. Have documented procedures been established and maintained for implementing corrective action and preventive action? | 5  4  3  2  1 |
| 5  4  3  2  1 | 2. Are changes in the documented procedures that result from corrective or preventive actions recorded? | 5  4  3  2  1 |
|  | 3. Do the procedures for corrective action include: |  |
| 5  4  3  2  1 | 3.1 The effective handling of customer complaints and reports of product or service nonconformities? | 5  4  3  2  1 |
| 5  4  3  2  1 | 3.2 The documented investigation of the cause of nonconformities relating to product, service, process, and the quality system? | 5  4  3  2  1 |
| 5  4  3  2  1 | 3.3 The determination of the corrective action needed to eliminate the cause of nonconformities? | 5  4  3  2  1 |
| 5  4  3  2  1 | 3.4 The application of controls to ensure that effective corrective action is taken? | 5  4  3  2  1 |
|  | 4. Do the procedures for preventative action include? |  |
| 5  4  3  2  1 | 4.1 The use of appropriate sources of information to detect, analyze, and eliminate potential causes of nonconformities? | 5  4  3  2  1 |
| 5  4  3  2  1 | 4.2 The determination of the steps to deal with any problems requiring preventive action? | 5  4  3  2  1 |
| 5  4  3  2  1 | 4.3 The initiation of preventive actions and application of controls to ensure effectiveness? | 5  4  3  2  1 |
| 5  4  3  2  1 | 4.4 The insurance that associated procedures are changed as a result of preventative actions? | 5  4  3  2  1 |

Summation A — Difference

**50** − ☐ = ☐

Any A Item of < 4 reflects a need in that category.

00-10 = Excellent
11-20 = Needs Work
21-30 = Strong Need
31-50 = Very Strong Need

Any B Item of < 4 reflects a need for improved commitment in that category.

## Needs Assessment Inventory (continued)

| In your view, with what success is this being achieved in your company? | 4.15 Handling, Storage, Packaging, Preservation, and Delivery | In your view, how important is this item? |
|---|---|---|
| 5  4  3  2  1<br>Column A | Instructions: Read the assessment question/statement and circle your response in Column A and B; total column A and enter in the marked box. | 5  4  3  2  1<br>Column B |
| 5  4  3  2  1 | 1. Are methods of handling product in place that prevent damage or deterioration? | 5  4  3  2  1 |
| 5  4  3  2  1 | 2. Are designated storage areas or stock rooms provided? | 5  4  3  2  1 |
| 5  4  3  2  1 | 2.1 Are appropriate methods for authorizing receipt and dispatch to and from such areas defined? | 5  4  3  2  1 |
| 5  4  3  2  1 | 2.2 Is the condition of the product in stock assessed at appropriate intervals? | 5  4  3  2  1 |
| 5  4  3  2  1 | 3. Are the packaging and marking processes controlled to the extent necessary to ensure conformance to specified requirements? | 5  4  3  2  1 |
| 5  4  3  2  1 | 4. Are appropriate methods for the preservation and segregation of product applied? | 5  4  3  2  1 |
| 5  4  3  2  1 | 5. Have proper arrangements been made for the protection of the product quality after final inspection and test, including during delivery, where contractually specified? | 5  4  3  2  1 |

Summation A — ☐ = Difference ☐

**35** − ☐ = ☐

00-07 = Excellent
08-14 = Needs Work
15-22 = Strong Need
23-35 = Very Strong Need

Any A Item of < 4 reflects a need in that category.

Any B Item of < 4 reflects a need for improved commitment in that category.

## Needs Assessment Inventory (continued)

| In your view, with what success is this being achieved in your company?<br>5 4 3 2 1<br>Column A | 4.16 Control and Retention of Quality Records<br><br>Instructions: Read the assessment question/statement and circle your response in Column A and B; total column A and enter in the marked box. | In your view, how important is this item?<br>5 4 3 2 1<br>Column B |
|---|---|---|
| 5 4 3 2 1 | 1. Have documented procedures been established and maintained for the identification, collection, indexing, access, filing, storage, maintenance, retention, and disposition of quality records? | 5 4 3 2 1 |
| 5 4 3 2 1 | 2. Are pertinent supplier and sub-contractor quality records an element of this data? | 5 4 3 2 1 |
| 5 4 3 2 1 | 3. Are quality records legible and readily retrievable? | 5 4 3 2 1 |
| 5 4 3 2 1 | 4. Are quality records stored in facilities that provide a suitable environment to minimize damage, deterioration, or loss. | 5 4 3 2 1 |

Summation A − ☐ = Difference ☐

20

00-04 = Excellent
05-08 = Needs Work
09-12 = Strong Need
13-20 = Very Strong Need

Any A Item of < 4 reflects a need in that category.

Any B Item of < 4 reflects a need for improved commitment in that category.

## Needs Assessment Inventory (continued)

| In your view, with what success is this being achieved in your company?<br>5  4  3  2  1<br>Column A | 4.17 Internal Quality Audits<br><br>Instructions: Read the assessment question/statement and circle your response in Column A and B; total column A and enter in the marked box. | In your view, how important is this item?<br>5  4  3  2  1<br>Column B |
|---|---|---|
| 5  4  3  2  1 | 1. Have documented procedures been established and maintained for planning and implementing internal quality audits? | 5  4  3  2  1 |
| 5  4  3  2  1 | 2. Do the internal quality audits verify whether the quality activities and related results comply with planned arrangements and do they determine the effectiveness of the quality system? | 5  4  3  2  1 |
| 5  4  3  2  1 | 3. Are the internal quality audits scheduled on the basis of status and importance of the activity to be audited? | 5  4  3  2  1 |
| 5  4  3  2  1 | 4. Are internal quality audits carried out by personnel independent of those having direct responsibility for the activity being audited? | 5  4  3  2  1 |
| 5  4  3  2  1 | 5. Are the audit results recorded and brought to the attention of the personnel having responsibility in the area audited? | 5  4  3  2  1 |
| 5  4  3  2  1 | 6. Has timely corrective action been taken for the deficiencies found during the audits? | 5  4  3  2  1 |
| 5  4  3  2  1 | 7. Do follow-up audit activities record the implementation and effectiveness of the corrective action taken? | 5  4  3  2  1 |
| 5  4  3  2  1 | 8. Do the results of the internal quality audit form an integral part of management review activities? | 5  4  3  2  1 |

Sumation A — Difference

[ 40 ] − [   ] = [   ]

00-08 = Excellent
09-16 = Needs Work
17-24 = Strong Need
25-40 = Very Strong Need

Any A Item of < 4 reflects a need in that category.

Any B Item of < 4 reflects a need for improved commitment in that category.

## Needs Assessment Inventory *(continued)*

| In your view, with what success is this being achieved in your company?<br>5  4  3  2  1<br>Column A | 4.18 Training<br><br>Instructions: Read the assessment question/statement and circle your response in Column A and B; total column A and enter in the marked box. | In your view, how important is this item?<br>5  4  3  2  1<br>Column B |
|---|---|---|
| 5  4  3  2  1 | 1. Have documented procedures been established and are they maintained for identifying training needs? | 5  4  3  2  1 |
| 5  4  3  2  1 | 2. Is training of all personnel performing activities affecting quality provided for? | 5  4  3  2  1 |
| 5  4  3  2  1 | 3. Have personnel performing specific assigned tasks been qualified on the basis of appropriate education, training, or experience? | 5  4  3  2  1 |
| 5  4  3  2  1 | 4. Are appropriate records of training maintained? | 5  4  3  2  1 |

Summation A — Difference

**20** — ☐ = ☐

00-04 = Excellent
05-08 = Needs Work
09-12 = Strong Need
13-20 = Very Strong Need

Any A Item of < 4 reflects a need in that category.

Any B Item of < 4 reflects a need for improved commitment in that category.

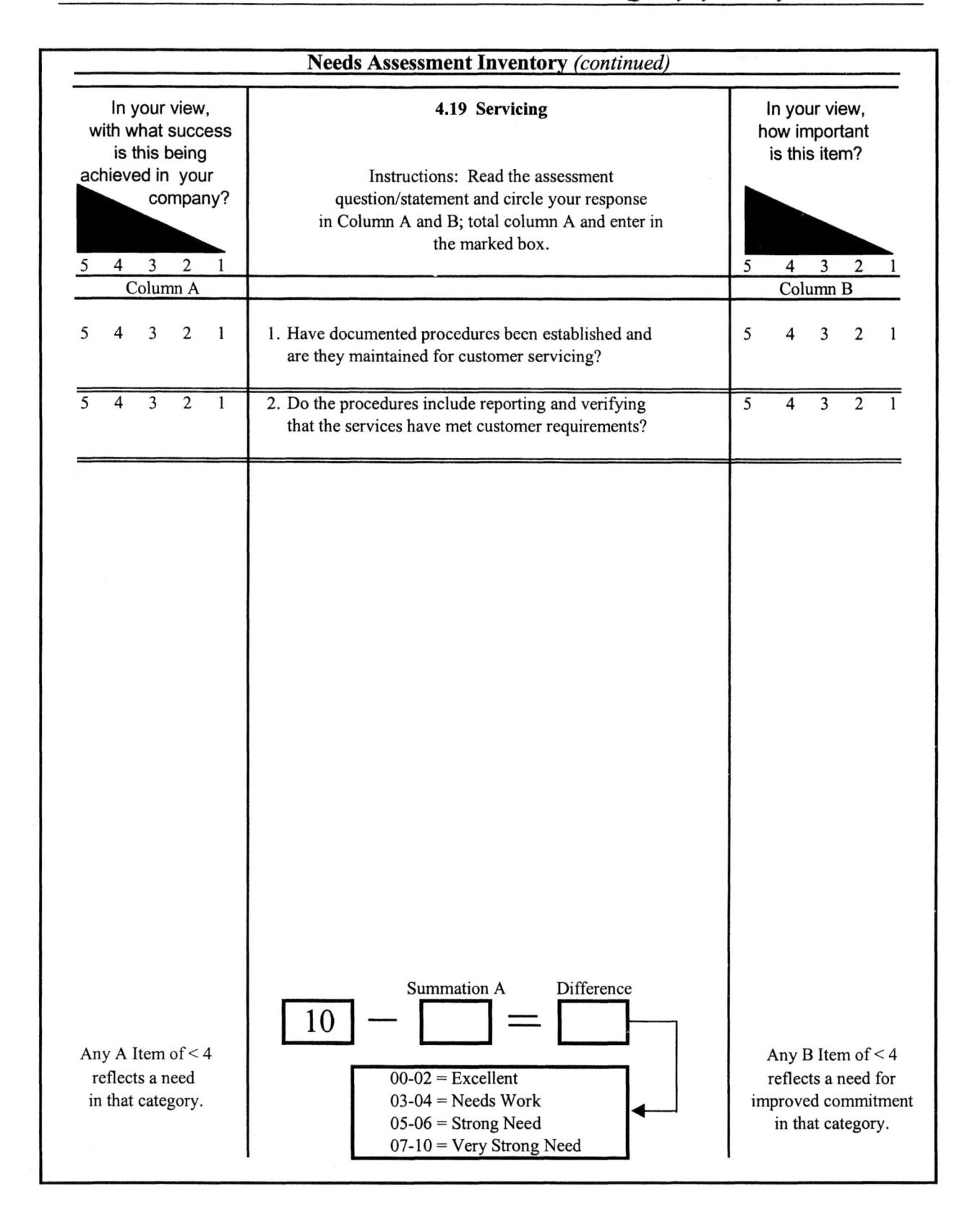

## Needs Assessment Inventory (continued)

| In your view, with what success is this being achieved in your company?<br><br>5  4  3  2  1<br>Column A | 4.19 Servicing<br><br>Instructions: Read the assessment question/statement and circle your response in Column A and B; total column A and enter in the marked box. | In your view, how important is this item?<br><br>5  4  3  2  1<br>Column B |
|---|---|---|
| 5  4  3  2  1 | 1. Have documented procedures been established and are they maintained for customer servicing? | 5  4  3  2  1 |
| 5  4  3  2  1 | 2. Do the procedures include reporting and verifying that the services have met customer requirements? | 5  4  3  2  1 |

Summation A     Difference

$\boxed{10} - \boxed{\phantom{X}} = \boxed{\phantom{X}}$

00-02 = Excellent
03-04 = Needs Work
05-06 = Strong Need
07-10 = Very Strong Need

Any A Item of < 4 reflects a need in that category.

Any B Item of < 4 reflects a need for improved commitment in that category.

## Needs Assessment Inventory (continued)

| In your view, with what success is this being achieved in your company?<br><br>5  4  3  2  1<br>Column A | 4.20 Statistical Techniques<br><br>Instructions: Read the assessment question/statement and circle your response in Column A and B; total column A and enter in the marked box. | In your view, how important is this item?<br><br>5  4  3  2  1<br>Column B |
|---|---|---|
| 5  4  3  2  1 | 1. Has the need for and use of statistical techniques for establishing, controlling, and verifying process capability and product characteristics been identified? | 5  4  3  2  1 |
| 5  4  3  2  1 | 2. Have documented procedures been established and are they maintained to implement and control the application of the statistical techniques identified? | 5  4  3  2  1 |

Sumation A — Difference

10 − ☐ = ☐

00-02 = Excellent
03-04 = Needs Work
05-06 = Strong Need
07-10 = Very Strong Need

Any A Item of < 4 reflects a need in that category.

Any B Item of < 4 reflects a need for improved commitment in that category.

| \multicolumn{4}{c|}{**Needs Assessment Listing**<br>**Ranked by Need**<br>Complete this Needs Assessment by listing the self-assessment numbers contained in the Block marked "Difference" of each section. Then rank in order of magnitude, the largest number (greatest need) first and the smallest number last.} |
|---|---|---|---|
| **Section** | **Difference Number** | **Rank** | **Comments** |
| 4.1 Management Commitment | | | |
| 4.2 Quality System | | | |
| 4.3 Contract Review | | | |
| 4.4 Design Control | | | |
| 4.5 Document & Data Control | | | |
| 4.6 Purchasing & Supplier Control | | | |
| 4.7 Control of Customer Supplied Product | | | |
| 4.8 Product Identification and Traceability | | | |
| 4.9 Process Control (Work Control) | | | |
| 4.10 Inspection & Testing | | | |
| 4.11 Control of Inspection, Measuring & Test Equipment | | | |
| 4.12 Inspection & Test Status | | | |
| 4.13 Control of Non-conforming Product | | | |
| 4.14 Corrective & Preventive Action | | | |
| 4.15 Handling, Storage, Packaging, Preservation, & Delivery | | | |
| 4.16 Contol of Quality Records | | | |
| 4.17 Internal Quality Audits | | | |
| 4.18 Training | | | |
| 4.19 Servicing | | | |
| 4.20 Statistical Techniques | | | |

## Needs Assessment Inventory

| In your view, with what success is this being achieved in your company?<br><br>5  4  3  2  1<br>Column A | Instructions: Read the assessment question/statement and circle your response in Column A and B; total column A and enter in the marked box. | In your view, how important is this item?<br><br>5  4  3  2  1<br>Column B |
|---|---|---|
| 5  4  3  2  1 |  | 5  4  3  2  1 |
| 5  4  3  2  1 |  | 5  4  3  2  1 |
| 5  4  3  2  1 |  | 5  4  3  2  1 |
| 5  4  3  2  1 |  | 5  4  3  2  1 |
| 5  4  3  2  1 |  | 5  4  3  2  1 |
| 5  4  3  2  1 |  | 5  4  3  2  1 |
| 5  4  3  2  1 |  | 5  4  3  2  1 |
| 5  4  3  2  1 |  | 5  4  3  2  1 |
| 5  4  3  2  1 |  | 5  4  3  2  1 |
| 5  4  3  2  1 |  | 5  4  3  2  1 |
| Any A Item of < 4 reflects a need in that category. | Summation A    Difference<br>[ 50 ] − [  ] = [  ]<br><br>00-10 = Excellent<br>11-20 = Needs Work<br>21-30 = Strong Need<br>31-50 = Very Strong Need | Any B Item of < 4 reflects a need for improved commitment in that category. |

# Chapter 6

# QUALITY SYSTEM IMPLEMENTATION PLAN DEVELOPMENT

## IMPORTANCE OF PLANNING

Before launching into a Quality System effort of the magnitude required within most organizations, one should put together an overview of a plan. Planning should be done even before the hiring of any quality-specific personnel so as to fit the right person(s) with the requirements as well as to determine the need for such personnel.

Planning is one of the most difficult tasks an organization has to perform. In the process of planning, many members of the organization will have the sense that "we aren't getting the work done that is so evidently in need of doing. Why don't we just get on with it?" This mindset is precisely why so many organizations work at addressing short-term rather than long-term issues and symptoms rather than root causes of organizational problems.

Planning is tedious, hard work. But nothing an organization does can ultimately benefit it more than the time it spends in planning. It is planning that allows an organization to be sure that each action it takes adds a step in its journey towards accomplishing its mission. It is planning that allows an organization to have a sense of control over its endeavors, and to know that success in that endeavor is attainable.

Planning! Without a doubt, is the most important factor that determines the cost, speed, and effectiveness of a Quality System and, therefore, the success of installation and implementation.

*There is no substitute for good planning!*

## PLANNING ELEMENTS

The plan elements for implementing an ISO 9000-Based Quality System may vary depending on where the organization is relative to their respective quality journey. It should also be noted that the implementation of an ISO 9000-Based Quality System is one step or phase of the larger implementation of a TQM Process (see Chapter 19).

Determination of the needed plan elements may wait until after the initial self-assessment is completed and results analyzed. The needed plan elements may be determined through a "brainstorming" process, by using a typical shopping list developed for a complete journey plus any customized elements required by the specific organization.

## Typical Shopping List of ISO 9000 Quality System Plan Elements

- Audits/assessments
- Mission Statement
- Quality Policy
- Organizational goals
- Quality Structure
- Quality System Manual
- Unit Quality System Manual (as applicable for operating divisions or affiliated companies)
- Quality System Controlling Procedures
- Work Process Procedures
- Work Process Instructions/Checklists
- Determination of training types required
- Determination of Primary Work Processes
- Determination of the baseline training requirements
- Determination of personnel categories
- Development of a Title Matrix
- Position Description Manual
- Delegation of Authority Manual
- Organization Charts Manual
- Determination of special training requirements
- Comparison of each employee against requirements
- Document training
- Development of training courses
- Preparation of New Hire Plan for each personnel category

Presentation of the ISO 9000 Implementation Plan and overall schedule might look like what is shown in Figure 6-1.

# Quality System Implementation Plan Development / 59

| Plan Element | Month 1 | Month 2 | Month 3 | Month 4 | Month 5 | Month 6 | Month 7 | Month 8 | Month 9 | Month 10 | Month 11 | Month 12 | Month 13 | Month 14 | Month 15 |
|---|---|---|---|---|---|---|---|---|---|---|---|---|---|---|---|
| 1. Audits/Assessments | Status Audit | | | | | X..Develop Internal Audit Procedures & Checklists....X | | | Develop Schedule | Select/Qualify Internal Auditors | | Pre-Assessment | | | ISO Unit Audit |
| 2. Mission Statement | | Drafts Reviewed | Final Approved | X........Distribution....X | | | | | | | | | | | |
| 3. Quality Policy | | Drafts Reviewed | Final Approved | X........Distribution....X | | | | | | | | | | | |
| 4. Organizational Goals | | Assignment Made | Draft Reviewed | Final Approved | X.........Distribution......X | | | | | | | | | | |
| 5. Establish Quality Structure | Define Structure | Finalize Structure | | | | | | | | | | | | | |
| 6. Corporate Quality System Manual | | QSM Draft Complete | QSM Rev & Approved | QSM Issued | | | | X........QSM Training.............X | | | | QSM Submittal | | | |
| 7. Unit Quality System Manual (As applicable) Divisions, Affiliated Companies | | | | Unit QSM Prepared | | Corporate Review | Issue | | | | | QSM Submittal | | | |
| 8. Common/Controlling Procedures | | Define List | X.........Draft/Review/Issue..........X | | | | | X..Common Procedure Training...X and Implementation | | | | | | | |
| 9. Work Process Procedures | | Define List | Finalize List & number | X.........Draft/Review/Issue..........X | | | | | X..........Work Process Procedure..........X Training & Implementation | | | | | | |
| 10. Work Instructions | | | Define List | Finalize List & number | X.........Draft/Review/Issue..........X | | | | X..........Work Instruction..........X Training & Implementation | | | | | | |
| 11. Work Instruction Check Lists | | | Define List | Finalize List & number | X.........Draft/Review/Issue..........X | | | | X..........Work Instruction..........X Training & Implementation | | | | | | |
| 12. Training - Determination of Types Required | Types Determined | | | | | | | | | | | | | | |
| 13. Training - Determination of Primary Work Processes | | Define List | Finalize List | | | | | | | | | | | | |
| 14. Training - Determine Baseline Training Requirements | | Inputs Received | Consolidate Inputs | Issue Cons List | Final List Approved | | | | | | | | | | |
| 15. Training - Determine Personnel Categories | | Inputs Received | Consolidate Inputs | Issue Cons List | Final List Approved | X...Prepare Job Descriptions......X | | | | | | | | | |
| 16. Training - Determine Special Training Requirements | | | | Consolidate Inputs Received | Issue Cons List | Final List Approved | | | | | | | | | |
| 17. Training - Compare Each Person against Requirements | | | | | Compare w/ Reqm't's | | | Compare w/ Special | X...Incorporate in Training Budget/Plan...X | | | | | | |
| 18. Training - Documentation | | | X..Determine Record...X Requirements | | Establish Method | X...........Develop Software..........X | | | | X............Update Records.........X | | | | | |
| 19. Training - Develop Courses | | | | | X.........Develop Training Courses (In-House or Outside)...X | | | | | | | | | | |
| 20. Training - Prepare New Hire Plan for each Personnel Category | | | | | X.........Develop New Hire Training Plan/Method.........X | | | | | | | | | | |

**Figure 6-1. ISO 9000 Implementation Plan/Overall Schedule**

## Arrangement of Plan Elements

After having determined the plan elements listing, they should be arranged in a priority order and numbered. They do not have to be in a sequence-of-occurrence order.

Tied to each plan element are all of the tasks associated with that element and the corresponding schedule for each. Configuration of the elements, tasks, and schedule into a project schedule, as illustrated, allows good visibility and tracking by senior management. One should be cautioned, however, not to make the schedule too detailed or complex, such that one is managing the schedule and its presentation rather than the plan elements.

The plan element and schedule presentation should show the relationship between the various tasks of each element and have a timeline showing status on a monthly basis.

A monthly report would include this timeline as well as a written status of each plan element, including actions in process and responsibility for such.

In the following chapters of this book, each of the listed plan elements is presented in detail.

# Chapter 7

# THE QUALITY POLICY

## IMPORTANCE OF THE QUALITY POLICY

ISO 8402 paragraph 3.4 states:

*Quality Policy: The overall quality intentions and direction of an organization as regards to quality, as formally expressed by top management.*

**Note:** The Quality Policy forms one element of the corporate policy and is authorized by top management.

ISO 9001 paragraph 4.1.1 states:

*The supplier's management with executive responsibility shall define and document its policy for quality, including objectives for quality and its commitment to quality. The Quality Policy shall be relevant to the supplier's organizational goals and the expectations and needs of its customers. The supplier shall ensure that this policy is understood, implemented, and maintained at all levels in the organization.*

The Quality Policy is the first section of a company's Quality System Manual and, in conjunction with the company's values, principles, mission, and vision, should capture the essence of the organization.

Existence = What I do (an individual or organization).

Essence = Who I am (as an individual or organization).

## Elements of the Quality Policy

The *Values and Principles Statement* of an organization denotes the "who I am" and sets the "culture" resulting from the organization's background.

The *Mission Statement* of an organization denotes "why we exist," and ties into the value-added and primary work processes. The Mission Statement should consider factors such as: outputs, customers, processes, inputs, and suppliers.

The *Vision Statement* denotes "how we wish to exist" and includes such considerations as:

- How we treat each other
- How we treat customers
- How we maintain health, environment, and safety
- How we help our community and nation
- How we grow our business

```
                              QUALITY
                              POLICY
                    ↗           ↑           ↖
      VALUES                                      VISION
      PRINCIPLES            MISSION
      Who we are            Why we exist          How we wish to exist

      Culture                                     How we:
      Background            Outputs               Treat each other;
                            Customers             Treat customers;
                            Processes             Maintain health,
                            Inputs                   environment and safety;
                            Suppliers             Help our community and nation;
                                                  Grow our business
```

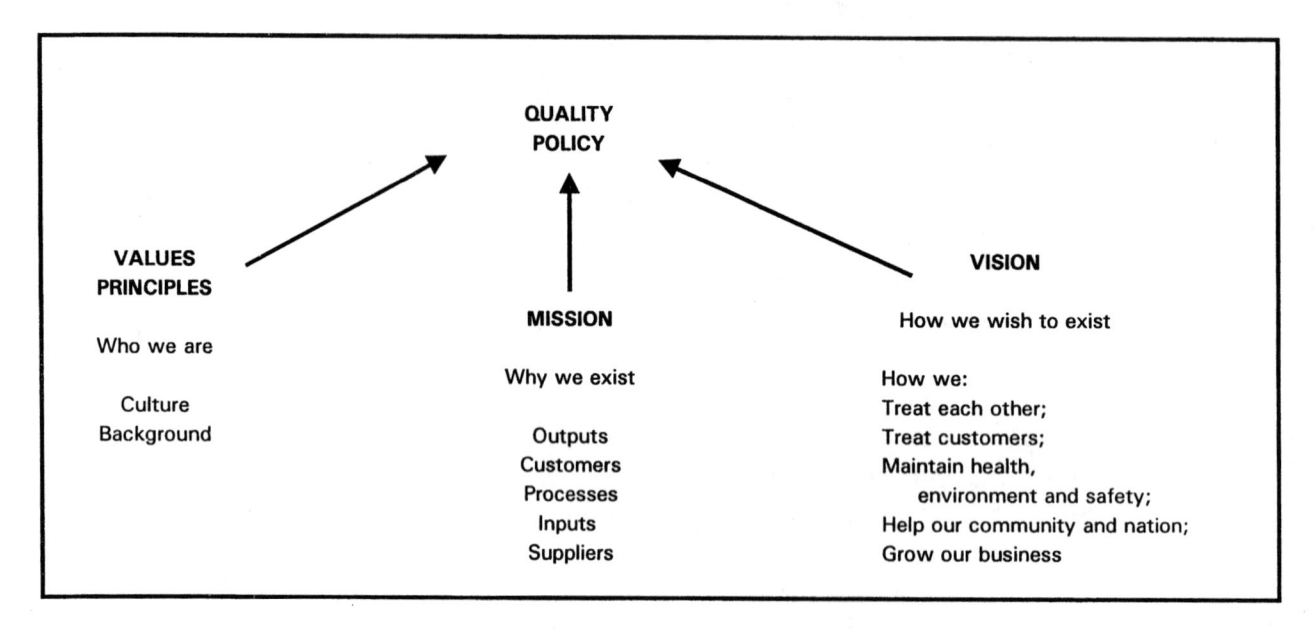

**Figure 7-1. Quality Policy Development**

These four elements—values, principles, mission, and vision—feed the Quality Policy, which then becomes the vehicle for communicating "the overall quality intentions and direction of the organization" to the organization.

The steps to develop a Quality Policy are clear and relate directly to the above listed elements.

## QUALITY POLICY DEVELOPMENT STEPS

### Step 1—Code of Ethics

Step 1, the organization's values and principles, is generally contained in the organization's Code of Ethics, which is given to and understood by each employee.

Development of a Code of Ethics is a very personal organizational matter. The Code of Ethics should be kept very simple, easy to read, and easy to understand.

The Code of Ethics might address such items as:

- Integrity
- Credibility
- Confidentiality of information
- Compliance with laws and regulations
- Services—manner offered
- Conflicts of interest

The organization's background and culture help determine the "who I am" of the organization, which is encompassed by the Code of Ethics.

The senior manager or staff should develop the Code of Ethics for the organization, if it does not already exist. If it does exist, it may need to be reviewed and updated to reflect any changes.

Distribution methods of the Code of Ethics may include:

- Directly to each employee
- As a part of the quality system manual
- Through group meetings

### Step 2—Mission Statement

Step 2 is the development and distribution of a Mission Statement.

A Mission Statement is a clear, concise affirmation (50 words or less) of the unique reason or purpose for the existence and efforts of the organization.

Developing a Mission Statement may be a rather lengthy process but it is the foundation statement for the work of the organization and, therefore, significant time and effort should be given to its development.

One of the values of keeping a Mission Statement to fifty (50) words or less is to make it possible for employees to remember the mission of the organization as they plan their day-to-day work.

The Mission Statement should reflect the values that drive the organization.

The Mission Statement should answer the following questions:

- What business are we in?
- Who are our customers?
- How do we want our customers to know us?

The Mission Statement should be clear, short, and include more than one task. It should be something everyone can easily understand and remember, and it should be something that should be hung on the wall.

Remember that the Mission Statement should not describe any activities unless the activities are an intricate part of the *mission* of the organization.

Mission Statement example:

> *The mission of the American Bureau of Shipping is to serve the public interest as well as the needs of our clients by promoting the security of life, property and the natural environment primarily through the development and verification of standards for the design, construction, and operational maintenance of marine-related facilities.*

The Mission Statement may be displayed in any manner desired. Some possibilities include:

- On business cards (reverse side)
- As a wall display in conference rooms
- As a wall display in individual offices
- In all proposals/literature

- In the Quality System Manual

Distribution of the Mission Statement may be delegated to a Communications Continuous Improvement Team (C-CIT) or other designated team or individual.

**Note:** Some ISO 9000 auditors have required that there be some method to ensure that any displayed or distributed Mission Statement is the latest version. This could be accomplished by having it signed and dated as a part of the original document.

## Step 3—Vision Statement

Step 3 is the development and sharing of the vision of the organization. Presentation of the organization's Vision Statement can take almost any form and be called by a number of different names, so long as it shares the "How we wish to exist" message.

Typical subjects addressed in a Vision Statement include:

- Teamwork
- Organizational effectiveness
- Leadership
- Commitment
- Innovation
- Communications

When preparing the Vision Statement, consider the "How we wish to exist" listing shown in Figure 7-1.

The vision is perhaps best developed by senior management.

## Step 4—Preparation and Setup

Step 4 is the actual preparation of the Quality Policy guidelines. Here is a sample setup.

## Purpose

To make it clear where management stands on quality, to know where the company is headed.

The Quality Policy of an organization is too important to be left to those responsible for the acceptance of the product or service.

## What Is the Quality Policy?

If a formal policy is not established by the management of the organization, then the personnel will select their own—individually.

## What the Quality Policy Should Not Be

1. The Quality Policy should not be a treatise on the "economics of quality."

2. The Quality Policy should not have a number in it.

3. The Quality Policy should not indicate any method of deviating from it.

4. The Quality Policy should not delegate the responsibility for evaluating performance to the policy.

5. The Quality Policy should not be hidden in a book reserved for executive personnel only. It should be stated and publicized until everyone knows, understands, and believes it.

## Management Team Agreement

It is vital that each member of operating management understand and agree with this policy, and more important—implement it.

## Quality Policy Guidelines

1. Short and to the point

2. Containing the name of the company

The Quality Policy may be displayed in any manner desired. Some possibilities include:

- On business cards (reverse side)
- On wall displays in conference rooms

- On wall display in individual offices
- In all proposals/sales literature
- Within the Quality System Manual (not an option—it *must* be contained here)
- On the inside cover of all manuals
- Network computer screens when logging onto the system each day

Distribution of the Quality Policy may be delegated to a Communications Quality Improvement Team (C-QIT) or other designated team or individual.

**Note:** Some ISO 9000 auditors have required that there be some method to ensure that any distributed or displayed Quality Policy is the latest version. This could be accomplished by having it signed and dated as a part of the original document.

## Example of Quality Policy—American Bureau of Shipping

*It is the policy of the American Bureau of Shipping to provide quality services in support of our mission and to be responsive to the individual and collective needs of our clients as well as those of the public at large. All our client commitments, supporting actions, and services delivered must be recognized as expressions of quality. We pledge to monitor our performance as an ongoing activity and to strive for continuous improvement.*

## CONCLUSION

1. The organization's values and principles, mission, and vision are key inputs in the development of the organization's Quality Policy.

2. The Values and Principles Statement of an organization denotes the "who I am" and sets the "culture" resulting from the organization's background.

3. The Mission Statement of an organization denotes "why we exist" and ties into the value-added and primary work process.

4. The Vision Statement of an organization denotes "how we wish to exist."

5. The Quality Policy is a clear statement of where management stands on quality.

68 / *Implementing an ISO 9000-Based Quality System*

6. Management's responsibility is to ensure that the Quality Policy is understood, implemented, and maintained at all levels of the organization.

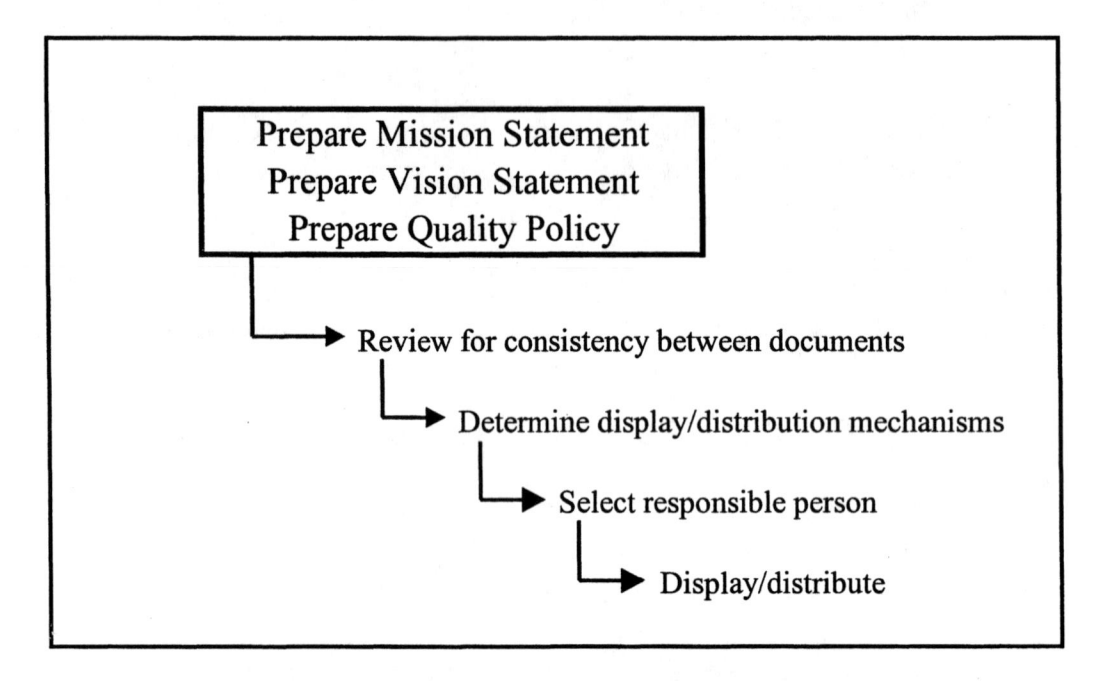

```
┌─────────────────────────────────┐
│  Prepare Mission Statement      │
│  Prepare Vision Statement       │
│  Prepare Quality Policy         │
└─────────────────────────────────┘
         │
         └──▶ Review for consistency between documents
                   │
                   └──▶ Determine display/distribution mechanisms
                             │
                             └──▶ Select responsible person
                                       │
                                       └──▶ Display/distribute
```

**Figure 7-2. Quality System Implementation Plan—Step 1**

# Chapter 8

# QUALITY SYSTEM RELATIONSHIP DIAGRAM

Figure 8-1 defines the relationship of the ISO 9000 major elements in one figure. The generic version of this figure (without the QSM Section Listing and the Quality System Procedure Listings) can be customized for each company or organization and used as a Quality System Implementation training tool.

As detailed in Chapter 7, the Quality Policy input drivers include the company values and principles, mission, and vision. The Quality Policy itself is the main driver of the QSM and is contained in the first section, as shown in Chapter 9. Additional QSM drivers include the ISO 9000 selected standard requirements and the organization's Quality Goals.

## QUALITY SYSTEM MANUAL

The Quality System Manual (QSM) is defined simply as "a high level document that adequately describes the organization's Quality System." The QSM section makeup is depicted in the Table of Contents of the QSM. A typical representation is shown in Figure 8-2, which can be customized as discussed in Chapter 9.

An overall Quality System description of one or two pages for use in proposals and customer distribution in lieu of the entire QSM is of benefit. This document is a condensed description of the Quality System. It is not considered a controlled document.

The QSM is considered the highest level, or Level 1, of the Quality System documentation structure.

Level 2 of this structure is the Quality System Procedures, sometimes called Controlling Procedures. The Quality System Procedures are documentation that detail the requirements and controlling factors applicable to the entire organization. These procedures are referenced by name in the QSM (for those that the selected ISO 9000 Standard requires) and themselves reference to a specific QSM section.

70 / *Implementing an ISO 9000-Based Quality System*

A typical Quality System Procedure Listing is depicted in Figure 8-1 and can be customized, as discussed in Chapter 10.

**Table of Contents - QS Manual**

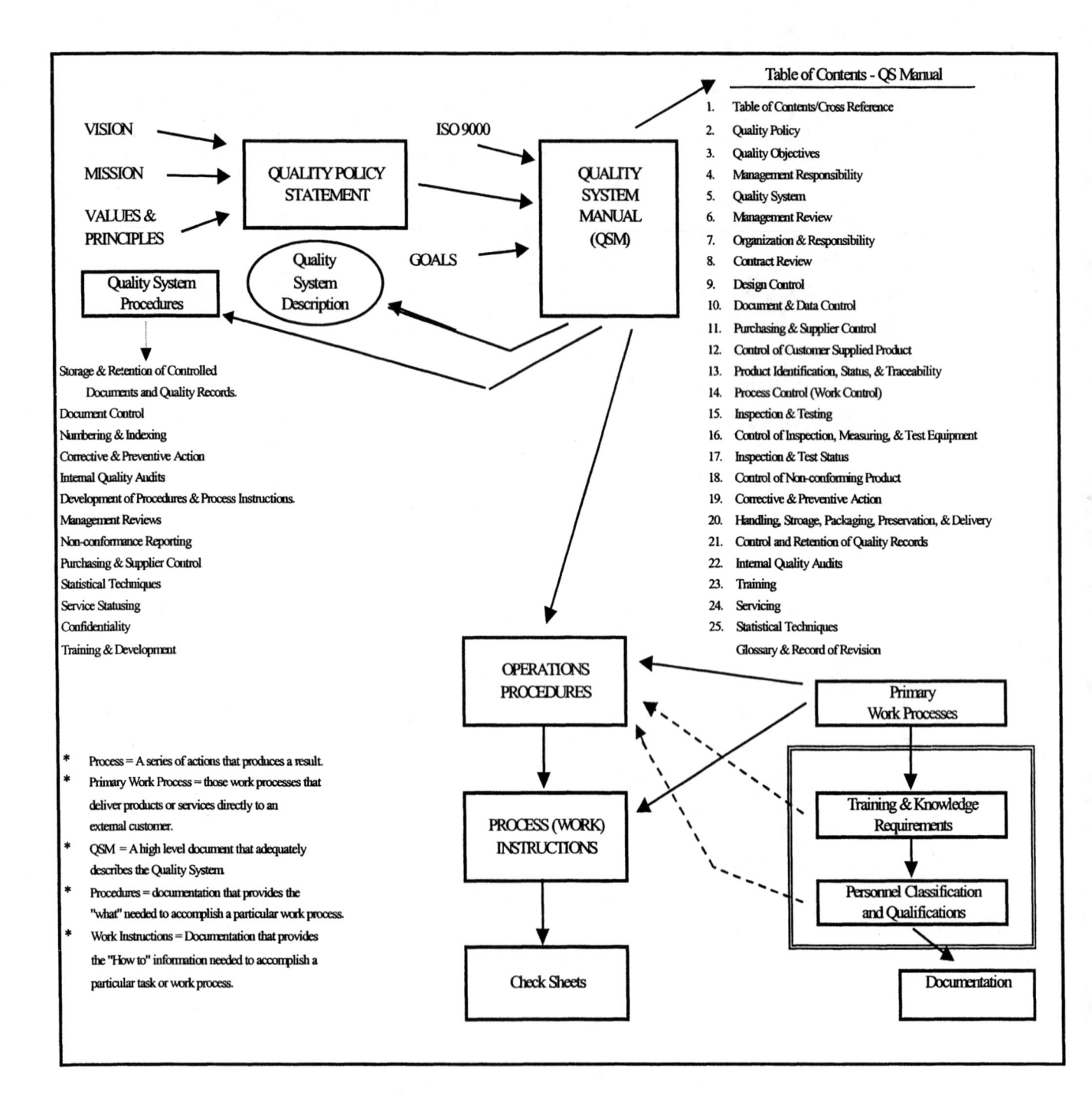

1. Table of Contents/Cross Reference
2. Quality Policy
3. Quality Objectives
4. Management Responsibility
5. Quality System
6. Management Review
7. Organization & Responsibility
8. Contract Review
9. Design Control
10. Document & Data Control
11. Purchasing & Supplier Control
12. Control of Customer Supplied Product
13. Product Identification, Status, & Traceability
14. Process Control (Work Control)
15. Inspection & Testing
16. Control of Inspection, Measuring, & Test Equipment
17. Inspection & Test Status
18. Control of Non-conforming Product
19. Corrective & Preventive Action
20. Handling, Stroage, Packaging, Preservation, & Delivery
21. Control and Retention of Quality Records
22. Internal Quality Audits
23. Training
24. Servicing
25. Statistical Techniques

Glossary & Record of Revision

**Quality System Procedures:**
- Storage & Retention of Controlled Documents and Quality Records.
- Document Control
- Numbering & Indexing
- Corrective & Preventive Action
- Internal Quality Audits
- Development of Procedures & Process Instructions.
- Management Reviews
- Non-conformance Reporting
- Purchasing & Supplier Control
- Statistical Techniques
- Service Statusing
- Confidentiality
- Training & Development

* Process = A series of actions that produces a result.
* Primary Work Process = those work processes that deliver products or services directly to an external customer.
* QSM = A high level document that adequately describes the Quality System.
* Procedures = documentation that provides the "what" needed to accomplish a particular work process.
* Work Instructions = Documentation that provides the "How to" information needed to accomplish a particular task or work process.

**Figure 8-1. Quality System Procedure Listing**

*Quality System Relationship Diagram / 71*

* Process = A series of actions that produces a result.
* Primary Work Process = those work processes that deliver products or services directly to an external customer.
* QSM = A high level document that adequately describes the Quality System.
* Procedures = documentation that provides the "what" needed to accomplish a particular work process.
* Work Instructions = Documentation that provides the "How to" information needed to accomplish a particular task or work process.

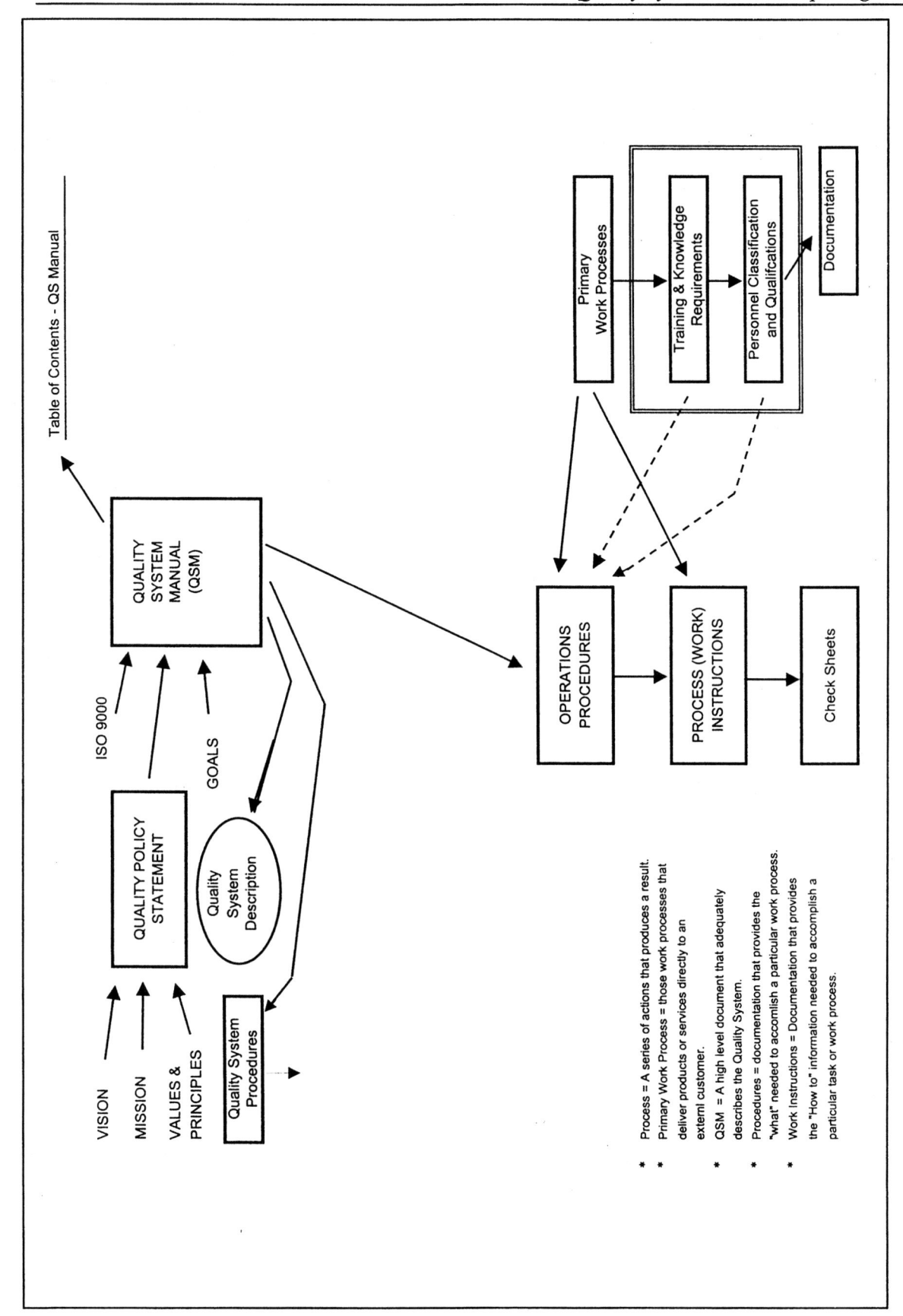

**Figure 8-2. Quality System Relationship Diagram**

The next step in the Quality System Relationship Diagram is *not* to develop the Quality System and Operations Procedures. Many companies and organizations jump right into this step and cause themselves a great deal of re-work and complication as a result. Instead, determine the organization's Primary Work Processes, as discussed in Chapter 11, listing them and grouping them in accordance with their respective categories, as explained in the text of the chapter.

Following the Primary Work Process listing is the determination of the Associated Training and Knowledge Requirement (Chapter 12) and Personnel Classifications and Qualifications for each (Chapter 13).

The output of this effort will be the simplest grouping of the resulting Procedures and Work Instructions, which encompass all of the Primary Work Processes.

A few organizations choose *not* to go this route, electing to concentrate on a product-oriented system rather than a process-oriented system (see Chapter 11). When doing so, however, remember that the ISO 9000 Standards are process-oriented standards, not product-oriented standards.

The Quality System Work Process Related Procedures Form is Level 3 of the system hierarchy; Level 4 is the Work Instructions.

The Check Sheets shown are actually a part of the Work Instructions as detailed in Chapter 15.

## Conclusion

The following chapters carry the Quality System Implementation through the details of preparing each of the elements shown on the Quality System Relationship Diagram. It is a guide to assist in maintaining the proper relationship between the Quality System elements and as a very useful training tool during and after implementation. Keep it updated as you progress through the implementation process.

# Chapter 9

# QUALITY SYSTEM MANUAL

## QUALITY SYSTEM MANUAL PREPARATION

Companies or organizations in the process of implementing or planning to implement an ISO 9000-based Quality System need a document that describes the system in a way suitable for presentation to the ISO 9000 auditor, to customers, and for internal use. Such a document is generally called a Quality Manual or Quality System Manual (QSM).

A Quality System Manual needs to demonstrate for the reader that the Quality System is complete with regard to the requirements of the ISO 9000 Standard selected.

Some organizations really get carried away in the preparation of a QSM, making it so complex and full of information and references that the purpose for which it serves is completely missed. The QSM should be kept *simple*. There is no need nor requirement to make it other than a simple, high-level document that adequately describes the Quality System and its requirements to its readers.

Remember, the QSM is the outside person's entry document into your organization's Quality System.

Although the 1987 ISO 9000 Standard did not require a QSM, the 1994 revision to the ISO 9000 Standard does require a Quality System Manual.

The 1994 ISO 9001, Paragraph 4.2.1 states:

*The supplier shall establish, document, and maintain a quality system as a means of ensuring that product conforms to specified requirements. The supplier shall prepare a quality manual covering the requirements of this International Standard. The quality manual shall include or make references to the quality system procedures and outline the structure of the documentation used in the quality system.*

Note the key words *"outline the structure."*

## Assessment

An ISO 9000 auditor will examine your organization's QSM against the ISO 9000 requirements, verify that all of the requirements are met, and then audit your organization against your own QSM. Therefore, it behooves you to make the QSM as "auditor friendly" as possible and as close to the ISO 9000 Standard arrangement as possible. Doing so allows a great deal of standardization between QSMs of all companies. So why not make use of it, unless you want to reinvent the wheel every time (not a cost-effective option).

A proper QSM can be completed within one week after the Mission Statement, Quality Policy, Quality Objectives, and Quality Organizational Structure have been determined.

The QSM must describe, at all times, the Quality System as it currently is. When changes are made within the system, appropriate changes must be made to the QSM immediately.

**Caution**: The QSM is the top level, controlling document. Therefore, one must be careful of the "tail wagging the dog" syndrome, and compare any proposed changes within the Quality System with the QSM requirements and their effect on the QSM. Remember, the QSM represents the ISO 9000 Standard requirements and must maintain that representation.

## Distribution and Control

The QSM must be widely available to company personnel. Managers at all levels must be familiar with the Quality System Manual requirements with which they must comply and for which they are responsible.

The QSM should provide a "broad brush" description of how quality is managed (not a detailed set of instructions) and reference the next tier of documentation, which is the Quality System Procedures. This reference is done in a generic manner, not by specifics.

The QSM is considered a "controlled document."

A simple approach to the development of a QSM is presented in the following process steps. Remember, there is no required way and, with each organization being different, there could be innumerable ways that requirements would be met.

If your organization already has a QSM, don't scrap it. Simply compare it to the ISO 9000 requirements or to the process steps listed here, noting the deficiencies and upgrading as necessary.

An ISO 9001-based QSM has been chosen as the basis of this presentation because it contains all of the ISO requirements. Should an ISO 9002 or 9003 QSM be desired, simply leave out the sections not applicable.

As in any other endeavor associated with the implementation of a Quality System, planning the task of writing the QSM is important for success. A part of this planning is the selection of the person, team, or task group that will be responsible for the QSM production process and for the QSM maintenance and distribution.

## Foundation Material

Another part of the preparation phase is the obtaining of the QSM foundation material, which was developed in an earlier chapter.

- Mission Statement
- Quality Policy
- Code of Ethics
- Quality Objectives

Finally, before launching into the writing process, decide upon the QSM format and structure, considering such items as:

- Cover page design
- Packaging of the QSM
- Determination of QSM sections to be included
- Each QSM section page header
- A standardized page layout

# 76 / Implementing an ISO 9000-Based Quality System

```
┌─────────────────────┐      ┌──────────────────────────┐
│ Decide responsible  │─────▶│ 1. Production Process    │
│ person/team/task    │      │ 2. Maintenance/          │
│ group for QSM       │◀─────│    Distribution          │
│ preparation         │      └──────────────────────────┘
└──────────┬──────────┘
           ▼
┌─────────────────────┐      ┌──────────────────────────┐
│ Obtain QSM          │─────▶│ 1. Mission Statement     │
│ foundation          │      │ 2. Quality Policy        │
│ material            │      │ 3. Code of Ethics        │
│                     │◀─────│ 4. Quality Objectives    │
└──────────┬──────────┘      └──────────────────────────┘
           ▼
┌─────────────────────┐
│ Determine the       │
│ Quality             │
│ Structure           │
└──────────┬──────────┘
           ▼
┌─────────────────────┐      ┌──────────────────────────────┐
│ Determine QSM       │─────▶│ 1. Cover page                │
│ Format and          │      │ 2. Binding                   │
│ Structure           │      │ 3. Sections to be included   │
│                     │◀─────│ 4. Section page header       │
└──────────┬──────────┘      │ 5. Section page standard     │
           ▼                  │    layout                    │
┌─────────────────────┐      │ 6. Prepare distribution      │
│ Prepare each        │      │    matrix                    │
│ individual          │      └──────────────────────────────┘
│ section             │
└──────────┬──────────┘
           ▼
┌─────────────────────┐
│ Package as          │
│ draft of final      │
│ version             │
└──────────┬──────────┘
           ▼
┌─────────────┐ (Not OK) ┌─────────────┐      ┌──────────────────┐
│ Modify QSM  │◀─────────│ Have QSM    │─────▶│ 1. External      │
│ draft       │          │ reviewed    │      │    review        │
│ (as         │          │             │◀─────│ 2. Internal      │
│ necessary)  │          │             │      │    review        │
└──────┬──────┘          └──────┬──────┘      └──────────────────┘
       │                   (OK) ▼
       │                 ┌─────────────┐      ┌──────────────────┐
       └────────────────▶│ Prepare     │      │ Receive & file   │
                         │ Transmittal │─────▶│ copy of          │
                         │ Record forms│      │ transmittal      │
                         └──────┬──────┘      │ record           │
                                ▼             └────────┬─────────┘
                         ┌─────────────────┐           ▼
                         │ Distribute QSM  │  ┌──────────────────┐
                         │ w/transmittal   │  │ Maintain QSM to  │
                         │ according to    │─▶│ ensure it truly  │
                         │ the distribution│  │ represents the   │
                         │ matrix          │  │ Quality System   │
                         └─────────────────┘  │ at all times     │
                                              └──────────────────┘
```

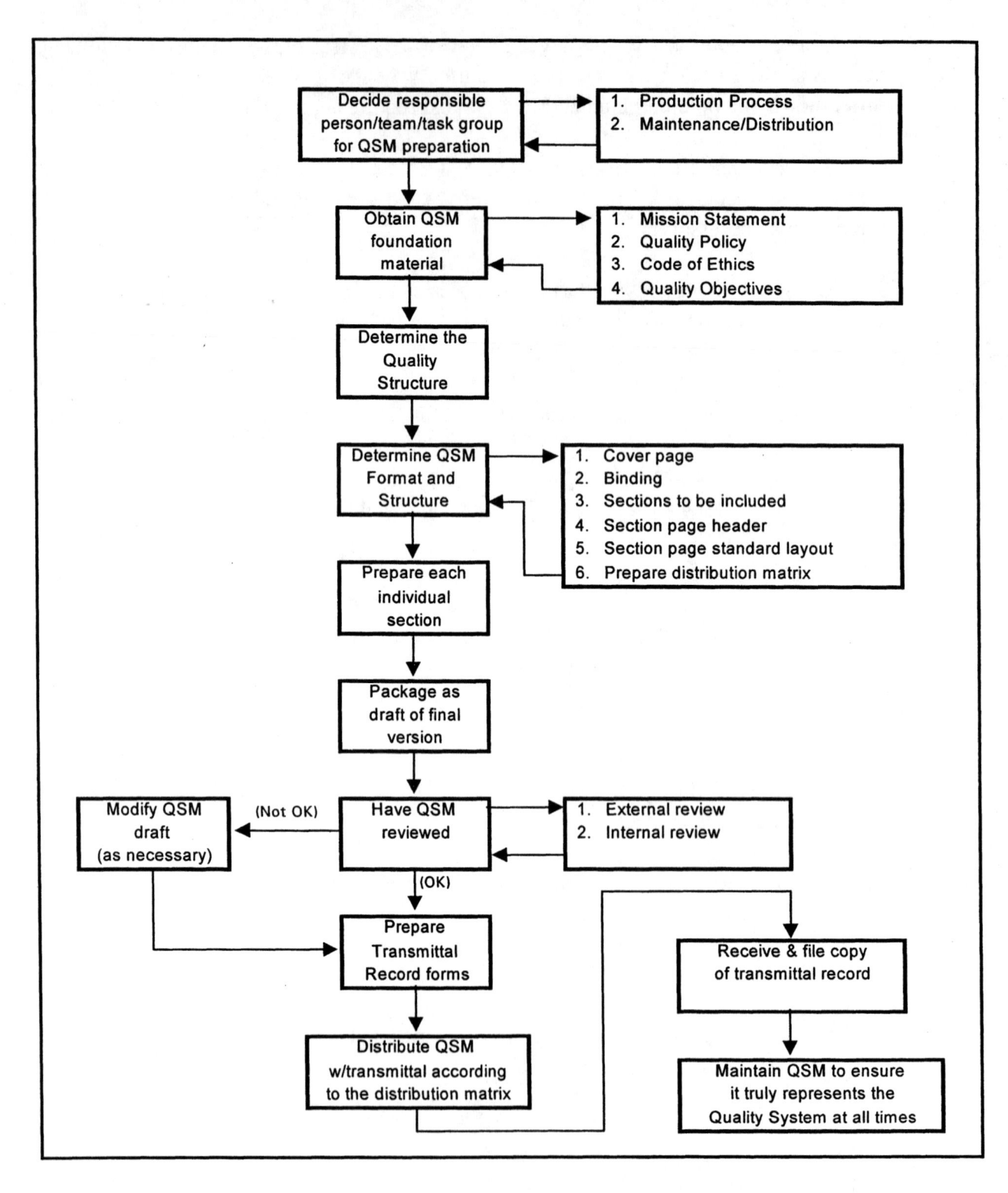

**Figure 9-1. The Development Process of a Quality System Manual**

# Quality System Description

A brief description, which is not a controlled document, may be prepared for use in marketing or as general information to provide to customers or suppliers in lieu of the complete Quality System Manual. An applied example of such is as follows:

---

**ABS**  **QUALITY SYSTEM DESCRIPTION**

ABS is a world-wide company which is structurally comprised of Corporate, three Operating Divisions (ABS Americas, ABS Europe and ABS Pacific) and affiliated companies. ABS as a Classification Society is comprised of ABS Corporate and the three Operating Divisions.

The ABS Quality System is modular in design and allows the ABS Classification Society to meet the ISO 9001 requirements within its decentralized, worldwide structure while maintaining consistency between the structural units (Divisions). The ABS Quality System utilizes a single ISO Certificate for the more than 100 offices worldwide.

The Quality System is documented in three tiers:

1) Quality Systems Manual, 2) Procedures, both quality system procedures and operations procedures, and 3) Process Instructions and checklists.

The first tier, the Quality System Manual, establishes the overall requirements for the quality system. It provides the Quality Policy, the general philosophy with regards to quality, and a broad description of "what" is to be done. The Quality System Manual provides the framework for the overall Quality System and provides the top down controls, standards, consistency and procedures to maintain a cohesive system.

The second tier, Procedures, provide a more descriptive outline of "what" is to be done and also "who", "where", "when" and sometimes in a very broad sense "how" that work process is to be accomplished.

The third tier, the Process Instructions, provide explicit detail of "how" the specific task is to be accomplished. Check sheets provide a sequence and record of what is to be done.

The ultimate responsibility for the implementation of the Quality System in each Division resides with the Chief Operating Officer (COO) of that Division, with direction and guidance provided by the Corporate Continuous Improvement Steering Committee. A Continuous Improvement Steering Committee has also been formed in each Division to assist the COO.

The Director of Total Quality is the Corporate Management Quality Representative who, irrespective of other responsibilities, has the responsibility to ensure the implementation, maintenance and continued improvement of the Quality System worldwide.

## QSM Section Development

The layout of each QSM section should also be consistent, including the paragraph numbering method.

Paragraph numbering should be sequential with sub-paragraphs also numbered.

### 2.0 Reference Documents

#### 2.1 ISO 9001, Paragraph 4.1.1

It is suggested that QSM section paragraphs 1 and 2 of each section be the same, except for content, i.e., *Purpose* and *Reference Documents*, respectively. The remaining paragraphs are customized, being organization dependent.

Although there is no set requirement for section titles or groupings within the QSM, the following list as applied to a manufacturing organization is suggested as being logical and user friendly.

Obviously, the presentation sequence is determined by each organization; but it is strongly suggested that it be given very careful consideration. Some organizations group all of the ISO 9001, Paragraph 4.1 items together in one QSM section titled Management Responsibility. However, I am of the opinion that the elements Quality Policy, Quality Objectives, Management Review, Organization and Responsibilities are so vital that they should have their own QSM section outside of the Management Responsibility section. Either way will work fine and be acceptable.

Whether the Glossary and Record of Revision is in the front or back of the manual makes no difference. I prefer the back, making a more presentable package.

Sufficient material is presented here to prepare a QSM that will not only meet the ISO requirements but also be very serviceable and user friendly.

In a service organization's QSM, all ISO 9001 categories should be addressed, even though they do not literally apply. The intent of the ISO 9000 requirements must still be met.

In addition, avail yourself of several good examples of Quality System Manuals. Most companies don't mind your using their QSM as a benchmark, but be sure to ask permission. There are also a number of books containing, in my opinion, poor examples of Quality System Manuals. Your best bet is to use a real case example.

## QSM Sections—Shopping List

Cross Referenced to ISO 9001

|   | Foreword/Certification | |
|---|---|---|
| 1 | Table of Contents and Cross Reference | 4.1.2 |
| 2 | Quality Policy | 4.1.1 |
| 3 | Quality Objectives | 4.1.1 |
| 4 | Management Responsibility | 4.1 |
| 5 | Quality System | 4.2 |
| 6 | Management Review | 4.1.3 |
| 7 | Organization and Responsibilities | 4.1.2.1 |
| 8 | Contract Review | 4.3 |
| 9 | Design Control | 4.4 |
| 10 | Document and Data Control | 4.5 |
| 11 | Purchasing and Supplier Control | 4.6 |
| 12 | Control of Customer Supplied Product | 4.7 |
| 13 | Product Identification, Status and Traceability | 4.8 |
| 14 | Process Control | 4.9 |
| 15 | Inspection and Testing | 4.10 |
| 16 | Control of Inspection, Measuring and Test Equipment | 4.11 |
| 17 | Inspection and Test Status | 4.12 |
| 18 | Control of Non-Conforming Product | 4.13 |
| 19 | Corrective and Preventive Action | 4.14 |
| 20 | Handling, Storage, Packaging, Preservation, and Delivery | 4.15 |
| 21 | Control and Retention of Quality Records | 4.16 |
| 22 | Internal Quality Audits | 4.17 |
| 23 | Training | 4.18 |
| 24 | Servicing | 4.19 |
| 25 | Statistical Techniques | 4.20 |
|   | Glossary | |
|   | Record of Revision | 4.5.2 |

This QSM Shopping List does not have to match the contents of the ISO 9001-1994 Standard. An example would be 18, Control of Nonconforming Product, which is necessary for a manufacturing organization but not for a service organization. In the case of a service organization, this section may be titled Client Supplied Product and

Materials, which may be only drawings or information. Some other QSM sections that would change for a service organization include:

| | |
|---|---|
| Section 9: | Service Design Control |
| Section 11: | Purchaser and Supplier Control (Subcontracting) |
| Section 12: | Control of Customer Supplied Product |
| Section 13: | Project Identification, Status, and Traceability |
| Section 15: | (Would be included in Section 14) |
| Section 16: | Measurement Control System |
| Section 17: | (Would be included in Section 13) |
| Section 18: | Not applicable |

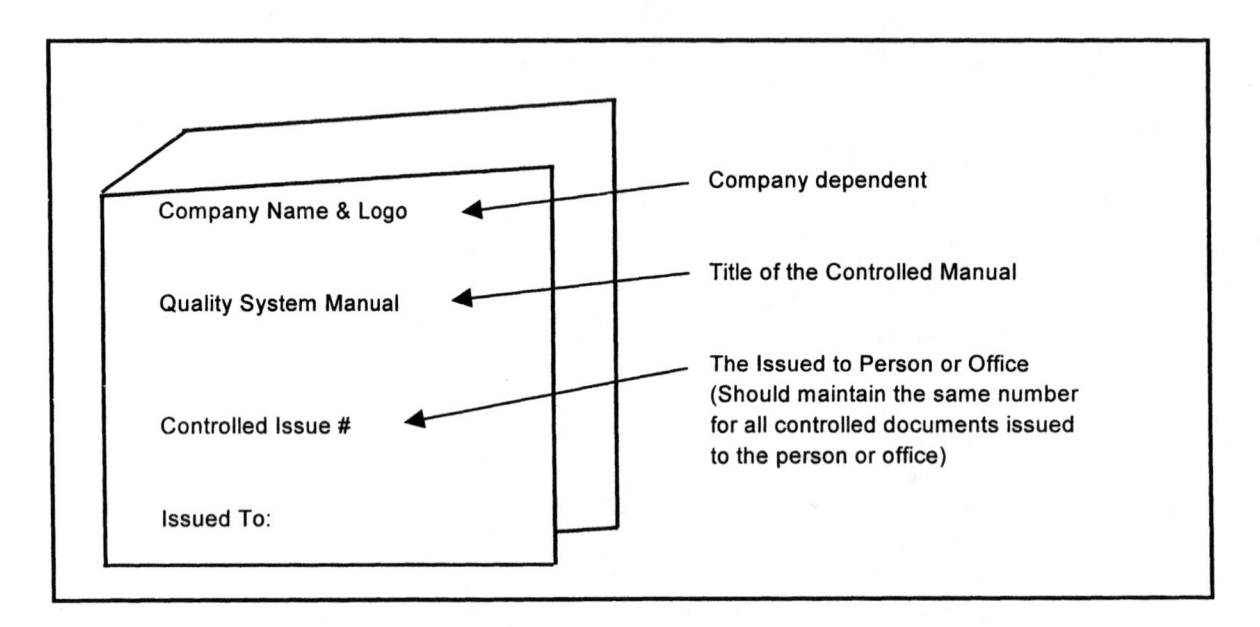

**Figure 9-2. Cover and Packaging of Quality Safety Manual**

## Cover and Packaging

The cover page (reference Figure 9-2) should be insertable and changeable, allowing for easy update. A specific color might help identify the QSM (such as blue or green). A three-ring binder packaging is most convenient. Using a case bound or spiral binding does not allow for easy individual section updates (a necessity).

## Standard Page Header

The QSM consists of a number of individually controlled sections (about 24). Each page of each section must be consistent in the use of the header and in terms of its format. Each section of the QSM needs to be individually controlled, carrying its own section revision level.

Determination of the specific QSM format (i.e., standard header information, footer information, and general presentation arrangement) is under the control of the individual organization or company (reference Figure 9-3).

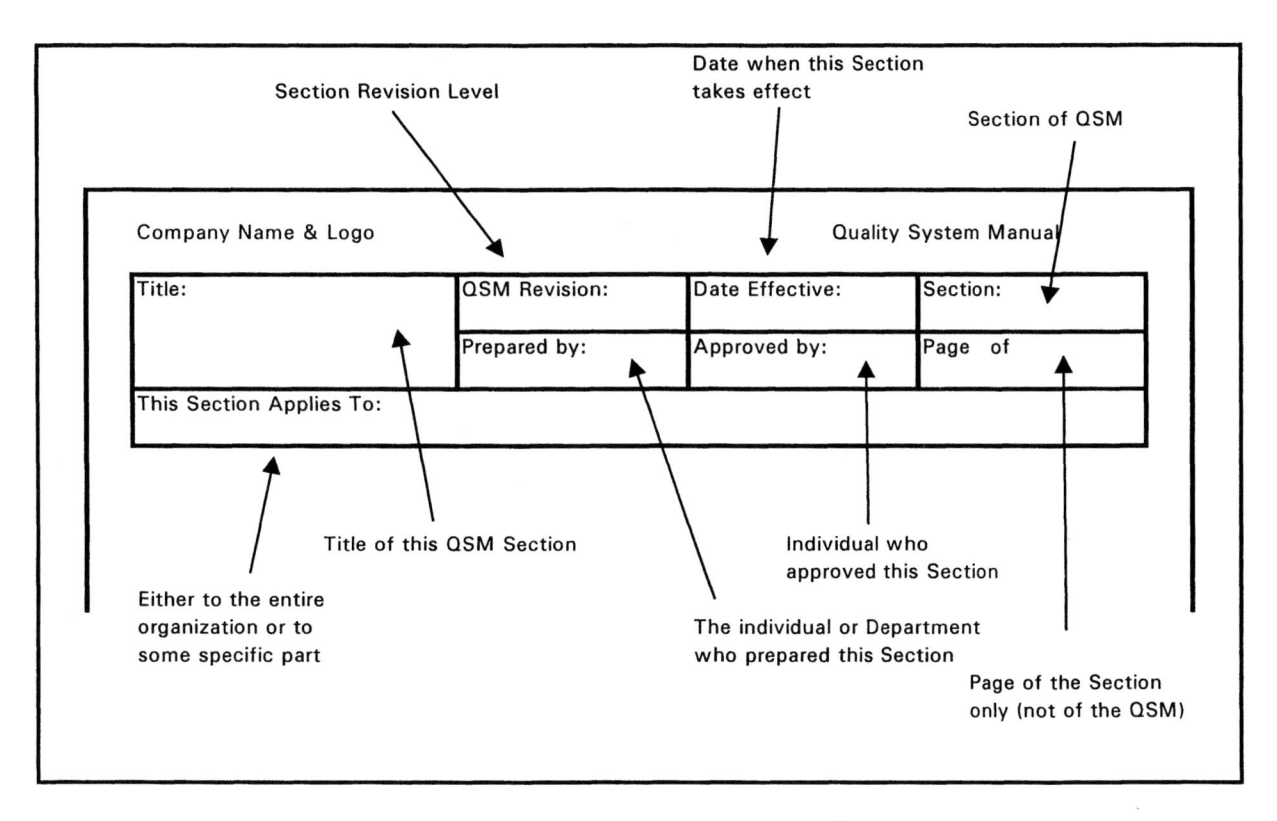

**Figure 9-3. Standardized Format for the QSM**

## Foreword/Certification

The Foreword/Certification does not normally carry a QSM section number and is located first in the manual. A typical Foreword/Certification content is shown in Figure 9-4. An applied example of such is also shown.

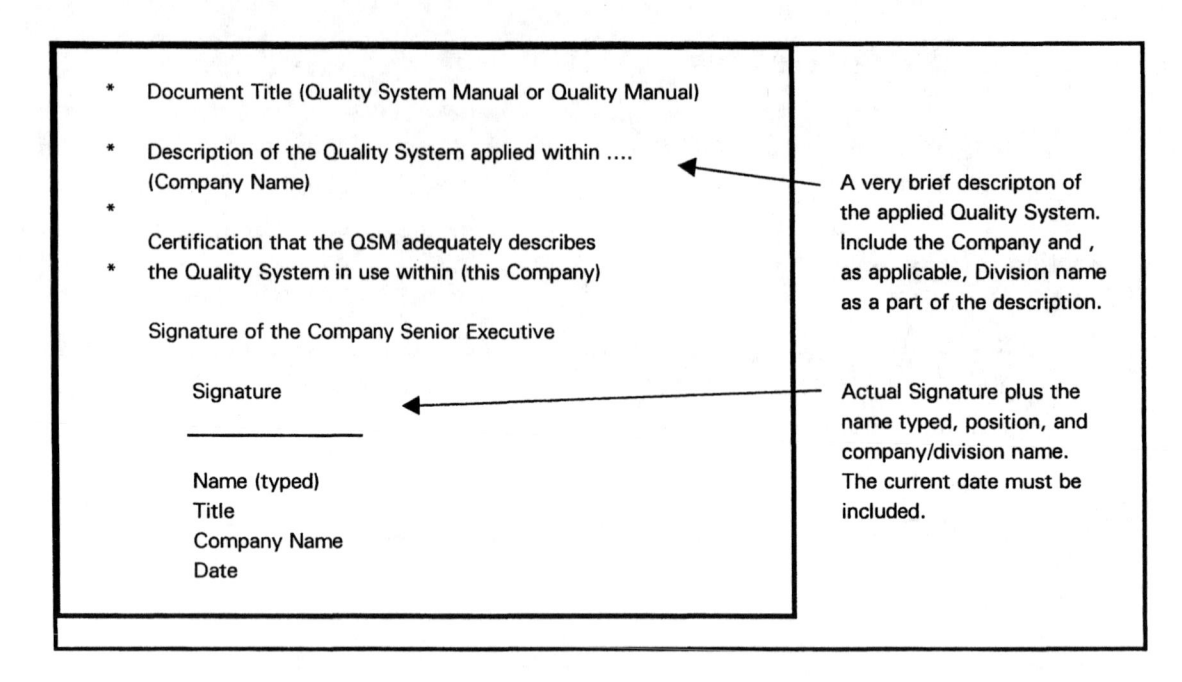

82 / *Implementing an ISO 9000-Based Quality System*

```
*   Document Title (Quality System Manual or Quality Manual)

*   Description of the Quality System applied within ....
    (Company Name)
*
    Certification that the QSM adequately describes
*   the Quality System in use within (this Company)

    Signature of the Company Senior Executive

        Signature
        _____

        Name (typed)
        Title
        Company Name
        Date
```

A very brief descripton of the applied Quality System. Include the Company and, as applicable, Division name as a part of the description.

Actual Signature plus the name typed, position, and company/division name. The current date must be included.

**Figure 9-4. Foreword/Certification Content**

## Table of Contents—Cross Reference

This section of the QSM is normally Section 1 and must be updated every time any of the other sections are updated.

| Title: | QSM Revision: | Date Effective: | Section: 1 |
|---|---|---|---|
|  | Prepared by: | Approved by: | Page  of |
| This Section Applicable to: |  |  | Volume: |

| QSM Section | Section Title | Section Revision | ISO 9000 Cross Reference |

— Standard Page Heading

— Selected ISO 9000 Standard Cross = Referenced paragraph

— The revision level of each QSM Section

— The QSM Section Title

— The QSM Section Number

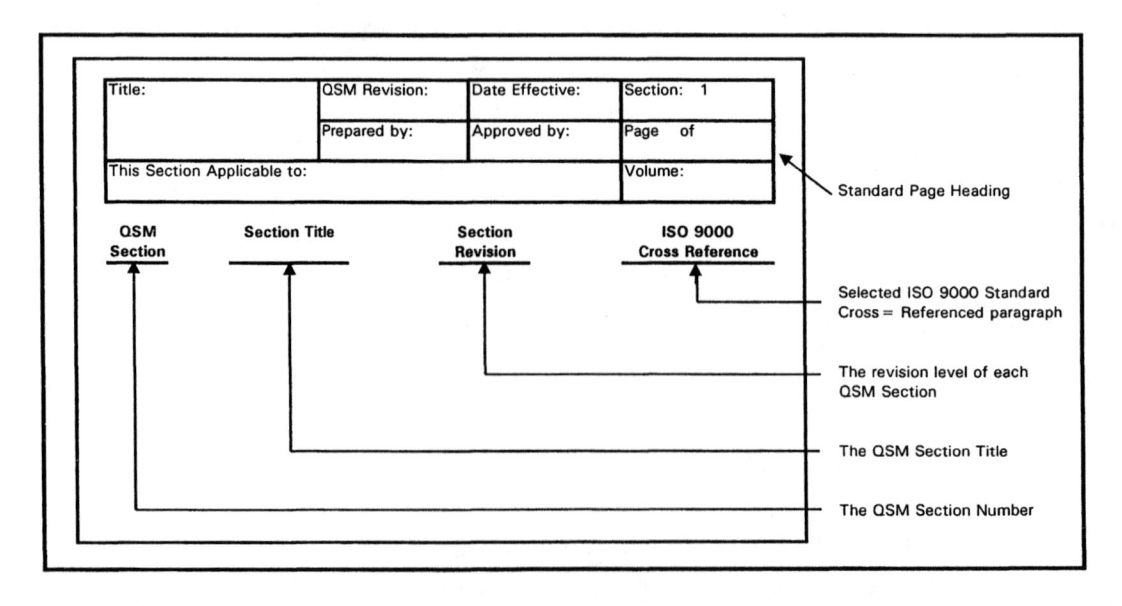

**Figure 9-5. Cross Referenced Table of Contents**

# QUALITY SYSTEM MANUALS—APPLIED EXAMPLES

## ABS Corporate Quality System Manual—Applied Example

One of the key objectives of "ABS 2000" is to instill an emphasis on quality and quality management in all aspects of ABS activities. Our goals are to totally integrate quality into everything we do and to enable ABS to become a model of quality management for other companies to follow. The foundation for this effort is the establishment of the quality system as described in this manual throughout ABS and its affiliated companies.

The Quality System Manual describes the ABS Quality System as defined by the International Association of Classification Societies (IACS) and the International Organization for Standardization (ISO). It is designed to meet all aspects of both IACS and ISO 9001 requirements with ABS's decentralized, worldwide structure while maintaining consistency between the structural units (Divisions).

The ABS Quality System will serve as a means of ensuring that ABS services conform to requirements through the preparation and effective implementation of procedures and work instructions as well as through concentration on quality education program for all our employees that includes team effectiveness, problem solving skills, and the identification of quality parameters for all of our activities.

Our goal is to instill in all ABS employees a common focus on client satisfaction and to forge and maintain an identification with the important words: safety and quality; with safety defining what we do and quality defining how we do it.

The Quality System Manual shall be distributed and maintained on a controlled copy basis.

Frank J. Iarossi
Chairman & CEO
22 June 1994

| ABS Corporate Quality System Manual |||||
|---|---|---|---|---|
| Title: TABLE OF CONTENTS & CROSS-REFERENCE | QSM Revision: 15 | Date Effective: 1 March 98 | Section: | 1 |
| | Prepared by: R.A. Giuffra | Approved by: R.J. Murphy | Page: | 1 of 1 |
| Applicable to: This section is applicable to all of ABS |||Volume: | 1 |

| ABS SECTION | REV. | CROSS-REFERENCE TO: ISO 9001 | IACS SECT. |
|---|---|---|---|
| 1  Table of Contents & Cross Reference | 15 | 4.5.2 | 4.5.2 |
| 2  Quality Policy | 5 | 4.1.1 | 4.1.1 |
| 3  Quality Objectives | 3 | 4.1.1 | 4.1.1 |
| 4  Management Responsibilities | 2 | 4.1 | 4.1 |
| 5  Quality System | 7 | 4.2 | 4.2 |
| 6  Management Review | 6 | 4.1.3 | 4.1.3 |
| 7  Organization & Responsibility | 10 | 4.1.2.1 | 4.1.2.1 |
| 8  Contract Review | 5 | 4.3, 4.1.2.2 | 4.3, 4.1.2.2 |
| 9  Service Design Control | 6 | 4.4 | 4.4 |
| 10 Document & Data Control | 8 | 4.5 | 4.5 |
| 11 Purchasing & Supplier Control | 9 | 4.6 | 4.6 |
| 12 Client Supplied Materials | 3 | 4.7, 4.10 | 4.7, 4.10 |
| 13 Project Identification & Traceability | 5 | 4.8, 4.12 | 4.8, 4.12 |
| 14 Process Control | 4 | 4.9, 4.10 | 4.9, 4.10 |
| 15 Measurement Control System | 5 | 4.11 | 4.11 |
| 16 Corrective and Preventive Action | 6 | 4.13, 4.14 | 4.13, 4.14 |
| 17 Handling, Strorage, Packaging, & Traceability | 2 | 4.15 | 4.15 |
| 18 Control and Retention of Quality Records | 5 | 4.16 | 4.16 |
| 19 Internal Quality Audits | 7 | 4.17 | 4.17 |
| 20 Training | 4 | 4.18 | 4.18 |
| 21 Customer Servicing | 4 | 4.19 | 4.19 |
| 22 Statistical Techniques | 2 | 4.20 | 4.20 |
| Glossary | 7 | N/A | N/A |
| Record of Revision | 15 | 4.5.2 | 4.5.2 |

**APPLIED EXAMPLE**

# Quality System Manual Elements—Applied Example

## Quality Policy

| Company Name | | | Quality System Manual | |
|---|---|---|---|---|
| Title: Quality Policy | QSM Revision: | Date Effective: | Section: | 2 |
| | Prepared by: | Approved by: | Page | of |
| This Section Applicable to: | | | Volume: | 1 |

← Standard Page Heading

**1.0 Purpose**
The purpose of this section is to establish the Quality Policy for (Name of Company)

← State the purpose of this Section of the Manual.

**2.0 Reference Document**
2.1 ISO 9001, paragraph 4.1.1

← Refer to the appropriate ISO 9001 Standard Paragraph.

**3.0 Mission Statement**
3.1 The following is the Mission Statement adopted by the Management of (Name of Company)

The Mission of ......................

← Present the Mission Statement of the Organization here.

**4.0 Quality Policy Statement**
4.1 The following is the Quality Policy Statement adopted by the Management of (Name of Company)

It is the Policy of ........................

← Present the Quality Policy Statement of the Organization here

**5.0 General Comments**
5.1 Our Quality Policy means ......................
5.2 Our clients confidence must be gained by the Products and Services we offer:

_____
_____
_____

← State the meaning of the Quality Policy in the eyes of the Clients, Suppliers, Employees, Stock Holders, and Public interest.

← List the methods. They must be measurable and demonstratable to an auditor.

5.3 All (Company Name) activities must be carried out in accordance with the (Company Name) code-of-ethics.

**6.0 Quality Policy Implementation**
The ways in which the (Company Name) Quality Policy is implemented include:
6.1
6.2
6.3   (Listing)
6.4
6.6

← List the specific methods. These must be measurable and demonstratable to the auditor.

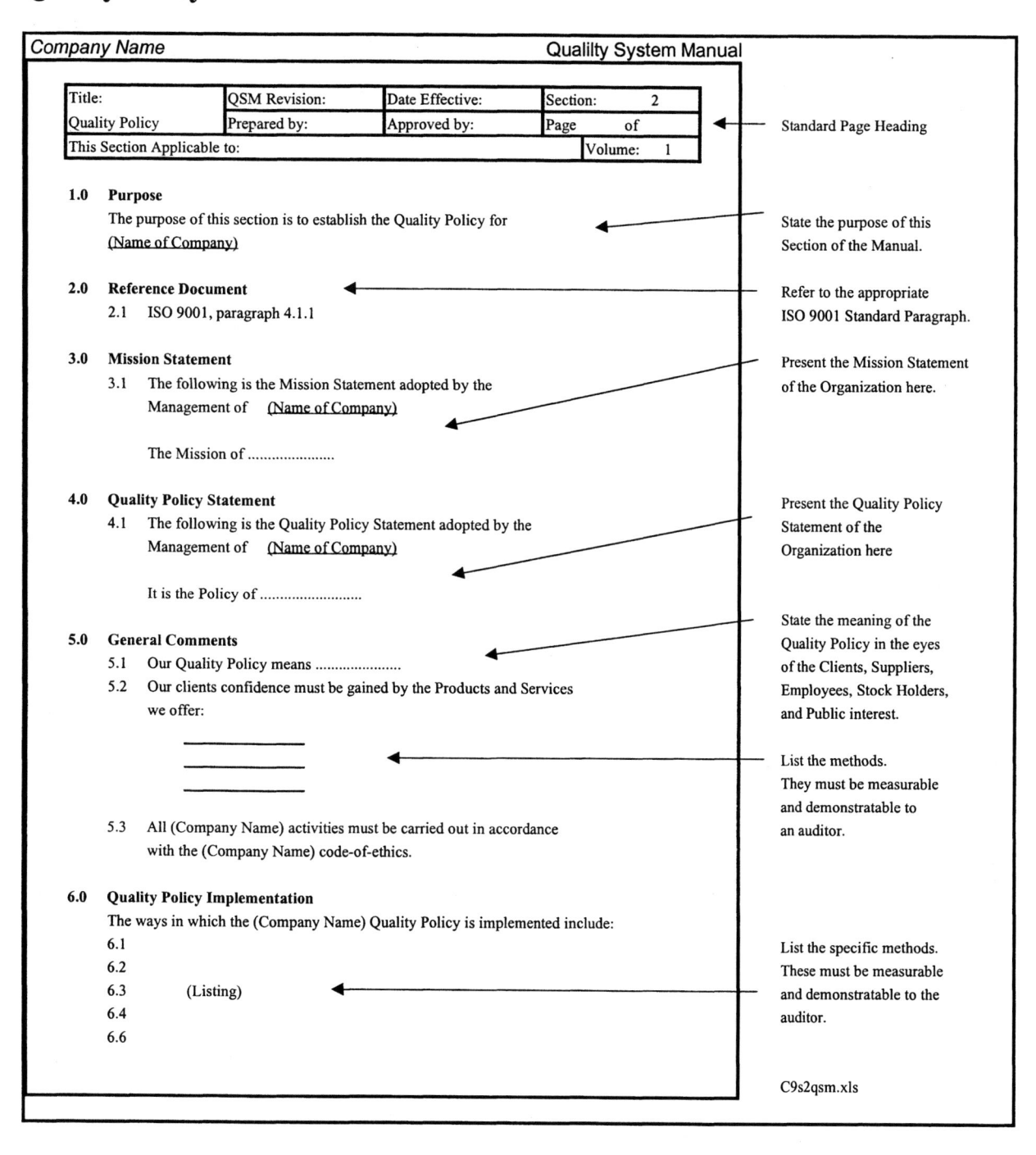

C9s2qsm.xls

86 / *Implementing an ISO 9000-Based Quality System*

# Quality Objective

| Company Name | | | Quality System Manual | |
|---|---|---|---|---|
| Title: Quality Objectives | QSM Revision: Prepared by: | Date Effective: Approved by: | Section: 3 Page of | |
| This Section Applicable to: | | | Volume: 1 | |

◄—— Standard Page Heading

**1.0 Purpose**

The purpose of this section is to establish the Quality Objectives of the (Name of Company)

◄—— State the purpose of this Section of the Manual.

**2.0 Reference Document**

2.1  ISO 9001, paragraph 4.1.1

◄—— Refer to the appropriate ISO 9001 Standard Paragraph.

**3.0 Quality Objectives**

The Quality Objectives of (Company Name) are:
3.1
3.2
3.3     (Listing of Quality Objectives)
3.4
3.5
3.6

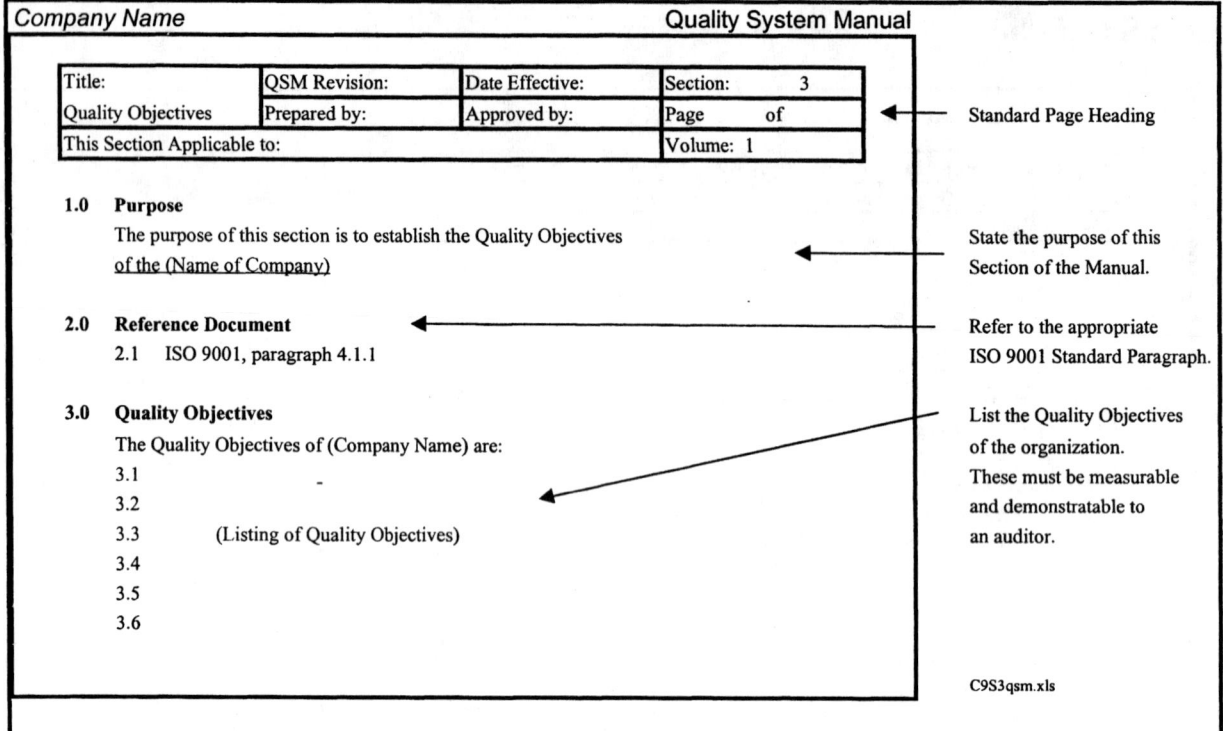

List the Quality Objectives of the organization. These must be measurable and demonstratable to an auditor.

C9S3qsm.xls

**Examples of Quality Objectives might include:**

3.1  To serve and respond to the needs of its customers through continuous improvement of its services and products.

3.2  To establish and nurture a culture and mindset throughout the company that is focused on customer satisfaction.

3.3  To create and maintain an environment for our employees that encourages teamwork, cooperation, innovative thinking, leadership, problem solving, decisionmaking, and a commitment to continuous improvement.

3.4  To continuously develop, implement, review, and improve systems and procedures to ensure consistency regardless of where the work is performed.

3.5  To continuously improve the value of our products and services to our clients by implementing quality into all aspects of our business.

3.6  To reduce cycle time and to remove non-value added work through process mapping, resulting in improved responsiveness to our clients needs.

3.7  To achieve and maintain ISO 9001 Series Quality System Certifications.

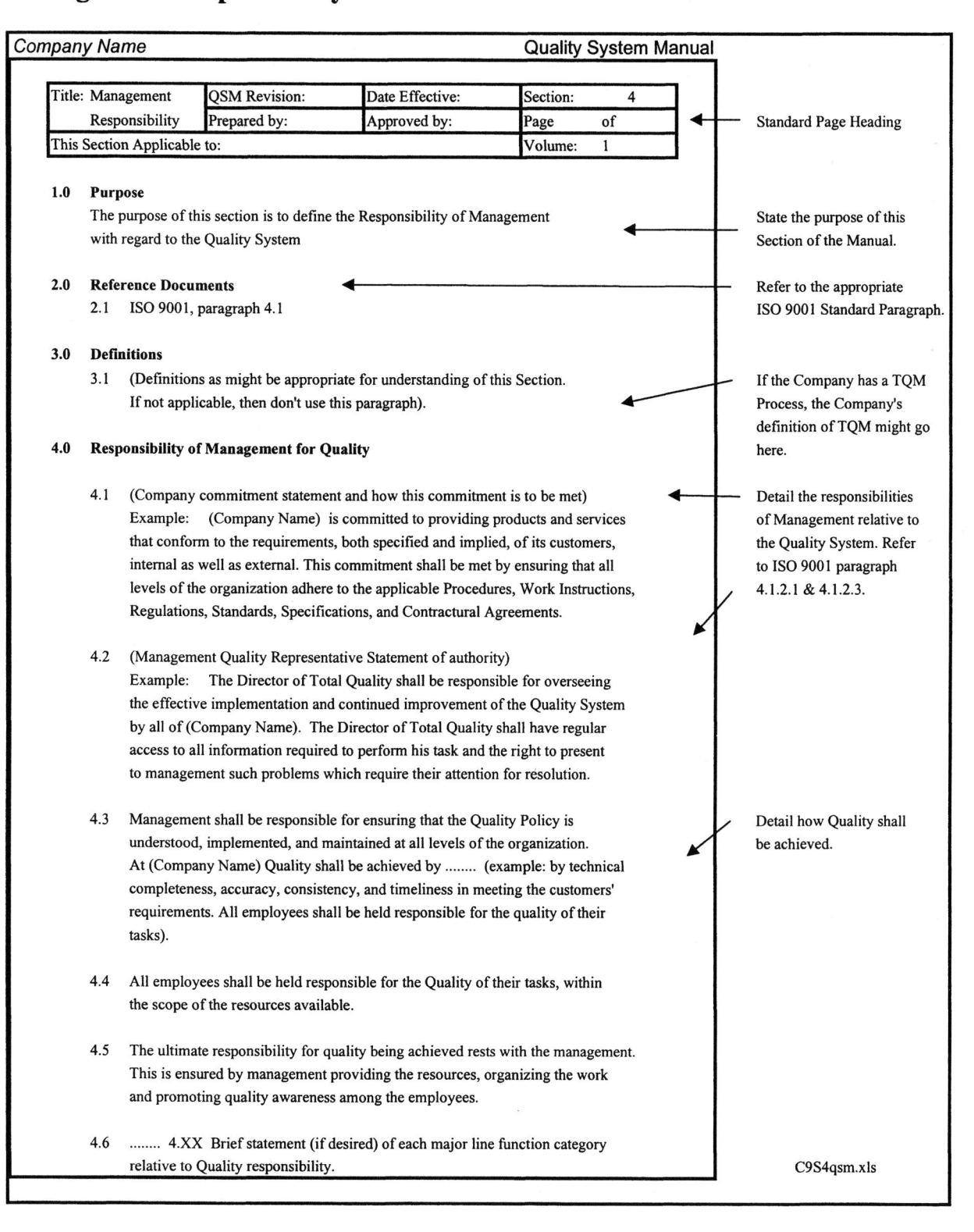

# Management Responsibility

| Company Name | | | Quality System Manual | |
|---|---|---|---|---|
| Title: Management Responsibility | QSM Revision: Prepared by: | Date Effective: Approved by: | Section: Page | 4 of |
| This Section Applicable to: | | | Volume: | 1 |

← Standard Page Heading

**1.0 Purpose**
The purpose of this section is to define the Responsibility of Management with regard to the Quality System

← State the purpose of this Section of the Manual.

**2.0 Reference Documents**
2.1 ISO 9001, paragraph 4.1

← Refer to the appropriate ISO 9001 Standard Paragraph.

**3.0 Definitions**
3.1 (Definitions as might be appropriate for understanding of this Section. If not applicable, then don't use this paragraph).

← If the Company has a TQM Process, the Company's definition of TQM might go here.

**4.0 Responsibility of Management for Quality**

4.1 (Company commitment statement and how this commitment is to be met)
Example: (Company Name) is committed to providing products and services that conform to the requirements, both specified and implied, of its customers, internal as well as external. This commitment shall be met by ensuring that all levels of the organization adhere to the applicable Procedures, Work Instructions, Regulations, Standards, Specifications, and Contractural Agreements.

← Detail the responsibilities of Management relative to the Quality System. Refer to ISO 9001 paragraph 4.1.2.1 & 4.1.2.3.

4.2 (Management Quality Representative Statement of authority)
Example: The Director of Total Quality shall be responsible for overseeing the effective implementation and continued improvement of the Quality System by all of (Company Name). The Director of Total Quality shall have regular access to all information required to perform his task and the right to present to management such problems which require their attention for resolution.

4.3 Management shall be responsible for ensuring that the Quality Policy is understood, implemented, and maintained at all levels of the organization. At (Company Name) Quality shall be achieved by ........ (example: by technical completeness, accuracy, consistency, and timeliness in meeting the customers' requirements. All employees shall be held responsible for the quality of their tasks).

← Detail how Quality shall be achieved.

4.4 All employees shall be held responsible for the Quality of their tasks, within the scope of the resources available.

4.5 The ultimate responsibility for quality being achieved rests with the management. This is ensured by management providing the resources, organizing the work and promoting quality awareness among the employees.

4.6 ........ 4.XX Brief statement (if desired) of each major line function category relative to Quality responsibility.

C9S4qsm.xls

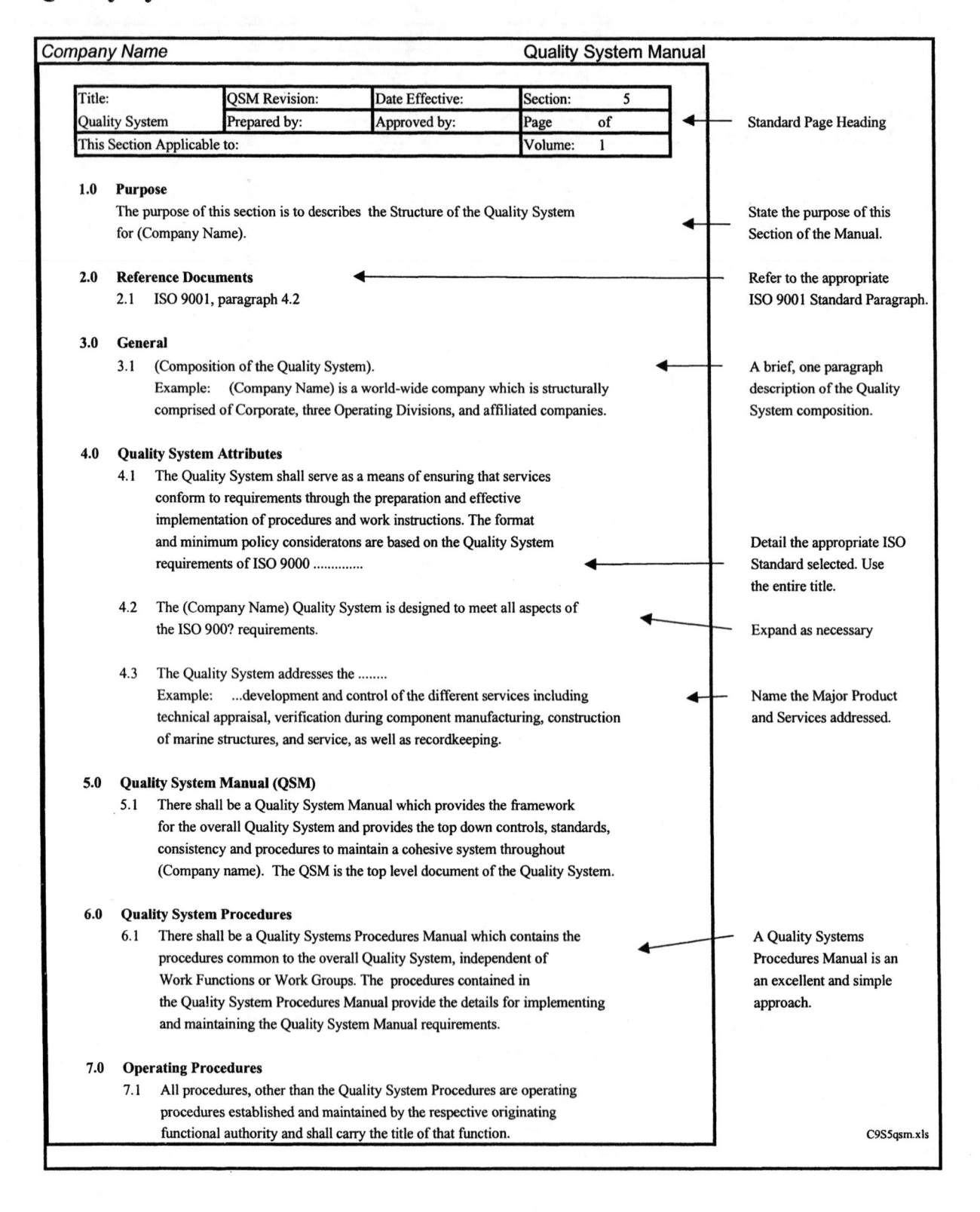

# Quality System

| Company Name | | | Quality System Manual | |
|---|---|---|---|---|
| Title: Quality System | QSM Revision: Prepared by: | Date Effective: Approved by: | Section: 5 Page of | |
| This Section Applicable to: | | | Volume: 1 | |

— Standard Page Heading

**1.0 Purpose**

The purpose of this section is to describes the Structure of the Quality System for (Company Name).

— State the purpose of this Section of the Manual.

**2.0 Reference Documents**

2.1 ISO 9001, paragraph 4.2

— Refer to the appropriate ISO 9001 Standard Paragraph.

**3.0 General**

3.1 (Composition of the Quality System).
Example: (Company Name) is a world-wide company which is structurally comprised of Corporate, three Operating Divisions, and affiliated companies.

— A brief, one paragraph description of the Quality System composition.

**4.0 Quality System Attributes**

4.1 The Quality System shall serve as a means of ensuring that services conform to requirements through the preparation and effective implementation of procedures and work instructions. The format and minimum policy consideratons are based on the Quality System requirements of ISO 9000 ..............

— Detail the appropriate ISO Standard selected. Use the entire title.

4.2 The (Company Name) Quality System is designed to meet all aspects of the ISO 900? requirements.

— Expand as necessary

4.3 The Quality System addresses the ........
Example: ...development and control of the different services including technical appraisal, verification during component manufacturing, construction of marine structures, and service, as well as recordkeeping.

— Name the Major Product and Services addressed.

**5.0 Quality System Manual (QSM)**

5.1 There shall be a Quality System Manual which provides the framework for the overall Quality System and provides the top down controls, standards, consistency and procedures to maintain a cohesive system throughout (Company name). The QSM is the top level document of the Quality System.

**6.0 Quality System Procedures**

6.1 There shall be a Quality Systems Procedures Manual which contains the procedures common to the overall Quality System, independent of Work Functions or Work Groups. The procedures contained in the Quality System Procedures Manual provide the details for implementing and maintaining the Quality System Manual requirements.

— A Quality Systems Procedures Manual is an an excellent and simple approach.

**7.0 Operating Procedures**

7.1 All procedures, other than the Quality System Procedures are operating procedures established and maintained by the respective originating functional authority and shall carry the title of that function.

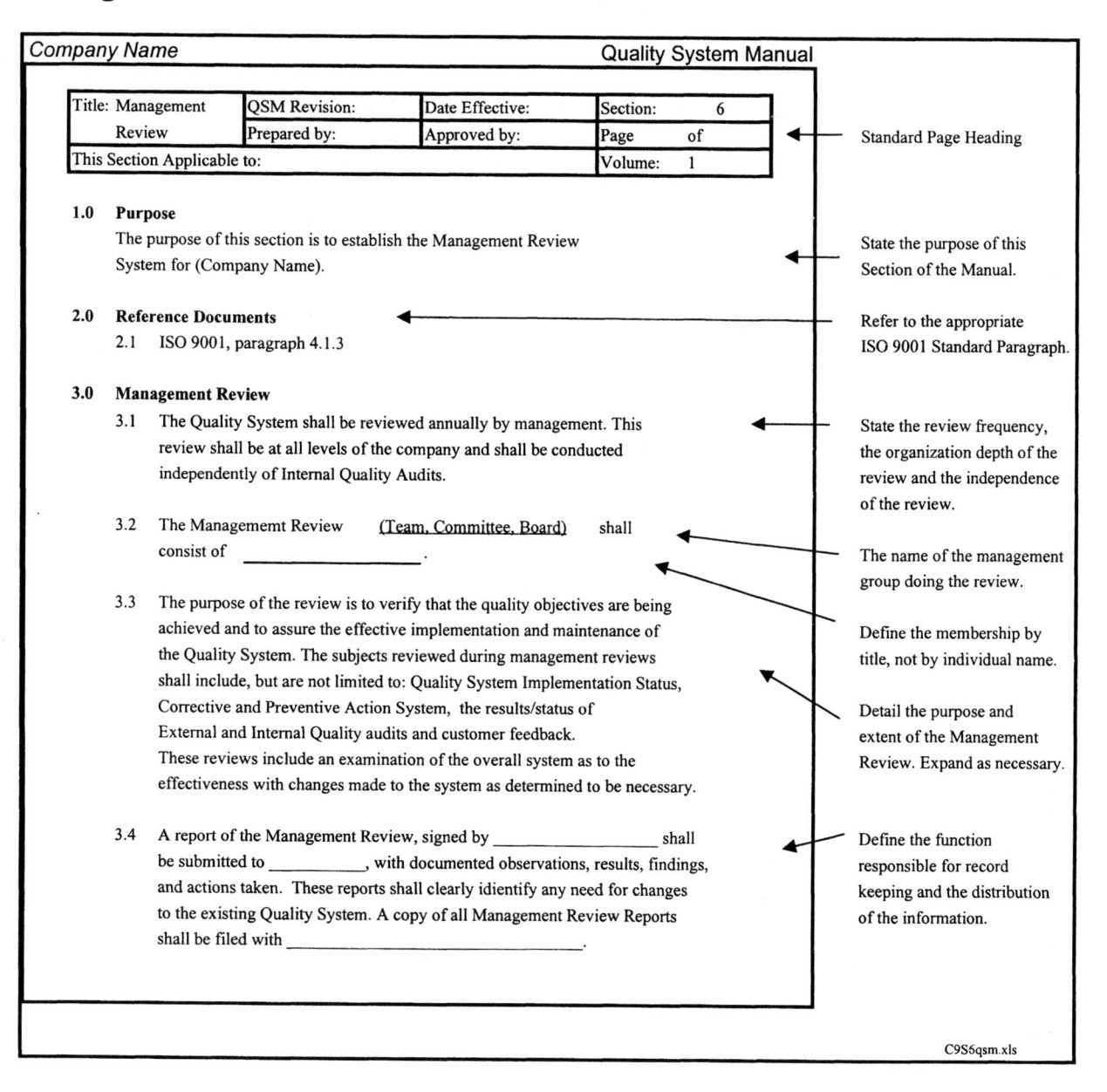

# Management Review

| Company Name | | | Quality System Manual | |
|---|---|---|---|---|
| Title: Management Review | QSM Revision: | Date Effective: | Section: | 6 |
| | Prepared by: | Approved by: | Page | of |
| This Section Applicable to: | | | Volume: | 1 |

*← Standard Page Heading*

**1.0 Purpose**
The purpose of this section is to establish the Management Review System for (Company Name).

*← State the purpose of this Section of the Manual.*

**2.0 Reference Documents**
   2.1   ISO 9001, paragraph 4.1.3

*← Refer to the appropriate ISO 9001 Standard Paragraph.*

**3.0 Management Review**

   3.1   The Quality System shall be reviewed annually by management. This review shall be at all levels of the company and shall be conducted independently of Internal Quality Audits.

*← State the review frequency, the organization depth of the review and the independence of the review.*

   3.2   The Managememt Review _(Team, Committee, Board)_ shall consist of _____.

*← The name of the management group doing the review.*

*Define the membership by title, not by individual name.*

   3.3   The purpose of the review is to verify that the quality objectives are being achieved and to assure the effective implementation and maintenance of the Quality System. The subjects reviewed during management reviews shall include, but are not limited to: Quality System Implementation Status, Corrective and Preventive Action System, the results/status of External and Internal Quality audits and customer feedback. These reviews include an examination of the overall system as to the effectiveness with changes made to the system as determined to be necessary.

*Detail the purpose and extent of the Management Review. Expand as necessary.*

   3.4   A report of the Management Review, signed by _____ shall be submitted to _____, with documented observations, results, findings, and actions taken. These reports shall clearly idientify any need for changes to the existing Quality System. A copy of all Management Review Reports shall be filed with _____.

*← Define the function responsible for record keeping and the distribution of the information.*

C9S6qsm.xls

# Organization and Responsibilities

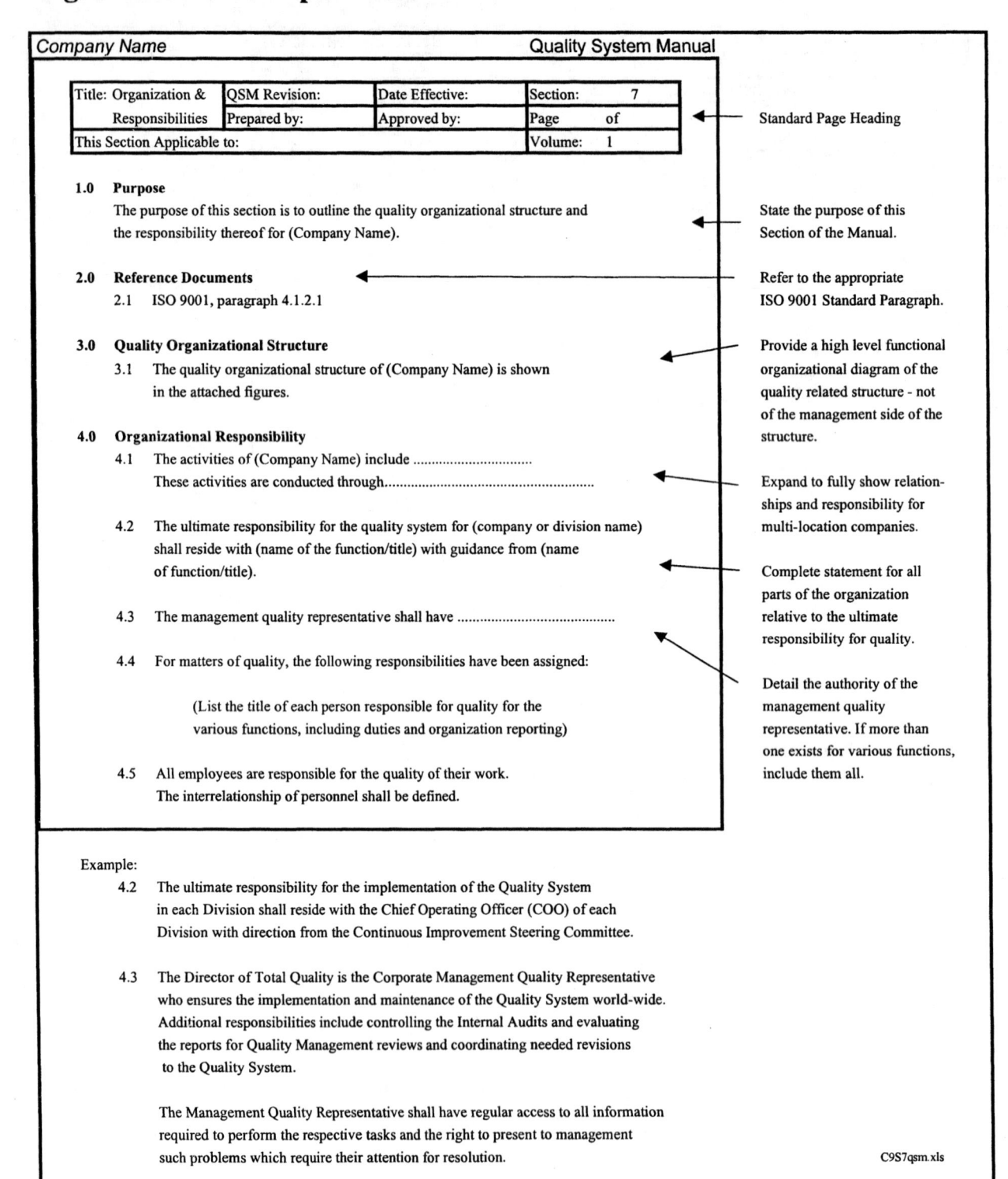

| Company Name | | | Quality System Manual | |
|---|---|---|---|---|
| Title: Organization & Responsibilities | QSM Revision: | Date Effective: | Section: | 7 |
| | Prepared by: | Approved by: | Page | of |
| This Section Applicable to: | | | Volume: | 1 |

→ Standard Page Heading

**1.0 Purpose**
   The purpose of this section is to outline the quality organizational structure and the responsibility thereof for (Company Name).

   ← State the purpose of this Section of the Manual.

**2.0 Reference Documents**
   2.1 ISO 9001, paragraph 4.1.2.1

   ← Refer to the appropriate ISO 9001 Standard Paragraph.

**3.0 Quality Organizational Structure**
   3.1 The quality organizational structure of (Company Name) is shown in the attached figures.

   ← Provide a high level functional organizational diagram of the quality related structure - not of the management side of the structure.

**4.0 Organizational Responsibility**
   4.1 The activities of (Company Name) include .................................
       These activities are conducted through.........................................................

   ← Expand to fully show relationships and responsibility for multi-location companies.

   4.2 The ultimate responsibility for the quality system for (company or division name) shall reside with (name of the function/title) with guidance from (name of function/title).

   ← Complete statement for all parts of the organization relative to the ultimate responsibility for quality.

   4.3 The management quality representative shall have ...........................................

   4.4 For matters of quality, the following responsibilities have been assigned:

       (List the title of each person responsible for quality for the various functions, including duties and organization reporting)

   ← Detail the authority of the management quality representative. If more than one exists for various functions, include them all.

   4.5 All employees are responsible for the quality of their work.
       The interrelationship of personnel shall be defined.

Example:

   4.2 The ultimate responsibility for the implementation of the Quality System in each Division shall reside with the Chief Operating Officer (COO) of each Division with direction from the Continuous Improvement Steering Committee.

   4.3 The Director of Total Quality is the Corporate Management Quality Representative who ensures the implementation and maintenance of the Quality System world-wide. Additional responsibilities include controlling the Internal Audits and evaluating the reports for Quality Management reviews and coordinating needed revisions to the Quality System.

   The Management Quality Representative shall have regular access to all information required to perform the respective tasks and the right to present to management such problems which require their attention for resolution.

# Contract Review

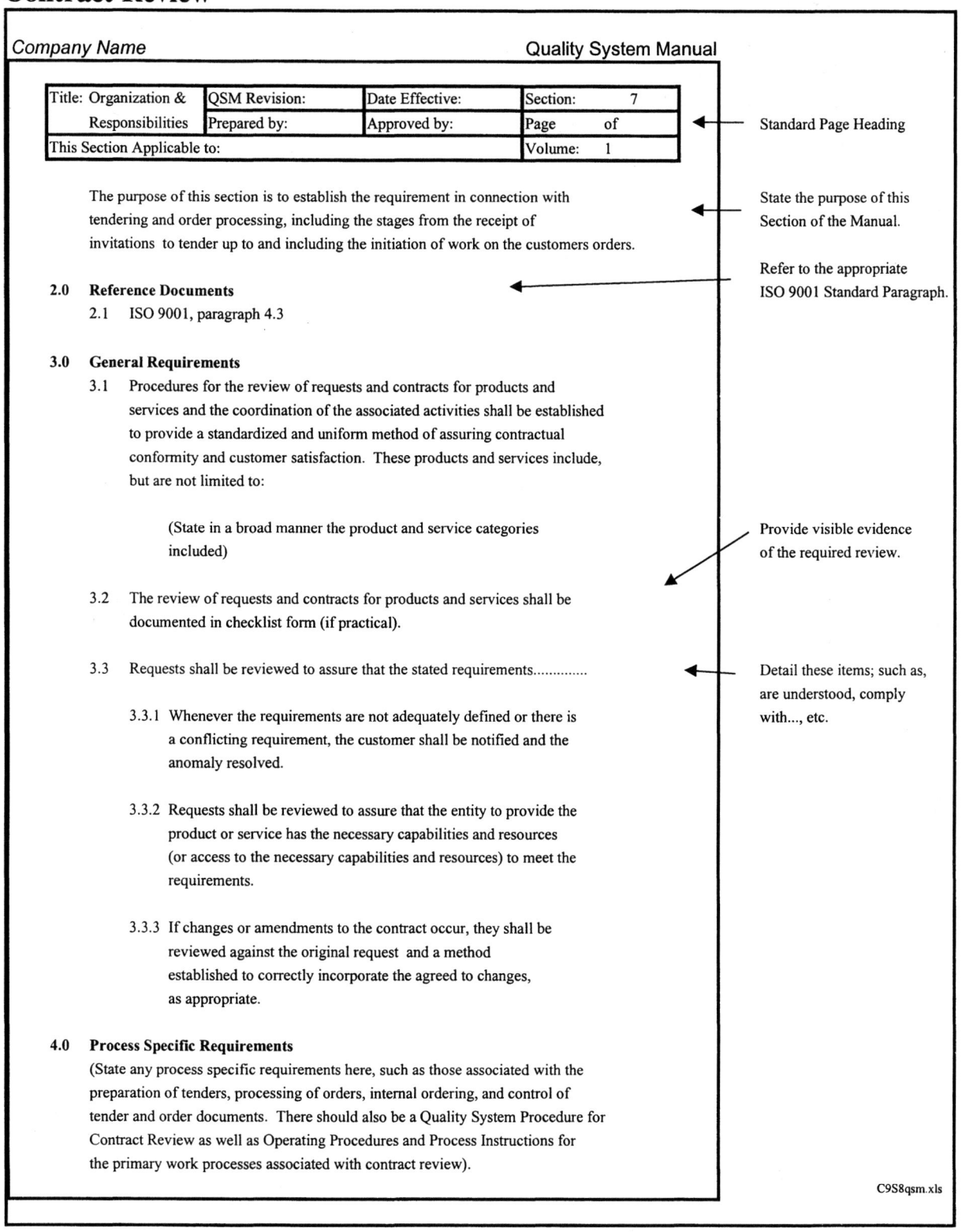

| Company Name | | | Quality System Manual | |
|---|---|---|---|---|
| Title: Organization & Responsibilities | QSM Revision: | Date Effective: | Section: | 7 |
| | Prepared by: | Approved by: | Page | of |
| This Section Applicable to: | | | Volume: | 1 |

*Standard Page Heading*

The purpose of this section is to establish the requirement in connection with tendering and order processing, including the stages from the receipt of invitations to tender up to and including the initiation of work on the customers orders.

*State the purpose of this Section of the Manual.*

**2.0 Reference Documents**
    2.1   ISO 9001, paragraph 4.3

*Refer to the appropriate ISO 9001 Standard Paragraph.*

**3.0 General Requirements**

    3.1   Procedures for the review of requests and contracts for products and services and the coordination of the associated activities shall be established to provide a standardized and uniform method of assuring contractual conformity and customer satisfaction. These products and services include, but are not limited to:

          (State in a broad manner the product and service categories included)

    3.2   The review of requests and contracts for products and services shall be documented in checklist form (if practical).

*Provide visible evidence of the required review.*

    3.3   Requests shall be reviewed to assure that the stated requirements..............

*Detail these items; such as, are understood, comply with..., etc.*

          3.3.1   Whenever the requirements are not adequately defined or there is a conflicting requirement, the customer shall be notified and the anomaly resolved.

          3.3.2   Requests shall be reviewed to assure that the entity to provide the product or service has the necessary capabilities and resources (or access to the necessary capabilities and resources) to meet the requirements.

          3.3.3   If changes or amendments to the contract occur, they shall be reviewed against the original request and a method established to correctly incorporate the agreed to changes, as appropriate.

**4.0 Process Specific Requirements**
(State any process specific requirements here, such as those associated with the preparation of tenders, processing of orders, internal ordering, and control of tender and order documents. There should also be a Quality System Procedure for Contract Review as well as Operating Procedures and Process Instructions for the primary work processes associated with contract review).

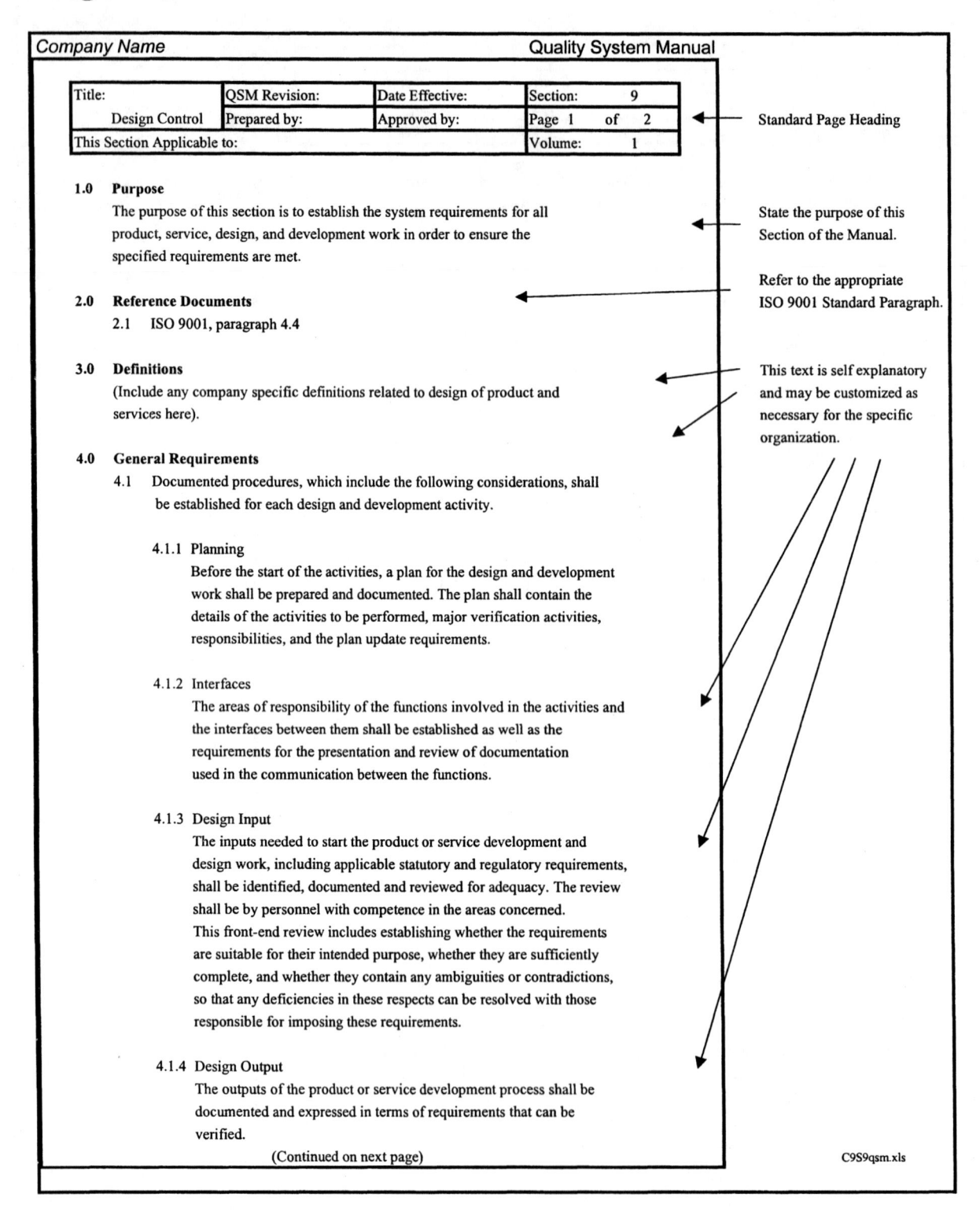

# Design Control

| Company Name | | | Quality System Manual | |
|---|---|---|---|---|
| Title: Design Control | QSM Revision: | Date Effective: | Section: | 9 |
| | Prepared by: | Approved by: | Page 1 of 2 | |
| This Section Applicable to: | | | Volume: | 1 |

**1.0 Purpose**

The purpose of this section is to establish the system requirements for all product, service, design, and development work in order to ensure the specified requirements are met.

*← State the purpose of this Section of the Manual.*

**2.0 Reference Documents**

2.1 ISO 9001, paragraph 4.4

*← Refer to the appropriate ISO 9001 Standard Paragraph.*

**3.0 Definitions**

(Include any company specific definitions related to design of product and services here).

*← This text is self explanatory and may be customized as necessary for the specific organization.*

**4.0 General Requirements**

4.1 Documented procedures, which include the following considerations, shall be established for each design and development activity.

    4.1.1 Planning

    Before the start of the activities, a plan for the design and development work shall be prepared and documented. The plan shall contain the details of the activities to be performed, major verification activities, responsibilities, and the plan update requirements.

    4.1.2 Interfaces

    The areas of responsibility of the functions involved in the activities and the interfaces between them shall be established as well as the requirements for the presentation and review of documentation used in the communication between the functions.

    4.1.3 Design Input

    The inputs needed to start the product or service development and design work, including applicable statutory and regulatory requirements, shall be identified, documented and reviewed for adequacy. The review shall be by personnel with competence in the areas concerned.
    This front-end review includes establishing whether the requirements are suitable for their intended purpose, whether they are sufficiently complete, and whether they contain any ambiguities or contradictions, so that any deficiencies in these respects can be resolved with those responsible for imposing these requirements.

    4.1.4 Design Output

    The outputs of the product or service development process shall be documented and expressed in terms of requirements that can be verified.

(Continued on next page)

*Standard Page Heading (annotation for top block)*

## Design Control—*Continued*

| Company Name | | | Quality System Manual | |
|---|---|---|---|---|
| Title: Design Control | QSM Revision: Prepared by: | Date Effective: Approved by: | Section: 9 Page 2 of 2 | |
| This Section Applicable to: | | | Volume: 1 | |

← Standard Page Heading

4.2 Design Review
Formal documented reviews of the design shall be planned and conducted at appropriate stages of the design process. The principals participating in each design review shall include representatives of all functions concerned with the design stage being reviewed as well as any other required specialist personnel. Records of such reviews shall be maintained as quality records.

4.3 Design Verification
Verification of the design at appropriate stages shall be performed and documented. The question subject to verification shall include whether the design satisfies the provisions of the input requirements and the requirements of the customer, including any specific regulatory requirements and whether the design is appropriate with regard to the resources available.

    4.3.1 Design verification may include activities such as:
        - repetition of calculations in a different manner and by a different person,
        - tests and demonstrations,
        - design review,
        - comparison with similar or proven design.

4.4 Design Changes
All design changes and modifications shall be identified, reviewed, documented, and approved before their execution. Acceptance shall always be obtained by those functions directly affected by the changes.

← This text is self explanatory and may be customized as necessary for the specific organization.

C9S9cqsm.xls

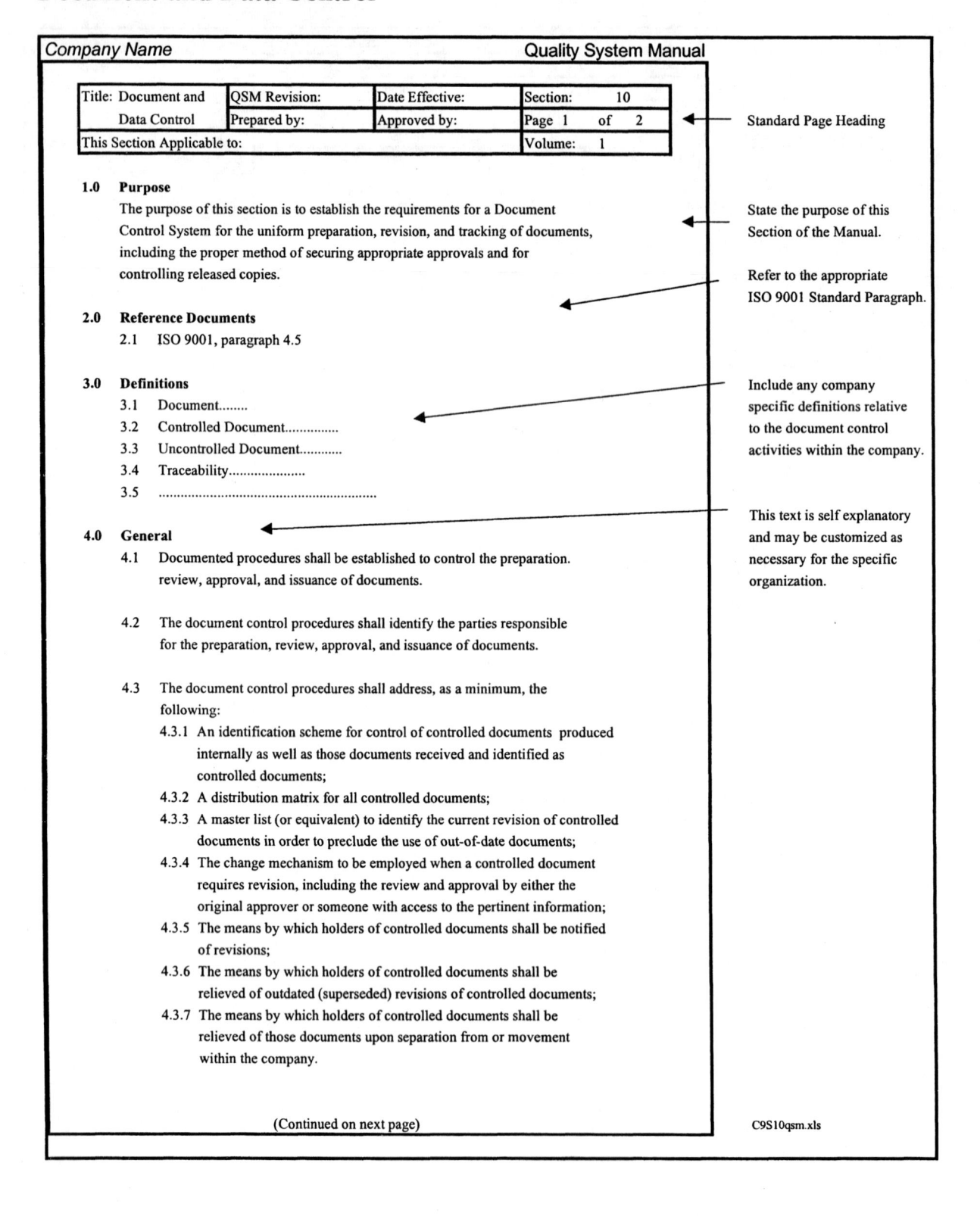

## Document and Data Control

| Company Name | | | Quality System Manual | |
|---|---|---|---|---|
| Title: Document and Data Control | QSM Revision: | Date Effective: | Section: | 10 |
| | Prepared by: | Approved by: | Page 1 of 2 | |
| This Section Applicable to: | | | Volume: 1 | |

→ Standard Page Heading

**1.0 Purpose**
The purpose of this section is to establish the requirements for a Document Control System for the uniform preparation, revision, and tracking of documents, including the proper method of securing appropriate approvals and for controlling released copies.

→ State the purpose of this Section of the Manual.

→ Refer to the appropriate ISO 9001 Standard Paragraph.

**2.0 Reference Documents**
2.1  ISO 9001, paragraph 4.5

**3.0 Definitions**
3.1  Document........
3.2  Controlled Document...............
3.3  Uncontrolled Document............
3.4  Traceability.....................
3.5  ............................................................

→ Include any company specific definitions relative to the document control activities within the company.

**4.0 General**
4.1  Documented procedures shall be established to control the preparation. review, approval, and issuance of documents.

→ This text is self explanatory and may be customized as necessary for the specific organization.

4.2  The document control procedures shall identify the parties responsible for the preparation, review, approval, and issuance of documents.

4.3  The document control procedures shall address, as a minimum, the following:
    4.3.1 An identification scheme for control of controlled documents produced internally as well as those documents received and identified as controlled documents;
    4.3.2 A distribution matrix for all controlled documents;
    4.3.3 A master list (or equivalent) to identify the current revision of controlled documents in order to preclude the use of out-of-date documents;
    4.3.4 The change mechanism to be employed when a controlled document requires revision, including the review and approval by either the original approver or someone with access to the pertinent information;
    4.3.5 The means by which holders of controlled documents shall be notified of revisions;
    4.3.6 The means by which holders of controlled documents shall be relieved of outdated (superseded) revisions of controlled documents;
    4.3.7 The means by which holders of controlled documents shall be relieved of those documents upon separation from or movement within the company.

(Continued on next page)

C9S10qsm.xls

# Document and Data Control—*Continued*

| Company Name | | | Quality System Manual | |
|---|---|---|---|---|
| Title: Document and Data Control | QSM Revision: | Date Effective: | Section: 10 | |
| | Prepared by: | Approved by: | Page 2 of 2 | |
| This Section Applicable to: | | | Volume: 1 | |

← Standard Page Heading

4.4 The distribution of controlled copies shall be in accordance with an approved distribution list.

4.5 Required references shall be made available to all employees for appropriate processes under their responsibility. These include but are not limited to:
   1) contracts and specifications;
   2) government regulations;
   3) technical standards;
   4) organization charts;
   5) employee benefits handbook (as applicable);
   6) computer software manuals (as applicable);
   7) ....................(other).

*Customize the listing as necessary for your specific requirements.*
*Only major categories and major documents need to be listed.*

4.6 Only controlled documents shall be used for work affecting quality. References used in work affecting quality shall be identified in the associated quality record or project file for the respective project. Under no circumstances shall an uncontrolled copy of a controlled document be used for work affecting quality. Controlled documents shall include:

   1) The Quality System Manual;
   2) Quality System Procedures;
   3) Operating Procedures and Process Instructions;
   4) Position Description Manual;
   5) Technical Software Master List (as applicable);
   6) Delegation of Authority Manual;
   7) ..................... (other)

*Customize the listing as necessary for your specific requirements.*

C9S10cqm.xls

Examples of definitions:
   **Controlled Document:** Any document issued to a particular department or individual that has been uniquely identified as a "controlled document" and is traceable for recall.

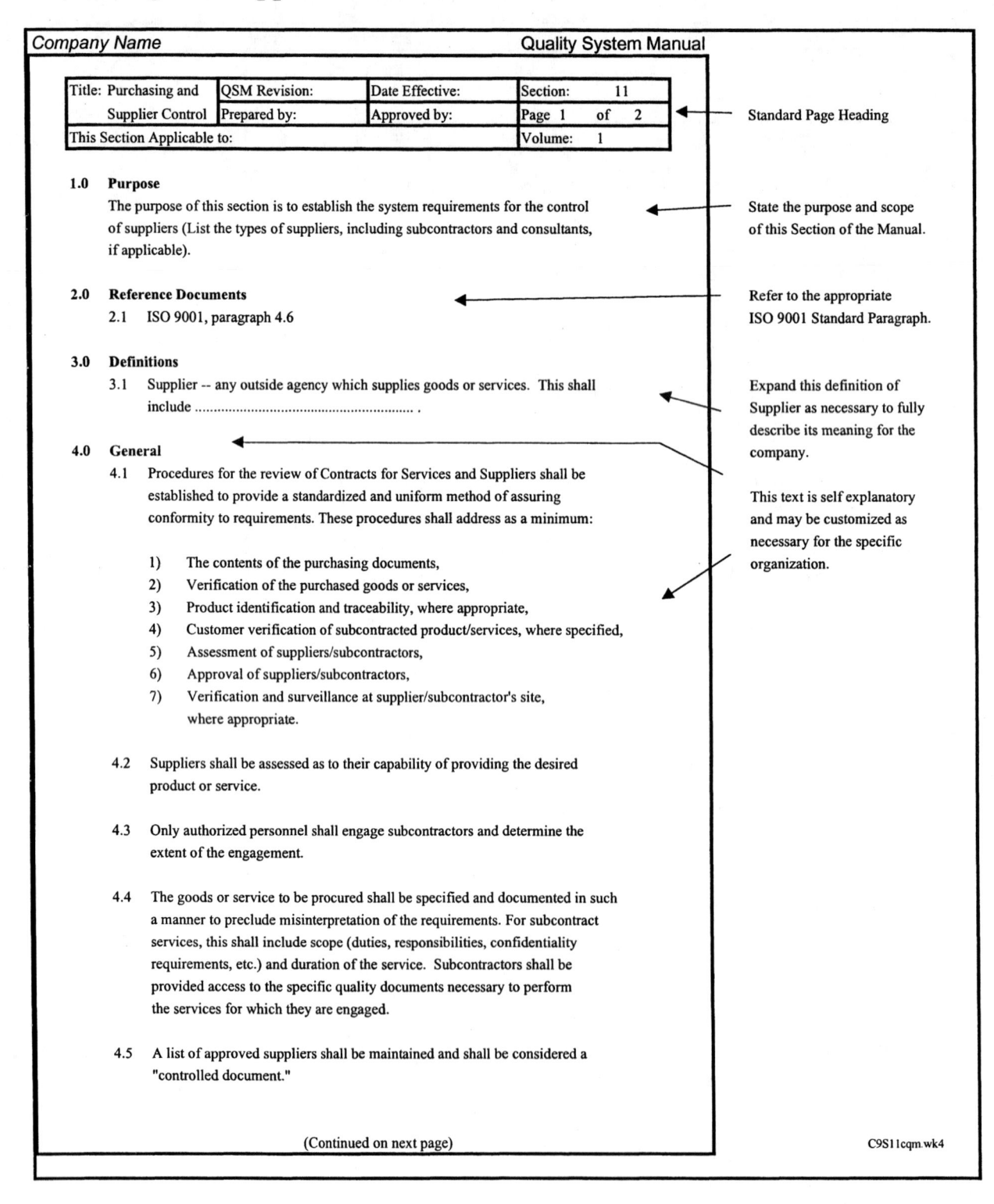

## Purchasing and Supplier Control

| Company Name | | | Quality System Manual | |
|---|---|---|---|---|
| Title: Purchasing and Supplier Control | QSM Revision: | Date Effective: | Section: | 11 |
| | Prepared by: | Approved by: | Page 1 of 2 | |
| This Section Applicable to: | | | Volume: 1 | |

*← Standard Page Heading*

**1.0 Purpose**

The purpose of this section is to establish the system requirements for the control of suppliers (List the types of suppliers, including subcontractors and consultants, if applicable).

*← State the purpose and scope of this Section of the Manual.*

**2.0 Reference Documents**

2.1 ISO 9001, paragraph 4.6

*← Refer to the appropriate ISO 9001 Standard Paragraph.*

**3.0 Definitions**

3.1 Supplier -- any outside agency which supplies goods or services. This shall include .......................................................... .

*← Expand this definition of Supplier as necessary to fully describe its meaning for the company.*

**4.0 General**

4.1 Procedures for the review of Contracts for Services and Suppliers shall be established to provide a standardized and uniform method of assuring conformity to requirements. These procedures shall address as a minimum:

1) The contents of the purchasing documents,
2) Verification of the purchased goods or services,
3) Product identification and traceability, where appropriate,
4) Customer verification of subcontracted product/services, where specified,
5) Assessment of suppliers/subcontractors,
6) Approval of suppliers/subcontractors,
7) Verification and surveillance at supplier/subcontractor's site, where appropriate.

*This text is self explanatory and may be customized as necessary for the specific organization.*

4.2 Suppliers shall be assessed as to their capability of providing the desired product or service.

4.3 Only authorized personnel shall engage subcontractors and determine the extent of the engagement.

4.4 The goods or service to be procured shall be specified and documented in such a manner to preclude misinterpretation of the requirements. For subcontract services, this shall include scope (duties, responsibilities, confidentiality requirements, etc.) and duration of the service. Subcontractors shall be provided access to the specific quality documents necessary to perform the services for which they are engaged.

4.5 A list of approved suppliers shall be maintained and shall be considered a "controlled document."

(Continued on next page)

C9S11cqm.wk4

## Purchasing and Supplier Control—*Continued*

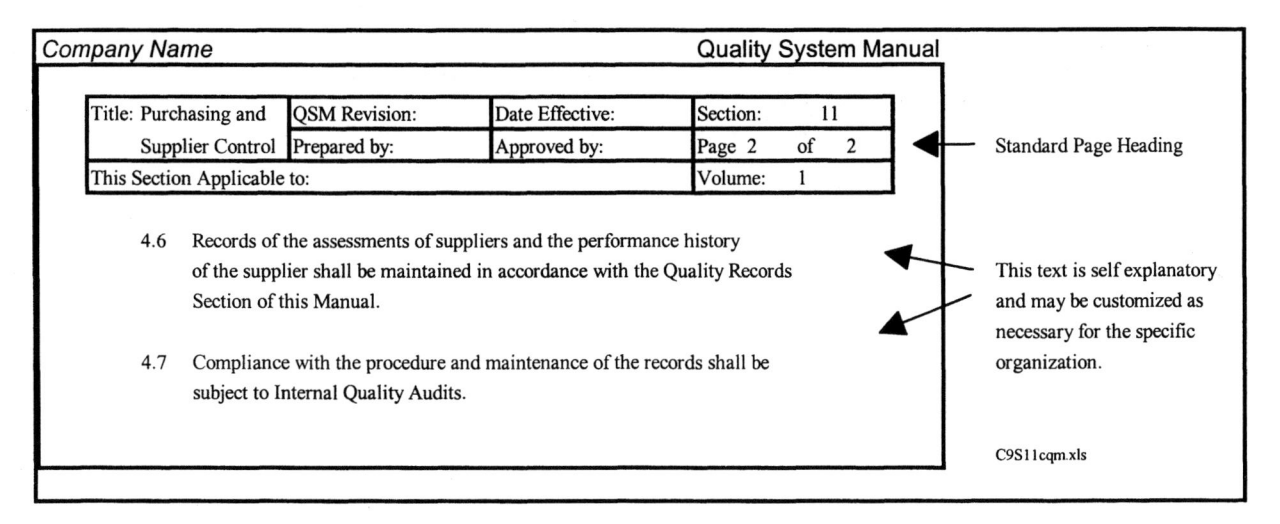

| Company Name | | | Quality System Manual | |
|---|---|---|---|---|
| Title: Purchasing and Supplier Control | QSM Revision: Prepared by: | Date Effective: Approved by: | Section: 11 Page 2 of 2 | |
| This Section Applicable to: | | | Volume: 1 | |

◄— Standard Page Heading

4.6 Records of the assessments of suppliers and the performance history of the supplier shall be maintained in accordance with the Quality Records Section of this Manual.

4.7 Compliance with the procedure and maintenance of the records shall be subject to Internal Quality Audits.

◄— This text is self explanatory and may be customized as necessary for the specific organization.

C9S11cqm.xls

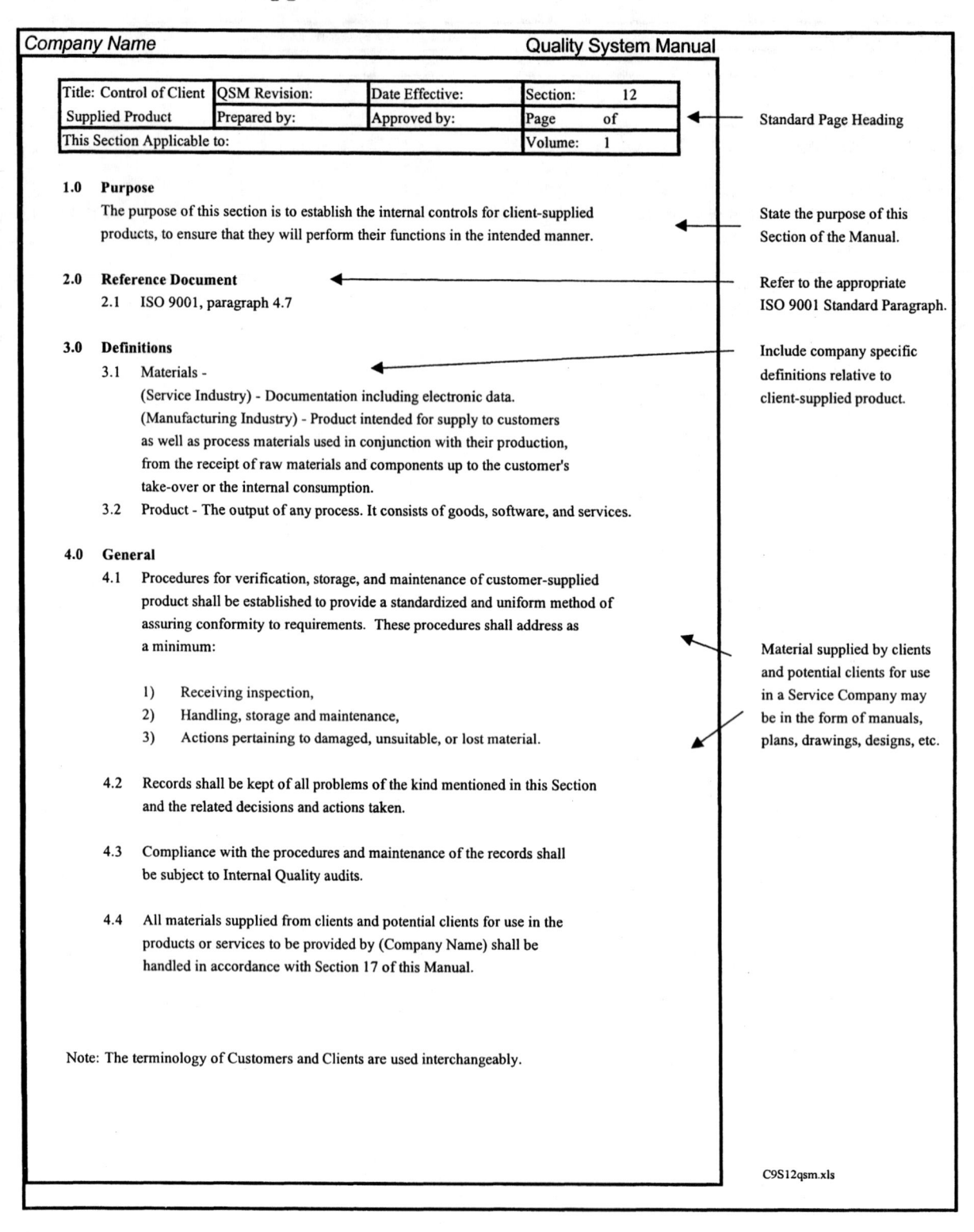

## Control of Client Supplied Product

| Company Name | | | Quality System Manual | |
|---|---|---|---|---|

| Title: Control of Client Supplied Product | QSM Revision: | Date Effective: | Section: | 12 |
|---|---|---|---|---|
| | Prepared by: | Approved by: | Page | of |
| This Section Applicable to: | | | Volume: | 1 |

◄──── Standard Page Heading

**1.0 Purpose**
The purpose of this section is to establish the internal controls for client-supplied products, to ensure that they will perform their functions in the intended manner.

◄──── State the purpose of this Section of the Manual.

**2.0 Reference Document**
 2.1 ISO 9001, paragraph 4.7

◄──── Refer to the appropriate ISO 9001 Standard Paragraph.

**3.0 Definitions**
 3.1 Materials -
   (Service Industry) - Documentation including electronic data.
   (Manufacturing Industry) - Product intended for supply to customers
   as well as process materials used in conjunction with their production,
   from the receipt of raw materials and components up to the customer's
   take-over or the internal consumption.
 3.2 Product - The output of any process. It consists of goods, software, and services.

◄──── Include company specific definitions relative to client-supplied product.

**4.0 General**
 4.1 Procedures for verification, storage, and maintenance of customer-supplied
   product shall be established to provide a standardized and uniform method of
   assuring conformity to requirements. These procedures shall address as
   a minimum:

   1) Receiving inspection,
   2) Handling, storage and maintenance,
   3) Actions pertaining to damaged, unsuitable, or lost material.

◄──── Material supplied by clients and potential clients for use in a Service Company may be in the form of manuals, plans, drawings, designs, etc.

 4.2 Records shall be kept of all problems of the kind mentioned in this Section
   and the related decisions and actions taken.

 4.3 Compliance with the procedures and maintenance of the records shall
   be subject to Internal Quality audits.

 4.4 All materials supplied from clients and potential clients for use in the
   products or services to be provided by (Company Name) shall be
   handled in accordance with Section 17 of this Manual.

Note: The terminology of Customers and Clients are used interchangeably.

C9S12qsm.xls

# Product Identification and Traceability—Manufacturing Industry

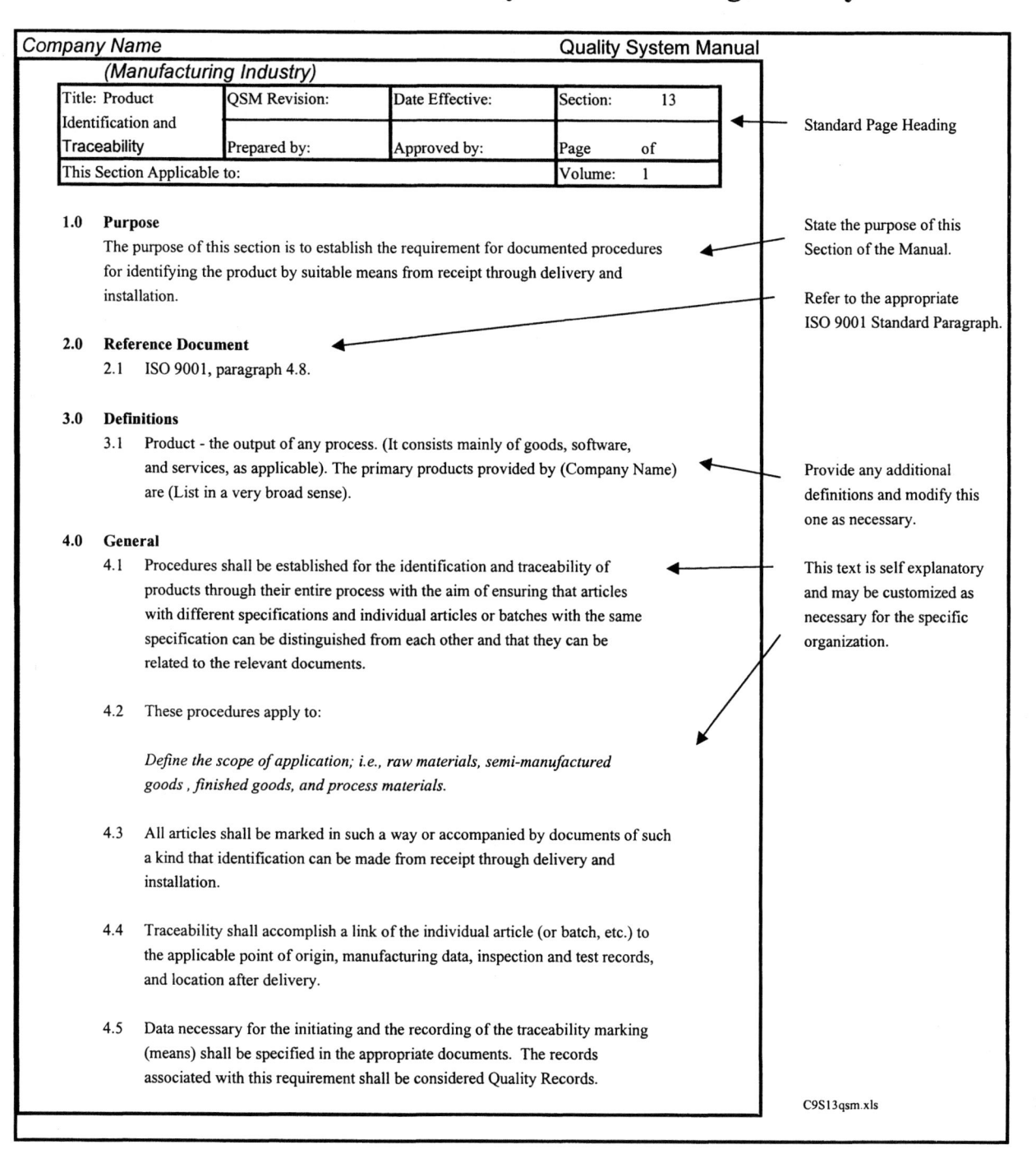

| Company Name | | | Quality System Manual | |
|---|---|---|---|---|
| *(Manufacturing Industry)* | | | | |
| Title: Product Identification and Traceability | QSM Revision: | Date Effective: | Section: | 13 |
| | Prepared by: | Approved by: | Page | of |
| This Section Applicable to: | | | Volume: | 1 |

*← Standard Page Heading*

### 1.0 Purpose

The purpose of this section is to establish the requirement for documented procedures for identifying the product by suitable means from receipt through delivery and installation.

*← State the purpose of this Section of the Manual.*

### 2.0 Reference Document

2.1 ISO 9001, paragraph 4.8.

*Refer to the appropriate ISO 9001 Standard Paragraph.*

### 3.0 Definitions

3.1 Product - the output of any process. (It consists mainly of goods, software, and services, as applicable). The primary products provided by (Company Name) are (List in a very broad sense).

*← Provide any additional definitions and modify this one as necessary.*

### 4.0 General

4.1 Procedures shall be established for the identification and traceability of products through their entire process with the aim of ensuring that articles with different specifications and individual articles or batches with the same specification can be distinguished from each other and that they can be related to the relevant documents.

*← This text is self explanatory and may be customized as necessary for the specific organization.*

4.2 These procedures apply to:

*Define the scope of application; i.e., raw materials, semi-manufactured goods, finished goods, and process materials.*

4.3 All articles shall be marked in such a way or accompanied by documents of such a kind that identification can be made from receipt through delivery and installation.

4.4 Traceability shall accomplish a link of the individual article (or batch, etc.) to the applicable point of origin, manufacturing data, inspection and test records, and location after delivery.

4.5 Data necessary for the initiating and the recording of the traceability marking (means) shall be specified in the appropriate documents. The records associated with this requirement shall be considered Quality Records.

C9S13qsm.xls

# Product Identification and Traceability—Service Industry

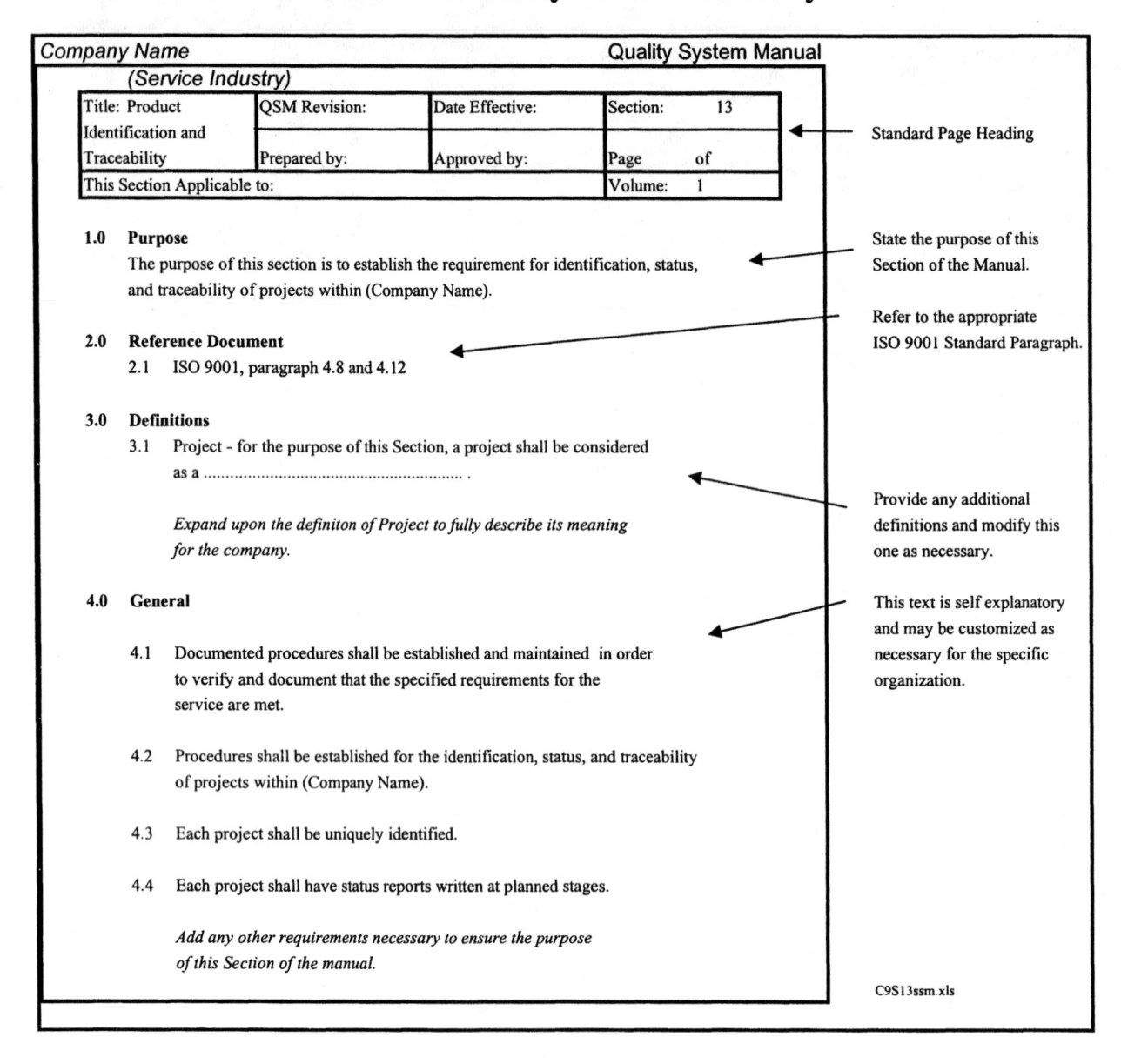

| Company Name | | | Quality System Manual | |
|---|---|---|---|---|
| *(Service Industry)* | | | | |
| Title: Product Identification and Traceability | QSM Revision: | Date Effective: | Section: | 13 |
| | Prepared by: | Approved by: | Page | of |
| This Section Applicable to: | | | Volume: | 1 |

*← Standard Page Heading*

**1.0 Purpose**

The purpose of this section is to establish the requirement for identification, status, and traceability of projects within (Company Name).

*← State the purpose of this Section of the Manual.*

**2.0 Reference Document**

2.1 ISO 9001, paragraph 4.8 and 4.12

*← Refer to the appropriate ISO 9001 Standard Paragraph.*

**3.0 Definitions**

3.1 Project - for the purpose of this Section, a project shall be considered as a ............................................................. .

*Expand upon the definiton of Project to fully describe its meaning for the company.*

*← Provide any additional definitions and modify this one as necessary.*

**4.0 General**

4.1 Documented procedures shall be established and maintained in order to verify and document that the specified requirements for the service are met.

*← This text is self explanatory and may be customized as necessary for the specific organization.*

4.2 Procedures shall be established for the identification, status, and traceability of projects within (Company Name).

4.3 Each project shall be uniquely identified.

4.4 Each project shall have status reports written at planned stages.

*Add any other requirements necessary to ensure the purpose of this Section of the manual.*

C9S13ssm.xls

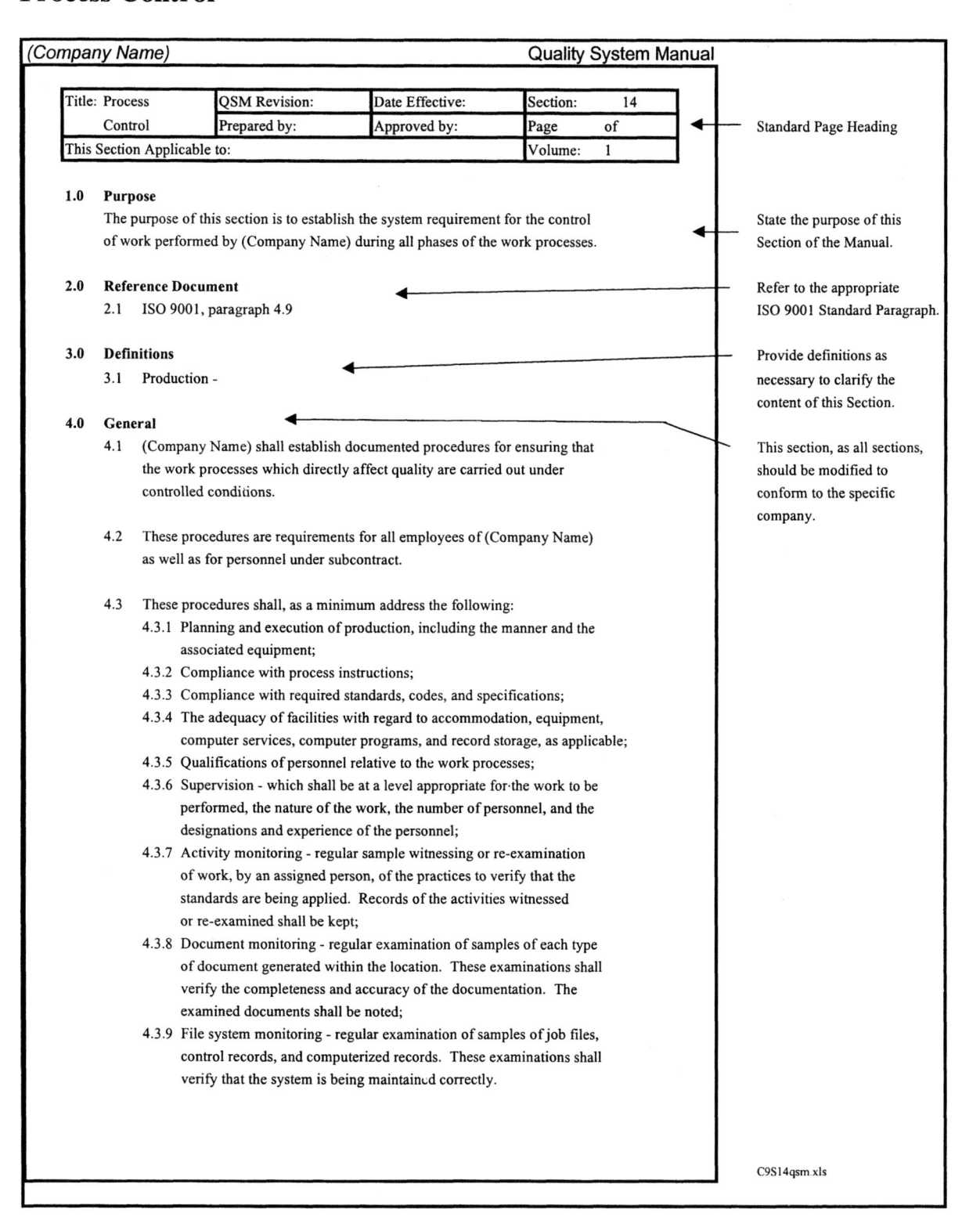

# Process Control

| (Company Name) | | | Quality System Manual | |
|---|---|---|---|---|
| Title: Process Control | QSM Revision: | Date Effective: | Section: | 14 |
| | Prepared by: | Approved by: | Page | of |
| This Section Applicable to: | | | Volume: | 1 |

*Standard Page Heading*

**1.0 Purpose**

The purpose of this section is to establish the system requirement for the control of work performed by (Company Name) during all phases of the work processes.

*State the purpose of this Section of the Manual.*

**2.0 Reference Document**

2.1 ISO 9001, paragraph 4.9

*Refer to the appropriate ISO 9001 Standard Paragraph.*

**3.0 Definitions**

3.1 Production -

*Provide definitions as necessary to clarify the content of this Section.*

**4.0 General**

4.1 (Company Name) shall establish documented procedures for ensuring that the work processes which directly affect quality are carried out under controlled conditions.

*This section, as all sections, should be modified to conform to the specific company.*

4.2 These procedures are requirements for all employees of (Company Name) as well as for personnel under subcontract.

4.3 These procedures shall, as a minimum address the following:

4.3.1 Planning and execution of production, including the manner and the associated equipment;

4.3.2 Compliance with process instructions;

4.3.3 Compliance with required standards, codes, and specifications;

4.3.4 The adequacy of facilities with regard to accommodation, equipment, computer services, computer programs, and record storage, as applicable;

4.3.5 Qualifications of personnel relative to the work processes;

4.3.6 Supervision - which shall be at a level appropriate for the work to be performed, the nature of the work, the number of personnel, and the designations and experience of the personnel;

4.3.7 Activity monitoring - regular sample witnessing or re-examination of work, by an assigned person, of the practices to verify that the standards are being applied. Records of the activities witnessed or re-examined shall be kept;

4.3.8 Document monitoring - regular examination of samples of each type of document generated within the location. These examinations shall verify the completeness and accuracy of the documentation. The examined documents shall be noted;

4.3.9 File system monitoring - regular examination of samples of job files, control records, and computerized records. These examinations shall verify that the system is being maintained correctly.

C9S14qsm.xls

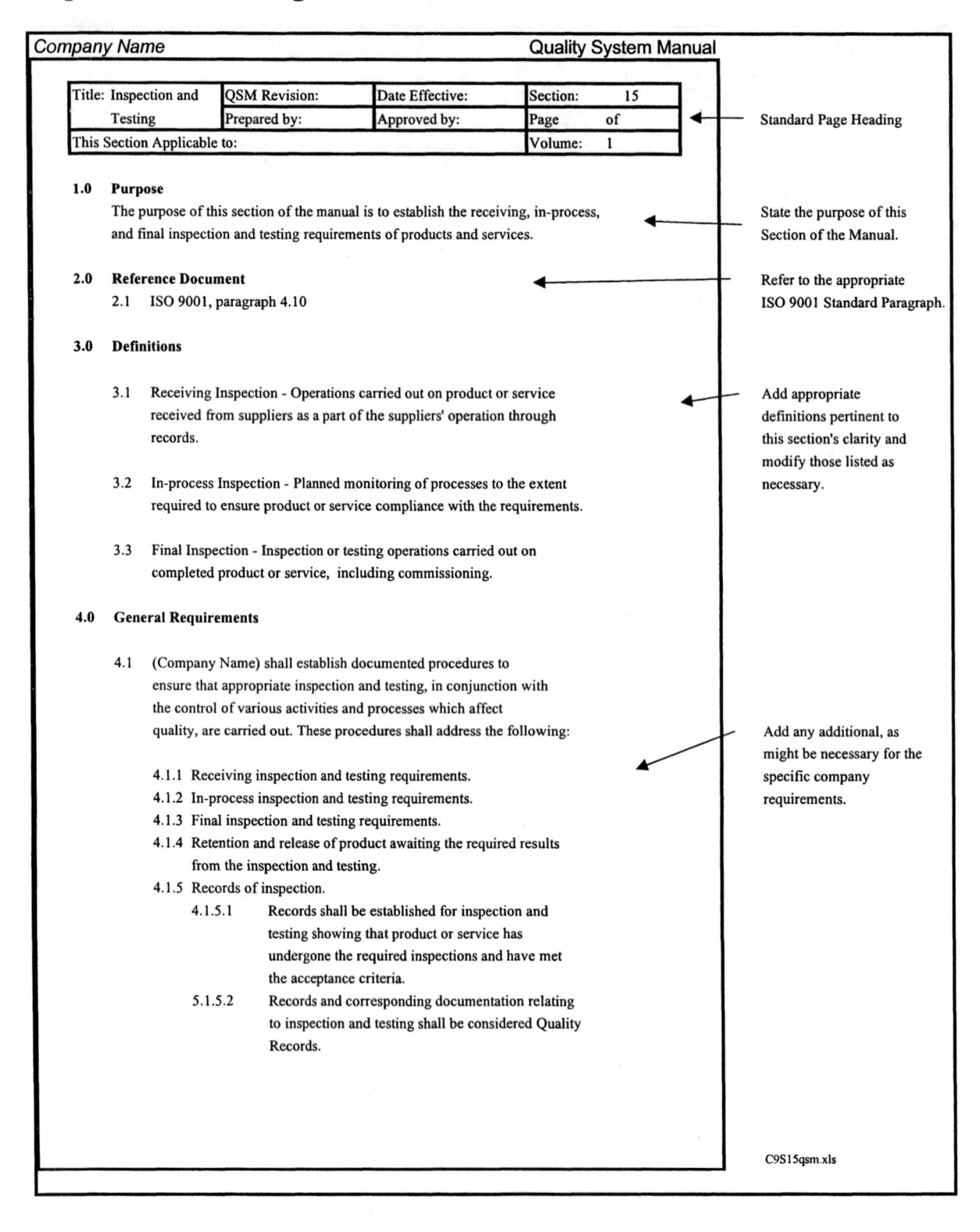

## Inspection and Testing

| Company Name | | | Quality System Manual | |
|---|---|---|---|---|
| Title: Inspection and Testing | QSM Revision: | Date Effective: | Section: | 15 |
| | Prepared by: | Approved by: | Page | of |
| This Section Applicable to: | | | Volume: | 1 |

*Standard Page Heading*

**1.0 Purpose**

The purpose of this section of the manual is to establish the receiving, in-process, and final inspection and testing requirements of products and services.

*State the purpose of this Section of the Manual.*

**2.0 Reference Document**

2.1 ISO 9001, paragraph 4.10

*Refer to the appropriate ISO 9001 Standard Paragraph.*

**3.0 Definitions**

3.1 Receiving Inspection - Operations carried out on product or service received from suppliers as a part of the suppliers' operation through records.

3.2 In-process Inspection - Planned monitoring of processes to the extent required to ensure product or service compliance with the requirements.

3.3 Final Inspection - Inspection or testing operations carried out on completed product or service, including commissioning.

*Add appropriate definitions pertinent to this section's clarity and modify those listed as necessary.*

**4.0 General Requirements**

4.1 (Company Name) shall establish documented procedures to ensure that appropriate inspection and testing, in conjunction with the control of various activities and processes which affect quality, are carried out. These procedures shall address the following:

    4.1.1 Receiving inspection and testing requirements.
    4.1.2 In-process inspection and testing requirements.
    4.1.3 Final inspection and testing requirements.
    4.1.4 Retention and release of product awaiting the required results from the inspection and testing.
    4.1.5 Records of inspection.
        4.1.5.1 Records shall be established for inspection and testing showing that product or service has undergone the required inspections and have met the acceptance criteria.
        5.1.5.2 Records and corresponding documentation relating to inspection and testing shall be considered Quality Records.

*Add any additional, as might be necessary for the specific company requirements.*

C9S15qsm.xls

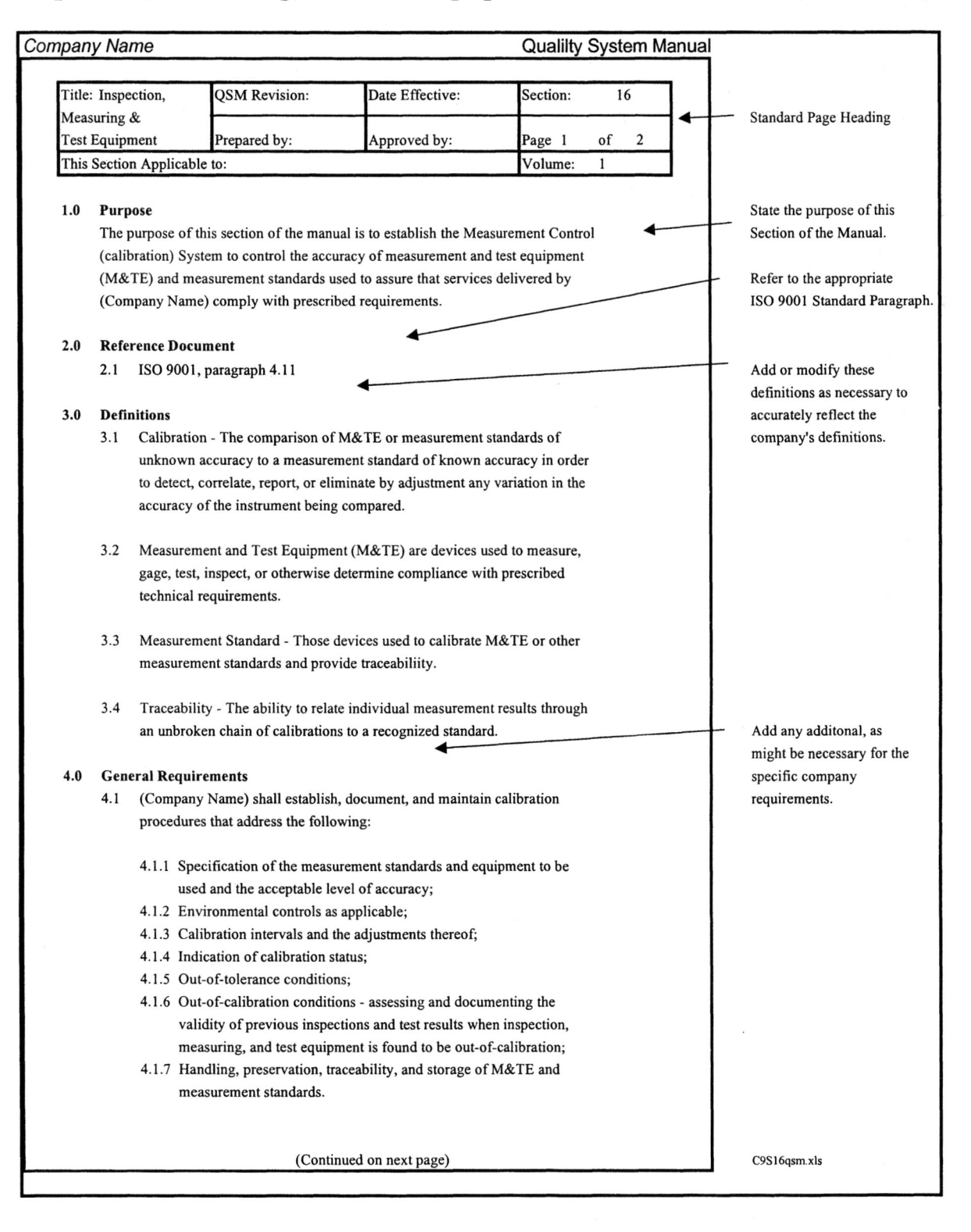

# Inspection, Measuring, and Test Equipment

| Company Name | | | Quality System Manual | |
|---|---|---|---|---|
| Title: Inspection, Measuring & Test Equipment | QSM Revision: | Date Effective: | Section: 16 | |
| | Prepared by: | Approved by: | Page 1 of 2 | |
| This Section Applicable to: | | | Volume: 1 | |

← Standard Page Heading

**1.0 Purpose**

The purpose of this section of the manual is to establish the Measurement Control (calibration) System to control the accuracy of measurement and test equipment (M&TE) and measurement standards used to assure that services delivered by (Company Name) comply with prescribed requirements.

State the purpose of this Section of the Manual.

Refer to the appropriate ISO 9001 Standard Paragraph.

**2.0 Reference Document**

2.1 ISO 9001, paragraph 4.11

Add or modify these definitions as necessary to accurately reflect the company's definitions.

**3.0 Definitions**

3.1 Calibration - The comparison of M&TE or measurement standards of unknown accuracy to a measurement standard of known accuracy in order to detect, correlate, report, or eliminate by adjustment any variation in the accuracy of the instrument being compared.

3.2 Measurement and Test Equipment (M&TE) are devices used to measure, gage, test, inspect, or otherwise determine compliance with prescribed technical requirements.

3.3 Measurement Standard - Those devices used to calibrate M&TE or other measurement standards and provide traceabiliity.

3.4 Traceability - The ability to relate individual measurement results through an unbroken chain of calibrations to a recognized standard.

Add any additonal, as might be necessary for the specific company requirements.

**4.0 General Requirements**

4.1 (Company Name) shall establish, document, and maintain calibration procedures that address the following:

    4.1.1 Specification of the measurement standards and equipment to be used and the acceptable level of accuracy;

    4.1.2 Environmental controls as applicable;

    4.1.3 Calibration intervals and the adjustments thereof;

    4.1.4 Indication of calibration status;

    4.1.5 Out-of-tolerance conditions;

    4.1.6 Out-of-calibration conditions - assessing and documenting the validity of previous inspections and test results when inspection, measuring, and test equipment is found to be out-of-calibration;

    4.1.7 Handling, preservation, traceability, and storage of M&TE and measurement standards.

(Continued on next page)

C9S16qsm.xls

## Inspection, Measuring, and Test Equipment—*Continued*

| Company Name | | | | Quality System Manual | |
|---|---|---|---|---|---|
| Title: Inspection, Measuring & Test Equipment | QSM Revision: | Date Effective: | Section: | | 16 |
| | Prepared by: | Approved by: | Page 2 | of | 2 |
| This Section Applicable to: | | | Volume: | | 1 |

← Standard Page Heading

4.2 (Company Name) shall maintain a calibration history for company owned M&TE. The history shall detail equipment type, a unique identification number, location of the equipment, method of calibration, acceptance criteria, and action taken when equipment is found to be out of calibration.

4.3 (Company Name) shall assure that any subcontractor used for providing calibration services has the calibration system, equipment, facility, and disciplines required to assure compliance with the requirements of the service contract.

4.4 All equipment used in the verification process, whether or not it is owned by (Company Name), shall have been calibrated to an appropriate recognized standard, either directly or by a unit that has been calibrated in accordance with a recognized standard.

4.5 The verification of measuring equipment calibration shall be included in each applicable work process check sheet or report.

4.6 Calibration history and records shall be considered Quality Records.

4.7 ............................. .

*Add additional company specific requirements as necessary.*

← The text is self explanatory and may be customized as necessary for the specific organization.

C9S16ssm.xls

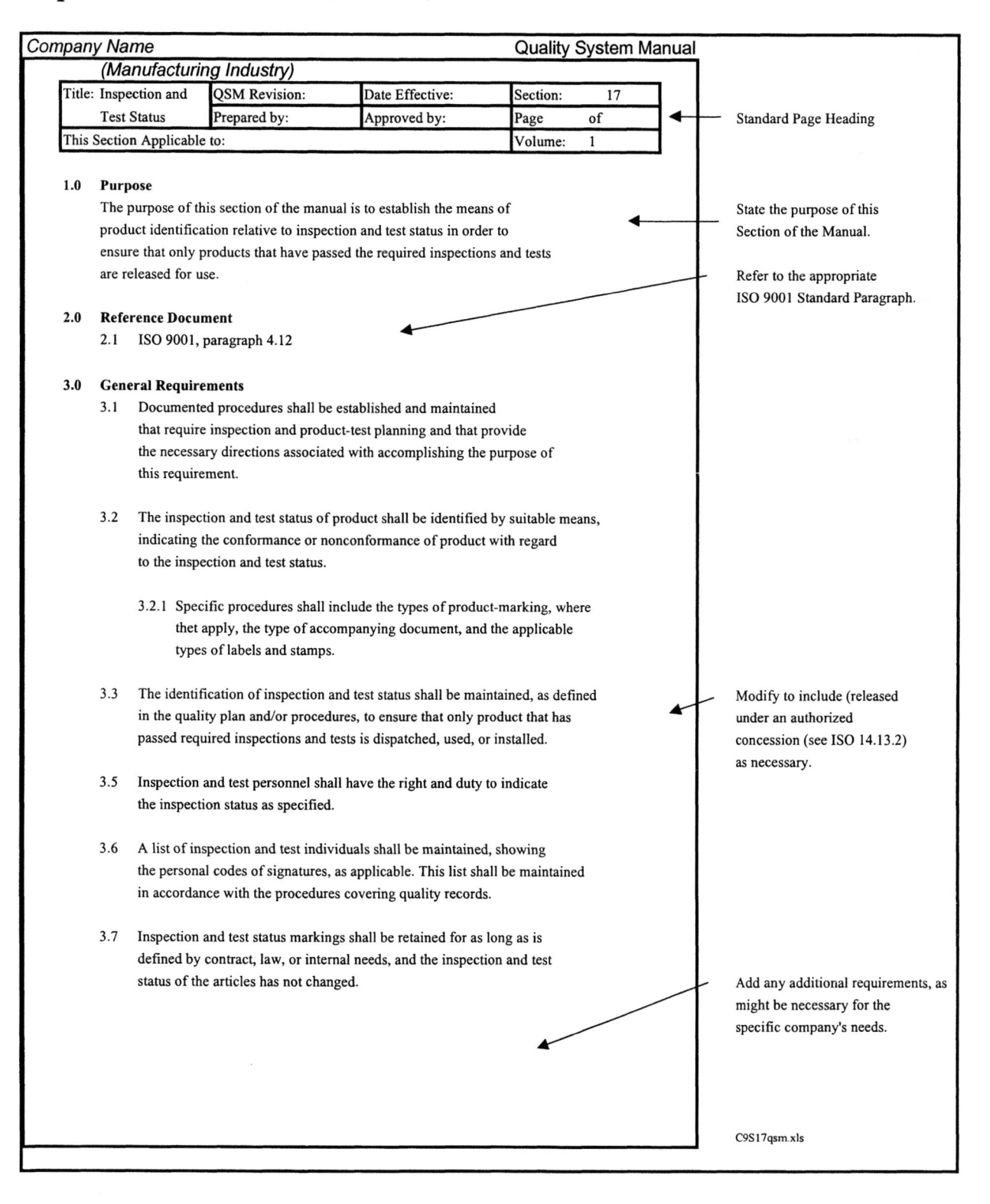

# Inspection and Test Status

| Company Name (Manufacturing Industry) | | | Quality System Manual | |
|---|---|---|---|---|
| Title: Inspection and Test Status | QSM Revision: | Date Effective: | Section: | 17 |
| | Prepared by: | Approved by: | Page | of |
| This Section Applicable to: | | | Volume: | 1 |

← Standard Page Heading

**1.0 Purpose**

The purpose of this section of the manual is to establish the means of product identification relative to inspection and test status in order to ensure that only products that have passed the required inspections and tests are released for use.

← State the purpose of this Section of the Manual.

← Refer to the appropriate ISO 9001 Standard Paragraph.

**2.0 Reference Document**

2.1 ISO 9001, paragraph 4.12

**3.0 General Requirements**

3.1 Documented procedures shall be established and maintained that require inspection and product-test planning and that provide the necessary directions associated with accomplishing the purpose of this requirement.

3.2 The inspection and test status of product shall be identified by suitable means, indicating the conformance or nonconformance of product with regard to the inspection and test status.

    3.2.1 Specific procedures shall include the types of product-marking, where thet apply, the type of accompanying document, and the applicable types of labels and stamps.

3.3 The identification of inspection and test status shall be maintained, as defined in the quality plan and/or procedures, to ensure that only product that has passed required inspections and tests is dispatched, used, or installed.

← Modify to include (released under an authorized concession (see ISO 14.13.2) as necessary.

3.5 Inspection and test personnel shall have the right and duty to indicate the inspection status as specified.

3.6 A list of inspection and test individuals shall be maintained, showing the personal codes of signatures, as applicable. This list shall be maintained in accordance with the procedures covering quality records.

3.7 Inspection and test status markings shall be retained for as long as is defined by contract, law, or internal needs, and the inspection and test status of the articles has not changed.

← Add any additional requirements, as might be necessary for the specific company's needs.

C9S17qsm.xls

# Control of Nonconforming Product—Manufacturing Industry

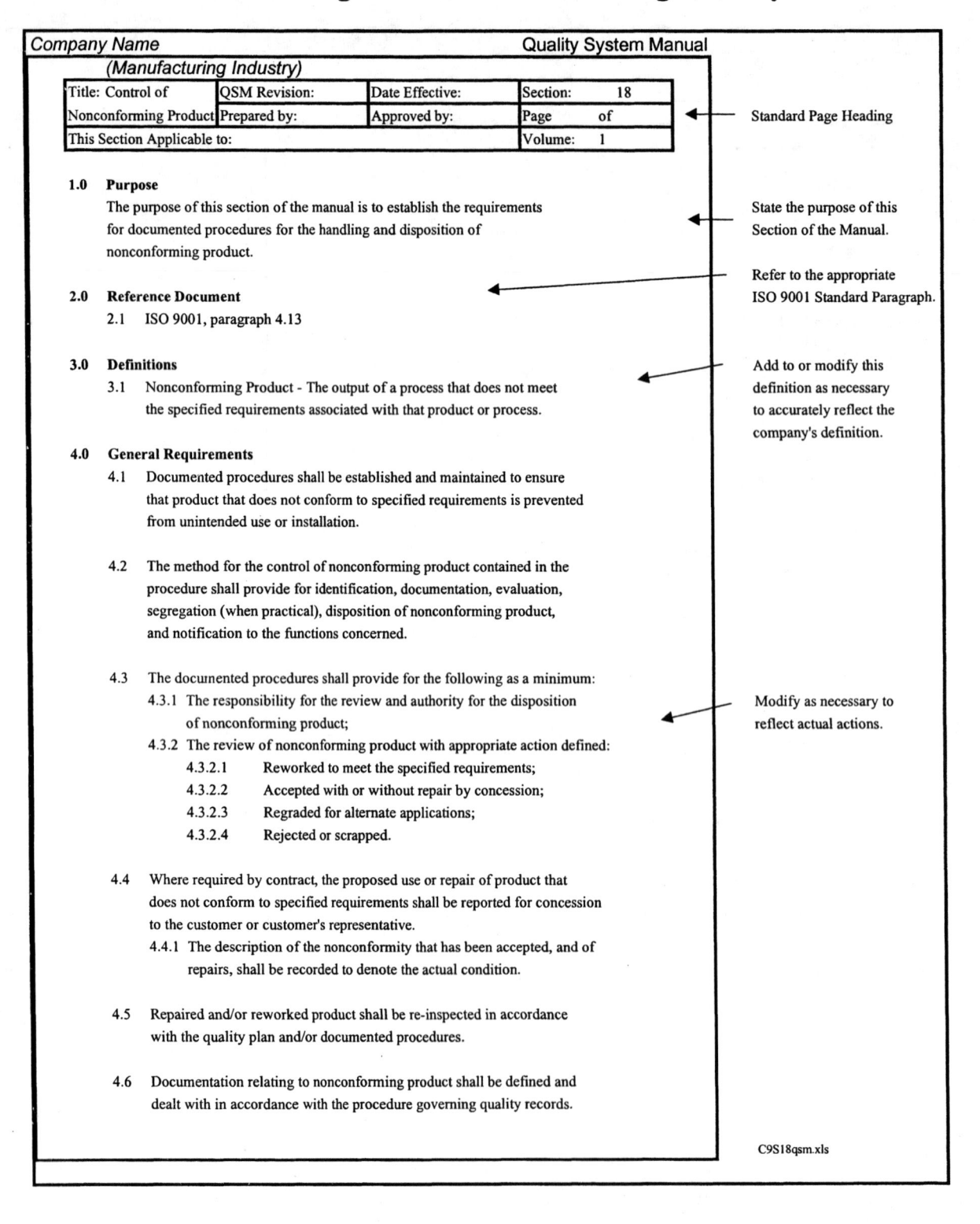

| Company Name | | | Quality System Manual | |
|---|---|---|---|---|
| (Manufacturing Industry) | | | | |
| Title: Control of Nonconforming Product | QSM Revision: | Date Effective: | Section: | 18 |
| | Prepared by: | Approved by: | Page | of |
| This Section Applicable to: | | | Volume: | 1 |

*← Standard Page Heading*

**1.0 Purpose**
The purpose of this section of the manual is to establish the requirements for documented procedures for the handling and disposition of nonconforming product.

*← State the purpose of this Section of the Manual.*

**2.0 Reference Document**
    2.1   ISO 9001, paragraph 4.13

*← Refer to the appropriate ISO 9001 Standard Paragraph.*

**3.0 Definitions**
    3.1   Nonconforming Product - The output of a process that does not meet the specified requirements associated with that product or process.

*← Add to or modify this definition as necessary to accurately reflect the company's definition.*

**4.0 General Requirements**

    4.1   Documented procedures shall be established and maintained to ensure that product that does not conform to specified requirements is prevented from unintended use or installation.

    4.2   The method for the control of nonconforming product contained in the procedure shall provide for identification, documentation, evaluation, segregation (when practical), disposition of nonconforming product, and notification to the functions concerned.

    4.3   The documented procedures shall provide for the following as a minimum:
        4.3.1   The responsibility for the review and authority for the disposition of nonconforming product;
        4.3.2   The review of nonconforming product with appropriate action defined:
            4.3.2.1    Reworked to meet the specified requirements;
            4.3.2.2    Accepted with or without repair by concession;
            4.3.2.3    Regraded for alternate applications;
            4.3.2.4    Rejected or scrapped.

*← Modify as necessary to reflect actual actions.*

    4.4   Where required by contract, the proposed use or repair of product that does not conform to specified requirements shall be reported for concession to the customer or customer's representative.
        4.4.1   The description of the nonconformity that has been accepted, and of repairs, shall be recorded to denote the actual condition.

    4.5   Repaired and/or reworked product shall be re-inspected in accordance with the quality plan and/or documented procedures.

    4.6   Documentation relating to nonconforming product shall be defined and dealt with in accordance with the procedure governing quality records.

C9S18qsm.xls

# Corrective and Preventive Action

| Company Name | | | Quality System Manual | |
|---|---|---|---|---|
| Title: Corrective and Preventive Action | QSM Revision: | Date Effective: | Section: | 19 |
| | Prepared by: | Approved by: | Page 1 of 2 | |
| This Section Applicable to: | | | Volume: 1 | |

◄──── Standard Page Heading

**1.0 Purpose**

The purpose of this section of the manual is to establish the requirements for documented procedures for implementing corrective and preventive action.

◄──── State the purpose of this Section of the Manual.

**2.0 Reference Document**

2.1 ISO 9001, paragraph 4.14 (and 4.13 for Service Industry)

◄──── Refer to the appropriate ISO 9001 Standard Paragraph.

**3.0 Definitions**

3.1 Corrective Action - Action taken to eliminate the causes of an existing nonconformance, nonconforming service, or other undesirable situation.

◄──── Add to or modify these definitions as necessary to accurately reflect the company's definitions.

3.2 Preventive Action - Action taken to eliminate the causes of a potential nonconformance, nonconforming service, or other undesirable situation.

3.3 Nonconformance - Nonfulfillment of a specified requirement.

3.4 Product - The output of any process. It consists of goods, software, and services.

3.5 Corrective Action Request (CAR) - A documented request either to improve the quality system, a procedure, a work instruction, or to initiate an internal investigation into the cause of a nonconformance for the purpose of applying corrective and preventive action.

3.6 Corrective Action System (CAS) - The system for identifying, analyzing, and implementing improvements and corrective action in (Company Name) products, services, and processes.

**4.0 General**

4.1 Documented procedures shall be established and maintained for the identification of nonconforming products and services and for implementing corrective and preventive action.

◄──── This text is self explanatory and may be modified as necessary for the specific organization.

    4.1.1 Any corrective or preventive action taken to eliminate the causes of actual or potential nonconformances shall be to a degree appropriate to the magnitude of problems and commensurate to the risks encountered.

4.2 These procedures shall, as a minimum, include the requirements for:

    4.2.1 The recording of nonconformances and the actions taken;

    4.2.2 The investigating of client complaints:

        4.2.2.1 Where investigation finds that the service was nonconforming, corrective action shall be taken;

(continued on next page)

C9S19qsm.xls

## Corrective and Preventive Action—*Continued*

| Company Name | | | Quality System Manual | |
|---|---|---|---|---|
| Title: Corrective and Preventive Action | QSM Revision: | Date Effective: | Section: | 19 |
| | Prepared by: | Approved by: | Page 2 of 2 | |
| This Section Applicable to: | | | Volume: | 1 |

*Standard Page Heading*

    4.2.3  The investigating of the cause of the nonconformance relating to product, process, and quality system, and recording the results of the investigation;

    4.2.4  The evaluation and determination of actions to be taken to eliminate the cause of the nonconformance;

    4.2.5  The applying of controls to ensure that corrective actions are taken and that they are effective;

    4.2.6  The analyzing of all procedures, practices, quality records, audit results, service reports, and customer complaints to detect and eliminate potential causes of nonconformances;

    4.2.7  The implementing of and recording of changes in procedures resulting from corrective and/or preventive action;

    4.2.8  Target dates for the implementation of the identified corrective action(s) or preventive action(s);

    4.2.9  The ensurance that relevant information on actions taken is submitted for management review.

*Add to or modify these definitions as necessary to accurately reflect the company's definitions.*

4.3  The corrective action initiating source shall be clearly defined and described.

4.4  Corrective actions shall be documented, followed-up, and tracked for effectiveness.

**5.0  Effectiveness Verification**

    5.1  The responsibility for ensuring that follow-up to verify the effectiveness of the corrective or preventive action shall be clearly stated and described. The follow-up may involve a temporary increase in the information provided to management, measurements, or arrangements for an internal audit.

**6.0  Clarification and Appeal**

    6.1  For external audits where a nonconformance is not clearly understood, the auditor shall be questioned. Once clearly understood, if the non-conformance is questionable, it shall be appealed by the (Company Name) representative to the auditing body.

    6.2  For internal audits, where a nonconformance is not clearly understood, the originator shall be questioned. Once clearly understood, if the nonconformance is questionable, it shall be appealed to the respective Quality Steering Committee (or to whomever is appropriate).

*This text is self explanatory and may be modified as necessary for the specific organization.*

C9S19ssm.xls

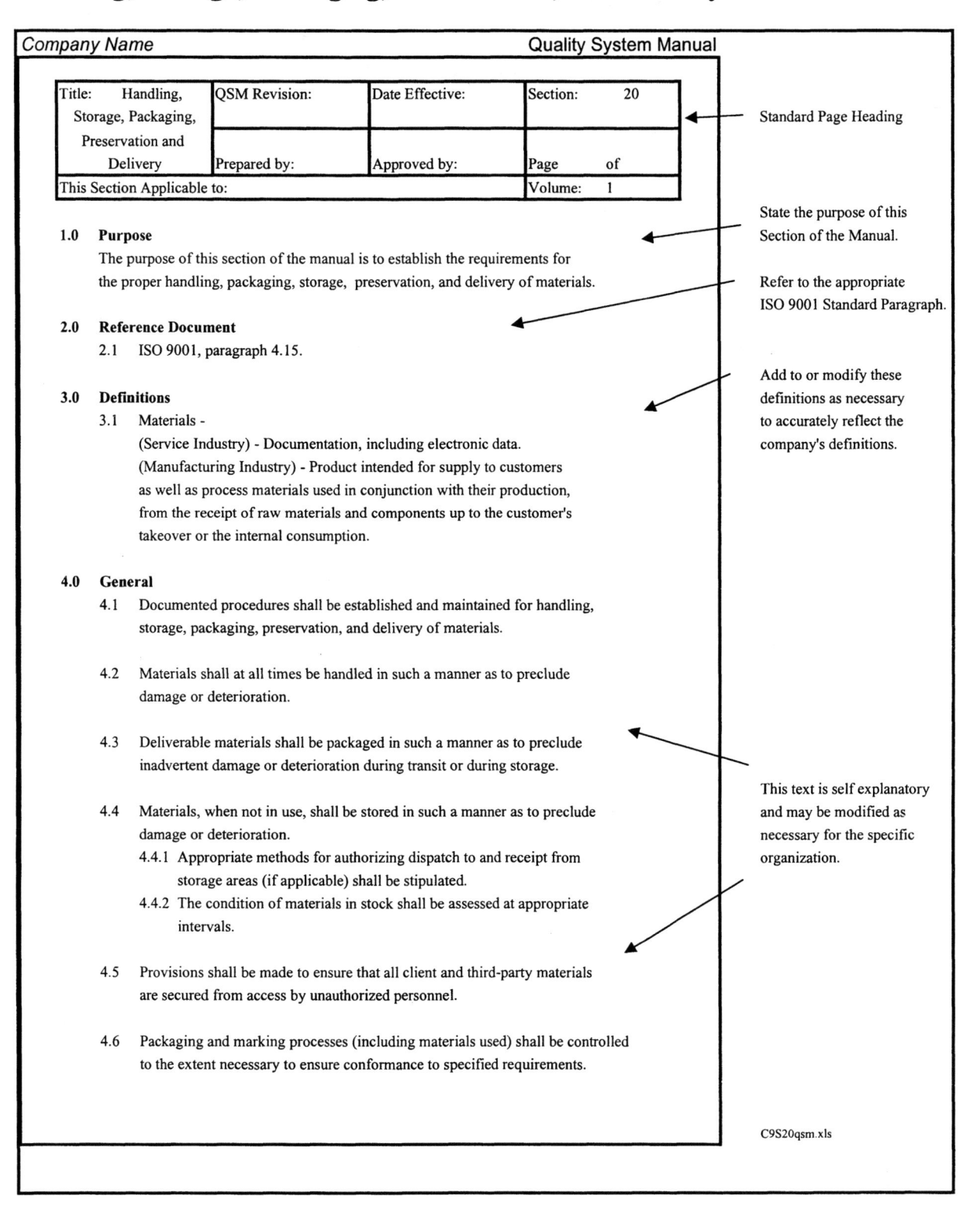

# Handling, Storage, Packaging, Preservation, and Delivery

| Company Name | | | Quality System Manual | |
|---|---|---|---|---|
| Title: Handling, Storage, Packaging, Preservation and Delivery | QSM Revision: | Date Effective: | Section: | 20 |
| | Prepared by: | Approved by: | Page | of |
| This Section Applicable to: | | | Volume: | 1 |

*Standard Page Heading*

1.0 **Purpose**

The purpose of this section of the manual is to establish the requirements for the proper handling, packaging, storage, preservation, and delivery of materials.

*State the purpose of this Section of the Manual.*

*Refer to the appropriate ISO 9001 Standard Paragraph.*

2.0 **Reference Document**

2.1 ISO 9001, paragraph 4.15.

3.0 **Definitions**

3.1 Materials -
(Service Industry) - Documentation, including electronic data.
(Manufacturing Industry) - Product intended for supply to customers as well as process materials used in conjunction with their production, from the receipt of raw materials and components up to the customer's takeover or the internal consumption.

*Add to or modify these definitions as necessary to accurately reflect the company's definitions.*

4.0 **General**

4.1 Documented procedures shall be established and maintained for handling, storage, packaging, preservation, and delivery of materials.

4.2 Materials shall at all times be handled in such a manner as to preclude damage or deterioration.

4.3 Deliverable materials shall be packaged in such a manner as to preclude inadvertent damage or deterioration during transit or during storage.

4.4 Materials, when not in use, shall be stored in such a manner as to preclude damage or deterioration.

4.4.1 Appropriate methods for authorizing dispatch to and receipt from storage areas (if applicable) shall be stipulated.

4.4.2 The condition of materials in stock shall be assessed at appropriate intervals.

*This text is self explanatory and may be modified as necessary for the specific organization.*

4.5 Provisions shall be made to ensure that all client and third-party materials are secured from access by unauthorized personnel.

4.6 Packaging and marking processes (including materials used) shall be controlled to the extent necessary to ensure conformance to specified requirements.

C9S20qsm.xls

## Control and Retention of Quality Records

Quality Records shall include pertinent subcontractor records.

Note: Quality records may be in the form of any type of media, such as hard copy or electronic data.

**4.0 General**
- 4.1 Documented procedures shall be established and maintained for the control, identification, collection, indexing, access, filing, storage, maintenance, and dispositon of quality records.

- 4.2 The procedure as a minimum shall address the following:
    - 4.2.1 The environmental conditions for the safeguarding of quality records;
    - 4.2.2 The retention periods for quality records;
    - 4.2.3 The person(s) responsible for the safe-keeping of quality records;
    - 4.2.4 The person(s) responsible for reviewing quality records prior to filing;
    - 4.2.5 What documents shall be kept at which location;
    - 4.2.6 A file identification procedure;
    - 4.2.7 Back-up requirements;
    - 4.2.8 Requirements for periodic examination;
    - 4.2.9 Retrieval procedure.

This text is self explanatory and may be modified as necessary for the specific organization.

C9S21qsm.xls

# Quality Audits

| Company Name | | | Quality System Manual | |
|---|---|---|---|---|
| Title: Internal Quality Audits | QSM Revision: Prepared by: | Date Effective: Approved by: | Section: Page | 22 of |
| This Section Applicable to: | | | Volume: | 1 |

← Standard Page Heading

**1.0 Purpose**

The purpose of this section of the manual is to establish the requirements for Internal Quality Audits for (Company Name). ← State the purpose of this Section of the Manual.

**2.0 Reference Document**

2.1 ISO 9001, paragraph 4.17. ← Refer to the appropriate ISO 9001 Standard Paragraph.

**3.0 General**

3.1 Documented procedures shall be established and maintained for planning and implementing internal quality audits to verify whether quality activities and related results comply with planned arrangements and to determine the effectiveness of the quality system.

3.2 Internal quality audits shall be scheduled on the basis of the status and importance of the activity to be audited.

3.3 Internal quality audits shall be carried out by personnel independent of those having direct responsibility for the activity being audited.

3.4 Internal audit checklists shall be developed for each function to be audited.

3.5 An internal audit report shall be generated of the findings and observations made during the internal audit. The report shall be distributed to the manager of the audited area for evaluation and response, if required. A copy of the report shall be sent to the Management Quality Representative.

3.6 Nonconformances shall be dispositioned in accordance with Section 19 of this manual. An appropriate time frame for the response and implementation of corrective and preventive action shall be established.

3.7 Implementation of corrective action(s) shall be verified for adequacy and effectiveness.

3.8 Auditors shall be trained through a company approved auditor/assessor course.

3.9 The results of internal quality audits form an integral part of the input to management review activities.

← This text is self explanatory and may be modified as necessary for the specific organization.

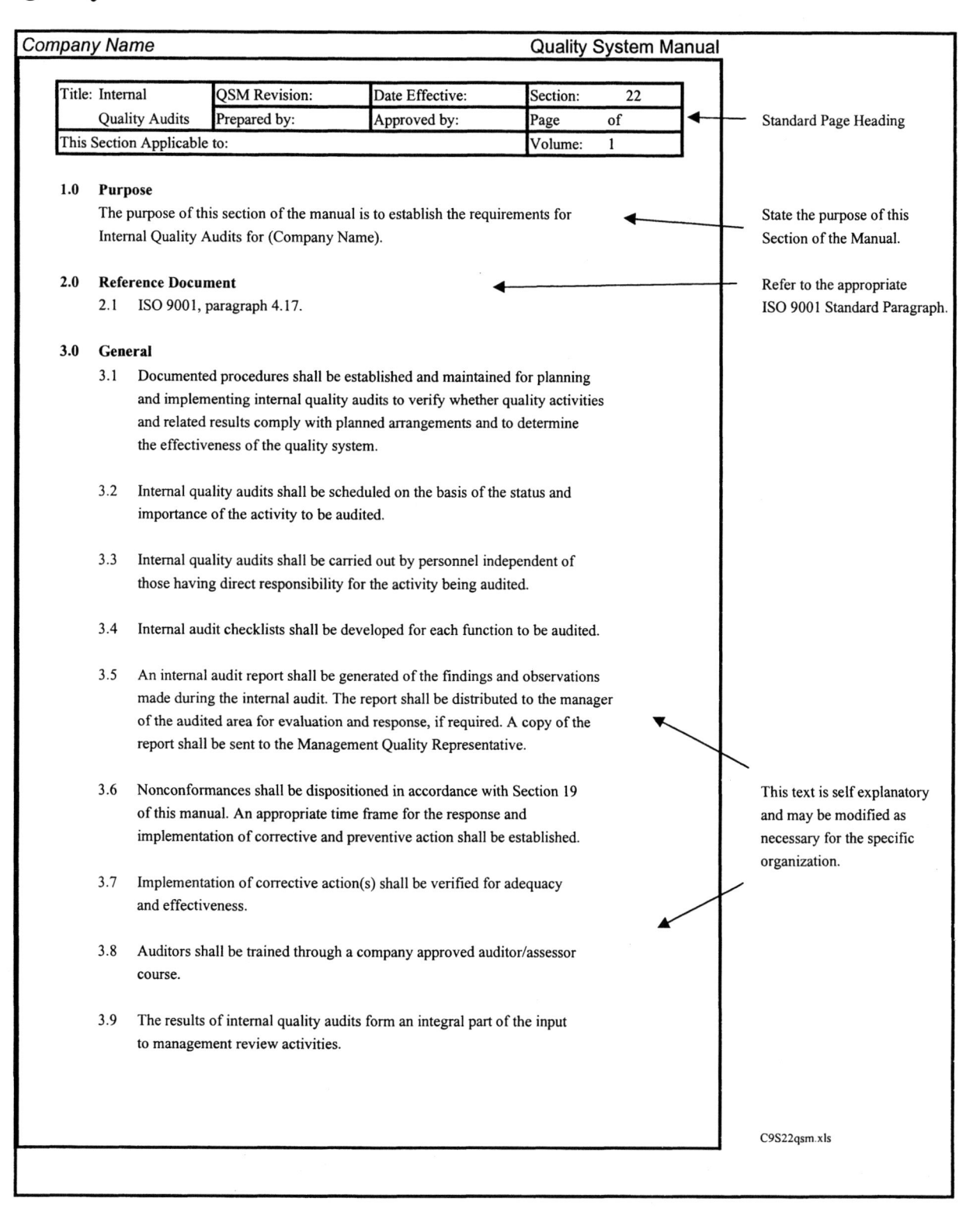

C9S22qsm.xls

# Training

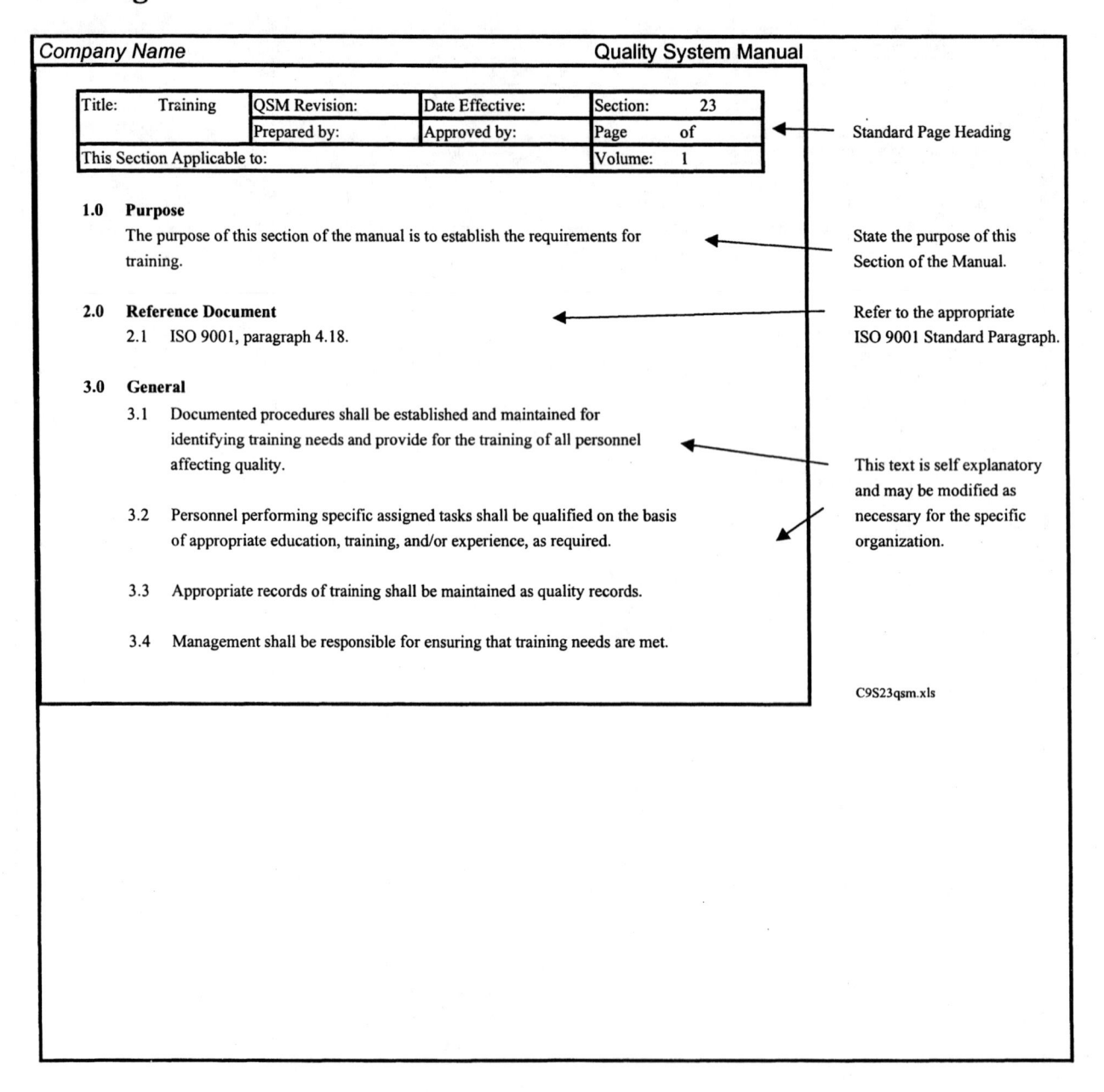

| Company Name | | | Quality System Manual | |
|---|---|---|---|---|
| Title: Training | QSM Revision: | Date Effective: | Section: | 23 |
| | Prepared by: | Approved by: | Page | of |
| This Section Applicable to: | | | Volume: | 1 |

⬅ Standard Page Heading

**1.0 Purpose**
The purpose of this section of the manual is to establish the requirements for training. ⬅ State the purpose of this Section of the Manual.

**2.0 Reference Document**
2.1 ISO 9001, paragraph 4.18. ⬅ Refer to the appropriate ISO 9001 Standard Paragraph.

**3.0 General**

3.1 Documented procedures shall be established and maintained for identifying training needs and provide for the training of all personnel affecting quality. ⬅ This text is self explanatory and may be modified as necessary for the specific organization.

3.2 Personnel performing specific assigned tasks shall be qualified on the basis of appropriate education, training, and/or experience, as required.

3.3 Appropriate records of training shall be maintained as quality records.

3.4 Management shall be responsible for ensuring that training needs are met.

C9S23qsm.xls

# Servicing

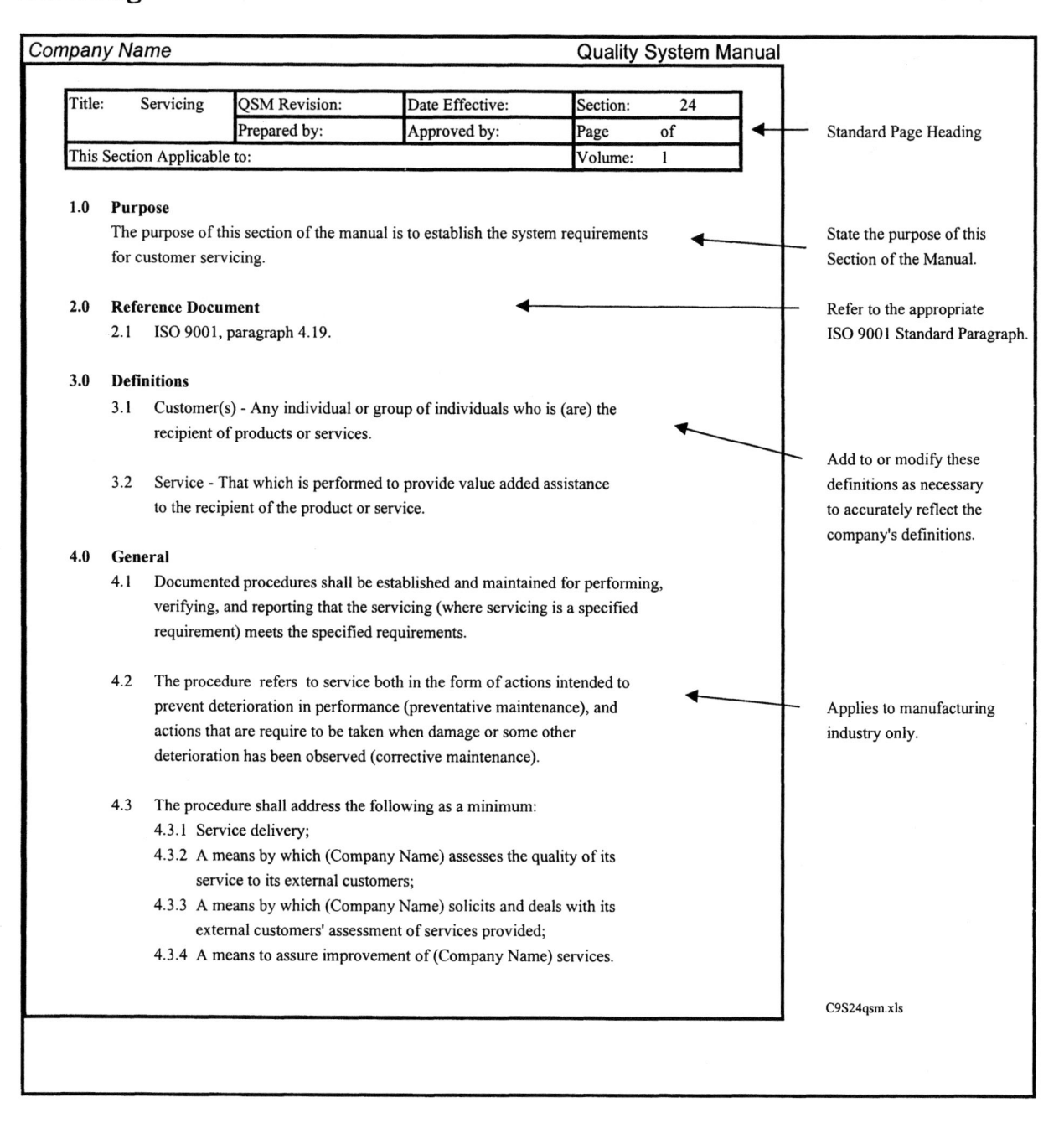

| Company Name | | | Quality System Manual | |
|---|---|---|---|---|
| Title: Servicing | QSM Revision: | Date Effective: | Section: | 24 |
| | Prepared by: | Approved by: | Page | of |
| This Section Applicable to: | | | Volume: | 1 |

◄──── Standard Page Heading

**1.0 Purpose**

The purpose of this section of the manual is to establish the system requirements for customer servicing. ◄──── State the purpose of this Section of the Manual.

**2.0 Reference Document**

2.1 ISO 9001, paragraph 4.19. ◄──── Refer to the appropriate ISO 9001 Standard Paragraph.

**3.0 Definitions**

3.1 Customer(s) - Any individual or group of individuals who is (are) the recipient of products or services.

3.2 Service - That which is performed to provide value added assistance to the recipient of the product or service.

◄──── Add to or modify these definitions as necessary to accurately reflect the company's definitions.

**4.0 General**

4.1 Documented procedures shall be established and maintained for performing, verifying, and reporting that the servicing (where servicing is a specified requirement) meets the specified requirements.

4.2 The procedure refers to service both in the form of actions intended to prevent deterioration in performance (preventative maintenance), and actions that are require to be taken when damage or some other deterioration has been observed (corrective maintenance). ◄──── Applies to manufacturing industry only.

4.3 The procedure shall address the following as a minimum:
 4.3.1 Service delivery;
 4.3.2 A means by which (Company Name) assesses the quality of its service to its external customers;
 4.3.3 A means by which (Company Name) solicits and deals with its external customers' assessment of services provided;
 4.3.4 A means to assure improvement of (Company Name) services.

C9S24qsm.xls

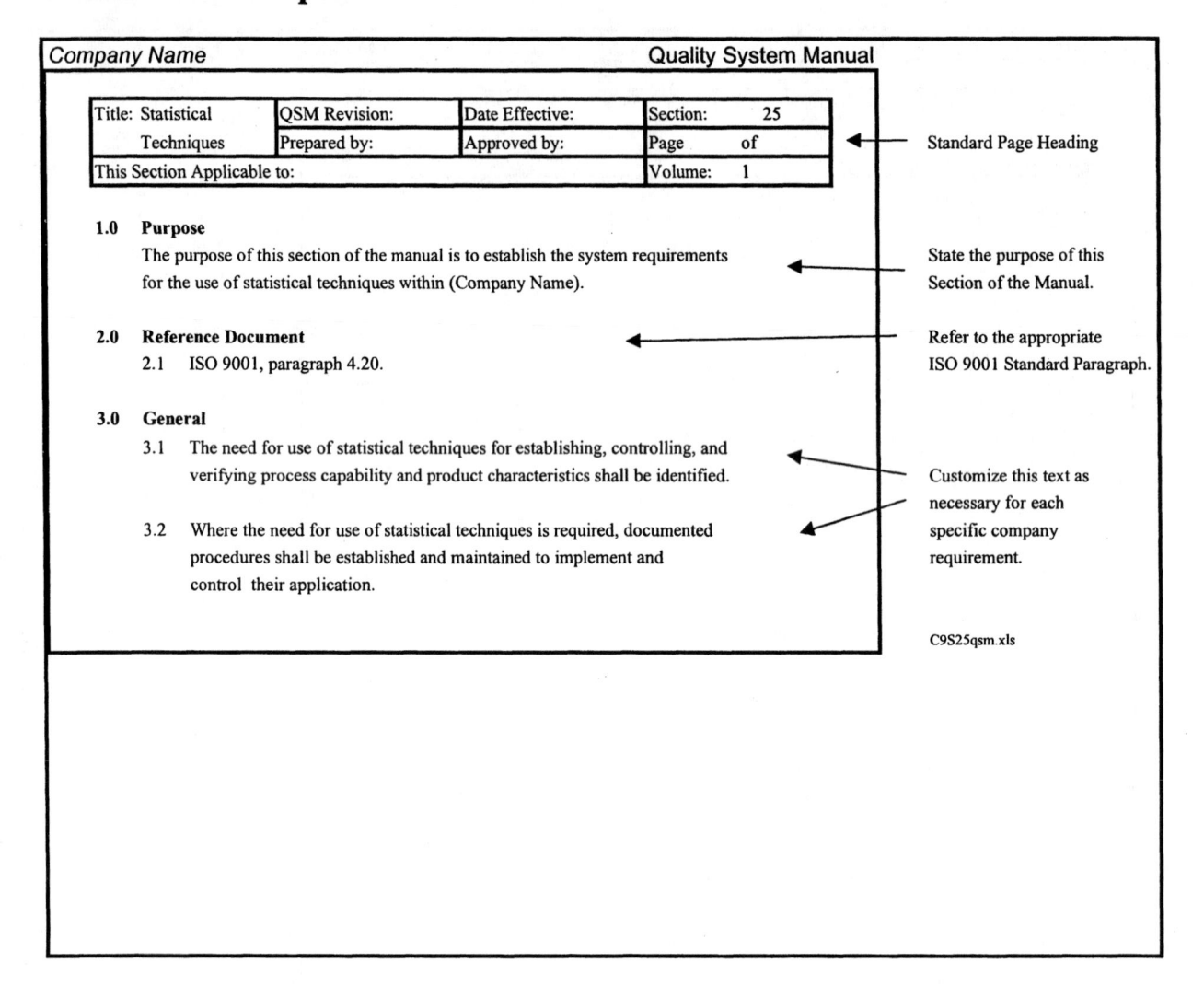

## Statistical Techniques

| Company Name | | | Quality System Manual | |
|---|---|---|---|---|
| Title: Statistical Techniques | QSM Revision: | Date Effective: | Section: | 25 |
| | Prepared by: | Approved by: | Page | of |
| This Section Applicable to: | | | Volume: | 1 |

— Standard Page Heading

**1.0 Purpose**
The purpose of this section of the manual is to establish the system requirements for the use of statistical techniques within (Company Name).

— State the purpose of this Section of the Manual.

**2.0 Reference Document**
2.1  ISO 9001, paragraph 4.20.

— Refer to the appropriate ISO 9001 Standard Paragraph.

**3.0 General**

3.1  The need for use of statistical techniques for establishing, controlling, and verifying process capability and product characteristics shall be identified.

3.2  Where the need for use of statistical techniques is required, documented procedures shall be established and maintained to implement and control their application.

— Customize this text as necessary for each specific company requirement.

C9S25qsm.xls

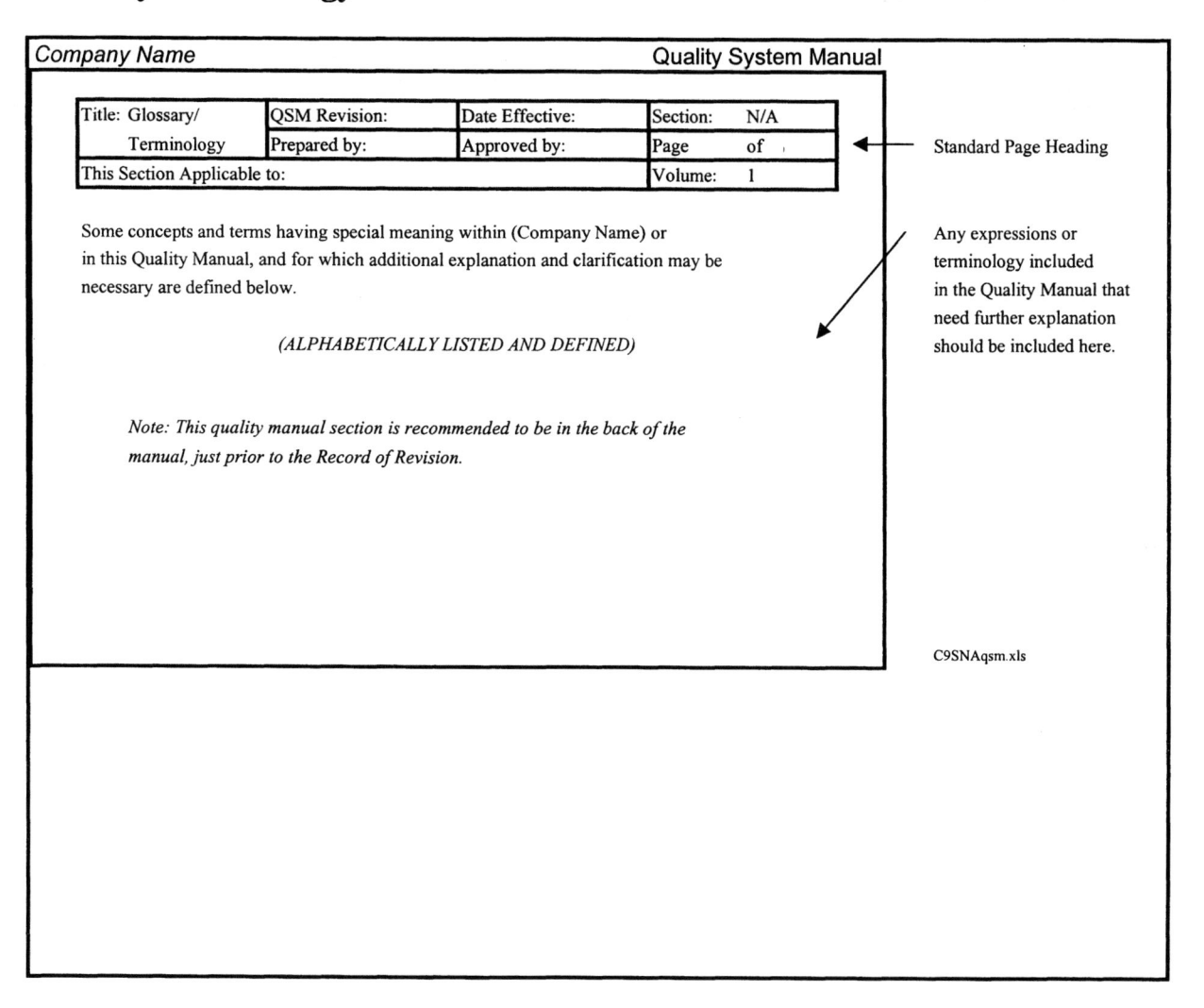

# Glossary/Terminology

| Company Name | | | Quality System Manual | |
|---|---|---|---|---|
| Title: Glossary/ Terminology | QSM Revision: | Date Effective: | Section: N/A | |
| | Prepared by: | Approved by: | Page of | |
| This Section Applicable to: | | | Volume: 1 | |

← Standard Page Heading

Some concepts and terms having special meaning within (Company Name) or in this Quality Manual, and for which additional explanation and clarification may be necessary are defined below.

*(ALPHABETICALLY LISTED AND DEFINED)*

Any expressions or terminology included in the Quality Manual that need further explanation should be included here.

*Note: This quality manual section is recommended to be in the back of the manual, just prior to the Record of Revision.*

C9SNAqsm.xls

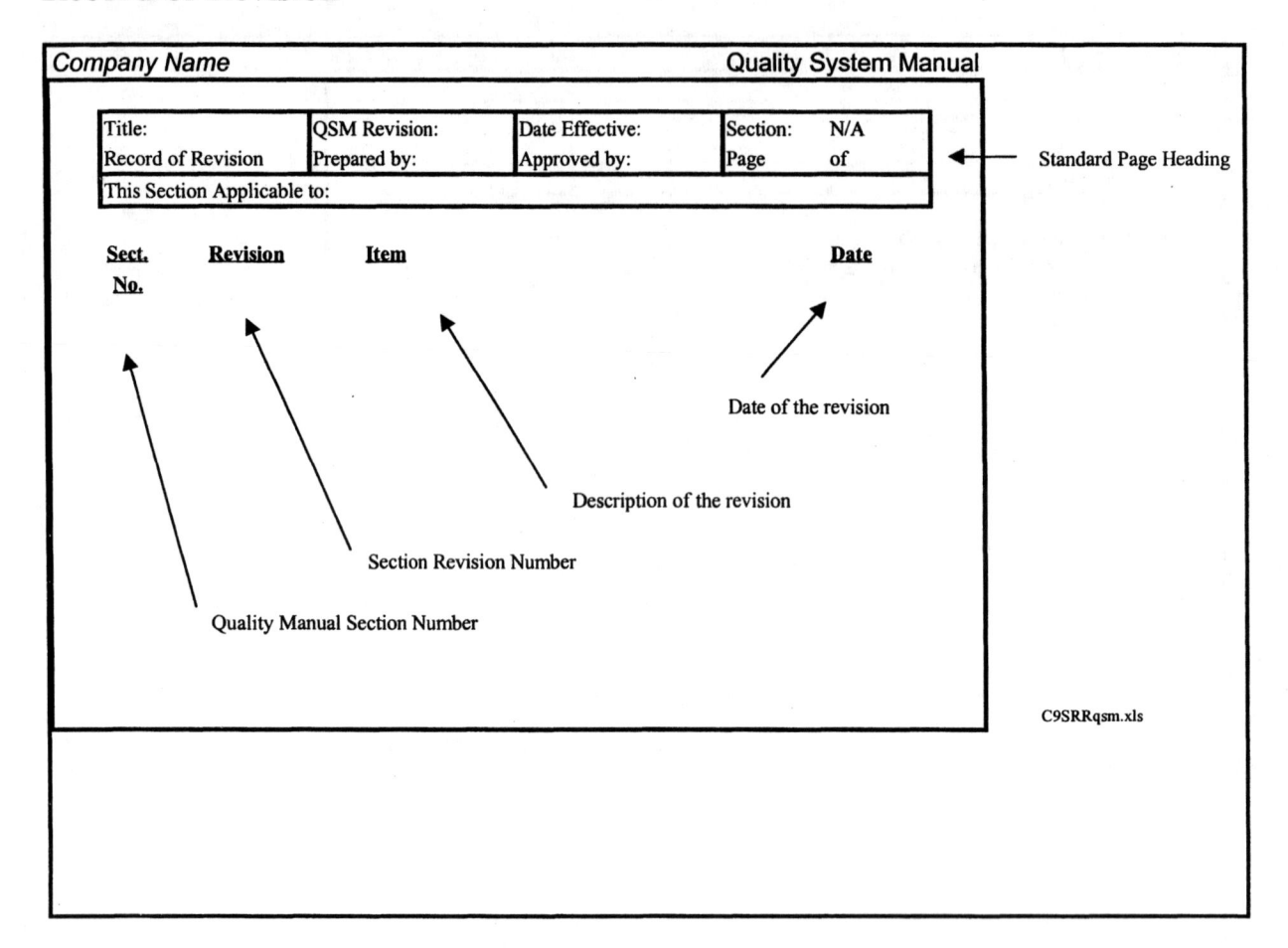

## Record of Revision

| Company Name | | | Quality System Manual | |
|---|---|---|---|---|
| Title: Record of Revision | QSM Revision: Prepared by: | Date Effective: Approved by: | Section: N/A Page of | ← Standard Page Heading |
| This Section Applicable to: | | | | |

**Sect. No.**     **Revision**     **Item**                                    **Date**

↑                  ↑                  ↑                                         ↑
│                  │                  │                                         │
│                  │                  │                                    Date of the revision
│                  │                  │
│                  │             Description of the revision
│                  │
│            Section Revision Number
│
Quality Manual Section Number

C9SRRqsm.xls

# Chapter 10

# QUALITY SYSTEM PROCEDURES

## RELATIONSHIP OF QUALITY SYSTEM PROCEDURES TO QUALITY SYSTEM

The Quality System Procedures are those that directly support the Quality System Manual of Chapter 9 and that are considered to be applicable to all operating and support functions. All procedures other than those designated as Quality System Procedures are *operating procedures*, **NOT** Quality System Procedures. There is often confusion over this issue, in that all procedures are sometimes mistakenly considered as Quality System Procedures.

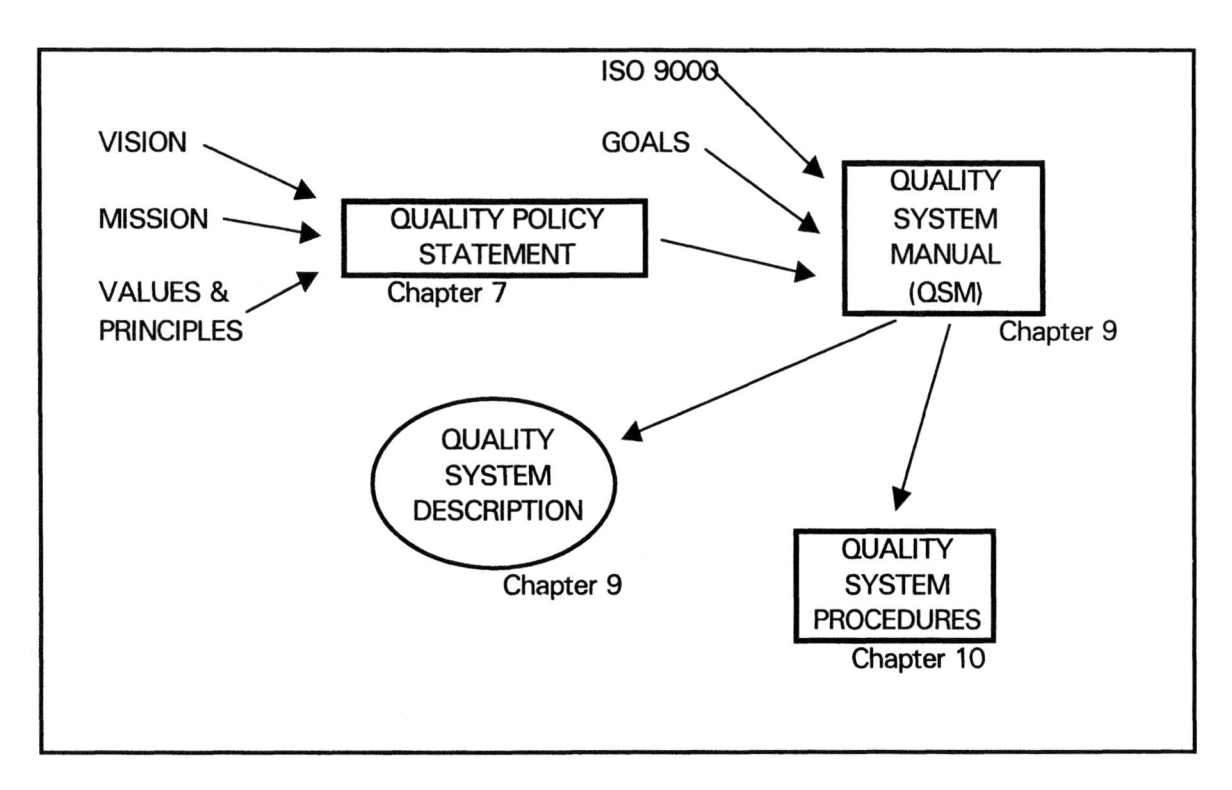

**Figure 10-1. Quality System Relationship Diagram Segment**

Where do the Quality System Procedures fit into the Quality System? How does one determine which ones to develop? What is their preparation method? Which are the key Quality System Procedures? Where does one start in their development? These are just a few of the questions that cross one's mind relative to the Quality System Procedures. It could appear to be an overwhelming task, but it is not when approached in a logical manner.

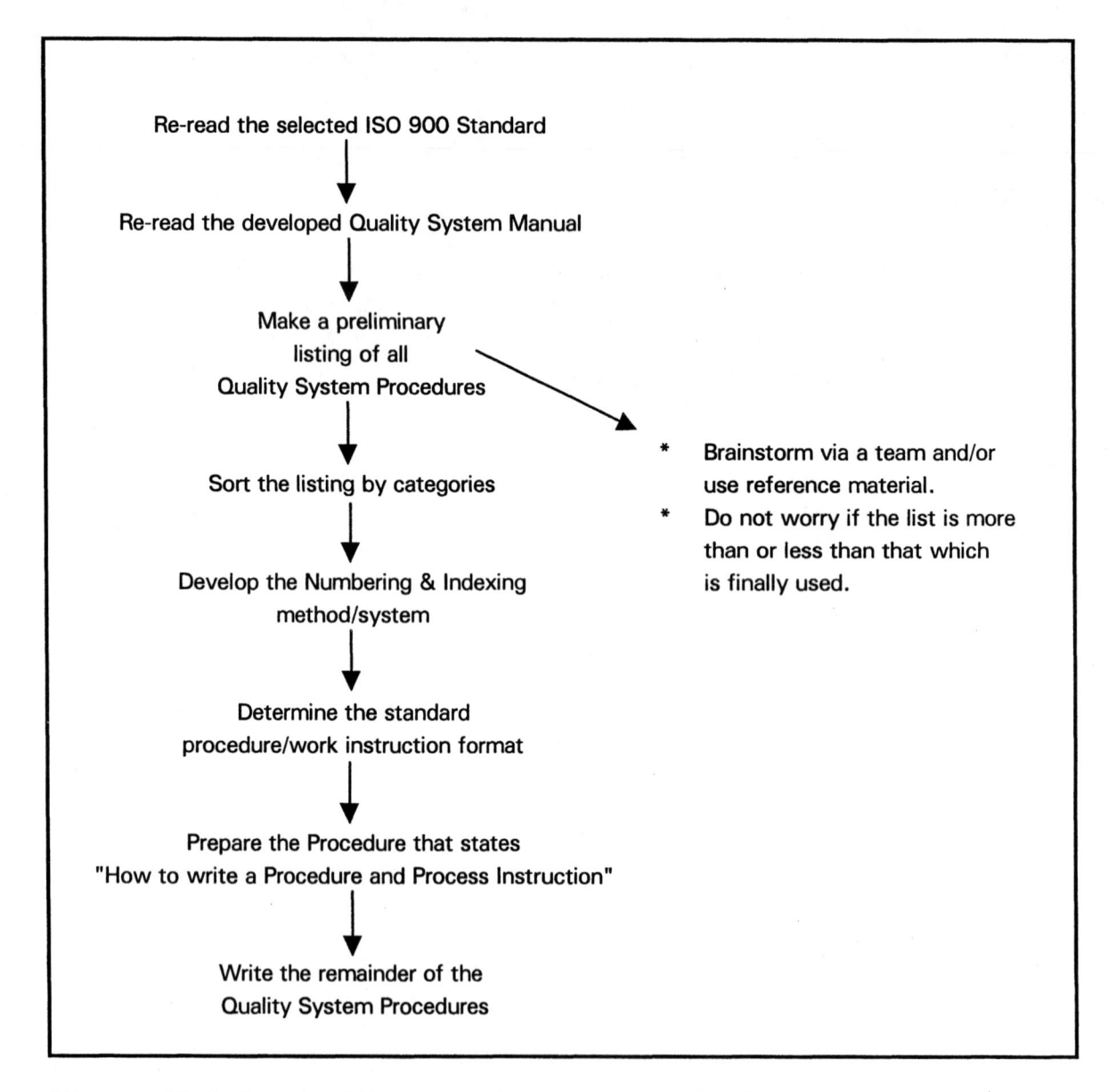

```
Re-read the selected ISO 900 Standard
                │
                ▼
Re-read the developed Quality System Manual
                │
                ▼
       Make a preliminary
          listing of all             ────────┐
     Quality System Procedures                │
                │                              ▼
                ▼                    *  Brainstorm via a team and/or
     Sort the listing by categories        use reference material.
                │                    *  Do not worry if the list is more
                ▼                        than or less than that which
     Develop the Numbering & Indexing     is finally used.
           method/system
                │
                ▼
        Determine the standard
     procedure/work instruction format
                │
                ▼
      Prepare the Procedure that states
  "How to write a Procedure and Process Instruction"
                │
                ▼
       Write the remainder of the
        Quality System Procedures
```

**Figure 10-2. Logical Manner Approach to the Development of Quality System Procedures**

# QUALITY SYSTEM PROCEDURES—A SHOPPING LIST

A shopping list of Quality System Procedures grouped into implementation categories might include the following:

**Those that apply to documentation**

- Storage and Retention of Controlled Documents and Quality Records
- Document and Data Control
- Numbering and Indexing
- Development of Operating Procedures and Work Instructions (Process Instructions)
- File Management and File Retention
- Correspondence Control

**Those that apply to work control or process control**

- Contract Review
- Design Control
- Product/Project Identification and Traceability
- Process Control and Checklists
- Handling, Storage, Packaging, Preservation, and Delivery
- Control of Customer Supplied Product

**Those that apply to quality control**

- Inspection and Testing
- Control of Inspection, Measuring, and Test Equipment
- Inspection and Test Status
- Control of Nonconforming Product

**Those that are training related**

- Training and Development

**Those that apply to corrective and preventive action**

- Corrective and Preventive Action
- Client Feedback
- Nonconformance Reporting

**Those that apply to the Quality System maintenance**

- Internal Quality Audit
- Internal Auditor Certification
- Statistical Techniques
- Management Reviews

**Those that apply to supplier control**

- Purchasing
- Subcontracted Technical Personnel
- Supplier Assessment and Control

**Those that are independent**

- Confidentiality

The following text provides some insight and details for each of the listed Quality System Procedures. The choice of use is determined by the amount of detail provided in the Quality System Manual (QSM). In general, the better choice is to keep the QSM at a high level, supplemented by the Quality System Procedures. Together, these two documents, the QSM and the Quality System Procedures must completely define the Quality System in accordance with the selected ISO 9000 Standard.

So let's get started with probably the single most important task, that of selection of an appropriate Numbering and Indexing System for all documentation required by the Quality System.

## DEVELOPING THE NUMBERING AND INDEXING SYSTEM

There are four basic types of documents to which the Numbering and Indexing must apply: Quality System Procedures, Work Instructions, Quality Records, and Position Descriptions.

Procedures state "what the requirements are." Work Instructions state "how the work is done" and are subservient to procedures. Quality Records are the documentation or visible evidence of the work having been done and are defined within each respective Quality System Procedure or Work Instruction. A Check Sheet is an example of a Quality Record. Position Descriptions are generally "stand alone" documents.

Procedures are Level 3 documents, as shown in Figure 10-3, and are associated with either a primary or supporting work process. Procedures are generally grouped together with other procedures into categories of processes. These categories are considered Level 2 documents in respect to the Numbering and Indexing System. The processes themselves are Level 1, the top level associated with the Numbering and Indexing System presented here.

The first step then is to define a Numbering System that will encompass all of the top level work functions, the categories of work within those work functions, the associated Work Process Procedures and the Work Instructions associated with each of the procedures. The Level 1 work functions might include Engineering, Manufacturing, Research and Development, Finance, Information Management, Human Resources, Legal, Office Services, Business Development (Sales/Marketing), etc. Within each work function of Level 1, there are a number of work categories. For example, within the Level 1 work function of manufacturing, the following work categories might be found: Shipping, Receiving, Production, Systems Test, Quality Control, and Process Control.

For each of the work categories, there is at least one procedure and could be as many as 99. For each procedure, there may be from 0 to 999 directly associated work instructions.

| Level 1 | | Level 2 | | Level 3 | | Level 4 | |
|---|---|---|---|---|---|---|---|
| Process | | Categories | | Procedure | | Work Instruction | |
| Number | Name | Number | Name | Number | Name | Number | Name |
| 001 | Engineering | 01 | | P01 | | W001 | |
| | | | There may be several Categories for each Process | | There may be several Procedures for each Category (minimum of 1) | W002 | |
| | | | | | | W003 | There may be several Work Instructions for each Procedure (minimum of 0) |
| | | | | | | W004 | |
| | | | | | | W005 | |
| | | | | P02 | | W001 | |
| | | | | | | W002 | |
| | | | | | | W003 | |
| | | 02 | | P01 | | W001 | |
| 002 | Manufacturing | 01 | | P01 | | W001 | |

Categories are grouped together with other categories which are associated with the same Process

Procedures are grouped together with other procedures into Categories of Processes

Work Instructions are grouped together with other work instructions which are associated with the same Procedure

Level 1    Work Process
Level 2    Categories of work within the Work Process
Level 3    Work Process Procedures
Level 4    Work Instructions

**Figure 10-3. Numbering and Indexing Method/System**

122 / *Implementing an ISO 9000-Based Quality System*

A sample format for each basic type of document for which the Numbering and Indexing must apply are shown in Figures 10-4 through 10-7. Of course, the intent of these samples is to trigger the development of one's own system. In so doing, one should keep in mind some key principles:

1. The numbering system must be:
   a. Simple, not complex
   b. Able to be easily computerized in such a manner that it can sort by selected fields

2. The number on each document must be "stand-alone," in that it refers upward to its associated document, but is unique in itself.

3. The numbers should not refer downward to subservient documents.

4. A number of documents may be Quality Records, but do not need to have a Quality Record Number applied if they contain the contract or project identification number in an obvious location. The project or contract number becomes the Quality Record Number.

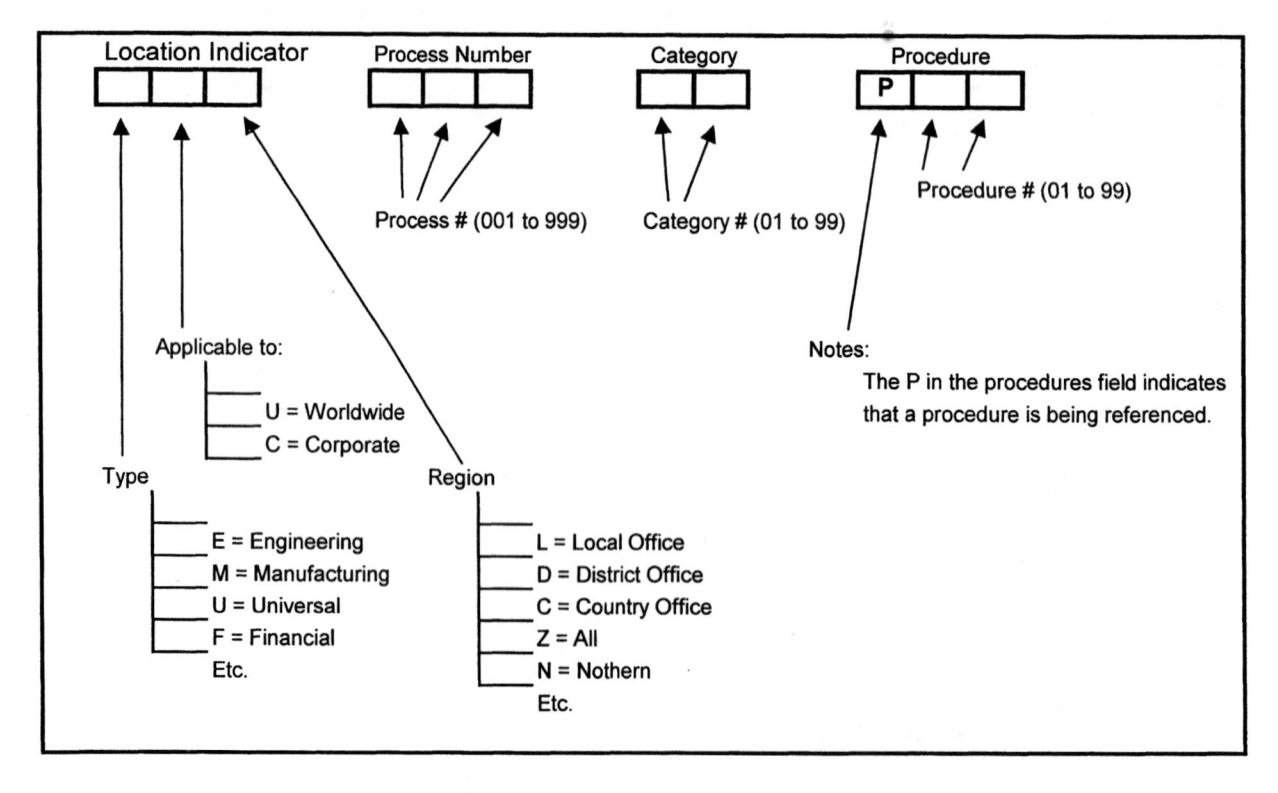

```
Location Indicator    Process Number    Category         Procedure
[ ][ ][ ]             [ ][ ][ ]         [ ][ ]           [P][ ][ ]

                      Process # (001 to 999)   Category # (01 to 99)   Procedure # (01 to 99)

Applicable to:                                          Notes:
   U = Worldwide                                           The P in the procedures field indicates
   C = Corporate                                           that a procedure is being referenced.
Type            Region

   E = Engineering        L = Local Office
   M = Manufacturing      D = District Office
   U = Universal          C = Country Office
   F = Financial          Z = All
   Etc.                   N = Nothern
                          Etc.
```

**Figure 10-4. Printed Number on Procedure—Sample Format**

## Quality System Procedures / 123

```
[Location Indicator] [Process Number] [Category] [Procedure: P] [Work Instruction] [Local Office or Department Code]
```

An additional Field is added for Work Instructions. By using the complete number, easy reference is made to the associated Procedure, Category, Work Process, and Location.

Work Instruction # (001 to 999)

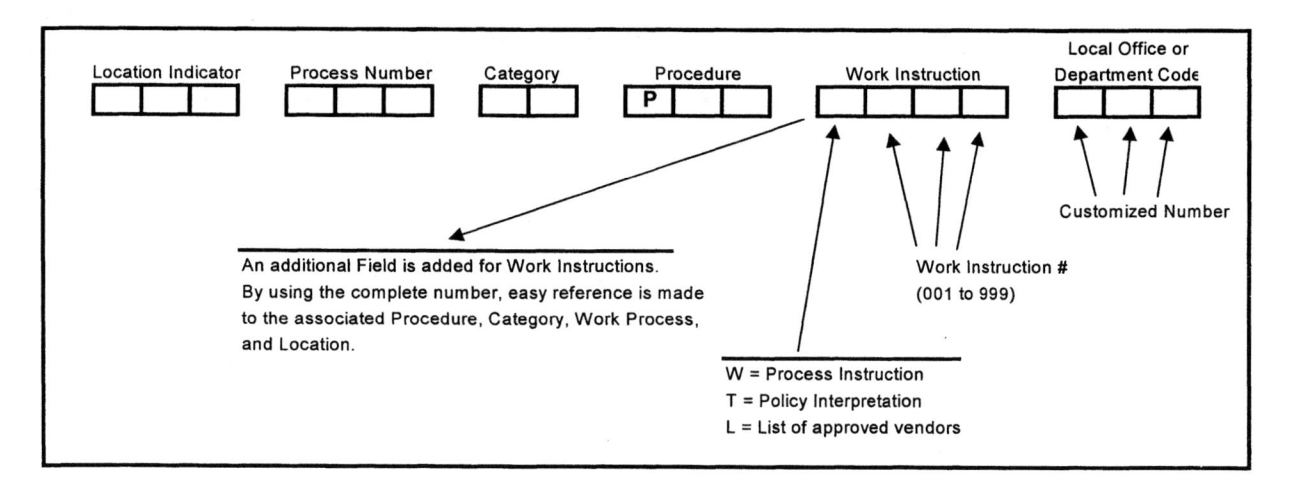

Customized Number

W = Process Instruction
T = Policy Interpretation
L = List of approved vendors

**Figure 10-5. Printed Number on Work Instruction—Sample Format**

```
[Document] [Date: D D M M M Y Y] [Number] [Office or Department Code]
```

The Date field is alpha numeric (05DEC94)

The Number field is sequential beginning at 001 for each type of Quality Record.

Customized Number Fields

Region:
- L = Local Office
- D = District Office
- C = country Office
- Z = All
- N = Northern
- Etc.

Applicable to:
- U = Worldwide
- C = Corporate

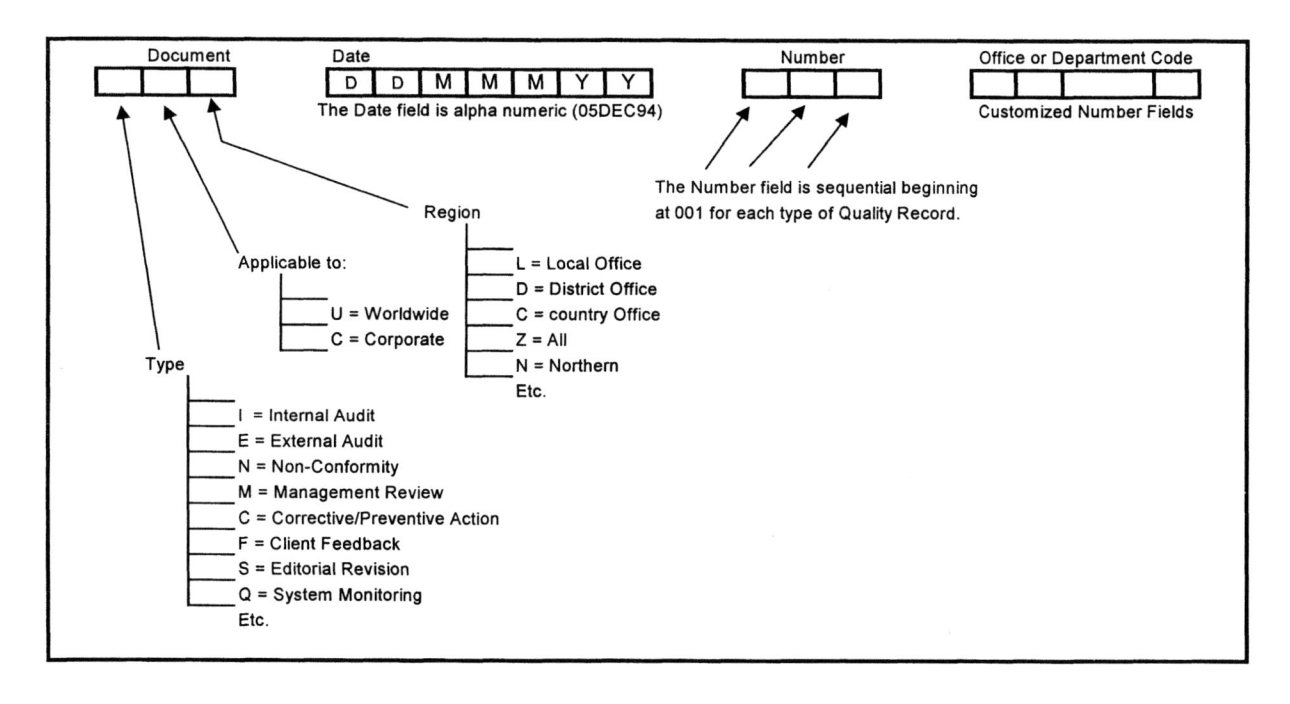

Type:
- I = Internal Audit
- E = External Audit
- N = Non-Conformity
- M = Management Review
- C = Corrective/Preventive Action
- F = Client Feedback
- S = Editorial Revision
- Q = System Monitoring
- Etc.

**Figure 10-6. Printed Number on Quality Records —Sample Format**

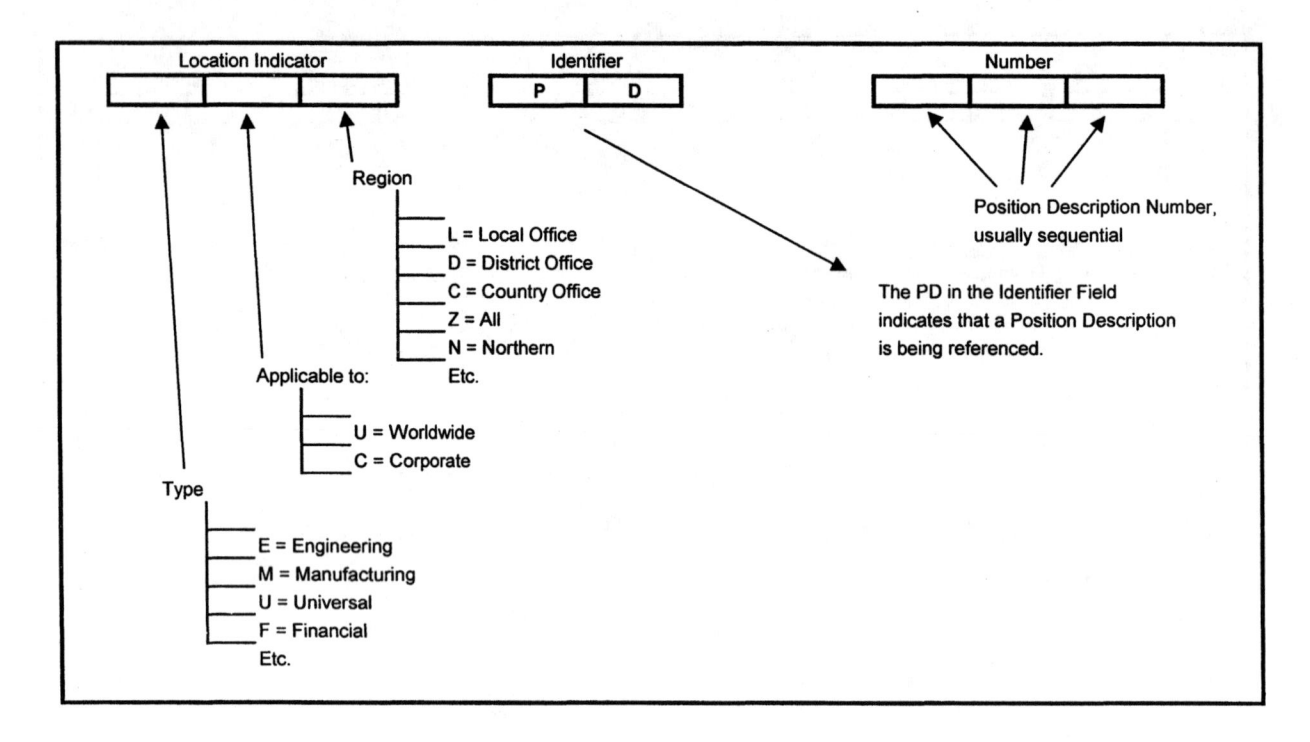

**Figure 10-7. Printed Number on Position Descriptions
—Sample Format**

## DETERMINE THE STANDARD FORMATS FOR PROCEDURES AND WORK INSTRUCTIONS

It is important for the entire organization to utilize a standard format for Procedures and Work Instructions in order to ensure overall consistency. These formats must be developed prior to initiating the writing/preparation process. Doing otherwise will create an uncontrollable situation, which is difficult and costly to correct. Creating a standard form using a word processing software program, with the formats already established, is a great assist in getting the job done right the first time.

### Procedure Title Block—Sample Standard Format

**Title block:** The title block should contain the title, revision number, date effective, procedure number, name of the preparer, approver's name, page number, and volume number (as applicable). The title block must be printed on each page of the procedure.

| The Title of the Procedure | | | Engineering, Manufacturing, Quality, HR, etc. (_____) **Procedure** | |
|---|---|---|---|---|
| Title | Revision Number: | Date Effective: | | Number: |
| | Prepared by: | Approved by: | | Page 1 of |
| Applicable to: | | | | Volume: |
| | | | | |

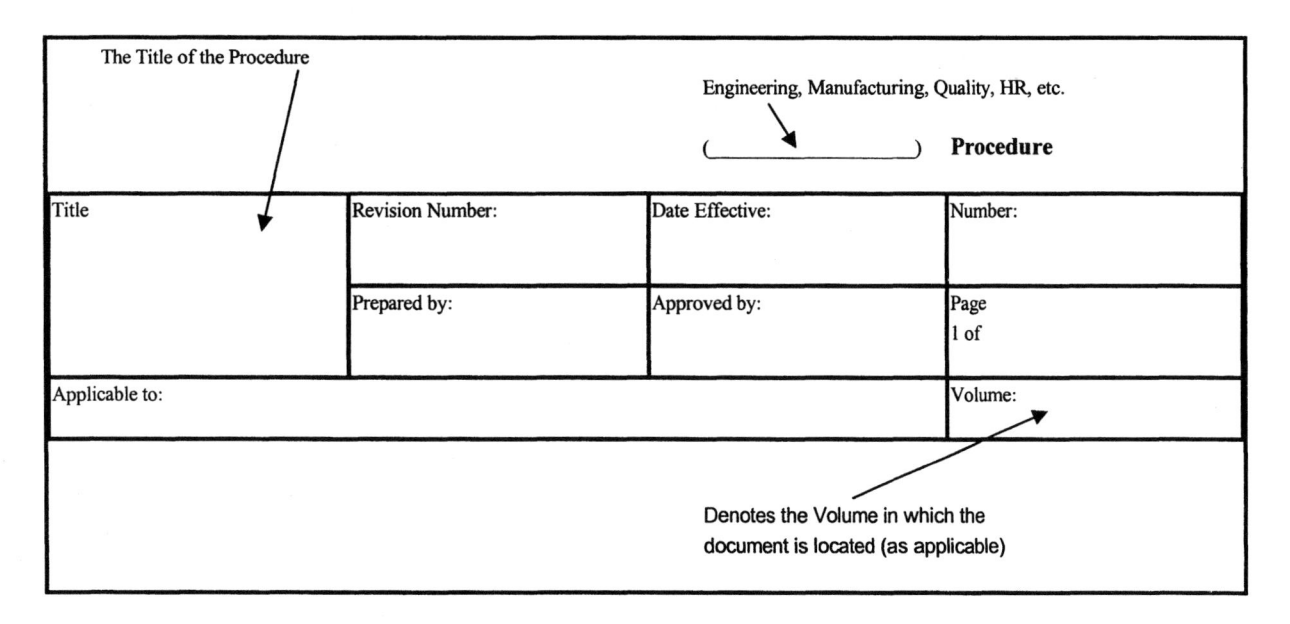

Denotes the Volume in which the document is located (as applicable)

**Figure 10-8. Procedure Title Block—Sample Standard Format**

| The Title of the Procedure | | | Engineering, Manufacturing, Quality, HR, etc. (_____) **Procedure** | |
|---|---|---|---|---|
| Title | Revision Number: | Date Effective: | | Number: |
| | Prepared by: | Approved by: | | Page 2 of |
| | | | | |

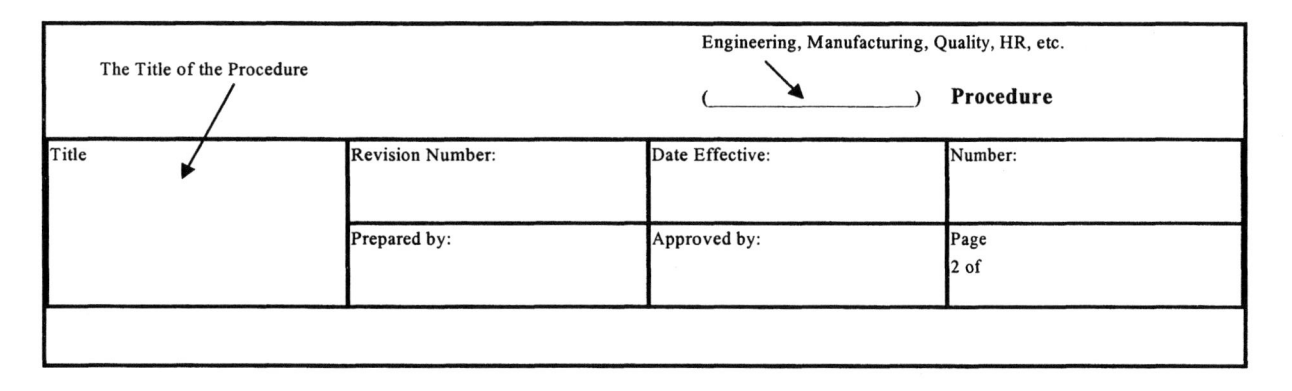

**Figure 10-9. Procedure Title Block for Subsequent Pages**

# Work Instruction Title Block—Sample Standard Format

**Title Block:** The title block should contain the title, revision number, date, work instruction number, name of the preparer, approver's name, page number, and volume number. The title block must be printed on each page of the Work Instruction.

| Title<br>(The Title of the Work Instruction →) | | Engineering, Manufacturing, Quality, HR, etc.<br>(_____↓_____) **Work Instruction** | |
|---|---|---|---|
| | Revision Number: | Date Effective: | Number: |
| | Prepared by: | Approved by: | Page<br>1 of |
| Applicable to: | | | Volume: → Used to denote in which volume the Work Instruction is located. |

**Figure 10-10. Work Instruction Title Block—Sample Standard Format**

| Title<br>(The Title of the Work Instruction →) | | Engineering, Manufacturing, Quality, HR, etc.<br>(_____↓_____) **Work Instruction** | |
|---|---|---|---|
| | Revision Number: | Date Effective: | Number: |
| | Prepared by: | Approved by: | Page<br>1 of |
| Figure 10-11 | | | |

**Figure 10-11. Work Instruction Title Block for Subsequent Sections**

Once the standard title blocks have been determined, it is time to standardize the content categories for both procedures and work instructions.

# DEVELOPMENT OF PROCEDURES AND WORK INSTRUCTIONS

This Quality System Procedures should state the requirements that govern the format, development, revision, control, and approval of Operating Procedures at all levels within the company. Operating Procedures are those that are identified by the function to which they relate (i.e., finance, human resources, manufacturing, engineering, marketing, quality, etc.).

This chapter is sectioned into two parts, the first for the Quality System Procedure itself and the second for those operating procedures and work instructions that are written in accordance with it.

## Procedure Table of Contents

The Table of Contents for the Quality System Procedure "Development of Procedures and Work Instructions" should include the following considerations:

### Contents

1.0 References
2.0 Scope
3.0 Description of the Procedure
    3.1 Definitions
    3.2 Numbering and Indexing
    3.3 New Procedure or Work Instruction Development and Review
    3.4 Local Procedure/Work Instruction Change or Development
    3.5 Revisions to Issued Procedures or Work Instructions
    3.6 Content and Format Requirements
4.0 Training and Knowledge
5.0 Responsibility
6.0 Quality Records
8.0 Confidentiality
9.0 Revision History
    Figures (1, 2,...)
    Check Sheets
    Attachments (A, B,...... )

# Explanation of Each Section of the Contents for the Quality System Procedure

## 1.0 References

All references directly associated with the Quality System Procedure or Work Instruction are listed in this section. When referencing a document, always indicate the number and index and include the complete title of the referenced document. The reference must be directly to the document containing the needed information. Never reference to a document that references to another document for the necessary information.

Examples of references:

1.1 Quality System Manual, Section 8, Volume 1.
1.2 Quality System Procedure, (title), (number), (other, as appropriate).

## 2.0 Scope

This section should state the scope of this specific procedure in a clear, concise manner and address the extent of the subject matter covered.

Example of a typical Scope Statement:

*This procedure addresses the initiation, development, revision and approval of Quality System and operating procedures at all levels within [company name]. Operating procedures include those identified by the function to which they relate (e.g., Engineering Procedures/Work Instructions, Manufacturing Procedures/Work Instructions, Quality System Procedures, etc.)*

## 3.0 Description of the Procedure

### 3.1 Definitions

All definitions that are necessary to fully understand this procedure and the terminology used within the procedure that are not standard should be included here.

Examples of typical definitions:

**Procedure**—defines what work is to be done and the responsibility for such work

**Work Instruction (Process Instruction)**—describes how to perform work categorically defined in a related procedure

**Local Procedure/Work Instruction**—deals solely with an office/department

**Worldwide (Company-wide) Procedure/Work Instruction**—those that are applicable to all offices/departments throughout the company

## 3.2 Numbering and Indexing

Included here is a statement that requires all procedures to be numbered and indexed in accordance with the Quality System Procedure, Numbering and Indexing (procedure number).

Example of the content of this section:

*Procedures and Work Instructions are numbered and indexed in accordance with the Quality System Procedure, Numbering and Indexing, QSZ-999-99-P03 Vol. 2.*

## 3.3 New Procedure or Work Instruction Development and Review

This section addresses the development, review, and approval requirements for operations-related procedures generated within the company. Perhaps the best way to demonstrate this section is by the use of a flow chart with accompanying words, as necessary, included in this section of the procedure.

Example of the content of this section:

*See Figure 10-1, New Procedure or Work Instruction Development Flow Diagram.*

### 3.3.1 New Procedure Development Worksheet

Consideration should be given to the use of a worksheet for gathering the necessary data and information for the preparation of the respective document. The worksheet of Attachment A is one such that can be used for determining the knowledge requirements one would need to perform the tasks associated with the document to be prepared. This is different from the training requirements, which is a listing of those skills that can be taught providing one had the basic knowledge as listed. The applicability (to what does the document apply) and the purpose of the procedure/work instruction should also be stated. The next major consideration is to outline (list) the process steps in the space provided. The completed worksheet will provide a good basis for the final document preparation.

| Date: | Applicability: |
|---|---|
| Division/Region/Office/Department: | |
| Procedure/Process Instruction Title: | Purpose: |
| Knowledge Requirements: | |
| | Procedure Outline (primary steps, components, deliverables) |
| Training Requirements: | |
| | Related Procedure(s): |
| | Related Work Instruction(s): |

Development of Procedures and Work Instructions, QSZ-999-99-P07     Attachment A - Revision 0     Page 1 of 1

**Figure 10-12. Procedure and Process Instruction Development Worksheet**

Example of the content of this section:

Prior to creating a new procedure/work instruction, a work process analysis should be performed to determine the following as they relate to the process under consideration.

- Applicability (which locations/offices/departments are affected)
- Scope (objective)
- Primary steps, components, and deliverables
- Knowledge requirements
- Training requirements

The Procedure/Work Instruction Development Worksheet (Attachment A), process mapping, or other analysis tools may be used to conduct the Work Process Analysis. This analysis is a working document and will not become a part of the procedure/work instruction.

### 3.3.2 New Procedure/Work Instruction Development

The development and review steps for a new procedure or work instruction should be listed here. Also, a flow diagram showing the document development steps may be included in a referenced figure located just prior to the attachments located at the end of the document.

Example of the content of this section:

*See Figure 1, New Procedure or Work Instruction Development Flow Diagram.*

1. *The originator initiates a New Procedure/Work Instruction Review and Approval Tracking Sheet (Attachment C), which accompanies the Procedure/Work Instruction throughout the review and approval process.*

2. *The Work Process Analysis, if utilized, and the Tracking Sheet shall be forwarded to the person responsible for the work process*

*and approval (the Corporate Responsible Person). See Section 1 of the Tracking Sheet.*

3. *If approved, the Procedure and Work Instruction Worksheet shall be used to develop the Procedure/Work Instruction.*

### 3.3.3 New Procedure/Work Instruction Review

The review requirements for a new procedure or work instruction should be stated in this section. One should also include a new Procedure Tracking Sheet to ensure that all requirements are met. This Tracking Sheet ensures that the responsible personnel have reviewed and approved the new document and provides evidence to an auditor that it has been done.

The responsible person for the process associated with the new procedure/work instruction may choose to assign a team or an individual to develop the document.

A matrix may be included that indicates by function the responsible persons for the various processes or product lines.

### 3.3.4 Developer of Procedure/Work Instruction

This section provides instructions to the developer of the document stating the format to be followed is that which is stated in the Quality System requirements. This section also states how the developer is to proceed after completion.

Example of the content of this section:

1. *The person (team) assigned to the development of the procedure/work instruction utilizes all necessary inputs and resources to develop the draft of the document in accordance with the requirements. The format is to follow the Quality System requirements.*

2. *Upon completion of development, the developer signs and dates the tracking sheet in the appropriate location (Section 3). The*

*developed document and associated tracking sheet are returned to the responsible person.*

### 3.3.5 Responsible Person Final Review

This section states the requirements for the final review by the responsible person for the associated process/product line. It also includes the instructions for the final sign-off of the associated Tracking Sheet.

### 3.3.6 Company Quality Organization Review and Processing for all Procedures/Work Instructions

The final review will be the quality organization within the company. This may be a single person who is responsible for ensuring that the form, fit, and function of the document is in order. This person/organization is also the one who is responsible for the controlled distribution of the generated document.

## 3.4 Local Procedure/Work Instruction Change or Development

When a procedure has been determined to be one that is locally applicable only, the development, change, and review requirements and the process for review must be stated here.

## 3.5 Revisions to Issued Procedures/Work Instructions

There are several reasons for revising issued procedures/work instructions that need to be detailed here.

### 3.5.1 Editorial Revisions

A simple method of addressing editorial revisions to procedures needs to be established with a simple initiating form. This method should be detailed here.

Editorial revisions are typos, grammatical errors, incorrect numbering and editorial inconsistencies in the Quality System Procedures or Work Instructions.

### 3.5.2 Substantive Revisions

A method of initiating and effecting changes to procedures or work instructions that are not editorial in nature needs to be established and detailed here. A tracking sheet to both initiate and track the changes through the process is the document that is normally used as a Quality Record for resulting procedure changes. Both procedures and work instructions that are applicable to the entire organization and those that are locally applicable need to be included.

### 3.5.3 Management Directed Revisions

Senior management may, at their discretion, make substantive changes to the procedures. The method for so doing should be described here.

## 3.6 Contents and Format Requirements

It is recommended that the contents of each operating procedure or work instruction be as indicated below. However, what is presented may be modified to fit the company requirements or those of the current operation.

**Development of Operating Procedures and Work Instructions—Contents Described**

The following describes the contents of the operating procedures and refers to Paragraph 3.6 content and format requirements of the Quality System Procedure, "Development of Procedures and Work Instructions."

*The contents of each procedure or process instruction shall be as indicated below, in the order presented.*

**Title Block**

A Title Block is required on all pages of the body of the Quality Procedure or Work Instruction. The required format and elements of a first page Title Block are shown at the top of Page 1 of this procedure. The Title Block for the second and subsequent pages is formatted as appears at the top of this page. In both cases, replace the words "Quality System Procedure" with the words

"Procedure" or "Work Instruction," preceded by the function to which it belongs, such as Finance, Human Resources, Engineering, etc.

**Note:** The designation above the Title Block should not be "Quality System Procedure" except for the Quality System Procedures themselves. For those procedures that are operating procedures, the designation should carry the respective function name (e.g., Engineering Procedure for procedures related to engineering matters, etc.).

### Table of Contents

A Table of Contents is required. It lists major section headings and subheadings, with associated starting page numbers. Important tables and figures, with their associated starting page numbers, may also be listed. Use the Table of Contents of Page 1 of this procedure as an example.

### List of Check Sheets

A list of work instructions is required. When process-related work instructions are attached to the Quality Procedure or Work Instruction, those work instructions shall be listed, in alphabetical order by work instruction letter, with associated revision numbers and dates. If there are not work instructions, state "None."

### List of Attachments

A list of attachments is required. When attachments are present, list attachments in alphabetical order by attachment letter, with associated revision numbers and dates. If there are no attachments, state "None."

### List of References

All references directly associated with the procedure shall be listed in this section. When referencing a document, the number and index shall always be indicated and include the complete title. The reference shall be directly to the document containing the needed information.

### Scope

This section is required if the scope or objective is not explicit in the title of the Quality Procedure or Work Instruction. The scope makes clear, up front, limits to the applicability of a procedure or work instruction; for example, specific limitations on who may perform a process or task; or to specifically limit the range of equipment or limited circumstances under which a procedure or work instruction applies.

### Description of the Procedure or Work Instruction

This section shall describe in a clear, concise manner what is to be done or how it is to be done. The description shall follow a logical sequence in order to achieve the objectives. The description may be in the form of logic flow diagrams coupled with text or text alone.

### Training and Knowledge

This section is conditionally required. It may detail training and knowledge requirements, or may refer to training and knowledge requirements prescribed in related documents.

If a process requires specific training and certification, a corresponding training form must be developed and referenced here. The Training Form may be a part of the procedure as it applies to all work instructions subservient to that procedure. This section may also describe cross-qualification for multiple processes, for example: "Certification in this procedure also qualifies the employee to perform ......... ."

### Responsibility

This section is required when technical, administrative, or managerial oversight responsibilities are not clear from the text of the Quality Procedure/Work Instruction, or go beyond those described in position descriptions, the Quality System Manual, or parent procedure in the case of a work instruction. If included, this section identifies personnel categories responsible for the work described in the document, and designates managerial oversight responsibilities.

### Quality Records

This section is required when records generated in compliance with a procedure or work instruction are auditable under the Quality System.

### Files

This section identifies external or internal records other than controlled documents and Quality Records. This section may not appear in all Quality Procedures or Work Instructions.

### Confidentiality

This section is required only if confidentiality requirements exceed the requirements of Quality System Procedure, Confidentiality, (procedure number).

### Revision History

This required section provides an abstract of substantive revisions to a procedure or process instruction. Each revised section is referred to by section number and, optionally, by title. Enough detail is provided to make the nature of the change clear to the reader. If revisions are extensive that line-by-line entries are not practical, the author may summarize the overall nature and/or scope of changes.

### Check Sheets

A work instruction may be added to the procedure when the procedure is of sufficient detail that it does not warrant an associated work instruction. This section may not appear in most procedures.

### Attachments

Attachments, when included, must carry a "footer" on each page that identifies the name of the procedure, the procedure number, the revision level of the procedure, and the number of pages in the attachment. Attachments of manuals, copyrighted materials, and other documents should be avoided.

## 4.0 Training and Knowledge

The following is an example of the text that should be included in this section:

*All initiators of new procedures or work instructions or changes to existing procedures or work instructions shall be familiar with the Quality System and the subject of the Quality Procedure or Work Instruction. Individuals who review and approve these documents are to have an understanding of the Quality System Manual and Quality System Procedures, their objectives, and implementation.*

## 5.0 Responsibility

The responsible functions for the development of the various procedures or work instructions should be detailed here.

## 6.0 Quality Records

The following is an example of the text that should be included in this section:

*All approved procedures or work instructions shall appear on the list of approved controlled documents, which is a controlled document and shall be maintained in accordance with Quality System Procedure, Storage and Retention of Controlled Documents, and Quality Records, (procedure number). These procedures and work instructions are to be distributed in accordance with Quality System Procedure, Document Control, (procedure number).*

*The completed Procedure or Work Instruction Review and Approval Tracking Sheets are Quality Records and act as Check Sheets for this process and shall be maintained in the files with the procedures in accordance with Quality System Procedure, Storage and Retention of Controlled Documents and Quality Records, (procedure number).*

## 7.0 Confidentiality

The following is an example of the text that should be included in this section:

*This document shall be controlled by the standard confidentiality policy in the Quality System Procedure, Confidentiality (procedure number).*

## 8.0 Revision History

The revision history of this specific procedure should be included here. Alternately, revisions may be marked in some manner within the text of the procedure (i.e., use of a vertical line on the side of the affected paragraph or the shading of the affected paragraph).

# PREPARE REMAINING QUALITY SYSTEM PROCEDURES

After completion of the two key Quality System Procedures—Numbering and Indexing, Development of Procedures and Work Instructions—have them reviewed by a third party as a "sanity" check. The tendency is to make them overly complicated rather than simple. Be sure to have them checked before going further.

Prepare the remaining Quality System Procedures in accordance with those just written. Have them reviewed and revise them as necessary.

One way to help in the preparation task is to obtain some reference examples for the type of operation that closely matches your own—service, manufacturing, etc.. Most companies are glad to provide these, sometimes at a cost to offset expenses if the demand is high. It is worth the effort in terms of assurance and time saved.

You should write the Quality System Procedures yourself, and ensure that they describe what you are currently doing. It is not necessary to re-engineer your current processes at this time. Remember, the Quality System for this part of the implementation process is simply writing down the overall guideline requirements.

Following the completion of the writing and review tasks, one must determine the following: the distribution list, the person responsible for their control, the printing and packaging method, the acknowledgment of receipt after distribution, training of personnel in the Quality System requirements, and follow-up to ensure compliance. These elements are straightforward and therefore not addressed here.

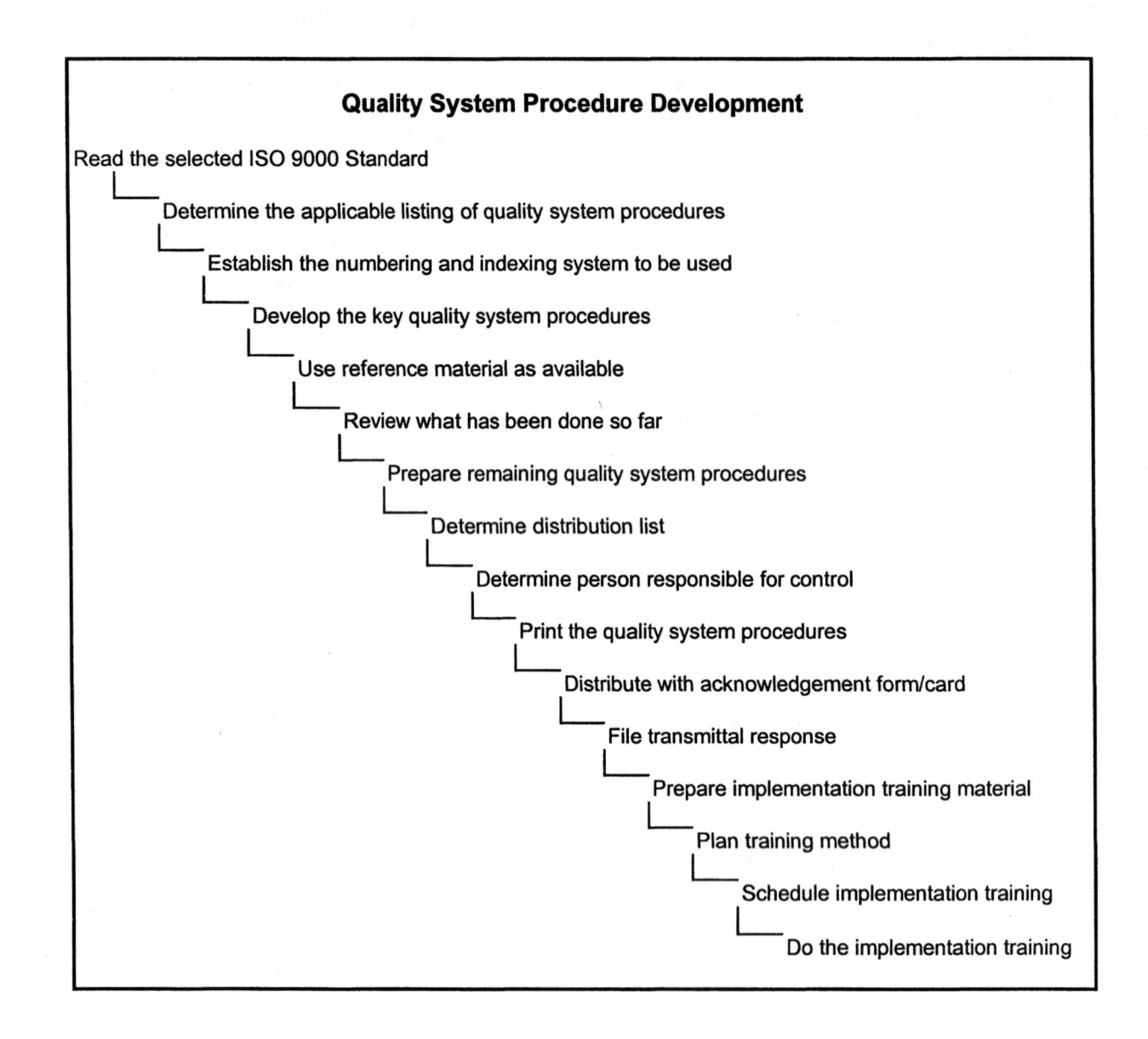

**Quality System Procedure Development**

Read the selected ISO 9000 Standard
└─ Determine the applicable listing of quality system procedures
　└─ Establish the numbering and indexing system to be used
　　└─ Develop the key quality system procedures
　　　└─ Use reference material as available
　　　　└─ Review what has been done so far
　　　　　└─ Prepare remaining quality system procedures
　　　　　　└─ Determine distribution list
　　　　　　　└─ Determine person responsible for control
　　　　　　　　└─ Print the quality system procedures
　　　　　　　　　└─ Distribute with acknowledgement form/card
　　　　　　　　　　└─ File transmittal response
　　　　　　　　　　　└─ Prepare implementation training material
　　　　　　　　　　　　└─ Plan training method
　　　　　　　　　　　　　└─ Schedule implementation training
　　　　　　　　　　　　　　└─ Do the implementation training

**Figure 10-13. Quality System Procedure Development**

## CONCLUSION

### Quality System Procedures

- What are they?
- Where do they fit?
- List preparation and determination?

### The key procedures (How to prepare them)

- Numbering and Indexing
- How to develop a Procedure and Work Instruction

### The rest of the Quality System common procedures (What are the guidelines?)

These are the questions that this chapter should have answered for you.

142 / Implementing an ISO 9000-Based Quality System

| Work Process Status Matrix<br>Quality System Procedures | High Level Work Process: | | Quality System Procedures | | Updated: (DATE) | | |
|---|---|---|---|---|---|---|---|
| PROCEDURE NAME | PROCEDURE NUMBER | DEVELOPMENT RESPONSIBILITY | PREPARATION STATUS | PROCEDURE REVIEW STATUS | PROCEDURE ISSUE STATUS | PROCEDURE TRAINING STATUS | AUDIT ASSIGNMENT | AUDIT STATUS |
| Storage and Retention of Controlled Documents and Quality Records | QSZ-999-99-P01 | TCD Department | Draft Completed 3/23/94 | Completed 3/30/94 | | | | |
| *Listing of all Quality System Procedures* | | | *Procedure number, assignment, and status maintained until procedure is issued and implemented* | | | | | |

**Figure 10-14. Sample Procedure Planning and Scheduling Document**

# Chapter 11

# PRIMARY WORK PROCESSES

## IDENTIFYING A PRIMARY WORK PROCESS

It is often tempting for a company to jump right into the writing of procedures and work instructions prior to determining which ones need to be written, which often leads to rework and confusion. It is far better to determine which procedures and work instructions are needed to fully describe the work done within the company or organization prior to the writing of any of them. One method of so doing is through the Primary Work Process approach presented in Figure 11-1.

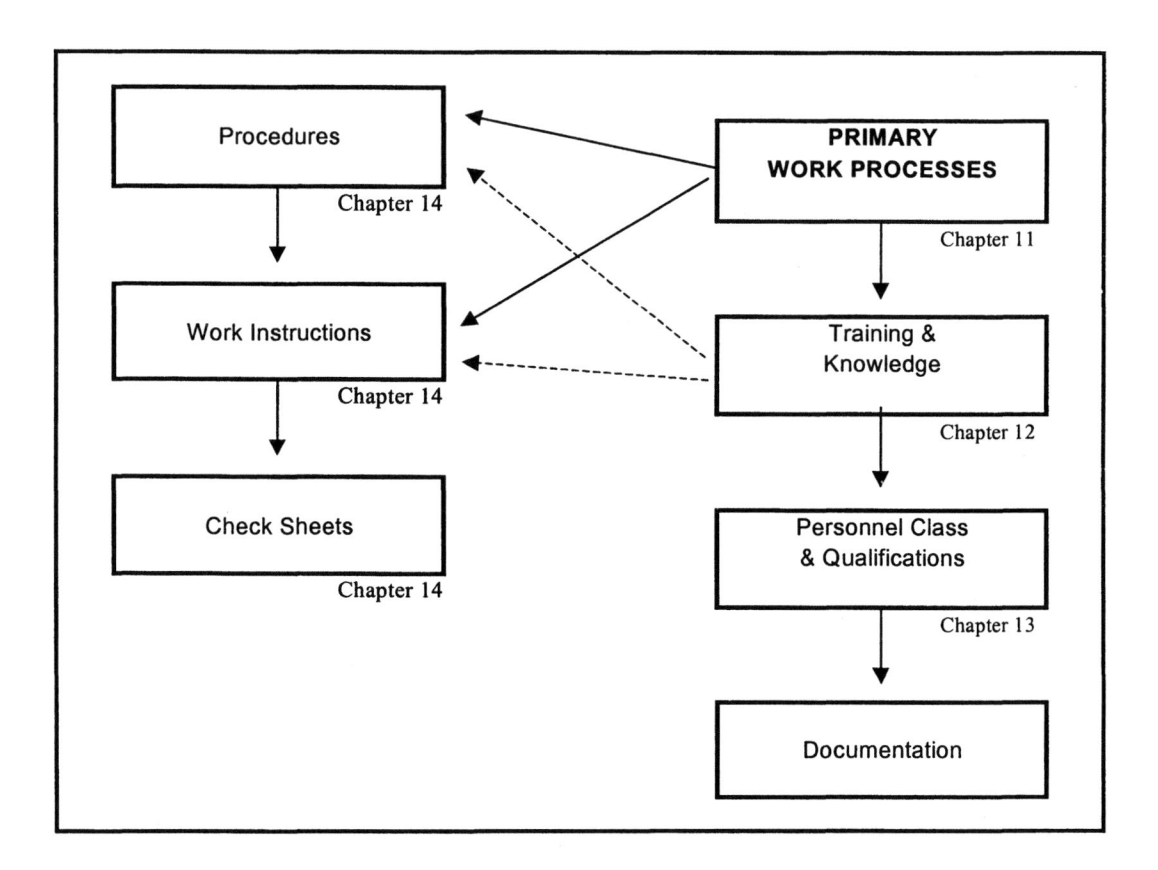

**Figure 11-1. Quality System Relationship Diagram**

## ESTABLISHING A PRIMARY WORK PROCESS

This Primary Work Process approach in determining the procedures and work instructions to be written is described in this and the following chapters:

| | | |
|---|---|---|
| Primary Work Processes | - | Chapter 11 |
| Training and Knowledge | - | Chapter 12 |
| Personnel Classification and Qualification | - | Chapter 13 |
| Work Process Procedures | - | Chapter 14 |
| Work Instructions | - | Chapter 15 |

A Primary Work Process (PWP) is one that delivers value-added outputs to a client or external customer (refer to Chapter 3 and Chapter 8 for the definition of "value-added"). By definition, every business has Primary Work Processes, the focus of the ISO 9000 Standards.

## Step 1—Determine Top Level Functions

The first step is to determine what are the top level (Level 1) functions performed within the organization or company and to name and number them in accordance with the previously developed "Numbering and Indexing" Quality System Procedure of Chapter 10. This determination can be accomplished in any way that works—individual effort, team effort, etc. Level 1 Function names might include Manufacturing, Engineering, Finance, Sales/Service, etc.

Figure 11-2 is a suggested format for the numbering and naming of the Level 1 functions. Figure 11-3 shows the actual function names for the American Bureau of Shipping as an applied example. The Level 1 Functions are high level and not to be confused with the Primary Work Processes described below.

**Level 1 - Work Function**

| Function | |
|---|---|
| Number | Name |
| 001 | |
| 002 | |
| 003 | |
| 004 | |
| 005 | |
| 006 | |

| 999 | |

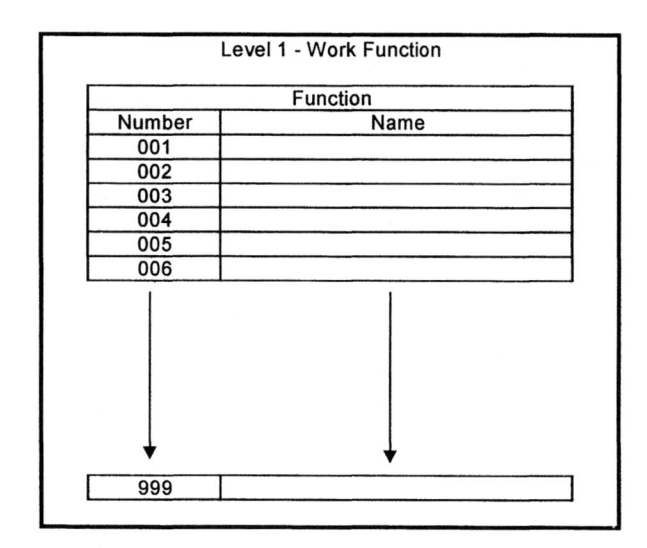

**Figure 11-2. Determination of Work Function Names**

**Level 1 - Work Function**

| Function | |
|---|---|
| Number | Name |
| 001 | Engineering |
| 002 | Survey |
| 003 | Technical Consistency |
| 004 | Regulatory Affairs |
| 005 | Marine Coordination |
| 006 | Corporate Services |
| 007 | Technical Applications |
| 008 | Rule Development |
| 009 | Financial Services |
| 010 | Research & Development |
| 011 | Information Management |
| 012 | Human Resources |
| 013 | Law |
| 014 | Government Services |
| 015 | Office Services |
| 016 | Business Development |

| 999 | |

**Figure 11-3. Applied Example—Work Functions**

## Step 2—List Primary Work Processes

The second step is to list all of the Primary Work Processes performed within the organization or company. The determination of the listing may again be through individual effort, team effort, interviews of personnel within each work function, etc. Once the listing is generated, group the listed processes into categories of work within each Level 1 Function and as described in the previously developed Quality System Procedure "Numbering and Indexing" of Chapter 10.

Since several Primary Work Processes may fall into one category of work within a function, the category should carry a name that is appropriate to the grouping. Figure 11-4 is a continuation of a suggested format for displaying the Level 1 Functions and Level 2 Categories together.

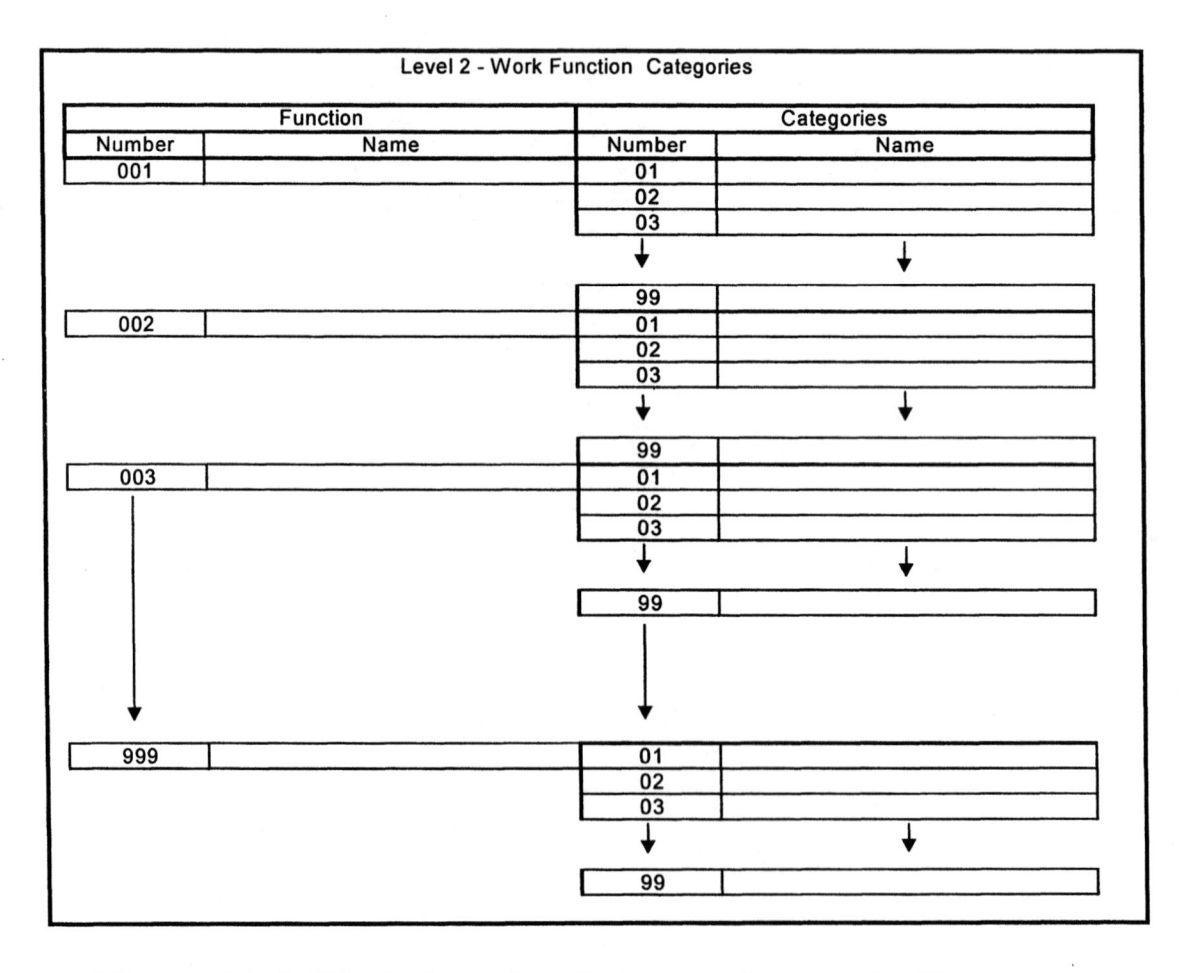

**Figure 11-4. Work Function Category Determination**

Figure 11-5 is the applied example of the American Bureau of Shipping.

| Level 2 - Work Function Categories - Applied Example ||||
|---|---|---|---|
| Function || Categories ||
| Number | Name | Number | Name |
| 001 | Engineering Review | 01 | Advanced Analysis |
|  |  | 02 | Engineering Services |
|  |  | 03 | Materials & Manufacturing |
|  |  | 04 | Offshore Engineering |
|  |  | 05 | Ship Engineering |
|  |  | 06 | Management Support |
|  |  | 99 | General |
| 002 | Survey | 01 | New Construction |
|  |  | 02 | After Construction |
|  |  | 03 | Materials & Equipment |
|  |  | 99 | General |
| 009 | Research & Development | 01 | Research/Development |
|  |  | 02 | Administrative |
| 999 | Controlling | 99 | Common |

**Figure 11-5. Category Determination—Applied Example**

# Step 3—Determine Which Processes Require Procedures

The third step is to determine which of the grouped Primary Work Processes require procedures to be written. Remember, a work process procedure states the process requirements—the "what is required" of the process; whereas, the associated work instruction(s) describe "how" the work is done. In general, every work process will require at least one procedure and could require several, with an upper limit of 99.

Once this determination has been made, assign a procedure name and number in accordance with the Quality System Procedure "Numbering and Indexing." Figure 11-6 is a continuation of a suggested format for displaying the Level 3 Procedures together with their associated categories and functions. Figure 11-7 is the applied example of the American Bureau of Shipping. An additional example is included in Chapter 14.

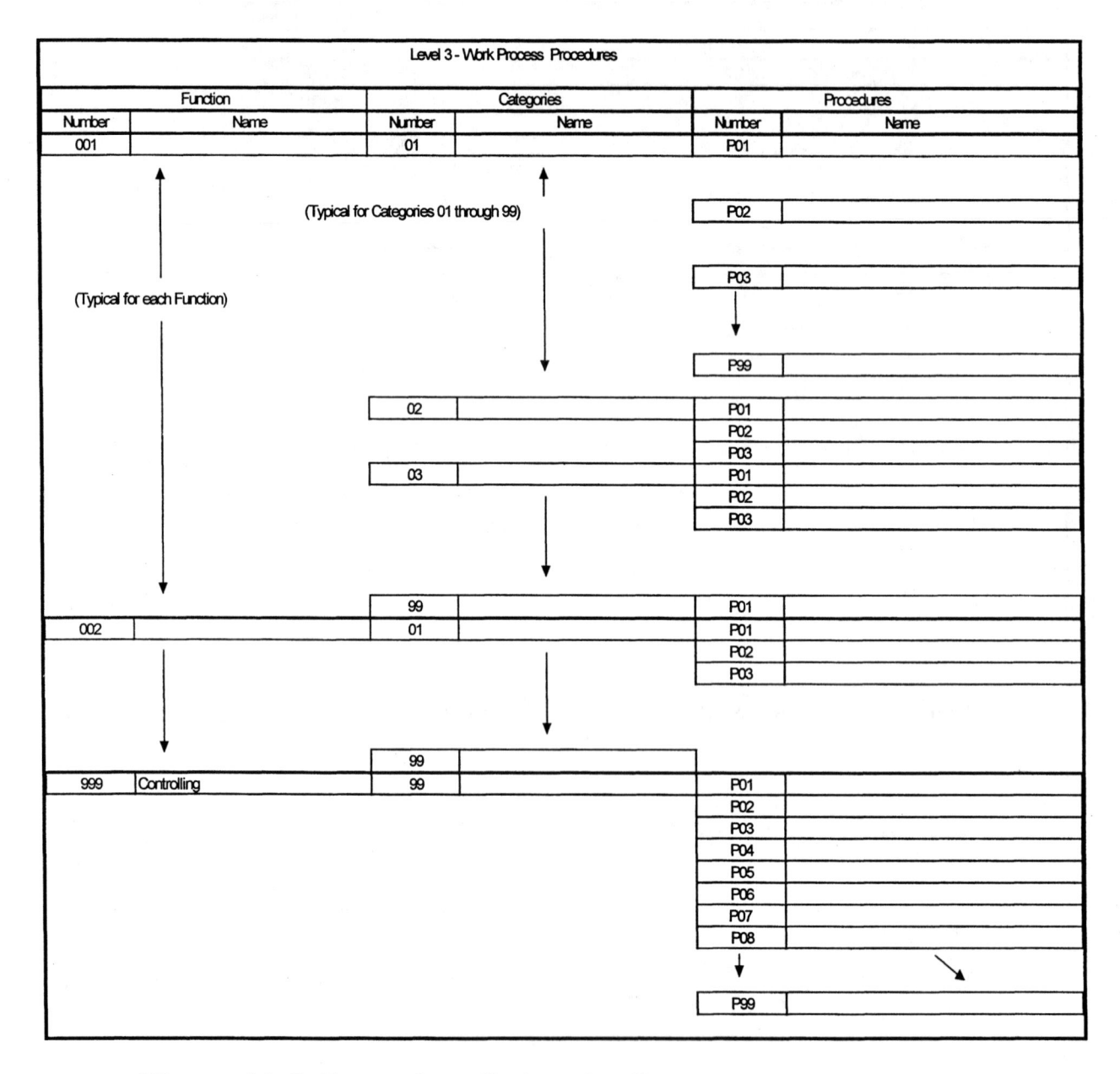

| Level 3 - Work Process Procedures |||||||
|---|---|---|---|---|---|
| Function || Categories || Procedures ||
| Number | Name | Number | Name | Number | Name |
| 001 |  | 01 |  | P01 |  |
|  |  |  | (Typical for Categories 01 through 99) | P02 |  |
|  | (Typical for each Function) |  |  | P03 |  |
|  |  |  |  | P99 |  |
|  |  | 02 |  | P01 |  |
|  |  |  |  | P02 |  |
|  |  |  |  | P03 |  |
|  |  | 03 |  | P01 |  |
|  |  |  |  | P02 |  |
|  |  |  |  | P03 |  |
|  |  | 99 |  | P01 |  |
| 002 |  | 01 |  | P01 |  |
|  |  |  |  | P02 |  |
|  |  |  |  | P03 |  |
|  |  | 99 |  |  |  |
| 999 | Controlling | 99 |  | P01 |  |
|  |  |  |  | P02 |  |
|  |  |  |  | P03 |  |
|  |  |  |  | P04 |  |
|  |  |  |  | P05 |  |
|  |  |  |  | P06 |  |
|  |  |  |  | P07 |  |
|  |  |  |  | P08 |  |
|  |  |  |  | P99 |  |

**Figure 11-6. Procedure Determination**

## Level 3 - Work Process Procedures - Applied Example

| Function | | Categories | | Procedures | |
|---|---|---|---|---|---|
| Number | Name | Number | Name | Number | Name |
| 001 | Engineering Review | 01 | Advanced Analysis | P01 | Structural Modelling, FEM - Static |
| | | | | P02 | Structural Modelling, FEM-Dynamic |
| | | | | P03 | Structural Response Analysis - Static |
| | | | | P04 | Structural Response Analysis - Dynamic |
| | | | | P05 | Fatigue and Fracture |
| | | | | P06 | Applied Forces |
| | | | | P07 | Structural Capability Analysis |
| | | | | P99 | Supply Structural Analysis Services |
| | | 02 | Engineering Services | | |
| | | 03 | Materials & Manufacturing | (Procedures listed as applicable - format as shown above and below) | |
| | | 04 | Offshore Engineering | | |
| | | 05 | Ship Engineering | | |
| | | 06 | Management Support | | |
| | | 99 | General | P01 | Consultants |
| | | | | P02 | Engineering Activity Monitoring |
| | | | | P03 | Letter Writing & Annotation of Plans |
| | | | | P04 | Stamping |
| | | | | P05 | Plan Hour Reporting |
| 002 | Survey | 01 | New Construction | (Procedures listed as applicable - format as shown above and below) | |
| | | 02 | After Construction | | |
| | | 03 | Materials & Equipment | | |
| | | 99 | General | | |
| 009 | Research & Development | 01 | Research/Development | P01 | Project Execution |
| | | 02 | Administrative | P01 | Project Planning |
| | | | | P02 | External Project Monitoring |
| 999 | Controlling | 99 | Common | P01 | Storage & Retention of Controlled Documents & Quality Records |
| | | | | P02 | Document Control |
| | | | | P03 | Numbering & Indexing |
| | | | | P04 | Training & Development |
| | | | | P05 | Corrective and Preventive Action |
| | | | | P06 | Internal Quality Audits |
| | | | | P07 | Procedure Development |
| | | | | P08 | Work Instruction Development |
| | | | | P22 | Client Satisfaction |

**Figure 11-7. Procedure Determination—Applied Example**

## Step 4—Determine Work Instructions

The fourth step is the determination of the necessary work instructions to support the work process procedures. A procedure does not always require a work instruction, but a work instruction must always be directly associated with a procedure. A procedure may have as many as 999 subservient work instructions; however, the average is perhaps one to four. The written Work Instructions should be named and numbered in accordance with the Quality System Procedure "Numbering and Indexing." It may be that the actual determination of the work processes cannot be done until the procedures are written, or at least outlined as to their content.

Figure 11-8 is a continuation of a suggested format for displaying the Level 4 Work Instructions together with their associated procedures, categories, and processes. The applied example of the American Bureau of Shipping is included in Chapter 15.

| Function | | Categories | | Procedures | | Work Instruction | |
|---|---|---|---|---|---|---|---|
| Number | Name | Number | Name | Number | Name | Number | Name |
| | | 01 | | P01 | | W001 | |
| | | | | | | W002 | |
| | | | | | | W00? | |
| | | | | P02 | | W001 | |
| | (Typical per Function) | | | | | W002 | |
| | | | | | | W00? | |
| | | | | P03 | | W001 | |
| | | | | | | W002 | |
| | | | | | | W00? | |
| | | 02 | | P01 | | W001 | |
| | | | | | | W002 | |
| | | | | | | W00? | |
| | | | | P02 | | W001 | |
| | | | | | | W002 | |
| | | | | | | W00? | |
| | | | | P03 | | W001 | |
| | | | | | | W002 | |
| | | | | | | W00? | |
| | | 03 | | P01 | | W001 | |
| | | | | | | W002 | |
| | | | | | | W00? | |
| | | | | P02 | | W001 | |
| | | | | | | W002 | |
| | | | | | | W00? | |
| | | | | P03 | | W001 | |
| | | | | | | W002 | |
| | | | | | | W00? | |
| | | 99 | General | P01 | | W001 | |
| | | | | | | W002 | |
| | | | | | | W00? | |
| | | | | P02 | | W001 | |
| | | | | | | W002 | |
| | | | | | | W00? | |
| | | | | P03 | | W001 | |
| | | | | | | W002 | |
| | | | | | | W00? | |

**Figure 11-8. Procedure and Work Instruction Listing**

## CONCLUSION

The following figure exhibits the steps to be taken in documenting the Primary Work Process:

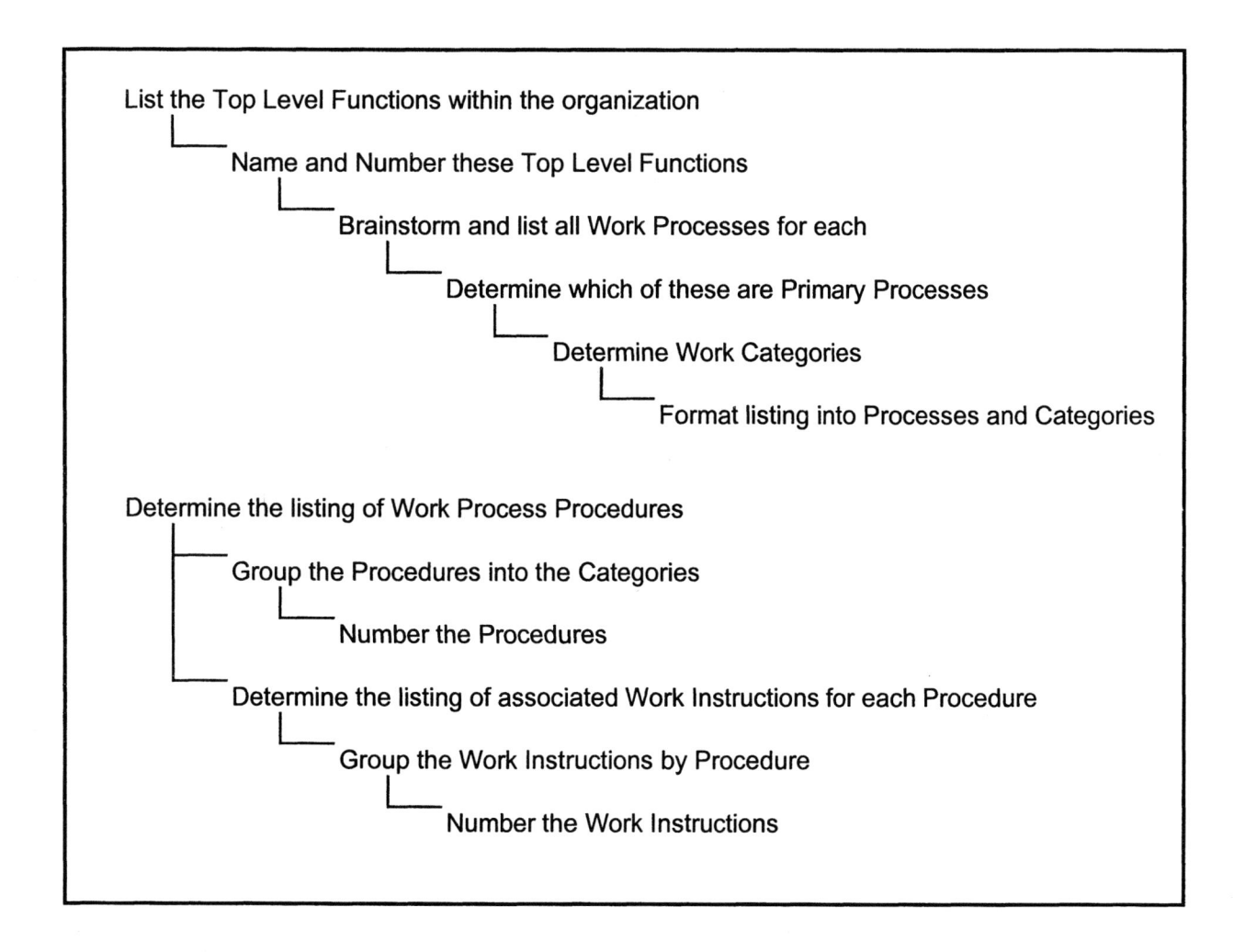

```
List the Top Level Functions within the organization
  └── Name and Number these Top Level Functions
        └── Brainstorm and list all Work Processes for each
              └── Determine which of these are Primary Processes
                    └── Determine Work Categories
                          └── Format listing into Processes and Categories

Determine the listing of Work Process Procedures
  ├── Group the Procedures into the Categories
  │     └── Number the Procedures
  └── Determine the listing of associated Work Instructions for each Procedure
        └── Group the Work Instructions by Procedure
              └── Number the Work Instructions
```

**Figure 11-9. Primary Work Processes Determination**

# Chapter 12

# TRAINING AND KNOWLEDGE REQUIREMENTS

Training and knowledge are two of the factors that control the quality of the output of the work processes (refer to Chapter 3, Primary Work Processes—Controlling Factors). If someone is placed into the work process without the necessary training and knowledge to perform the work, then opportunity for error is introduced into that process. Ensuring that employees have the proper training and knowledge to perform their work properly is a management responsibility.

The next step after determining what the work processes are, as done in Chapter 11, is to determine the necessary training and knowledge requirements for each of them. To do so, one might develop a work form similar to the one shown in Figure 12-1 for each of the work processes requiring procedures and work instructions. Refer also to Paragraph 3.3.1 of Chapter 10.

## TRAINING AND KNOWLEDGE WORKSHEET

The following is a brief description of the various fields and associated terminology of the Training and Knowledge Worksheet.

| | |
|---|---|
| **Procedure Title:** | The proposed title of the procedure to be developed. |
| **Applicability:** | The work functions for which this procedure will be applicable. |
| **Purpose:** | The stated purpose of this procedure. |
| **Procedure Outline:** | A "high level" listing of the primary steps, components, and deliverables associated with this procedure. |

**Related Procedure:** Listing of any related procedure that may be affected or referenced by this proposed procedure.

**Related Work Instruction:** Listing of any related work instruction that may be affected or referenced by this proposed procedure.

| Date: | Applicability: |
|---|---|
| Division/Region/Office/Department: | |
| Procedure/Process Instruction Title: | Purpose: |
| Knowledge Requirements: | |
| | Procedure Outline (primary steps, components, deliverables) |
| Training Requirements: | |
| | Related Procedure(s): |
| | Related Work Instruction(s): |
| Development of Procedures and Work Instructions, QSZ-999-99-P07 | Attachment A - Revision 0 — Page 1 of 1 |

**Figure 12-1. Training and Knowledge Determination Worksheet**

**Knowledge Requirements:** Listing/description of the "baseline" knowledge required by those performing the work required by this procedure. Knowledge includes educational background requirements.

**Training Requirements:** Listing/description of the necessary training requirements (completed or to be completed) for those performing the work required by this procedure.

## Training and Assessment

Consideration needs to be given to the assessment of training needs and the preparation of training courses and training materials necessary to ensure that employees are provided with the skills required for their employment.

In many companies, needs assessment determines the basis for the entire training program. Training needs assessment defines the process for comparing the existing employee skills with the skills currently required and projected to be required in the future. It takes into account employee turnover, budgetary constraints, technological developments, competing market trends, relevant legislation, and the labor market.

## Training Plan

A written Training Plan for each office/department should be maintained as a working document and include the results of the Training Needs Assessment. The Training Plan should consider new hire training, on-the-job training, self-administered training, and formal group training provided by both internal and external resources.

## On-the-Job Training

On-the-job training is generally preferred when the number of trainees in any one location is small, when a physical skill is involved, and when the material is difficult to communicate except by personal demonstration and participation. The persons providing on-the-job training shall have the technical expertise in the skills being taught. The instruction process should consist of, as a minimum:

- Explaining what is to be learned
- Demonstrating how the task is to be performed
- Requiring the trainee to perform the task
- Providing feedback on the trainee's performance
- Follow-up

## Group Training

Group training should be performed in the following cases:

- When other than a very small number of employees is involved
- When the purpose is to provide technical information, solve problems, or explain a method or procedure
- When input from several sources including the trainee may be required
- When the information or skills do not have to be demonstrated at the trainee's workplace

## Self-Administered Training

Self-administered training should be considered for subjects suitable and where extensive hands-on experience is not required. Printed and/or audio-visual materials are possibilities. Some objective measure of performance provided by the trainee is needed to demonstrate progress or proficiency in the targeted areas. Work Instructions can also be used for self-administered training in specific work processes with progress monitored by supervisory personnel.

## Budget Provisions for Training

Each manager needs to make suitable provisions in the budget for anticipated department training needs.

## Completion of Training Courses

Records need to be maintained and retained of the successful completion of any training course with the respective employee's personnel record updated. If available, the training database of employee vs. training taken should also be updated.

## Specific Process Training

When a Quality System Procedure or Work Instruction contains training requirements for specific work, each employee carrying out the process must be trained in accordance with those stated requirements and it must be documented.

Consideration should be given to the documentation of personnel versus the processes for which they are qualified in, perhaps, a training database, accessible by all managers making assignments of work.

Additional consideration should be given to developing a specific Quality System procedure for "Training and Development," which addresses all of the issues stated above as well as a procedure or work instruction for "Process Training Certification."

## Process Training Certification

Prior to any employee being qualified to carry out any process on an independent basis, the employee needs to be trained in accordance with the specific requirements of the Procedure/Work Instruction for the process being carried out. This process is usually contained in a Quality System Work Instruction or procedure en titled, "Process Training Certification." An example of the scope of such a document would be:

*This Work Instruction provides information on how training records are completed and what is needed to qualify or decertify an employee for work delineated in a Work Instruction or Procedure, as applicable.*

## CONCLUSION

The training of those who are in the direct process related to the delivery of the product or service to the customer is essential in order to reduce the possibility of problems affecting the quality of that product or service.

Training is a process-controlling factor that is the responsibility of management. The placing of someone in a process without the proper training invites quality problems. Each procedure or work instruction needs to state what the training and knowledge requirements are and each person performing those processes must be trained, and perhaps certified, in the respective process. Doing so will greatly improve consistency of the output and reduce nonconformances.

Quality System Procedures dealing with training need to be prepared. A company-wide training approach or plan needs to be in operation, one that considers feedback and is continually being improved. Individual training needs assessments are generally the beginning of a plan, followed by the plan, budget for implementing the plan, and, of utmost importance, the implementation and tracking of the training.

# Chapter 13

# POSITION DESCRIPTION MANUAL

---

The Position Description Manual is intended to provide personnel with a basic and comprehensive understanding of the job positions and reporting relationships within the company. The contents should include an introduction, a distribution listing, a job title matrix, and position descriptions for each position within the company.

The Position Description Manual is normally a controlled document issued from the Human Resource Department.

The Position Description Manual may be configured into meaningful sections or separate manuals, with consideration given for Support Staff, Professional Staff, and Operating Personnel. Any breakdown of personnel categories that make sense should be utilized.

## DESIGN OF POSITION DESCRIPTIONS

The position descriptions contained in the Position Description Manual(s) should be designed to meet the basic requirements of the company. Outlined in each are the general requirements, skills, and job knowledge needed for each position. Typical contents of a position description include:

**Title Block:** The title block would only be necessary if issued as a controlled document and would contain the Name of the Position, Revision Number, Date Effective, Position Description Number, Preparer's Name, Approver's Name, and Page Number.

**Title:** The title associated with the position

**Grade:** The salary grade(s) associated with the position

**General Summary:** A brief summary of the position

**Principal Duties and Responsibilities:** A listing of such by type

**Knowledge, Skills and Abilities Required:** A listing of these, including educational requirements and skills

**Working Conditions:** A description of the working environment

**Disclaimer Clause:** A disclaimer clause such as stated here might be a consideration:

*This position description is not intended, and should not be construed, to be an all inclusive list of responsibilities, skills, efforts, or working conditions associated with the job of the incumbent. It is intended to be an accurate reflection of the principal job elements for making a fair decision regarding the pay structure of the job.*

**Reporting Relationships:** A description of the reporting structure of the position

**Revision History:** If issued as a controlled document, this is a description of the revisions made to the respective position description.

An example of a Position Description is shown below.

## Title Matrix

The Title Matrix contained in the Position Description Manual is simply a matrix of grades/levels (not necessarily salary grades or levels) that show all position titles within each grade/level across the entire company. One advantage of having a Title Matrix is to ensure a visible consistency of position titles versus the actual grade/level and associated responsibilities. An example of a Title Matrix is shown in Figure 13-2.

| QUALITY MANAGEMENT | | | |
|---|---|---|---|
| POSITION DESCRIPTION | Revision Number: 1 | Date Effective: 1 April 1997 | Number ACZ-PD-014 |
| Total Quality Management | Prepared by: | Approved by: | Page 1 of 2 |

**Title:** Director of Total Quality Management

*General Summary*

Responsible for the promotion, support, and assurance of continuous improvement in the quality of the management process and the products of the work processes. The purpose is to continuously improve the basic work processes to achieve total customer satisfaction and improve business results by eliminating wasted and non-value added activities.

The role of the Director of Total Quality Management is one of a pro-active catalyst working in partnership with the Senior Management Team.

**Principal Duties and Responsibilities**

1. Planning and support to the Senior Management Team in the implementation of the Total Quality Management Strategy throughout the company.

2. To act as quality specialist to the Senior Management Team by pro-actively facilitating the integration of quality into the planning, marketing, finance, engineering, operations, and all other business processes.

3. To support the Management Team in applying quality and cycle time tools to drive work improvements in achieving annual objectives and longer-term goals.

4. To support management in defining and implementing effective means for measuring and managing customer satisfaction, quality, and cycle time improvement.

5. To be personally responsible to support senior management in upgrading their knowledge and skills in Total Quality Management (TQM).

**Figure 13-1. Position Description Example**

**Knowledge, Skills, and Abilities Required**

1. A bachelor's degree in a non-liberal arts field.

2. Practical experience relating to quality, the marine industry, program management, and supervision.

3. Formal training in a recognized Quality Management System.

**Disclaimer Clause**

This position description is not intended, and should not be construed, to be an all inclusive list of responsibilities, skills, efforts, or working conditions associated with the job of the incumbent. It is intended to be an accurate reflection of the principal job elements essential for making a fair decision regarding the pay structure of the job.

**Working Conditions**

Work will normally be performed in an air-conditioned office environment with a comfortable setting. May encounter stressful situations prevalent in a senior management position. Will travel frequently and will entertain clients and business associates as deemed appropriate.

**Reporting Relationships**

Reports directly to the Chairman and Chief Executive Officer.

*Revision History*

| Revision Number | Revision Summary | Effective Date |
|---|---|---|
| 0 | Initial Issue | 2 April 1993 |
| 1 | Revised position description manual | 1 April 1996 |

Figure 13-1. Position Description Example—*Continued*

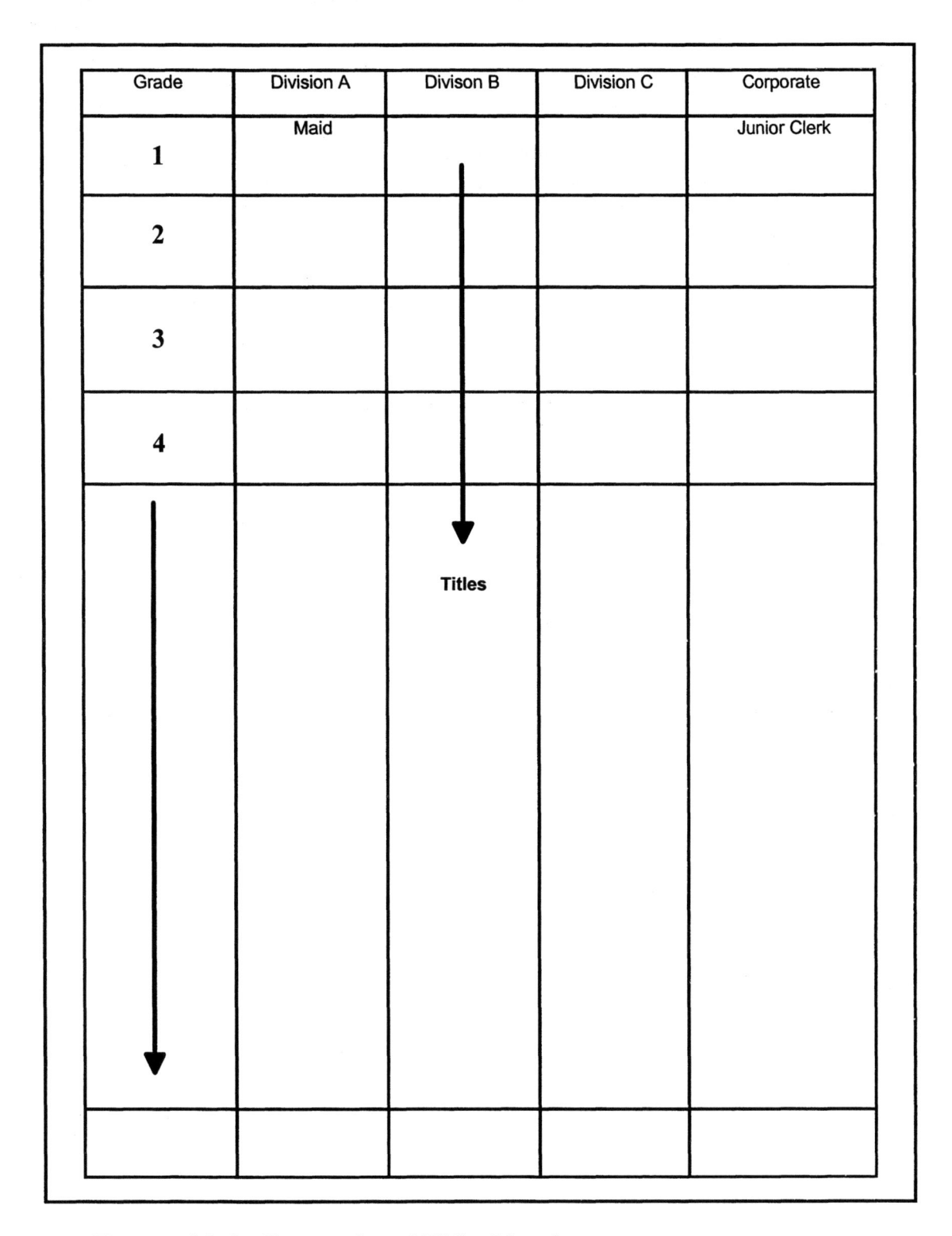

| Grade | Division A | Divison B | Division C | Corporate |
|---|---|---|---|---|
| 1 | Maid | | | Junior Clerk |
| 2 | | | | |
| 3 | | | | |
| 4 | | ↓ Titles | | |
| ↓ | | | | |

**Figure 13-2. Example of Title Matrix**

## ORGANIZATION CHARTS MANUAL

The Organization Charts Manual is normally a company confidential reference document rather than a controlled document. The need for an organization charts manual is highly dependent upon the size and structure of the company, as are its contents.

Traditional organizational charts and matrix cross-functional charts should be considered for inclusion. The Organization Charts Manual should be updated at least annually or when any significant changes occur.

Not all companies are of sufficient size to need an Organization Charts Manual. Even though this may be the case, organization charts in some configuration are still necessary and must be kept reasonably up-to-date.

Organization charts should be dated and signed with a distribution listing maintained to ensure any updates are sent to the same people/locations who received the original issue.

Local organization charts associated with departments and/or small offices are not usually included in the organization charts manual. Instead, they are maintained on a local basis. These local organization charts might also include the associated delegation of authority by each person's name on the chart.

Position
Persons name (A,B,....)

A = Signature authority
B = Designates "in-charge" when manager not in office

## DELEGATION OF AUTHORITY MANUAL

The Delegation of Authority Manual is also dependent upon the company size and structure relative to its existence. It is usually considered to be a controlled document with a defined format and controlled distribution. Companies that do not have an actual manual still need some documented means to cover the delegation of authority within the company.

An Introduction and a Table of Contents should be considered in the formatting of the manual.

## Introduction Section

The Introduction should be relatively short—no more than one or two pages—and should include the following:

**Objective/Scope:** A single paragraph describing the objective and scope of the Delegation of Authority Manual.

**Related Guidance:** Brief sentence length statements describing any related documents to the manual.

*Applied Example:*

*This Policy Statement represents only one of several media that define the management environment.*

- *Position descriptions set forth a general summary, principal duties and responsibilities, and other characteristics of each management position.*
- *Policies, organized by subject, define principles or "rules for action" governing the manner in which recurring types of situations in the conduct of business affairs are expected to be handled.*
- *Procedures and Work Instructions include the following components:*

## Contents Section

The Table of Contents should consider the following:

I. **Introduction:** To be structured as stated above.

II. **Organizational Overview**: Is usually one to three pages in length and describes, in summary form, the key features of the company's organization.

III. **The Concept of Delegation**: Reviews principles underlying the delegation of responsibility and authority and the corresponding accountability for performance and illustrates their application. This review should only be one to three pages in length.

**IV. Specific Delegations of Authority**: Delineates, by type of business transaction or decision, the level of authority delegated to the operating functions, as well as to executives and staff. The format may be in the form of matrices or written.

## Conclusion

Not all companies are large enough to need specific manuals for position descriptions, organization, and delegation of authority. However, each company needs these documents in some useable form.

# Chapter 14

# WORK PROCESS PROCEDURES, WORK INSTRUCTIONS, AND CHECK SHEETS— PREPARATION AND ASSIGNMENT

## WORK PROCESS PROCEDURES

The Quality System Manual has been written, the Quality System Procedures have either been completed or are well on their way, the procedures and associated work instructions have been listed and are grouped into categories and processes and have been numbered. Now it is time to begin the task of preparing the individual procedures, work instructions, and associated check sheets for the Primary Work Processes.

The key to success in accomplishing this task in the most expeditious and cost-effective manner is to spend the time to prepare a thought-out plan before launching the task. The steps of the planning process for this element of implementation should include:

1. Designate a team or department or individual within the organization to handle the logistics associated with assignment and tracking of this effort. This assigned entity should also be the designee for collecting and reviewing the completed documents for form, fit, and function.

2. Prepare a matrix of the procedures and work instructions to be done by extending the matrices developed in Chapter 10 for determining the listings. Reference Figure 14-2 and Figure 14-3.

3. Prepare a simple code to designate the status of each procedure and work instruction.

4. Prepare a sample of a typical procedure and a typical work instruction, which includes a checklist and a Training and Knowledge Worksheet. This sample should actually be one of the needed procedures and work instructions.

5. Determine who is best qualified to write each procedure and each work instruction within the entire organization. If possible, only one task should be

assigned to an individual. Place the names of the assignees on the matrix to be used for tracking the development process.

6. Prepare a software template on disk—one for the preparation of a procedure and one for the preparation of a work instruction. In this way, the developer only needs to complete the text and it can be easily edited and configured into the final form.

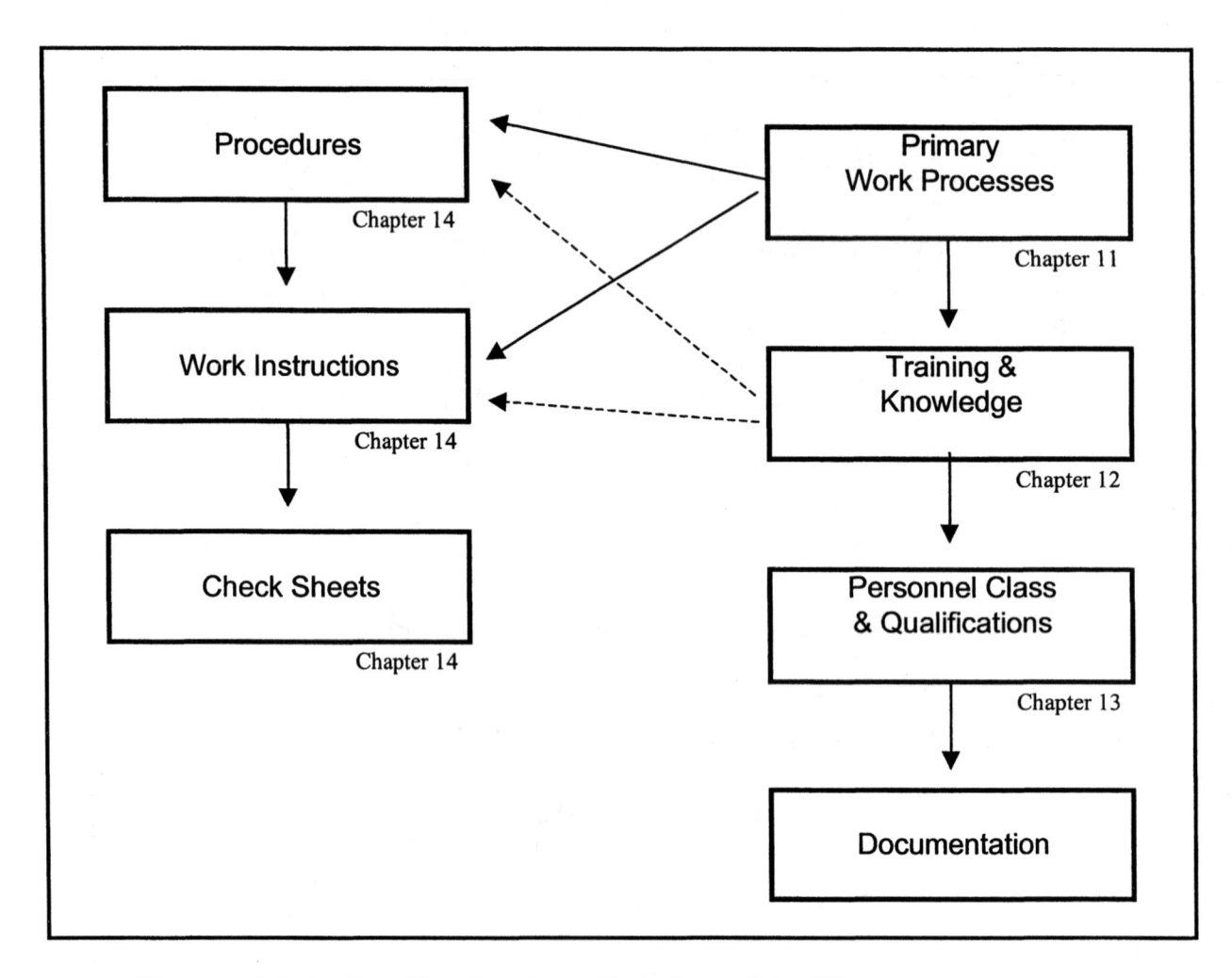

**Figure 14-1. Quality System Relationship Diagram**

# Work Process Procedures, Work Instructions, and Check Sheets—Preparation and Assignment / 169

| Level 1 | | Level 2 | | Level 3 | | | | | | |
|---|---|---|---|---|---|---|---|---|---|---|
| Process | | Categories | | Procedure | | | | | | |
| Number | Name | Number | Name | Number | Name | Procedure Number | Development Responsibility | Preparation Status | Review Status | Issue Status | Training Status |
| 001 | Engineering | 01 | There may be several Categories for each Process | P01 | There may be several Procedures for each Category (minimum of 1) | EWZ-001-01-P01 | Am Division | Complete | Under Review (DTQ) | Pending Review | To be completed |
| | | | | | | EWZ-001-01-P02 | Pac Division | Est. 9/1/96 | | | |
| | | | | P05 | | Example of completed Procedure Tracking Matrix | | | | | |
| | | 02 | | P01 | | | | | | | |
| 002 | Manufacturing | 01 | | P01 | | | | | | | |

- Complete Procedure Number
- Function/Person responsible for development of Procedure
- Development Status of the Procedure
- Procedure Technical & Completeness Review Status
- Issuance Status of the completed Procedure
- Status of Training of Personnel in the Procedure Contents

- Procedures are grouped together with other procedures into Categories of Processes
- Categories are grouped together with other categories that are associated with the same Process

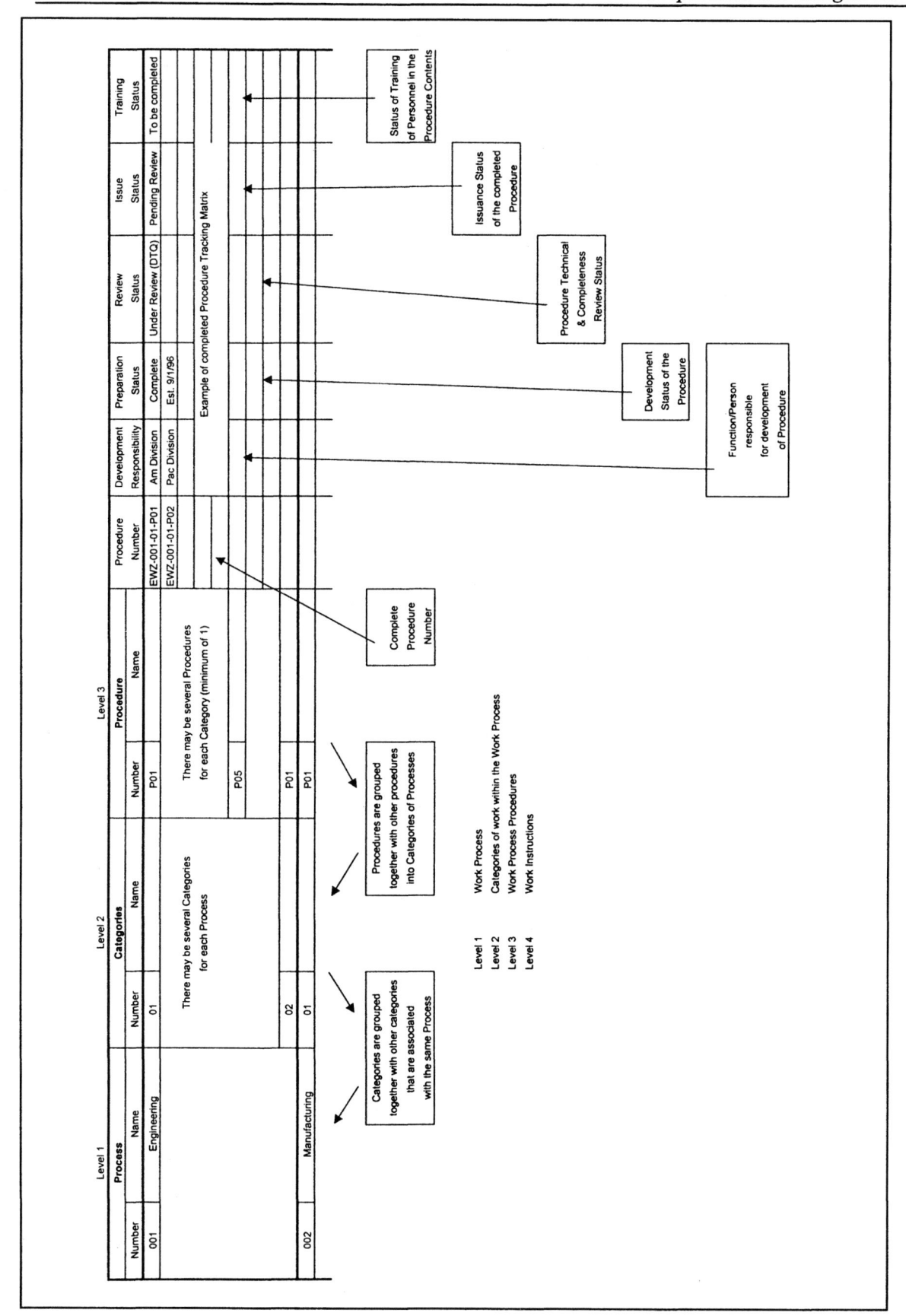

Level 1    Work Process
Level 2    Categories of work within the Work Process
Level 3    Work Process Procedures
Level 4    Work Instructions

**Figure 14-2. Assignment and Tracking Matrix for Operating Procedure Development**

170 / Implementing an ISO 9000-Based Quality System

| Level 3 Procedures || Level 4 |||||||
|---|---|---|---|---|---|---|---|
| | | Work Instruction | Work Instruction Number | Development Responsibility | Preparation Status | Review Status | Issue Status | Training Status |
| Number | Name | Name | Number | | | | | |
| P01 | | | | Am Division | Complete | Under Review (DTQ) | Pending Review | To be completed |
| | | | | Pac Division | Est. 9/1/96 | | | |
| P02 | | | | | | | | |

Example of completed Work Instruction Tracking Matrix

- Procedure Name
- Work Instruction Name
- Number assigned to each Work Instruction
- Function/Person responsible for development of Work Instruction
- Development Status
- Work Instruction Technical & Completeness Review Status
- Issuance Status of the completed Work Instruction
- Status of Training of Personnel in the Work Instruction Contents

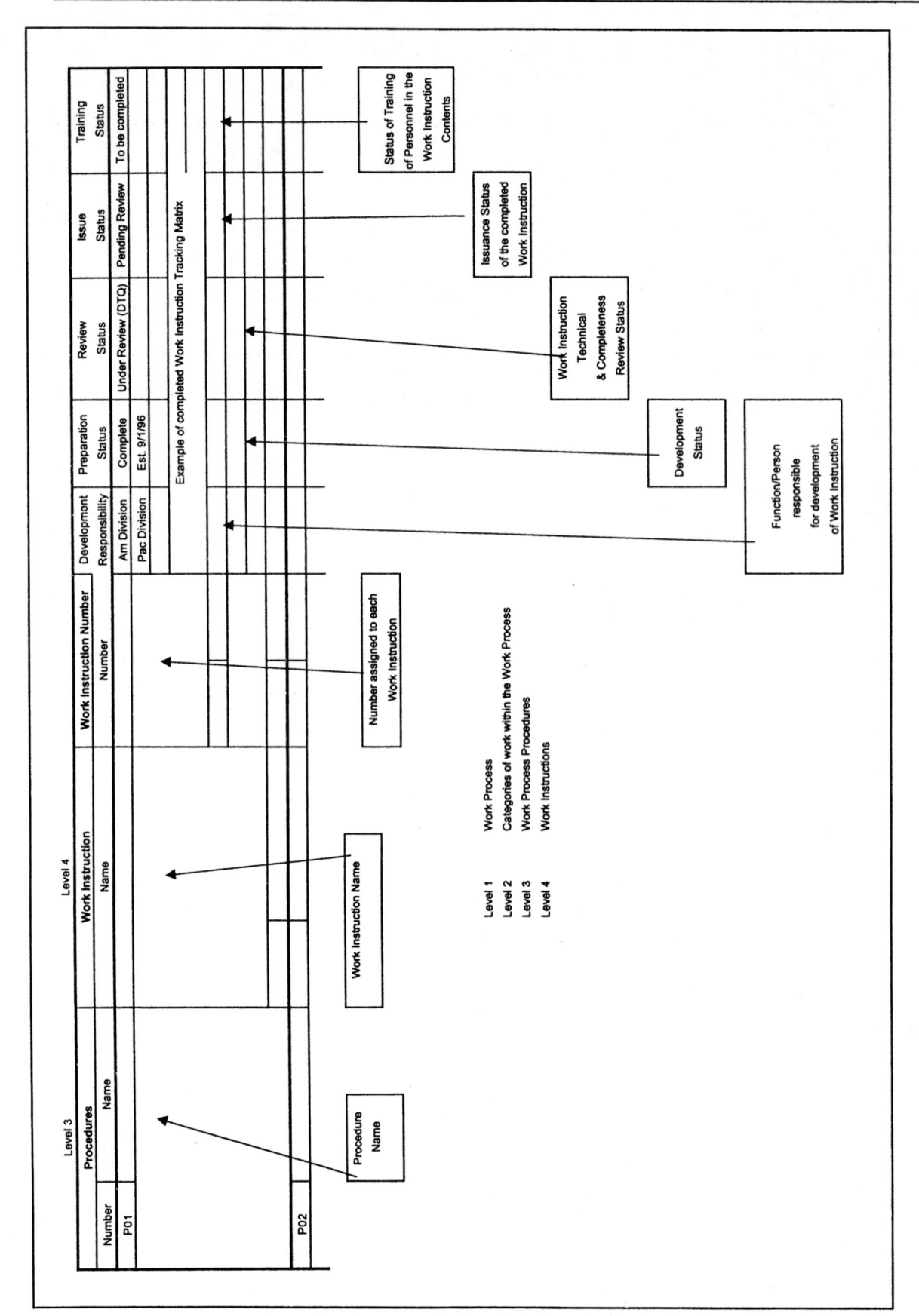

Level 1 — Work Process
Level 2 — Categories of work within the Work Process
Level 3 — Work Process Procedures
Level 4 — Work Instructions

**Figure 14-3. Assignment and Tracking Matrix for Work Instruction Development**

7. Prepare a packet for each developer that includes:

- Task assignment description (which procedure or work instruction to develop)
- Quality System Procedure (development of a Quality System Procedure or Work Instruction document)
- Sample Quality System Procedure or Work Instruction to be used as a guide
- Copy of the disk with the format pre-entered
- Where to call for help

8. Forward the packet to the developer. Be sure and gain agreement with the person's supervisor.

9. Monitor and track progress on the Tracking Matrix Chart.

The average time to develop a Quality System Procedure or Work Instruction is about two hours. If it takes longer, then too much detail is being generated.

The tendency is to make the Quality System Procedures or Work Instructions more complex than necessary. They should be kept simple, using flow charts where practical. The objective is to simply write down what you do, not what you would like to do. Keep it simple and make it more complex later if necessary. This approach is much easier than simplifying later.

Provide a "sanity" check for each completed document—an expert within the company in the respective technical field should be able to do this. Also, provide a format check to ensure the adherence to the Quality System Procedure requirements and to ensure documentation completeness. The assigned entity of Item 1 above can ensure this is accomplished.

## CHECK SHEETS

In conjunction with the development of Quality System Procedures or Work Instructions, one needs to consider the additional need for a Check Sheet. This guidance comes from another Quality System Procedure that needs to be considered, titled "Check Sheets." Such a procedure provides guidelines for when to use check sheets and addresses specific requirements when they are used.

## Definition of Check Sheets

Check Sheets are an assurance tool forming part of a work process control which

1. Assures all work processes are performed.

2. Provides evidence that all listed steps of a work process have been performed.

3. Supports consistent service delivery regardless of where or by whom the work process is performed.

## Check Sheets—General

Quality System Procedures have the purpose of stating the overall requirements of the process, but not how to do the process or how it is carried out. In addition, one Procedure may cover several work processes. Therefore, Procedures are not an alternate to the use of Check Sheets in carrying out of work.

Work Instructions, on the other hand, describe how the work is done in sufficient detail that would allow one to follow them and accomplish the work. As a result, the process instruction is usually too detailed for the experienced practitioner to need to use each time the process is carried out. In normal circumstances, the Work Instruction is used for training and certification of the practitioner to the process and for referral should the need arise during the performance of the associated work. Work Instructions are not usually used as Check Sheets, but could be.

Check Sheets are usually much more of a simplified document than a Work Instruction and are used as a reminder or memory jogger to the practitioner to ensure that he/she does not forget or bypass any steps that are important to the integrity of the associated process and it's being done right. Check Sheets also serve to ensure that the practitioner knows where he/she is when interruptions affect the work effort.

Check Sheets also serve as the document of record for verification that one is doing that which is written down in the associated work instruction or procedure. Finally, Check Sheets help to ensure that multiple practitioners are consistent in how they do their work, giving the client a consistent product.

Check Sheets should and must be simpler than Work Instructions, include only those items necessary to ensure that all pertinent steps that affect the integrity of the process output are covered and must take virtually no additional time to use as tracking tool/document.

## Criteria for the Use of Check Sheets

The use of a Check Sheet must be an evaluated decision, one that is challenged as to its value relative to the quality of the process output. The only question that must be asked relative to Check Sheets is, "How does one assure themselves and others that they have covered all of the key steps of the process and what is the visible evidence of such?" If one can adequately answer this question and show it with a simplified Check Sheet or none at all, then one meets the requirements.

The determination as to the requirement of a Check Sheet is by the process owner/manager based on informed judgments as to relative risks associated with doing (or not doing) the process consistently and the degree of confidence the manager requires to ensure the quality of the work performed.

## Purpose of Check Sheets

The purpose of Check Sheets is to assure that certain steps are carried out in a process. The completed Check Sheets are evidence that these steps were carried out and as such are considered quality records.

## Basis for Determining the Inclusion of a Check Sheet

Is a Check Sheet needed to ensure that the process is being carried out the same way, or consistently in all locations?

Is the Check Sheet needed to ensure that all critical items are checked prior to dispatch to the client?

Will the process or service quality suffer if a Check Sheet is not used?

## PREPARATION AND ASSIGNMENT

The preparation, assignment, and tracking progress until completion is the next step in the Quality System Implementation Process. The assigned person should be technically qualified to prepare the document and provided with the guidance examples and requirements to minimize variation between those preparing documents. Check Sheets should also be considered as to their need. Accountability and schedules should be established with monthly progress reports provided to management.

One should also keep in mind that all of the documents do not need to be completed before implementation, as they can be done in groupings. However, the entire set of documents that are envisioned to be needed should be planned and scheduled.

# Chapter 15

# CONTROLLED DOCUMENT ISSUANCE

ISO 9004-2 describes Documentation Control in the following manner:

*All documentation should be legible, dated (including revision dates), clear, readily identified, and carry authorization status.*

*Methods should be established to control the issue, distribution, and revision of documents. The methods should ensure that documents are:*

- *approved by authorized personnel;*
- *released and made available in the areas where the information is needed;*
- *understood and acceptable to user;*
- *removed when obsolete.*

The terminology generally accepted for documents meeting the above requirement is "controlled document," which carries the definition of: any document issued to a particular department or individual that is uniquely identified as a controlled document and is traceable for recall.

It is easy to get carried away in the classification of documents as *controlled*, even though it is not necessary for them to be so classified. In general, only those documents for which failure to use the latest revision will directly affect the end product or service need be classified as controlled documents.

Controlled documents normally include Work Process Procedures, Work Instructions, Quality System Manuals, Quality System Procedures, Technical Software lists, and any other documents that might be utilized in the production of product or service, including forms. In addition, management might decide to include other documents as controlled documents as a method of tracking and ensuring that the latest revisions are being utilized. Such documents might include Personnel Position Descriptions, Delegation of Authority Manual, Safety Manual, etc.

*176 / Implementing an ISO 9000-Based Quality System*

Being a controlled document implies that the document needs to be dated, numbered, signed, and the revision indicated (by date or number). There must also be a listing of who has received each specific document and a master listing of controlled documents showing the latest revision levels. A number of companies also require a signed acknowledgment of receipt of a controlled document and verified destruction of the outdated document.

A typical controlled document distribution list might look like that shown in Figure 15-1 and Figure 15-2. A typical master listing of controlled documents might look like that shown in Figure 15-3.

| Controlled Document Matrix 1 July 1996 | Location | Control Copy Number | Master List (Vol. 0) | Quality System Manual (Vol. 1) | Quality System Procedures & PIs (Vol. 2) | Worldwide Procedures & PIs (Vol. 3) | IS General Procedures & PIs (Vol. 3s) | IS Engineering Procedures & PIs (Vol. 4s) | IS Inspection/Consulting Procedures & PIs (Vol. 5s) | MS All Procedures & PIs (Vol. 4m) | Delegation of Authority Manual | Position Descriptions |
|---|---|---|---|---|---|---|---|---|---|---|---|---|
| Manager of Accounting | Singapore | 001 | X | X | X | X | X |  |  |  | X | X |
| Operations Manager | New York, NY | 026 | X | X | X | X | X | X | X | X | X | X |
| Engineering Manager | Houston, TX | 037 |  |  |  |  |  |  |  |  | X |  |
|  |  | 688 | X | X | X | X | X |  | X |  | X | X |
|  |  | 038 | X | X | X | X | X |  | X | X | X | X |
|  |  | 795 | X | X | X | X | X | X | X | X | X | X |
|  |  | 939 | X | X | X | X | X | X | X |  | X | X |
|  |  | 004 | X | X | X | X | X |  |  |  | X | X |
|  |  | 010 | X | X | X | X | X | X | X | X | X | X |
| Name of Office or Department or Function |  | 443 | X | X | X | X | X | X | X |  | X | X |
|  |  | 994 | X | X | X | X | X |  | X |  | X | X |
|  |  | 072 | X | X | X | X | X |  | X |  | X | X |
|  |  | 558 | X | X | X | X | X | X | X | X | X | X |
|  |  | 973 | X | X | X | X | X |  |  | X | X | X |
|  |  | 016 | X | X | X | X | X |  |  |  |  |  |
|  |  | 427 | X | X | X | X | X |  | X | X | X | X |
|  |  | 637 | X | X | X | X | X |  |  |  | X | X |
|  |  | 401 | X | X | X | X | X |  | X | X | X | X |
|  |  | 071 | X | X | X | X | X |  | X | X | X | X |
|  |  | 979 | X | X | X | X | X |  | X | X | X | X |
|  |  | 066 | X | X | X | X | X |  |  |  | X | X |
|  |  | 428 | X | X | X | X | X |  |  |  | X | X |
|  |  | 007 | X | X | X | X | X |  |  |  | X | X |
|  |  | 079 | X | X | X | X | X |  |  |  | X | X |
|  |  | 514 | X | X | X | X | X |  |  |  | X | X |
|  |  | 683 | X | X | X | X | X | X | X | X |  |  |
|  |  | 656 | X | X | X | X | X | X | X |  | X | X |

**Figure 15-1. A Typical Controlled Document Distribution Matrix for Offices/Departments/Functions**

Controlled Document Issuance / 177

| Personnel Controlled Document Distribution Matrix 1 July 1996 | | | Control Copy Number | Master List (Vol. 0) | Quality System Manual (Vol. 1) | Quality System Procedures & PIs (Vol. 2) | Worldwide Procedures & PIs (Vol. 3) | IS General Procedures & PIs (Vol. 3s) | IS Engineering Procedures & PIs (Vol. 4s) | IS Inspection/Consulting Procedures & PIs (Vol. 5s) | MS All Procedures & PIs (Vol. 4m) | Delegation of Authority Manual | Position Descriptions |
|---|---|---|---|---|---|---|---|---|---|---|---|---|---|
| | | Houston | 001 | X | X | X | X | X | | | | X | X |
| | | Singapore | 026 | X | X | X | X | X | X | X | X | X | X |
| | | DuBai | 037 | | | | | | | | | X | |
| | | | 688 | X | X | X | X | X | | X | | X | X |
| | | | 038 | X | X | X | X | X | | X | X | X | X |
| | | | 795 | X | X | X | X | X | X | X | X | X | X |
| | | | 939 | X | X | X | X | X | X | X | | X | X |
| | | | 004 | X | X | X | X | X | | | | X | X |
| Name of Person and Functional Title | | | 010 | X | X | X | X | X | X | X | X | X | X |
| | | | 443 | X | X | X | X | X | X | X | | X | X |
| | | | 994 | X | X | X | X | X | | X | | X | X |
| | | | 072 | X | X | X | X | X | | X | | X | X |
| | | | 558 | X | X | X | X | X | X | X | X | X | X |
| | | | 973 | X | X | X | X | X | | | X | X | X |
| | | | 016 | X | X | X | X | X | | | | | |
| | Location | | 427 | X | X | X | X | X | | X | X | X | X |
| | | | 637 | X | X | X | X | X | | | | X | X |
| | | | 401 | X | X | X | X | X | | X | X | X | X |
| | | | 071 | X | X | X | X | X | | X | X | X | X |
| | | | 979 | X | X | X | X | X | | X | X | X | X |
| | | | 066 | X | X | X | X | X | | | | X | X |
| | | | 428 | X | X | X | X | X | | | | X | X |
| | | | 007 | X | X | X | X | X | | | | X | X |
| | | | 079 | X | X | X | X | X | | | | X | X |
| | | | 514 | X | X | X | X | X | | | | X | X |
| | | | 683 | X | X | X | X | X | X | X | X | | |
| | | | 656 | X | X | X | X | X | X | X | | X | X |

**Figure 15-2. A Typical Controlled Document Distribution Matrix for Individuals**

| Quality System Procedure and Work Instruction Master List | Revision Number: 17 | Date Effective: 1 Sept. 96 | Section Number: 27 |
|---|---|---|---|
| Process: 999 - Controlling Category: 99 - Common | Prepared By: TCD | Approved by: | Page: 1 of 1 |

| Quality System Procedure/Work Instruction Name | Controlled Document Number | Revision Number | Revision Date | Volume Number |
|---|---|---|---|---|
| Storage & Retention of Controlled Documents & Quality Records | QSZ-999-99-P01 | 8 | | 2 |
| Document Control | QSZ-999-99-P02 | 9 | | 2 |
| Numbering & Indexing | QSZ-999-99-P03 | 7 | | 2 |
| Training & Development | QSZ-999-99-P04 | 8 | | 2 |
| Process Training Certification | QSZ-999-99-P04-W001 | 9 | | 2 |
| Corrective and Preventive Action | QSZ-999-99-P05 | 6 | | 2 |
| Internal Quality Audits | QSZ-999-99-P06 | 9 | | 2 |
| Internal Auditor Certification | QSZ-999-99-P06-W001 | 7 | | 2 |
| Development of Procedures & Work Instructions | QSZ-999-99-P07 | 4 | | 2 |
| Management Review | QSZ-999-99-P09 | 12 | | 2 |
| Non-conformance Reporting | QSZ-999-99-P15 | 10 | | 2 |
| Confidentiality | QSZ-999-99-P20 | 11 | | 2 |
| Client Feedback | QSZ-999-99-P22 | 8 | | 2 |
| Correspondence Control | QSZ-999-99-P23 | 9 | | 2 |
| File Management & Retention | QSZ-999-99-P25 | 5 | | 2 |
| Check Sheets | QSZ-999-99-P26 | 6 | | 2 |
| Supplier Assessment & Control | QSZ-999-99-P27 | 7 | | 2 |
| New Service Development | QSZ-999-99-P30 | 4 | | 2 |

**Figure 15-3. Typical Master Listing of Controlled Documents**

In acknowledgment of a controlled document one may use a bar coding and scanning approach or a signed and returned acknowledgment or any other suitable method such as e-mail. An example of each approach is shown in Figure 15-4 and Figure 15-5.

| Company Name | | | | |
|---|---|---|---|---|

**Controlled Document Transmittal Record**

Attached are controlled copies of approved documents. Please include these in your records and discard superseded copies. Please return one signed copy of this transmittal record to the undersigned within six weeks of receipt.

Date: _____   Initial Transmittal: _____   Revision Transmittal: _____

ISSUED TO:

Address:

Control Copy:

| Document Name | Document Number | Section Number | Revision Number | Revision Date |
|---|---|---|---|---|
|  |  |  |  |  |
|  |  |  |  |  |
|  |  |  |  |  |

I have received and filed these documents, and will thoroughly familiarize myself with their content before doing the work they govern:

_____
Document Recipient's Signature

_____
Date of Acknowledgment

Issuer of Document:

Name: _____
Title: _____
Address: _____
_____
_____

Document Control, QSZ-999-99-P02      Attachment A - Revision 1      Page 1 of 1

**Figure 15-4. Signed and Returned Acknowledgment—Applied Example**

180 / Implementing an ISO 9000-Based Quality System

---

**CONTROLLED DOCUMENT ACKNOWLEDGMENT CARD**

Enclosed are documents listed in the enclosed packing sheet. Retain these documents. Discard superseded copies. Sign and return this card within 6 weeks of receipt.

Recipient: D.P. Unger, Principal Engineer
Control Copy No.: 016
Issue Date: 18/01/87
Document Type & Sequence No.: 00-01
Bar Code

I have received and filed these documents, and will thoroughly familiarize myself with their content before doing the work they govern:

Sincerely,
*Signature*

_____
Signature/Date

Document Types:

| | |
|---|---|
| 00 | Master List |
| 01 | Quality System Manual |
| 02 | Quality System Procedures and Work Instructions |
| 03 | Worldwide Coordinated Procedures and Work Instructions |
| 04 | Engineering Procedures and Work Instructions |
| 05 | Survey Procedures and Work Instructions |
| 06 | Position Description Manual |
| 07 | Human Resources Procedures and Work Instructions |
| | .....ETC., ETC. |

[ Applied Example ]

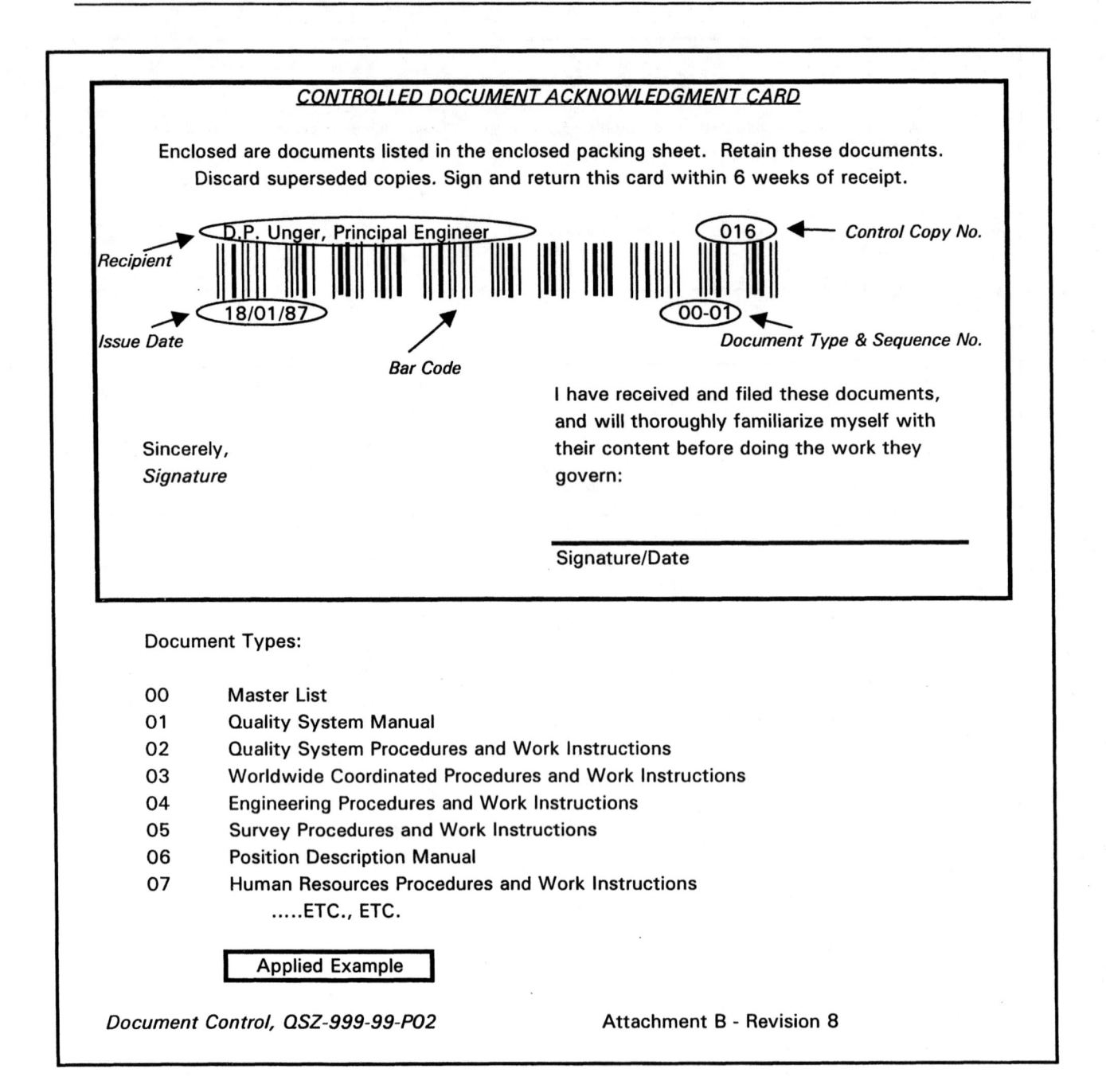

*Document Control, QSZ-999-99-P02*                    *Attachment B - Revision 8*

**Figure 15-5. Controlled Document Acknowledgment Card**

## CONCLUSION

There is no right or wrong way to issue controlled documents so long as a record is maintained of the people who have the documents so that it can be assured that these same people receive the latest revisions to the issued documents. This chapter offers examples of some methods for such tracking and confirmation of receipt of documents. In reality, the simplest method that meets the requirements is best.

# Chapter 16

# QUALITY SYSTEM IMPLEMENTATION INSTRUCTIONS

---

Distribution of the controlled documents has been made to the various offices/departments/individuals. Now comes the task of ensuring that those who receive these documents know what to do with them so that they become "just the way we do our work." This effort can be accomplished in a number of ways, but one of them is *not to let it happen without a planned effort*. The implementation of the system should be planned and executed, with feedback, just like any other step of the process needs to be in order to be successful.

The first task, then, is to determine the implementation plan for each office/country/region/etc. For single location companies, this plan may be for departments.

- Select the key person or task team charged with implementation.
- Determine the implementation method (modules or scattered).
    The *scattered approach* is to have no pre-planned groupings of documents.
    The *modular approach* is to group related documents together.
        A typical module might include:
            QSM Section
            Associated Quality System Procedure
            Supporting Procedure(s)/Documents
- Implement even if other organizations are not yet ready.
- Educate all participants of requirements and processes.
- Follow-up to ensure compliance and to work out any discovered problems.
- Begin with full effort.

## IMPLEMENTATION HANDBOOK

One method of Quality System Implementation is to prepare an ISO 9000 Implementation Instruction Handbook for use by all employees, issued in an uncontrolled manner to each office/department. This Implementation Instruction Handbook would have about a three-month life span, used mostly for training and as a guidance document.

The layout of such a handbook should be modular in nature, combining all of the procedures and work instructions into groups dependent on their respective content and providing explanations for each group.

A typical Quality System Implementation Handbook might include the following sections, with each section containing References, Immediate Actions, and Implementation Instructions. Not all modules will contain Immediate Actions. I have chosen to include all modules, even though it is very simplistic in order to be very clear as to the approach. Each module should be customized for the specific status of the company, some being further along than others in the process. Smaller, single sight companies will not need this handbook.

## Module 1—Quality System Implementation Plan

This module would be a one-page plan of implementation, which describes the deployment methodology.

## Module 2—Quality Policy

### References

- QSM Section 2

### Immediate Actions

1. Assess the Quality Policy and Mission Statement needs for each location and complete order form (attached). *Prepare a simple order form to be completed by those receiving the handbook.*
2. Recommendation is to have a minimum of one set in each geographical office location (not each employee office). For larger offices, such as regional, more copies or larger size copies may be desirable.
3. Order from *(name of individual)*. Coordinate your orders through your CISC.
4. Display when received.

### Implementation Instructions

1. Supervisors and above read QSM Section 2.
2. Managers and above may want to memorize both the Mission Statement and Quality Policy.

3. All employees familiarize themselves with the Quality Policy, Mission Statement, and Company Creed (if there is one).
4. Managers and above understand the General Comments section of the QSM Section 2. Each should know what it means to them and the work processes for which they are responsible.
5. Supervisors and above understand the Quality Policy Implementation section (Page 2 of Section 2 of the QSM). One method would be for each to write it out for group review with their team.

# Module 3—Quality Objectives

## References

- QSM Section 3
- Company Vision Statement (if there is one)

## Immediate Actions

1. Make Vision Statement available for all employees.

## Implementation Instructions

1. Read QSM Section 3 for understanding (supervisors and above).
2. All employees are provided with a copy of the Vision Statement and have read it.
3. Supervisors and above understand Quality Objectives and their part in accomplishing those objectives. One method would be for each to write their part out for review with their respective team.
    - What does each Objective mean to them and their job?
    - How do they measure success of these objectives?

# Module 4—Management Responsibility

## References

- QSM Section 4

### Implementation Instructions

1. CISC/CIT members and all managers read Section 4 of the QSM for understanding.
    - Know who your internal and external customers are.
    - Understand Section 4.1 of the QSM.
2. Management must especially understand Section 4.3 of the QSM.
    - What does this responsibility mean?
    - How is it carried out?

## Module 5—Quality System

### References

- QSM Section 5

### Implementation Instructions

1. Read Section 5 of the QSM (supervisors and above).
2. Gain an understanding of the structure of the company as stated in Section 5, Paragraph 3.1, General (all employees).
3. Understand the relationship of the QSM, Quality System Procedures, and Operating Procedures (supervisors and above).

## Module 6—Management Review

### References

- QSM Section 6
- Quality System Procedure, Management Review, *(Procedure Number)*

### Implementation Instructions

1. Applies to all CISC members and management
2. Establish method of Management Review, either through a Management Review Board or through a continuous Management Review as part of the CISC meetings. The review shall include:
    - Quality System Implementation Status
    - The Corrective and Preventive Action System

- External and Internal Audits
- Customer Feedback (Complaints)
3. Prepare a report in accordance with Section 6, Paragraph 3.4 of the QSM and the Management Review Procedure and submit to the Corporate CISC.
4. The timing for the first of these reviews should be after the initial audit schedule has been accomplished for all offices/departments.

## Module 7—Organization and Responsibilities

### References

- QSM Section 7
- Company Position Description Manual
- Company Organization Manual (charts)

### Implementation Instructions

1. All of management must be thoroughly familiar with the company's organization and responsibilities, including where to find associated organizational and responsibility information.
2. Supervisors and above should thoroughly familiarize themselves with the contents of Section 7 of the QSM and ensure that each is able to respond to auditor questions related to this section.

   Things to know include:
   1. Who is your Management Quality Representative?
   2. What is the responsibility of your function as related to products or services provided?
   3. What is the organizational structure for the organization of which you are a part?
   4. CISC/CIT members should know the head office and regional and district organization structure (as applicable) as well as fully understanding QSM Section 7.

## Module 8—Contract Review

### References

- QSM Section 8

- Listing of all applicable procedures associated with contract review, including as applicable: Review of Requests for Services, Initiation of Projects, and Contract Review
- Listing of other related documents as applicable, such as: Training Documentation System, Letter Writing, Report Issuance, General Reporting and QSM Section 21 (Control and Retention of Quality Records)

## Implementation Instructions

Everyone involved with this specific work process must understand and comply with the referenced documents for their respective part of this process.

1. Determine those individuals/departments involved in contract review and review of requests for service.
2. Provide each with the referenced material to read and study.
3. Implement the process as stated in the referenced documents.
4. Follow-up to ensure compliance and understanding.

# Module 9—Design Control

## References

- QSM Section 9
- Listing of all applicable procedures associated with Design Control, including as applicable: New Service Design, New Product Design, etc.

## Implementation Instructions

Everyone who is involved with this specific work process must understand and comply with the referenced documents for their respective part of Design Control.

1. Determine those individuals/departments involved in Design Control.
2. Provide each with the referenced material to read and study.
3. Implement the process as stated in the referenced documents.
4. Follow-up to ensure compliance and understanding.

## Module 10—Document and Data Control

### References
- QSM Section 10
- Quality System Procedure, Storage and Retention of Controlled Documents and Quality Records, *(Procedure Number)*
- Quality System Procedure, Numbering and Indexing *(Procedure Number)*

### Implementation Instructions

Each office/department must set up the Document and Data Control structure within which everyone in or out of that office must comply. Consideration might be given to a File Management Guide such that the basic file types within each office or department would be the same and carry the same file reference number.

1. Determine who or what group is responsible for "setting up" the Document Control System within each respective office/department.
2. Provide the referenced documents to each responsible individual or group for review and study.
3. Implement the process as stated in the referenced documents.
4. Follow-up to ensure compliance and understanding.

## Module 11—Purchasing and Supplier Control

### References

- QSM Section 11
- Quality System Procedure, Purchasing and Supplier Control *(Procedure Number)*
- Listing of all applicable procedures associated with Purchasing and Supplier Control, including as applicable, those associated with the use of subcontracted labor

### Implementation Instructions

Everyone involved in the process of purchasing and supplier control as well as those involved in the engagement of subcontractors who supply labor must understand and comply with the referenced documents.

1. Determine who is responsible for purchasing and supplier control within each respective office/department.
2. Provide the referenced documents to each of those responsible for review and study.
3. Implement the process as stated in the referenced documents.
4. Follow-up to ensure compliance and understanding.

## Module 12—Control of Customer Supplied Product

### References

- QSM Sections 12 and 20
- Listing of all applicable procedures associated with the Control of Customer Supplied Product

### Implementation Instructions

This module applies to everyone and every location that handles customer-supplied product (material or drawings) as defined in QSM Section 12. This product must be handled in accordance with QSM Section 20, Handling, Storage, Packaging, Preservation, and Delivery.

1. Determine who is responsible for Customer Supplier Product within each respective office/department.
2. Provide the referenced documents to each of those responsible.
3. Implement the process as stated in the referenced documents.
4. Follow-up to ensure compliance and understanding.

## Module 13—Product Identification, Status, and Traceability

### References

- QSM Section 13
- Project Identification and Traceability Procedure, as applicable *(Procedure Number)*
- Project Number Issuance Procedure, as applicable *(Procedure Number)*

## Implementation Instructions

This module applies to everyone at every location.

1. Determine the method in which each location will comply with the requirements of this module.
2. Train everyone at the location using the referenced documents.
3. Implement the process as required in the referenced documents.
4. Follow-up to ensure compliance and understanding.

# Module 14—Process Control (Work Control)

## References

- QSM Section 14
- All *(Company Name)* Quality System Procedures
- All *(Company Name)* Operating Procedures, Work Instructions, and associated Check Sheets
- Applicable Reference Documents

## Implementation Instructions

This module applies to all *(Company Name)* employees involved in Work Processes.

1. Make the Work Process Procedures and Work Instructions available to each employee involved in the respective work process.
2. If the employee is engaged in the work process, he/she must read the work process documents and comply with their requirements.
3. Implement the Work Process Procedures in accordance with the requirements after having been certified in accordance with the respective work process by the supervisor for that process. *(Note: This should be an academic step of the process, as the written work instructions should reflect how we do our work. If this is the case, the personnel who have been doing the work process are certainly qualified and only need to read the documentation for that process).*
4. Utilize the Check Sheets in accordance with the instructions of the associated Work Instruction.
5. Follow-up to ensure compliance and understanding.
6. **Note:** Supervisors carry a responsibility in this module.

## Module 15—Inspection and Testing

### References

- QSM Section 15
- Inspection and Testing Procedures, as applicable *(Procedure Numbers)*
- All other related procedures or work instructions associated with the subject of receiving, in-process and final inspection, and testing of products and services

### Implementation Instructions

This module applies to anyone involved in the inspection and testing of products or services throughout the associated process.

1. Determine the work categories involved and acquaint each person within those categories with the requirements associated with their respective work.
2. Set up a system to ensure compliance within each office/department performing associated work.
3. Follow-up to ensure compliance and understanding.

## Module 16—Control of Inspection, Measuring, and Test Equipment

### References

- QSM Section 16
- Any related procedures applicable to the control of test equipment, their handling, issuance, calibration, etc.

### Implementation Instructions

This module is generally applicable to manufacturing organizations that have a specific department to handle this requirement. They must, however, have procedures to cover what they do.

## Module 17—Inspection and Test Status

### References

- QSM Section 17
- Any related procedures applicable to product identification and test status in order to ensure that only product that has passed the required inspections and tests are released for use.

### Implementation Instructions

This module is generally applicable to manufacturing organizations but can also be applicable to service organizations that deliver approved drawings, software, etc.

1. Determine the work categories involved and acquaint each person within those categories with the requirements associated with their respective work.
2. Set up a system to ensure compliance within each office/department performing associated work.
3. Follow-up to ensure compliance and understanding.

## Module 18—Control of Nonconforming Product

### References

- QSM Section 18
- Quality System Procedure, Control of Nonconforming Product *(Procedure Number)*
- Any related procedures applicable to the control of nonconforming product

### Implementation Instructions

This module is generally only applicable to manufacturing organizations.

1. Determine the work categories involved and acquaint each person within those categories with the requirements associated with their respective work.
2. Set up a system to ensure compliance within each office/department performing associated work.
3. Follow-up to ensure compliance and understanding.

## Module 19—Corrective and Preventive Action

### References

- QSM Section 19
- Quality System Procedure, Corrective and Preventive Action *(Procedure Number)*
- Nonconformance Reporting Procedure, as applicable, *(Procedure Number)*
- Corrective and Preventive Action Handbook, as might be applicable. (**Note:** Such a handbook would be for information to employees of large companies with complex corrective and preventive action systems)

### Implementation Instructions

This module applies to all *(Company Name)* offices, departments, and every employee. It is the responsibility of the respective supervisor to implement.

1. Thoroughly review and understand the referenced documents (supervisors and up).
2. Set up the requirements of the Corrective and Preventive Action Procedures within each office/department location.
3. Train the office and field personnel in the use of the Corrective and Preventive Action System.
4. Make Corrective and Preventive Action Forms available (convenient).
5. Implement the process.
6. Follow-up to ensure compliance and understanding.

## Module 20—Handling, Storage, Packaging, Preservation, and Delivery

### References

- QSM Section 20
- Quality System Procedure, Handling, Storage, Packaging, Preservation, and Delivery *(Procedure Number)*
- Any procedure that addresses this subject, which may include Report Issuance or some specific procedures for service companies

## Implementation Instructions

This procedure will apply to all personnel in all offices.

1. Thoroughly review and understand the referenced documents (supervisors and up).
2. Train the office and field personnel.
3. Implement operation in accordance with the procedural requirements.
4. Follow-up to ensure compliance and understanding.

# Module 21—Control and Retention of Quality Records

## References

- QSM Section 21
- Quality System Procedure, Control and Retention of Quality Records *(Procedure Number)*
- Quality System Procedure, Document Control *(Procedure Number)*
- Quality System Procedure, Numbering and Indexing *(Procedure Number)*
- Quality System Procedure, Internal Quality Audits *(Procedure Number)*
- Quality System Procedure, Management Review *(Procedure Number)*
- Quality System Procedure, Check Sheets *(Procedure Number)*

## Implementation Instructions

This module applies to all *(Company Name)* offices and every employee and is the responsibility of the respective supervisor to implement.

1. Thoroughly review and understand the referenced documents (supervisors and up).
2. Set-up the procedural requirements within each office/department.
3. Train the office and field personnel.
4. Implement the process.
5. Follow-up to ensure compliance and understanding.

## Module 22—Internal Quality Audits

### References

- QSM Section 22
- Quality System Procedure, Internal Quality Audits *(Procedure Number)*
- Quality System Procedure, Corrective and Preventive Action *(Procedure Number)*
- Nonconformance Reporting Procedure, as applicable, *(Procedure Number)*

### Implementation Instructions

This module applies to all *(Company Name)* offices. In most cases, internal audits must be carried out for all offices prior to the ISO 9000 audit.

1. The Continuous Improvement Steering Committee members should thoroughly review the referenced documents for understanding of the requirements.

## Module 23—Training

### References

- QSM Section 23
- Quality System Procedure, Training *(Procedure Number)*
- Relative Human Resource Procedures associated with training with the corresponding procedure numbers. Examples might be: New Hire Training Plan/Process, Training Data Base, Hiring and Recruitment, and Position Description Procedure

### Implementation Instructions

This module applies to all *(Company Name)* offices/departments and is the responsibility of the respective supervisor to implement.

1. Become thoroughly familiar with the reference documents.
2. Establish the processes required by the procedures in each office/department.
3. Acquaint all employees with the process and process requirements.
4. Follow-up for compliance and understanding.

## Module 24—Servicing (Customer Servicing)

### References

- QSM Section 24
- Procedures relating to Customer Servicing should be included here including procedure numbers

### Implementation Instructions

Customer Servicing is everyone's responsibility.

1. Supervisors and above review and understand the referenced procedures.
2. Make all employees aware of the requirements, but especially those directly involved.
3. Implement in accordance with the referenced procedural requirements.
4. Follow-up to ensure compliance and understanding.

## Module 25—Statistical Techniques

### References

- QSM Section 25
- Listing of associated procedures and procedure numbers

### Implementation Instructions

This module applies to those who are responsible for all aspects associated with statistical techniques and describes the system requirements for their use. It may be part of a defined function responsibility associated with manufacturing or service or that of the quality-specific personnel who analyze nonconformances.

## CONCLUSION

This chapter deals with the Quality System and Operating System Implementation instructions. Actual implementation should be based on where the company is in its journey towards an ISO 9000 System. What is offered here is for a company that has multiple offices in many locations, utilizing a single Quality System for all (recommended method).

One should not make the implementation instructions more complex than necessary for the specific application. In many cases, this chapter would not be necessary. Remember, however, to plan the implementation, which is the real key to success. This should be coupled with follow-up to ensure understanding and compliance with the requirements of the plan.

# Chapter 17

# INTERNAL AUDITS

Internal audits are a key tool in determining whether or not the Quality System is properly designed, implemented, and effective in meeting the stated objective of the Quality System.

Overall internal audit responsibility is usually assigned to the Corporate Management Quality Representative. This representative is specifically responsible for:

- Maintaining overall internal audit scheduling
- Ensuring the qualifications of selected internal auditors
- Ensuring that the internal audits take place as scheduled
- Reviewing all internal audit reports for content and finding accuracy
- Assuring that corrective and preventive action has taken place relative to the audit findings
- Analyzing the findings for trends and the taking of appropriate actions

The Management Quality Representative should also report the results of internal audits and the overall effectiveness of the quality and operating systems to the Continuous Improvement Steering Committee or to senior management should there not be such a committee.

Audits are of fundamental importance to a Quality System. Because audits uncover system deficiencies, they are a very powerful tool in developing and improving a Quality System that will help to ensure processes are done right the first time and to help ensure a zero defect mentality. An effective internal audit program provides assurance that the documented quality and operating systems have been implemented and are maintained. Such a program also will verify that corrective and preventive actions are implemented to resolve nonconformances and verifies their effectiveness.

Internal audits are concerned with the company's operating procedures, products, services, the requirements of the ISO Standard, and customers. All offices/departments and activities that affect product or service quality should be included in the audit program, including Finance, Human Resources, Information Management, Manufacturing, Engineering, Business Development, etc.

The objectives of internal audits are to:

- Determine the conformity of the quality and operating system to specified requirements
- Determine the effectiveness of the quality and operating system in meeting the quality objectives
- Provide a basis for inputs directed at continuous improvement of the work processes
- Meet certification requirements

## AUDITOR TRAINING AND QUALIFICATIONS

Auditor training and qualifications are an important consideration in ensuring the effectiveness of the audit program. Formal auditor training is essential, although it need not be an IQA- or RAB-approved lead auditor course. However, I have found that having such training is a plus. Each internal auditor must be very familiar with the company's Quality System and the ISO 9000 Series Standard that has been selected. Finally, internal auditors should have experience, which can be a part of the internal auditor training and certification process. This usually involves, after training, the accompanying of an experienced auditor as an observer and then as the lead auditor.

It has been said that good auditors are born and not made. While we maintain that training can improve an auditor's skills, it is true that certain basic personal attributes are important when selecting internal auditor candidates. The successful auditors are open-minded and mature. They must be able to exercise sound judgment in employing analytical skills. They should have a "hound-dog" mentality to tenaciously follow nonconformance trails. Above all, they must be fair in their judgments and sensitive to the feelings and egos of those being audited.

## PLANNING AND CONDUCTING AN AUDIT

Planning and conducting the audit is the next essential element for the success of the internal audit program. A schedule of area activities to be audited must be established to ensure all elements of the quality and operating systems are audited annually, as a minimum. The frequency that an area or activity is audited is dependent upon several factors, such as the number of nonconformances found during the previous audit, severity of the nonconformances, the cost of possible nonconformances, the criticality of the function, the age of the process, experience of personnel performing the task, any special requirements of the customer, past history of problems and any adverse trends.

Responsibility for defining the scope and sample size of each audit is generally that of the Management Quality Representative. Often a generic internal audit checklist is prepared from which the audit categories can be selected. In addition, notification of the office/department/function to be audited needs to be given no later than four (4) weeks prior to the planned audit date. This is normally done by the selected lead auditor for the respective audit.

Unlike most external or third party audits, there is generally no requirement for a formal opening meeting, but some formalities should be observed. Before beginning the audit, the auditor should meet with the respective manager(s) to confirm awareness of the audit being performed and to set a time for a brief closing meeting involving the supervisors and managers of the audited functions. The manager or designee should accompany the auditor as an escort for the duration of the audit.

# INTERNAL AUDIT PLAN

An Internal Audit Plan is another essential part of making an internal audit successful. Such a plan should include:

- An audit schedule
- Applicable reference documents
- Responsibilities associated with the audit defined
- Provision for audit notification and verification 4 weeks prior to the audit
- A defined audit format
- Clear audit objectives and scope
- Flexibility to improvise
- Identified audit contact points
- Provision of confidentiality
- A planned report format and distribution

## AUDIT CHECKLIST

The use of an Audit Checklist is recommended, although the auditor should remain flexible and may use the checklist as a guide.

The checklist should identify:

- What you want to look at
- What you want to look for
- Whom you want to speak to
- What you want to ask

Numerical scoring is to be avoided to reduce subjectivity. Questions that can be answered "yes" or "no" or by a brief explanation are best.

When designing the content of a checklist, keep in mind that the completed audit will have accomplished the following:

- Determined the extent of conformance to existing policies, procedures, and work instructions
- Determined whether existing policies, procedures, and instructions comply with requirements
- Assured availability, understanding and use of policies, procedures, and work instructions
- Determined need for new documentation or changes to existing documentation

A properly designed internal audit checklist can be used as the Audit Report. The following text and figures are examples of such a combination.

## Cover Page

The cover page (Figure 17-1) contains the audit report number, name of the company, name of the office/function being audited, those interviewed during the audit, the audit team, audit dates, and signatures.

## Instructions Page

The second page of the document is an instruction page, an example of which is shown in Figure 17-2. This page should be customized for each specific company and checklisted, as might be applicable.

### *(Name of Office/Department)* and Reporting Functions

| Column Number | Office/Departments Audited | Personnel Interviewed |
|---|---|---|
| 1 | *(Name of Office/Department being audited)* | *(Names of personnel interviewed)* |
| 2 | **Function:** *(Additional internal functions audited)* | |
| 3 | **Function:** | |

**Audit Team/Signature(s):** *(Name)* (Lead Auditor)
*(Names of audit team members)*

**Audit Date(s):** *(Date internal audit was held)*

**Figure 17-1. Internal Audit Checklist Cover Page**

## (Name of Company)
## Quality System Internal Audit
## Checklist and Report—Instructions

### Introduction
This Internal Audit Checklist/Report is based on the requirements of the *(Company Name)* Quality System. The checklist is configured in such a manner so to allow customization by the audit team for the office or function(s) being audited.

Suggested improvements should be forwarded to the *(Name of responsible function for the maintenance of the Quality System)*.

### Checklist/Report Configuration
This Internal Audit Checklist/Report is configured in a manner that will allow the completed document to meet the requirements of the concluding audit report and the checklist for which the Audit Report is based. It is designed to be completed without having to be typed or computerized. Copies can be made for distribution and stapled together, while the original remains with the audited department or function.

### Internal Audit Function
The function for which this specific checklist and report is configured is for *(name of function)*.

### Audit Scope
The scope of the Internal Surveillance Audit is the evaluation of the operation in the audited office for compliance with the *(Name of Company)* Documented Policies and Procedures as contained in the Corporate Quality System Manual, Quality System Procedures, and Operations Procedures and Work Instructions.

### Audit Approach
The purpose of the audit is to collect objective evidence, through interviews with personnel and review of pertinent records to assess the level of compliance to the documented requirements. The approach is to be positive and constructive with open dialogue.

All previous audit findings will be reviewed for closeout and noted accordingly as a new finding or as closed-out in the conclusion of this report.

Audit items will be selected in advance by *(Name of Company)* for each specific audit cycle. Not every item listed in this document will be audited each time.
Each audited item must have a comment or note clarifying the sample size or audited details, even if there are no associated findings.

### Audit Finding Follow-up Action Plan
The audited function is reminded that Quality System Procedure *(procedure number and paragraph)* calls for a Follow-up Action Plan to be submitted within four (4) weeks of receipt of the Audit Report.

> Each audited item must have a comment or note clarifying the sample size or audited details, even if there are no associated findings.

**Figure 17-2. Audit Checklist Instructions Page**

**Internal Audit Categories**
Check the Items and Categories to be included in this audit

| | | |
|---|---|---|
| Category 1 | X | Quality Policy, Code of Ethics, Responsibility and Authority |
| Category 2 | X | Organization and Responsibilities |
| Category 3 | X | Training and Development |
| Category 4 | X | Document Control and Reference Documents |
| Category 5 | X | Change Notice and Instructions |
| Category 6 | X | Correspondence Control |
| Category 7 | X | File Management and Retention |
| Category 8 | X | Internal Quality Audits |
| Category 9 | X | Corrective and Preventive Action System |
| Category 10 | X | Confidentiality |
| Category 11 | X | Technical Libraries and Master Index |
| Category 12 | X | Technical Papers and Articles |
| Category 13 | X | Client Feedback |
| Category 14 | X | Supplier Assessment and Control |
| Category 15 | X | Subcontractor Control |
| Category 16 | X | Human Resources |
| Category 17 | X | Financial Services |
| Category 18 | X | Check Sheets |
| Category 19 | X | Proposal Preparation |
| Category 20 | X | Legal Review |
| Category 21 | X | Pricing Development |
| Category 22 | X | Administration of Fee Schedules |
| Category 23 | X | Project Identification and Traceability |
| Category 24 | X | Request for PID Numbers |
| Category 25 | X | Contract Project Management |
| Category 26 | X | Request for Service (Contract Review) |
| Category 27 | X | Project Execution |
| Category 28 | X | Work Flow Control |
| Category 29 | X | Miscellaneous |

**Figure 17-3. Listing of Internal Audit Categories**

206 / *Implementing an ISO 9000-Based Quality System*

| Item No. | Audit Topic/Reference(s) | Column Number Enter OK/NC/OBS/X as applicable. Leave Blank if not checked. ||| Finding Detailed/Notes/Comments |
|---|---|---|---|---|---|
| | | 1 Office | 2 | 3 | |
| | Quality Policy, Code of Ethics, Quality System Management Quality Policy Related Responsibility Quality System | | | | |
| | Category 1 | | | | |
| 1-1 | Is the Quality Policy available?<br><br>QSM 2, Vol. 1 | OK | | | The Quality Policy was posted and visible to everyone within the office and to those who come into the office. |
| 1-2 | Is the meaning of the Quality Policy understood by Management and Employees?<br><br>QSM 2, Vol. 1 | OK | | | Discussed the Quality Policy with the head of operations as well as various office staff. They were able to put the meaning of the quality policy into their own words. |
| 1-3 | Is the Code of Ethics available? Has it been provided to or presented to all employees? Is there visible evidence or interviewed evidence of this?<br><br>QSM 2, 6.0 Vol.1 | OBS | | | The March 94 version of the Code of Ethics was in evidence as well as the Sept 92 version, but interview with employees indicated a need for them to review it. *It is suggested that for both this and the Confidentiality Procedure, that a one page document be prepared with each employee's name and signature plus the current date be utilized as evidence.* See also Item 12-1. |
| 1-4 | Is management aware of how the Quality Policy is implemented within the organization?<br><br>QSM 2, 6.0 Vol. 1 | OK | | | Reviewed Volumes 1 (Quality System Manual) and Volume 2 (Quality System Procedures) with the management of the Office. |
| 1-5 | Are the Quality Objectives for the Organization known?<br><br>QSM 3, 3.0 Vol. 1 | OK | | | See Item 1-4 above. |
| Item No. | Audit Topic/Reference(s)<br><br>Quality Policy, Code of Ethics, Quality System Management Quality Policy Related Responsibility Quality System | Column Number Enter OK/NC/OBS/X as applicable. Leave Blank if not checked. ||| Finding Detailed/Notes/Comments |

**Figure 17-4 Typical Internal Audit Checklist Category—Completed**

|  | Category 1 - continued | 1 Office | 2 | 3 |  |
|---|---|---|---|---|---|
| 1-6 | Does Management know their responsibilities regarding Quality?<br><br>QSM 4, 4.0 Vol. 1 & QSM 7, 5.0 Vol.1 | OK |  |  | See Item 1-4 above. |
| 1-7 | Do Management and Employees understand the Quality System Structure?<br><br>QSM 5, 4.0 Vol. 1 | OK |  |  | Yes, as evidenced from interviews with the employees. |
| 1-8 |  |  |  |  |  |
| 1-9 |  |  |  |  |  |
| 1-10 |  |  |  |  |  |

**Figure 17-4—Continued**

## Typical Internal Audit Checklist—Example

An example of a typical checklist category that has been completed is shown in Figure 17-4. The checklist is generally made up from analysis of each of the Quality System Procedures (categories of which are contained in each of the functional checklists) and the respective operating procedures of the function being audited. There may be a different checklist for each function, such as Human Resources, Finance, Manufacturing, Engineering, etc.

## Conclusion Page—Example

The concluding page of the Internal Audit Checklist (Figure 17-5) contains the record of attendees at the opening meeting (if there was one) and the closing meeting. In addition, the auditor's summary remarks and recommendations are included. The distribution of the internal audit report is indicated.

## THE ADMINISTRATION OF INTERNAL AUDITS

This is another of the key elements in a successful internal audit program.

The manager/supervisor of the office/department being audited must be notified prior to an audit using established channels of communication. This is known as *audit notification*. The information provided should include the scope of the audit, auditor names, schedule, any support needs (rooms, phone, etc.), and other needed logistical information (flights, hotel, etc.).

If the audit team is composed of more than one auditor, a *pre-audit meeting* should be held with the auditors to review the purpose of the audit, scope, resources to be applied, who has authorized the audit criteria/standards and to answer any questions that might have arisen. The internal audit checklist to be used should be discussed and revised as necessary for the specific audit. This meeting could be held on the day of the audit.

The *lead auditor* must remain in control of the audit and the audit team. The lead auditor is responsible for the integrity of the audit. Support auditors can audit independently or as teams.

## Opening/Closing Meeting Attendance Register

**No Meeting Held** ☐

| Name | Opening | Closing |
|------|---------|---------|
| *(Names of individuals attending the meetings)* | X | X |
|  |  |  |
|  |  |  |
|  |  |  |
|  |  |  |
|  |  |  |

**Auditor Conclusion:**

The 4 nonconformances and 16 observations indicate that the Quality and Operating Systems procedures and operating instructions need to become more of "just the way we do our work" rather than additional tasks that must be done in addition to our work. Considering that this is the first audit in 3 years, the results are not as bad as they appear. The attitude of the office personnel is excellent and very cooperative.

*(EXAMPLE)*

**Auditor Recommendation:**

In accordance with the procedural requirements, an Action Plan is required to be submitted to the Lead Auditor, with copies to the Regional Quality Coordinator and Director of TCD within 4 weeks of receipt of this audit report. It is recommended that a follow-up audit be conducted in conjunction with the follow-up audit of the *(office name)* within the next 3 to 6 months.

*(EXAMPLE)*

**Distribution :**
Audited Office: ☐             Director of Total Quality: ☐
Regional QC: ☐                 Corporate Quality Coordinator: ☐

**Figure 17-5. Example of the Concluding Page of the Internal Audit Report**

One reason to team two auditors might be that one may have a stronger technical knowledge of the function being audited and the other stronger auditor process skills, but weak specific knowledge.

The *audit escorts* should allow persons being interviewed to answer all questions independently. Their function is to act as a guide and to ensure cooperation. It should be noted that an escort is not necessary for smaller offices, but may be a wise idea to ensure a third party presence and to clarify any misunderstandings that may occur.

The *collection of data* during the audit is also very important. The auditor should document the audit results as factually as possible. Objective evidence should be collected and only the facts recorded on the audit checklist.

## Auditor Meetings

Two types of auditor caucus meetings may be held as deemed necessary by the audit team: audit team meetings and daily briefings.

The duration of audit team meetings should be as brief as possible so that the auditee representatives are not kept waiting to continue the audit and so that valuable audit time is not wasted. It is a good idea to schedule audit team meetings as a part of the audit plan. This type of meeting is a private one for the audit team members only (the auditee representatives are not included). Audit team meetings are conducted to:

- Keep the audit team informed of developments
- Make revisions to the audit schedule
- Review and discuss evidence presented
- Examine observations and reach consensus on findings
- Inform team members of any change of assignments
- Have the team members examine confusing or complex issues or documents
- Determine the acceptability of compliance
- Examine specific documentation or evidence of compliance for pitfalls
- Develop the Audit Report as the audit progresses (begin drafting the report on the first day of the audit)

Two short meetings should be held with the auditee representatives daily. These are usually conducted in the morning and near the end of the audit day. In each of these meetings, the lead auditor takes the opportunity to advise the auditee of:

- Planned daily activities

- Any schedule changes
- Summary of observations and nonconformances (findings)
- Areas of concern

Such meetings keep the auditee informed of how the audit is progressing and gives the auditee the opportunity to produce any evidence of compliance or conformance in inconclusive areas of concern.

# The Finding Statement

The Finding Statement is the primary result of the internal audit. The statement should cite the specific Quality System or operating system requirement and the specific nonconformance or observation. Objective evidence should be included wherever possible (i.e. copies of records, instructions, etc., or references to such). It must be noted that sensitive data must not be copied. Although not recommended by this author, if the system contains categories of nonconformances, categorize the findings as either a major or minor. A major nonconformance is a finding that is systemic and puts product or service quality at risk. A minor nonconformance poses no immediate threat to product or service quality. An observation is a finding that, if not corrected, could lead to a nonconformance. For internal audits, it is recommended that only nonconformances (without major or minor classification) and observations be utilized. The associated definitions in such a case would be:

*Nonconformance = Nonfulfillment of a specified requirement*

*Observation = A detected weakness that, if not corrected, may result in a degradation of product or service quality*

At the conclusion of the internal audit a *closing meeting* should be held. The lead auditor should control and conduct the meeting. Thanks should be expressed for cooperation, the purpose of the audit summarized and the findings summarized with each one being reviewed. Copies of the audit summary should be provided. Recommendations and conclusions on the acceptability of the system can also be given at this time. An attendance roster is needed for the formal report later.

The Audit Report can either be the combined audit checklist as noted above or a separate report. In either case, the audit report should be completed as soon as possible after the conclusion of the audit (preferably before leaving the sight). The report should be factual and include:

- Name of audited organization
- Date and location of audit
- Purpose of audit
- Scope of audit
- Auditor(s) names
- Summary of the findings
- Checklist element by element assessment showing nonconformances and observations
- Conclusion and recommendations
- Exhibits (attendance rosters, nonconformance reports, and any pertinent documentation)

Equally important as the items that are included in the formal audit report are those items that should be excluded:

- Any confidential or proprietary information
- Any subjective opinions
- Unsolicited recommendations. In most cases, it is wise to omit solicited recommendations as well.
- Nit-pick items
- Emotional argumentative statements
- Items neither discussed nor mentioned during the closing meeting

The overall internal auditor's function is to determine whether a quality system is in place and its effectiveness. A single paragraph is sufficient for the statement of this analysis.

The Audit Report should be as simple, clear, and concise as possible. Based on the nature of the audit and the auditor's authority, it may be necessary to order the auditee to stop work on an order, project, or contract. The Audit Report must state exactly what work must be stopped.

## CORRECTIVE AND PREVENTIVE ACTION

Corrective and preventive action is the responsibility of the auditee and not the auditor. A Corrective and Preventive Action Response Plan that addresses the root cause of the finding and an action plan must be developed by the auditee. Provisions must be made for follow-up where functions of the effectiveness of any action taken as well as if the action was actually completed. Formal closure should not be done until verification is complete and a follow-up internal audit report is issued.

The internal audit results should be used as part of management reviews of the state of the quality and operating systems and their implementation. Future audits should use the results of past audits and serve as a basis to evaluate the effectiveness areas of the corrective and preventive action.

## CONCLUSION

Early in the Quality System Implementation, auditors can serve as a valuable teaching support to help those being audited to understand the requirements of the system and to help identify needed changes to help comply with the selected ISO 9000 Series Standard.

A well-designed and implemented internal quality audit program is vital in the successful implementation and the continuance of the Quality System. Without an effective internal quality audit process the Quality System will die in a relatively short period of time. One key to the success of such a program is to have a well-developed internal audit checklist (and report or combination checklist and report) and well trained internal auditors. Coupled with these two items is a good analysis of the audit results with follow-up of findings to resolution.

# Chapter 18

# CORRECTIVE AND PREVENTIVE ACTION SYSTEM

## ESTABLISHING AN EFFECTIVE SYSTEM

An effective Corrective and Preventive Action System (CPAS) is a key element of the quality process and is based on every employee becoming a problem identifier and, more importantly, a problem solver. An effective Corrective and Preventive Action System provides a mechanism for every employee to identify and communicate process improvement opportunities to management and for these opportunities to be evaluated with positive changes implemented. The CPAS also provides the means for addressing and tracking nonconformances.

The responsibility for the overall direction of the CPAS lies with the Continuous Improvement Steering Committee(s) or, if there is not such, with management. Any real success resulting from the CPAS must come from the commitment and dedicated effort of all employees as participants in the CPAS. The CPAS must be an integral part of the Total Quality Management Process or as part of an ISO 9000 Quality System. A CPAS is required in either case.

## Purpose of a Continuous Improvement Steering Committee

The purpose of the CPAS is to provide a structured and disciplined approach for identifying, analyzing, and implementing improvement opportunities related to work processes that support the company's mission and Quality Policy. Improvement opportunities include:

- Investigating root causes of nonconformances and the application of corrective and preventive actions
- Reducing the cycle time of work processes
- Making work processes more efficient
- Increasing customer satisfaction
- Improving the work environment
- Strengthening teamwork and communication at all levels of the organization

- Eliminating the cost associated with errors

## ORGANIZATION AND RESPONSIBILITIES

The Corrective and Preventive Action System does not replace the normal management functions of decision making and resource allocation. The teams described in this section solve problems and make recommendations, but it remains with the respective supervisors, managers, and senior managers to take final action.

### Continuous Improvement Steering Committee

The CISCs (reference Chapter 4 for further information) have the responsibility for the overall direction of the CPAS. In the absence of a CISC, management or a Management Quality Representative would have this responsibility. The CISCs are comprised of management personnel. Their functions related to the CPAS include:

- Establishing guidelines and priorities for operation of the CPAS
- Assuring that all employees are trained and the CPAS is operating efficiently at all levels within the organization
- Addressing major quality and cycle time issues
- Forming Corrective Action Teams (CATs) on critical quality matters
- Reviewing recommendations and taking action on recommendations
- Resolving Corrective and Preventive Action Requests (CPARs)

### Continuous Improvement Teams (CITs)

Continuous Improvement Teams (reference Chapter 4) manage parts of the Total Quality Management (TQM) process on behalf of the Continuous Improvement Steering Committee. In respect to the CPAS, these teams would be responsible for the above listing for their respective defined areas.

### Management and Supervisors Responsibilities

Managers and supervisors play a key role in the Corrective and Preventive Action System. Their responsibilities include:

- Educating and training employees on the benefits and use of the CPAS

- Encouraging employees to originate Corrective and Preventive Action Requests (CPARs), provide solutions to problems, and become involved in Corrective Action Teams (CATs)
- Responding quickly to all submitted CPARs
- Tracking the review and resolution status of departmental CPARs and providing timely feedback to originators on the actions taken
- Creating employee awareness and recognizing employee achievement
- Implementing approved recommendations in a timely and efficient manner

## Employee Responsibilities

For the Quality Process to work, employees at every level of the organization must be trained to use the quality tools and techniques by the Corrective and Preventive Action System. They must also participate in the CPAS by originating CPARs, by offering solutions to issues raised by CPARs, by becoming members of CATs and CITs, and by being committed to the principles of "continuous performance improvement" and "doing every task right the first time."

## Management System and Quality

Some companies have separated the Quality System from management systems and found out that it does not work. Employees will tend to separate the two as well and think of quality as an additional burden, additional work. Although it is paramount to remember that the Quality System does not manage the company, one must also remember that the Quality System is just one of the many management systems and processes of a successful company (reference Chapter 19). In fact, one major objective of management should be to have quality become "just the way we do our work." When this occurs, the word "quality" will disappear and become a natural part of our management systems and processes.

The management systems and processes of the company (reference Chapter 19) incorporate the Quality System. Management, acting as management, should identify and solve problems independent of the Corrective and Preventive Action System. One should not assign all of the management responsibilities for addressing management issues to quality. Doing so will cause problems, and will be detrimental to proper system integration. The Quality System must not be the only source of identifying inputs to management for business process improvements.

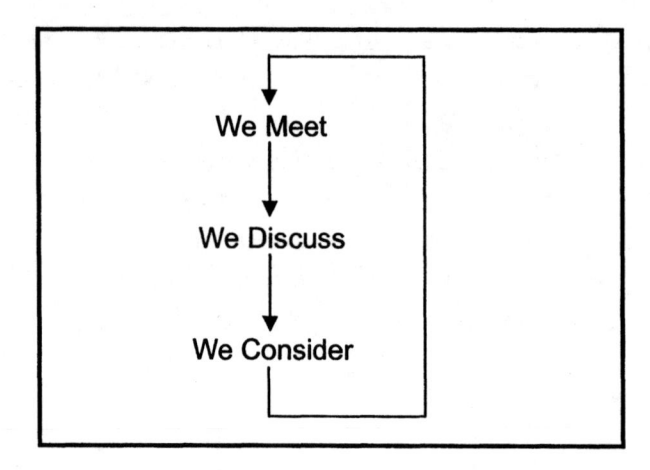

218 / *Implementing an ISO 9000-Based Quality System*

**Figure 18-1. Method of Addressing Problems in Many Companies**

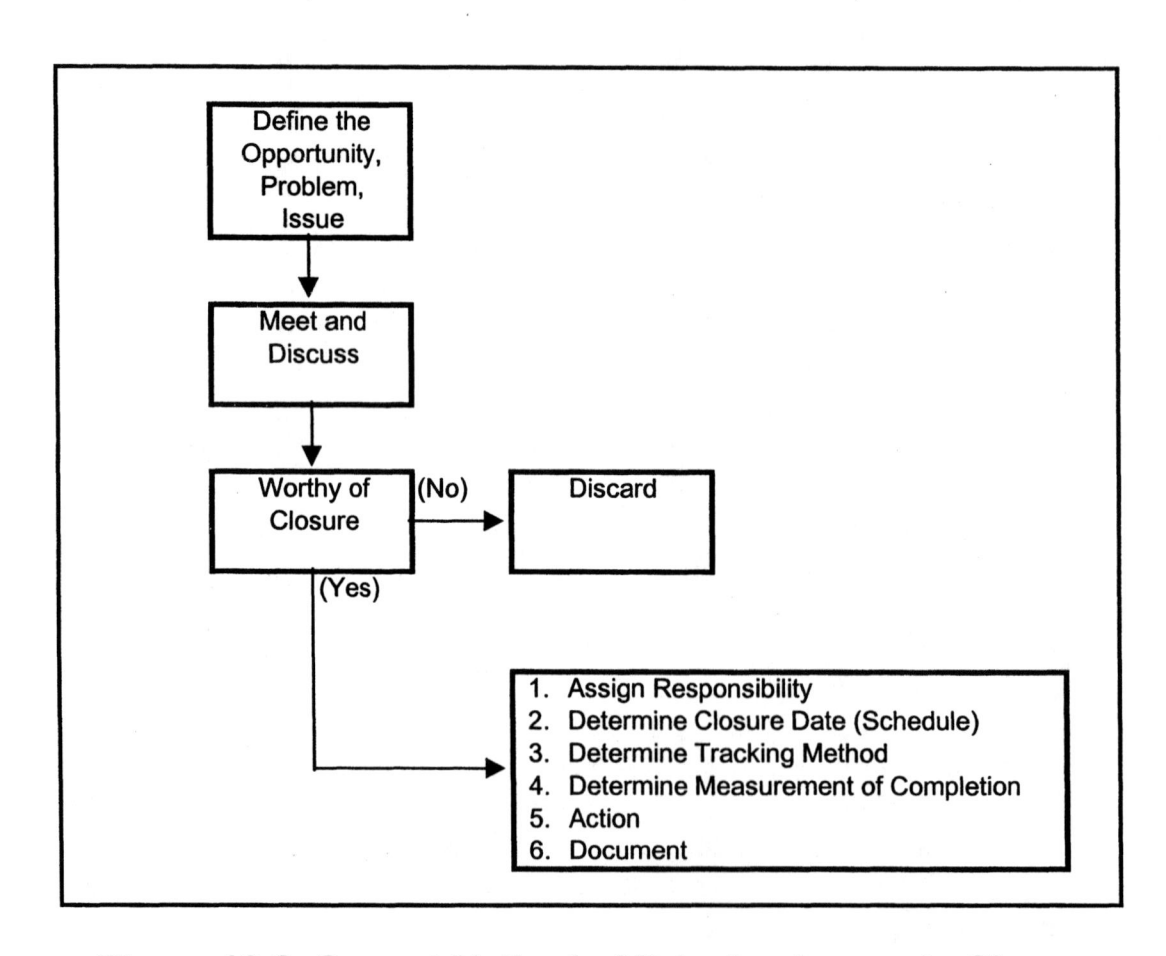

**Figure 18-2. Correct Method of Bringing Issues to Closure**

Who is really responsible for problem identification and solutions? Let's look at it this way: problem identification, analysis solution determination, decision to implement, implementation, and follow-up are all management system responsibilities, not Quality System responsibilities. If this is the case, then where does the Quality System, specifically, the Corrective and Preventive Action System, fit into the equation?

The Quality System needs to be supplemented by a consistent, company-wide methodology for addressing problems. One method is presented in Chapters 19 and 20 as part of the continuous improvement training provided to employees.

The Quality System must be supplemented with tools and techniques for problem identification, root cause determination, tracking, measurement, and follow-up for use by management, individuals or management appointed problem-solving teams. The use of these tools and techniques should be taught as part of the overall training program. The tools must teach all employees a common language associated with all aspects of problem identification and problem solving. Actual utilization of the method presented in Chapters 19 and 20 or equivalent method of problem identification and problem solving, the tools and techniques and the common language remains a management system decision, to be used or not used. One important additional quality-related attempt is to establish an environment that allows for effective problem identification and problem solving.

What is the real problem in most companies? The questions are, "Is the management system utilizing these tools and techniques to address and solve problems?" and "Is the management system fostering an environment conducive to problem identification and problem solving?" An observation of a number of companies has been that they do not use the identification and solving of problems within the established management system that has historically been set in place. One might say that they have identified problems as they surfaced, discussed them, considered them, and then repeated the process over and over again without performing the remainder of the steps leading to successful solution and close out. Instead, problems continue to surface without being solved, causing the organization to become problem saturated, which oftentimes causes organizational immobility.

If the established management system is not a problem-solving type of system and if an ISO 9000-based Corrective and Preventive Action System is introduced, the tendency is for management to use it in lieu of what they don't have but should have. This causes confusion and misuse of the CPAS.

Therefore, the statement made earlier that all problem identification, analysis, solution determination, decision to implement, implementation, and follow-up are management system responsibilities verifies that these are not Quality System responsibilities.

If the above is a valid scenario, then where does the Corrective And Preventive Action System fit into that scenario and why does the ISO 9000 Standard require it? Let's see if we can sort it out.

## USES OF THE CORRECTIVE AND PREVENTIVE ACTION SYSTEM

The Quality System, via the Quality System Manual and Quality System Procedures, provides the normalization for consistency and control purposes of the "documentation of what we do." In other words, it ensures that we write down what we do in our work processes in a consistent manner and that there is a formalized process for changes and control of this documentation.

The Corrective and Preventive Action System is the mechanism for change and improvement of the documented work process procedures and instructions and their associated work processes. These types of improvement opportunities come from those involved in the work processes and improvements are associated with those work processes. The CPAS is an all-employee, "bottom up" approach and requirement. This approach would be one of the parameters of the CPAS that is outside the less formal management system problem identification and problem solving responsibilities.

The Corrective and Preventive Action System is used to document nonconformances in order to track corrective action, investigation, preventive action, and follow-up to ensure effectiveness. The actual documentation of a nonconformance uses the CPAR form itself, no other form being necessary (reference Figure 18-3).

The Corrective and Preventive Action System is also used to document the findings of external audits. A CPAR is completed for each finding (nonconformance or observation). Again, this is for the purpose of tracking to closure, as stated above for nonconformances, as well as to provide formalized documentation, analysis, and follow-up.

The Corrective and Preventive Action System is also used to document negative customer feedback (complaints), when those complaints may affect work processes. The CPAR form is used to accomplish this and is tracked to closure as is done for nonconformances.

The Corrective and Preventive Action System is also used to track CPARs generated as a result of trend analysis. Should a trend be detected relative to customer feedback, analysis of internal or external audit findings, or any other trending gained from the application of statistical methods, it is documented and tracked through the use of the CPAS.

## Corrective and Preventive Action Requests (CPARs)

A properly designed and implemented Corrective and Preventive Action System allows any employee to originate a CPAR and assures that the CPAR will be considered by management with timely feedback to the originator. CPARs are used to:

- Identify problem areas associated with work processes (procedures and work instructions) that need corrective action
- Identify opportunities that will improve work processes and services
- Address identified nonconformances

A typical CPAR form might look like that shown in Figure 18-3, but can be customized to fit the respective company. For multiple office companies, it is recommended that only one CPAS be implemented using the same CPAR form. It is beneficial to have the CPAR form a color, such as yellow, so that the originals can easily be differentiated from copies.

The CPAR form should contain the following information:

- The name of the person to whom the CPAR is to be sent
- The name of the person who originated the CPAR
- The date initiated
- The office/department of the initiator
- The CPAR number (assigned by the Quality Coordinator or MQR in accordance with the quality system requirements)
- The reason for initiation (as a result of an opportunity for improvement, nonconformance, customer feedback, trend analysis)
- A description of the problem
- The CPAR recommendations of the initiator or auditee if the initiator is an internal auditor
- Investigation results for nonconformances and client feedback-related CPARs
- Actions taken to resolve the CPAR and signature of who has taken the action
- The target closure date

| | |
|---|---|
| **Corrective and Preventive Action Request (CPAR)** *Improving the way we do our work* ||
| To (QC): <br> From (CPAR Initiator) <br> Date:   Office/Dept: | CAR Number:* |

**Reason for Initiation:**

(OI)  ☐  Opportunity for Improvement of a Procedure of Process Instruction

(NC)  ☐  Nonconformance   Audit No./NC No. (if applicable) _____

(CF)  ☐  Client Feedback

| Description: | Source of CPAR/NC (check one) <br><br> Day-to-day operation ☐ <br> Client feedback ☐ <br> Internal audit ☐ <br> External audit ☐ <br> Management review ☐ <br> Trend analysis ☐ <br> Other ☐ <br> _____ |
|---|---|
| Affected document and section: | |

**CPAR Initiator's** (or Auditee if initiator is an Internal Auditor) **Recommendations:**

**\* CPAR Forwarding:**
    This issue could not be resolved locally and is herewith forwarded to the responsible
    CISC for resolution. See Section 3.3.6 of the procedure for additional guidance.

Sent to CISC on (date)   [        ]

*QC completes shaded areas.

**Investigation Results** (for non-conformance, client feedback, trend analysis related CARs):

Corrective and Preventive Action, (Procedure Number)      Attachment A - Revision 1      Page 1 of 2

# Figure 18-3. Corrective and Preventive Action Form

| Corrective and Preventive Action Request (CPAR) |
| --- |
| *Improving the way we do our work* |

**Action(s) taken to resolve the CPAR:**  Target Closure Date:

Action by: _____  Date: _____

Affects other processes:   Yes [ ]  (If yes, list them)   No [ ]

**Measure of completion and requirement for follow-up:**   (for nonconformance and client feedback related CPARs)
What measurement(s) will be used to determine that the CPAR resolution has been implemented?
_____

Who is responsible for follow-up action to ensure effectiveness?   _____

How is follow-up action verification of effectiveness to be accomplished?   _____
_____

**Corrective and Preventive Action Request Close-Out** (after implementation has been completed):

Closed-out by: _____   Comments:
Date: _____

**Closed-Out CPAR Distribution:**

|   |   |   | Name of Individual | Date Sent |
|---|---|---|---|---|
| 1. | CPAR Initiator | Copy | | |
| 2. | Supervisor/Office file w/attach | Copy | | |
| 3. | QC (w/attachments) | Original | | |
| 4. | Follow-up designee (NCs only) | Copy | | |
| 5. | Director, Total Quality (if the CPAR was handled by the CISC | Copy | | |
| 6. | CIT (if the CPAR was handled by the CIT) | Copy | | |
| 7. | Additional information copies, as needed | Copy | | |

Corrective and Preventive Action, (Procedure Number)   Attachment A - Revision 1   Page 2 of 2

**Figure 18-3—*Continued***

- Whether or not the CPAR affects other processes
- The measure of completion and requirement for follow-up stated on the CPAR form
- The close-out of the CPAR, with the signature and date of the authorized person closing it out
- The distribution of the closed-out CPAR and date of distribution

## Corrective and Preventive Action System—Definitions

The Corrective and Preventive Action System is the heart of successful continuance and improvement of any Quality System. For this reason, it is worthy of a great deal of detail.

To ensure that there is no miscommunication relative to the CPAS, the following definitions are offered for consideration:

**The Corrective and Preventive Action System (CPAS)**—the system for identifying, analyzing, and implementing improvements and corrective action in a company's products, services, and work processes.

**A Corrective and Preventive Action Request (CPAR)**—a documented request to improve a procedure, a work instruction, or to initiate an internal investigation of the cause of a nonconformance for applying corrective or preventive action.

**Product**—the output of any process. It consists mainly of goods, software, and services. The primary product of *(company name)* is *(list)*.

**Nonconformance**—non-fulfillment of a specified requirement.

**Opportunity for Improvement**—an input to the Corrective and Preventive Action System that is not initiated by a nonconformance, but is nevertheless an opportunity for improving a procedure or a work instruction.

**Corrective Action**—action to eliminate the causes of an existing nonconformance, nonconforming service, or other undesirable situation.

**Preventive Action**—action to eliminate the causes of a potential nonconformance, nonconforming service, or other undesirable situation.

**Assign**—for the purposes of the CPAS, the term "assign" means to transfer responsibility, with mutual consent, for action to an individual or group (i.e., team or committee).

## Corrective and Preventive Action System—Initiation

Any employee or subcontractor should be able to initiate a CPAR using the equivalent of the form shown in Figure 18-3. The CPAR is issued to document and track corrective and preventive action as a result of:

- Customer feedback
- Internal or external audit findings
- Analysis of trends associated with the following:
    - Customer data
    - Customer feedback
    - Nonconformances
    - Process monitoring
- Identify improvement opportunities that involve changes to procedures or work instructions that are beyond the originator's area of responsibility.
- Nonconformances

The CPAR initiator must be required to provide recommendations and obtain as many facts as possible before initiating the CPAR. If the CPAR initiator is an internal auditor, the originator recommendations are to be completed by the auditee.

In general, a CPAR is not needed to change a procedure or work instruction within one's own area of responsibility. These are documented and tracked according to the Quality System Procedure, Development of Procedures and Work Instructions, using the respective tracking sheet.

## Corrective and Preventive Action System—General Description

The intent should be for corrective and preventive actions to occur at the lowest possible organizational level. In addition, overall awareness by the respective Continuous Improvement Steering Committee is also necessary to ensure correct and documented resolutions. Such actions are intended to address situations that require correction and identify preventive action to diminish the opportunity for nonconforming services.

226 / Implementing an ISO 9000-Based Quality System

The simplified flow chart, Figure 18-4, shows an applied example of ABS for the path of a CPAR through the Corrective and Preventive Action System.

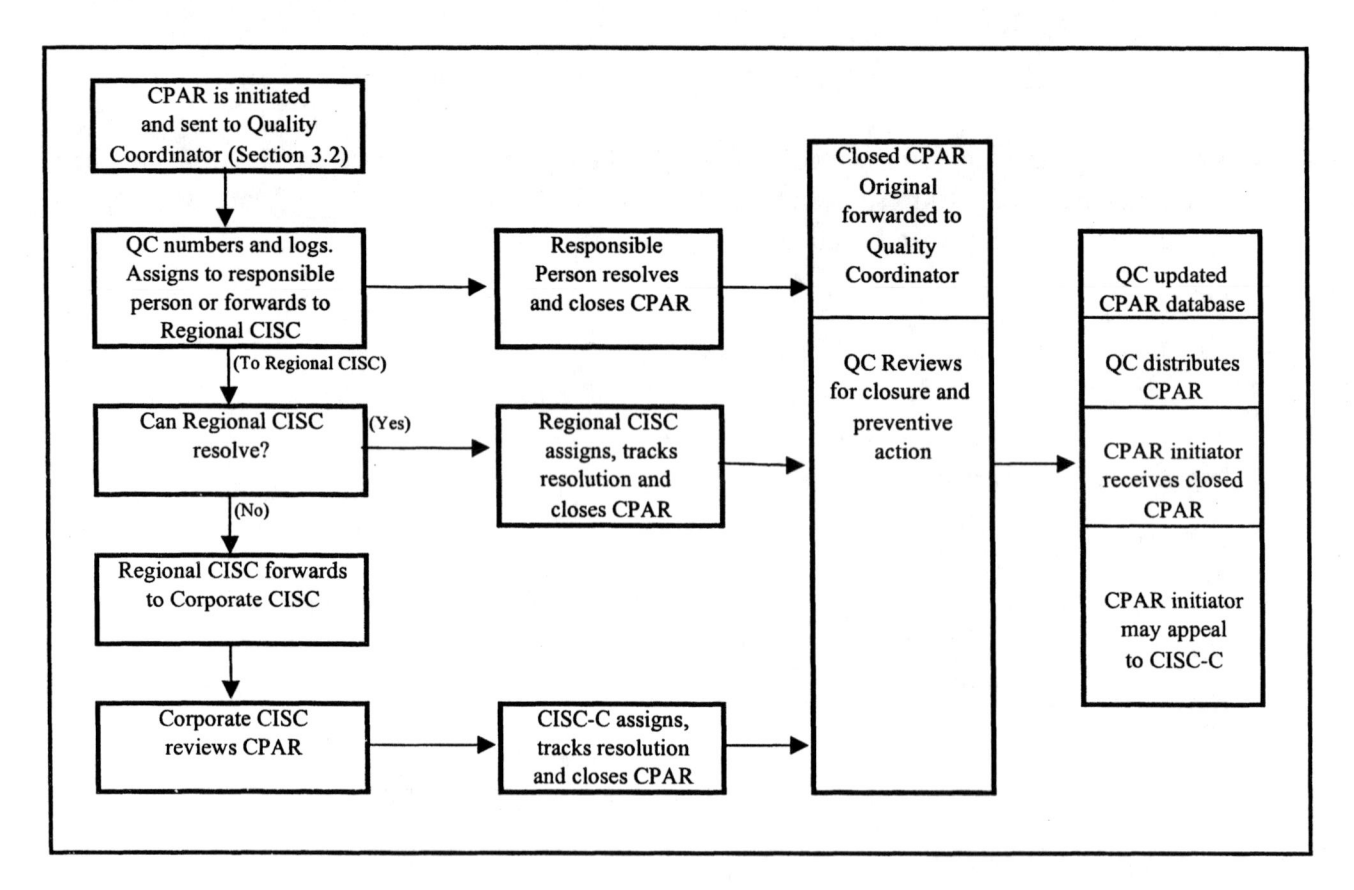

```
┌─────────────────────────────────────────────────────────────────────────────┐
│  ┌──────────────────┐                                                        │
│  │ CPAR is initiated│                                                        │
│  │ and sent to Quality                                                       │
│  │ Coordinator (Section 3.2)│                        ┌──────────────┐        │
│  └──────────────────┘                                │ Closed CPAR  │        │
│           │                                          │  Original    │        │
│           ▼                                          │ forwarded to │        │
│  ┌──────────────────┐      ┌──────────────┐          │   Quality    │  ┌──────────────┐
│  │ QC numbers and logs.│   │ Responsible  │          │ Coordinator  │  │ QC updated   │
│  │ Assigns to responsible│─▶│Person resolves│────────▶│              │  │ CPAR database│
│  │ person or forwards to │   │and closes CPAR│         └──────────────┘  └──────────────┘
│  │ Regional CISC     │      └──────────────┘                             ┌──────────────┐
│  └──────────────────┘                                ┌──────────────┐   │ QC distributes│
│      (To Regional CISC)                              │  QC Reviews  │   │     CPAR     │
│           │                                          │ for closure and  └──────────────┘
│           ▼                                          │  preventive  │   ┌──────────────┐
│  ┌──────────────────┐      ┌──────────────┐          │    action    │   │CPAR initiator│
│  │ Can Regional CISC│(Yes) │ Regional CISC │─────────▶│              │   │receives closed│
│  │    resolve?      │─────▶│assigns, tracks│          │              │   │    CPAR      │
│  └──────────────────┘      │resolution and │          │              │   └──────────────┘
│        (No)                │closes CPAR    │          │              │   ┌──────────────┐
│           ▼                └──────────────┘          │              │   │CPAR initiator│
│  ┌──────────────────┐                                │              │   │  may appeal  │
│  │ Regional CISC forwards│                           │              │   │  to CISC-C   │
│  │ to Corporate CISC │                               │              │   └──────────────┘
│  └──────────────────┘                                │              │
│           │                                          │              │
│           ▼                                          │              │
│  ┌──────────────────┐      ┌──────────────┐          │              │
│  │  Corporate CISC  │      │CISC-C assigns,│         │              │
│  │   reviews CPAR   │─────▶│tracks resolution│──────▶│              │
│  └──────────────────┘      │ and closes CPAR│        └──────────────┘
│                            └──────────────┘                          │
└─────────────────────────────────────────────────────────────────────────────┘
```

**Figure 18-4. Simplified Flow Diagram—Applied Example**

The design of the CPAS should consider a path for those CPARs that require immediate action, the effects on other work processes and an appeal process for those solutions in which the originator does not agree.

The completed CPAR forms are considered quality records and must be retained for presentation to the external and internal auditors.

## CONCLUSION

This chapter has presented considerations for a Corrective and Preventive Action System. The CPAS is essential, besides being required, for the success of the Quality System and its continuation. A working CPAS can provide management with insights and opportunities for continuous improvement of the work processes. It is a very formal, documented system and must not replace or be used in lieu of a very informal system of problem solving and continuous improvement. This informal system should be dominant and only involve the more formal CPAS when a change to a procedure or work instruction is necessary.

The CPAS is not an employee suggestion system and should never be used as such.

Each completed CPAR form should be a stand-alone document with all necessary attachments to make it so.

Software programs are commercially available for Corrective and Preventive Action Systems, but they must be selected with care since many of them do not meet the needs of the system. Unfortunately, one doesn't find this out until after both money and resources are wasted. It may be best to design one's own system by utilizing available off-the-shelf software.

It is important to keep the CPAR form as simple and easy to complete as possible, especially from the initiator's point of view. This may help to increase the number generated and forestall any excuses for not generating them.

# Chapter 19

# BEYOND ISO 9000 CERTIFICATION

Once the ISO 9000-based Quality System has been installed, implemented, and in operation, it comes time to think about where one goes next. In actuality, this should have been decided prior to launching the ISO 9000 process. However, this decision oftentimes is done afterwards. There are several choices a company can consider:

- To stop with ISO 9000 Certification and just maintain that system
- To continuously improve the work processes
- To proceed to improve all of the company's management systems and processes

The ISO 9000 Quality System is part of process management, which itself is only one of the management systems and processes necessary to really become a Malcolm Baldrige (or equivalent) Award-winning company. The ISO 9000-based Quality System may be thought of as representing Phase 1 in a company's Journey to Excellence. One can decide how far along this journey the respective company wishes to travel.

## JOURNEY TO EXCELLENCE

The Journey to Excellence approach recommended in response to *Beyond ISO 9000 Certification* is one which aligns the activities of all employees and all management systems and processes within the organization with the *common focus of customer satisfaction through continuous improvement of all activities, goods, and services*. Within this context, customer means a person or group, internal or external to the organization, to whom a service is provided.

The Journey to Excellence can be accomplished in *four concurrent phases,* as shown in Figure 19-1.

## Phase 1—Process Management

Phase 1 is the implementation of process management, which includes the installation of a Quality System based on the International Organization for Standardization (ISO) 9000 Series Standards. Phase 1 involves the following ten-step plan of action:

1. Senior management education and commitment
2. Quality awareness for all employees
3. Quality foundations—ISO 9000*
4. Establishment of operating procedures/work instructions
5. Education and training of all employees
6. Establishment of a communication and recognition system
7. Installation of a corrective and preventive action system
8. Setting of goals
9. Establishment of metrics company wide
10. Continued improvement and simplification of all company work processes

*ISO 9000 is the comprehensive general standard model for quality assurance in design development, production, installation, and servicing.

Phase 1 of the Journey to Excellence needs to be solidly installed and forms the foundation for the remainder of the Journey. Phase 1 completion is evidenced by the receipt of ISO Certification to either ISO 9001, 9002, or 9003.

## Phase 2—Improve the Processes

Phase 2 provides all employees the tools and techniques to continuously improve the foundation processes established in Phase 1. If a company decides not to take the complete Journey to Excellence, they should at least proceed through Phase 2. Key aspects of this phase of the journey are elimination of non-value added process steps, mapping of processes, barrier identification and removal, team problem solving and process improvement, planning and metrics.

### Part 1 of Phase 2—Continuous Improvement Training

Phase 1 of Phase 2 can be accomplished through an investment of 16 hours of intensive Tools for Continuous Improvement (TFCI) classroom training for every employee of the company. The end result of such training is the knowledge by the employee of how to use the tools and techniques applied to process improvement, and a systematic approach or way of thinking in so doing. Any of the tools and techniques can be used by the employee, as deemed needed at any particular time and in any relevant order.

## JOURNEY TO EXCELLENCE

**Management Systems**
1. Leadership
2. Information & Analysis
3. Strategic Planning
4. Human Resource Development and Management
5. Process Management
6. Business Results
7. Customer Focus & Satisfaction

**Phase 4**
Drivers
* Customer Value Alignment

Total Customer Satisfaction

**Phase 3**
Drivers
* Management System
* Performance Measurements
* Benchmarking
* Goal Setting

Management Systems Alignment

**Phase 2**
Drivers
* Process Mapping
* Cycle Time Reduction
* Teamwork
* Work Simplification
* Problem Solving

Continuous Improvement

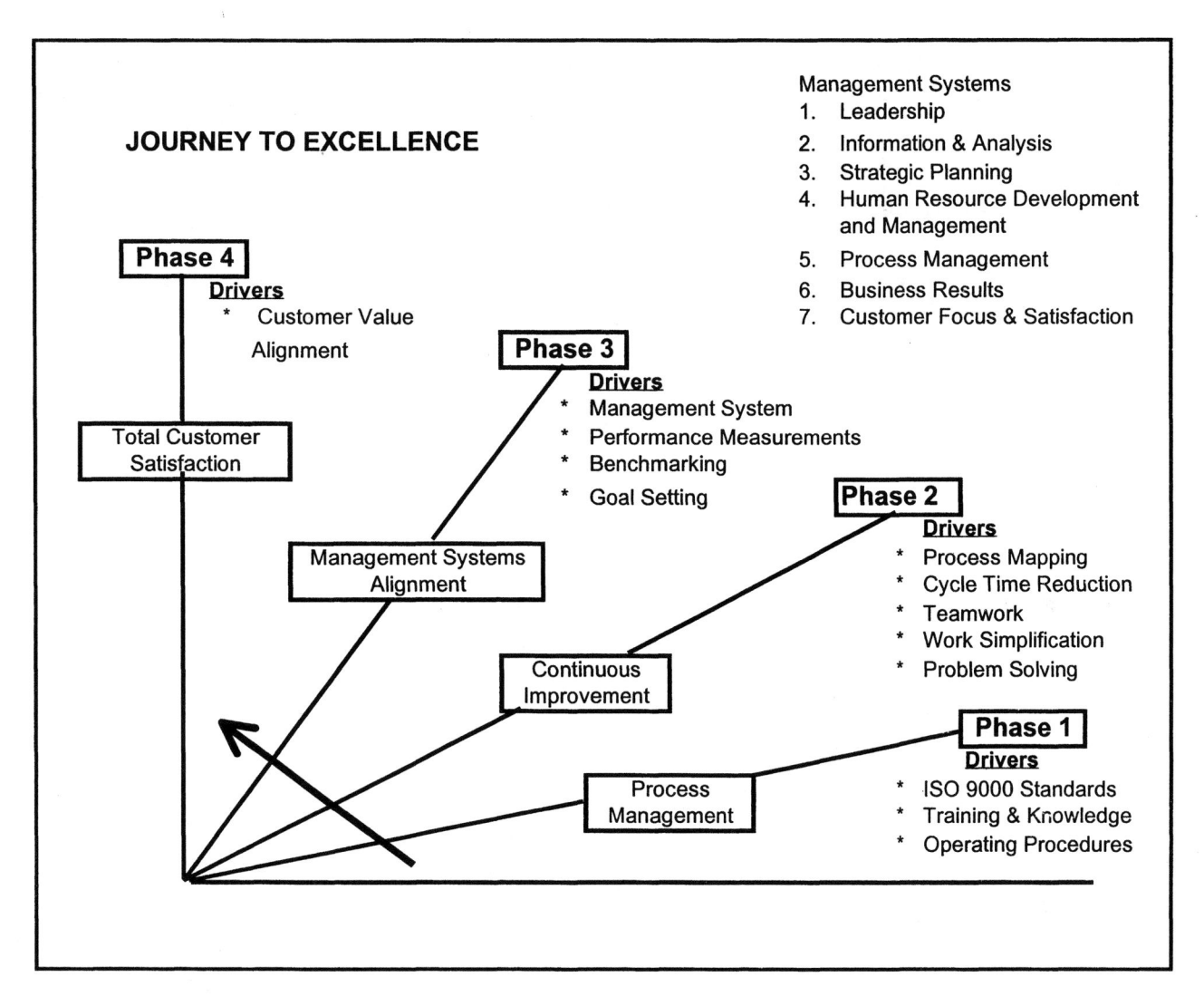

**Phase 1**
Drivers
* ISO 9000 Standards
* Training & Knowledge
* Operating Procedures

Process Management

**Figure 19-1. Journey to Excellence**

The TFCI training provides the employee with the tools and skills for process improvement. The tools that are provided by such training should include:

- Work Process Chart
- Histograms
- Pareto Charts
- PERT Chart
- Help-Hindrance Diagram
- Run Chart
- Cause-Effect Diagram

- Matrix Chart
- Gantt Chart
- Cost Benefits Chart

The techniques provided by TFCI training should include:

- How to prepare and analyze the cost and benefit of proposed improvements
- How to write a problem or opportunity for improvement statement
- How to define a process and scope the area for analysis
- How to measure the outputs of a process
- How to brainstorm causes and solutions
- How to prioritize solutions
- How to map work processes
- How to evaluate work processes relative to value added, necessary non-value added, and non-value added steps
- How to plan, implement, and measure the proposed improvement
- How to present the proposed improvement to management
- How to reduce/eliminate non-value adding steps from the work processes
- How to look at work processes innovatively
- How to work in teams

The skills taught during the TFCI training should include:

- How to actually apply all of the tools and techniques to a real project that is selected by the participant prior to the training. In other words, the training for the employee should include the solution of a problem or the improvement of a process as an integral part of the training.

The end result is the knowledge by the employee of how to use the tools and techniques applied to process improvement, and a systematic approach or way of thinking in so doing.

Any or all of the tools and techniques can be used by the employee, as deemed needed at any particular time and in any relevant order.

The TFCI training should simply be training for the employee to take back into his/her respective work environment and use in their efforts to effect continuous improvement.

### Part 2 of Phase 2—The Workplace Environment

Part 2 of the Phase 2 effort is in addition to the tools and techniques and establishes a workplace environment that will allow the employee to provide innovative solutions and ideas leading towards continuous improvement. Creation of this workplace environment oftentimes involves the changing of the culture of a company from one of very tight management control to one of control through leadership, processes, metrics, and accountability.

Phase 2 is aligned with the overall company objective, an example of which would be:

*Creating an environment for our employees that encourages innovative thinking, personal initiative, problem identification and problem solving, prevention, and commitment to continuous improvement and encouraging decisionmaking at the lowest practical levels.*

Part 2 of Phase 2 of the Journey to Excellence Plan involves a change of thought process from the traditional functional, hierarchical organizational structure to a matrix structure involving teams (cross-functional and departmental) and employee empowerment, with every employee becoming a "problem identifier" and "problem solver" and operating with a strong feeling of "I can make a positive difference." It also involves a change in mindset, to one where management is responsive to the needs of the work processes and employees are responsible for their work. To accomplish this it is necessary to establish a proper working environment that will both promote and allow for improvement opportunities to be identified and acted upon by employees in an innovative and empowered manner.

## Phase 3—Management Systems Alignment

Phase 3 is the establishment of management systems and processes where needed and the improvement of organizational effectiveness of those systems already established. Phase 3 maps the current management systems and processes and compares them to benchmarks from national and business standards, as well as to other world class companies.

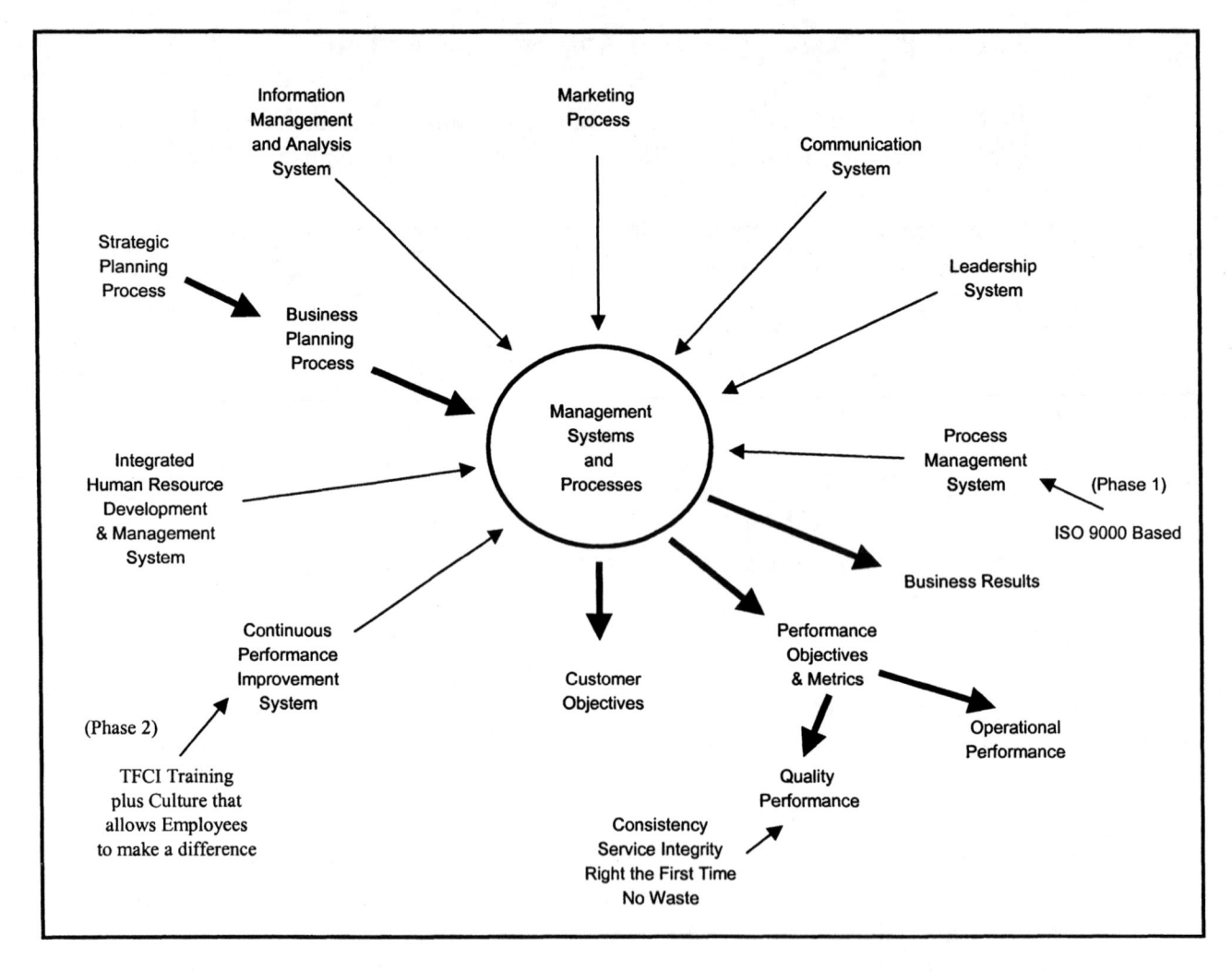

**Figure 19-2. Phase 3—Management Systems and Processes**

Some of the Management System Categories include (but are not limited to):

- Leadership
- Information and Analysis
- Strategic and Business Planning
- Human Resource Development and Management
- Process Management
- Business Results
- Customer Focus and Satisfaction

In considering the imperatives of each respective company's business, one must identify certain key strategic elements that must be incorporated into their plans if they are to compete effectively in the chosen markets. These elements deal with management systems and the alignment of such with the business objectives of the Journey to Excellence and are discussed below.

## Leadership

The responsibility for leadership strategy and its implementation belongs to the senior management team. This responsibility includes how the leadership translates the company's strategy into an effective overall organization and a management system that is performance based. Elements of this system include:

- Developing and maintaining an effective leadership system focused on individual development, high performance, and organizational learning
- Setting strategic direction
- Creating value and expectations
- Building company capabilities
- Building teamwork

## Information and Analysis

Information of all kinds must be managed for competitive advantage. In today's environment, the use of modern and efficient communications systems to support effective management decision is a must.

Measurements must be developed, tracked, and managed to show continually improving trends in overall quality, financial performance, core competencies, work process performance, employee satisfaction, cycle time reduction and customer satisfaction. These seven generic measurements should be regularly reported to the company's executive management.

The Information and Analysis System considers how well information from all systems is aggregated and analyzed to support reviews, business decisions, and planning. The system includes how competitive comparisons and benchmarking are used to drive improvement of overall company performance; rapid access and update of data capability; user needs considerations; reliability; selection and management of information. The Information and Analysis System is the "brain center" for the alignment of the company information system with its strategic directions.

## Strategic and Business Planning

A fact-based strategic and business planning and market planning process should be used to identify, select, and address those markets where the company has or can achieve competitive advantage.

The Strategic Planning System focuses on how strategy and plans are translated into key business drivers and includes such elements as:

- Operational performance requirements
- Customer performance requirements
- Long range view of key influences, challenges, and requirements that might affect the company's future opportunity and direction

The Business Planning System focuses on how well the plan is deployed throughout the organization and integrated into the review/measurement system and its effectiveness. The Business Planning System takes the key business drivers and translates them into:

- Action plans
- Spelling out the key performance requirements
- The alignment of work units
- How productivity, cycle time, and waste reduction are addressed
- The principal resources committed
- How alignment and consistency are achieved

## Human Resource Development and Management

The Integrated Human Resource Development and Management System ties the HR practices into and aligns them with the company's strategic directions. Included are the employee education, training, and development processes, the setting up of high performance work systems, employee well being and satisfaction, HR planning and evaluation, and employee incentive alignment.

The development of the entire workforce and the needs of a high performance workplace are addressed. The approach to enhance employee well being, satisfaction, and growth potential are addressed. Teamwork, employee recognition, employee compensation, job design, more employee discretion and decisionmaking, work environment, employee well being, and employee satisfaction are some of the other elements to be addressed.

## Process Management

A time-based management approach for understanding, managing, and continuously improving all key work processes and support to customers is recommended. The ISO 9000-based Quality System comprises the Quality Assurance System, which needs to be used throughout the company.

The Process Management System is the focal point for all key work processes and includes support services.

## Business Results

Measurements must be developed, tracked, and managed to show continually improving trends in the overall quality of the service delivery processes and in the support processes. Each category of service should be compared to the performances of industry leaders, with targets set to achieve world class performance and excellence.

Business Results include performance objectives and measures of quality performance, operational performance, competitive performance, and customer and market performance.

The Business Results provide a results focus for all processes and process improvement activities as well as "real time" information (measures or progress) for evaluation and improvement. Included are company operational and financial results, product and service quality results, and service performance results.

Measures also include comparative information and current level and trends for each.

## Customer Focus and Satisfaction

The Customer Focus and Satisfaction System is a closed-loop measurement and management system for identifying, understanding and fully satisfying customer requirements at competitive costs to the company and its customers. This system is the focal point for understanding in detail the voices of customers and the marketplace, with inputs coming from results and trends.

Included elements are customer relationship management (ease of customer access to information, complaint management, how customer follow-up is accomplished); customer market and knowledge (process for determining requirements and expectations, process for addressing future customer requirements and expectations); customer satisfaction results (customer dissatisfaction measurements, customer satisfaction measurements); customer satisfaction comparison (comparisons of gains and losses of customer accounts, and customer satisfaction relative to competitors, trends in gaining or losing market share).

### Communication System

The Communication System relates to how communicated information is "made real" throughout the company and reinforced through the organization and management system and work processes. This communicated information includes company values; company expectations; company directions; review of work process assessments, company performance, work unit performance.

The communications system must constantly reinforce "truth testing" and "walk the walk."

## Phase 4—Total Customer Satisfaction

Phase 4 is the alignment of the entire organization (people and processes) with the evolving needs of the company's targeted market. Phase 4 involves getting closer to the market (customers and competitor's customers) than the competitors do; being market driven; understanding customer needs and expectations; getting closer to customers and being customer driven.

## CONCLUSION

The foregoing Journey to Excellence is presented as one of the paths a company can take beyond ISO 9000 Certification. Any path, however, including the one presented, must have the full commitment of senior management from the very beginning, as they must be the champions for such a Journey to be successful. Planning the Journey prior to launch is essential, as is being willing to modify that plan en route.

Company-wide training in problem identification and problem solving is also a key factor in the success of the Journey, independent of the path chosen. All employees are involved in the effort.

It is much easier to stop the Journey after ISO 9000 Certification (Phase 1 of the Journey to Excellence presented), and many more companies do so than those who go forward. However, one need only ask those who have gone forward to see the positive results that are possible.

In reality, many companies are already on the Journey to Excellence, needing only to assess where they are and what gaps need to be filled in order to get to where they want to go.

As shown in the highlighted path of Figure 19-2, one very important consideration is the Strategic Planning Process through the Business Planning Process to the outputs of Customer Objectives, Performance Objectives and Metrics, Operational Performance, and Quality Performance. All employees should be tied into this path, with everything that they do supporting this path in some manner.

Notice that the Process Management System (Phase 1) in Figure 19-2 (the ISO 9000 Quality System) is only one small part of the overall Management Systems and Processes and that it is not at the center. Many people have the perception that the Quality System resides at the center and it may seem so sometimes, but it is very important that it be kept in its place. The Continuous Improvement System (Phase 2) is likewise only one part of the overall Management System and Process.

It is recommended that one obtain a copy of the Malcolm Baldrige National Quality Award Criteria for Performance Excellence (obtainable from the United States Department of Commerce). This document is an excellent model for Phase 3 of the Journey to Excellence and for Management Systems and Processes.

# Chapter 20

# CONTINUOUS IMPROVEMENT

As described in Chapter 19, continuous improvement is Phase 2 of the Journey to Excellence and is absolutely vital for a company if that company does not want to become stagnant and fall behind its competitors. It is an established fact that left alone, a company will improve. However, what distinguishes companies is the rate of improvement.

Will Rogers once said: *"You may be on the right track, but if you ain't moving fast enough you will get run over anyway."*

The same is true relative to continuous improvement. You may be on the right track of improvement, but one needs to move along that track at a pace that is faster than the competition. To do this, every employee needs to be a part of the continuous improvement process.

One method of accomplishing this is to set up the foundation for that improvement to take place. This is best accomplished by the establishment of procedures and work instructions that describe what and how the work is done by the respective company. Of course, the ISO 9000-based Quality System does this beautifully. Following this, one needs to train all employees in the tools for continuous improvement and to allow them the necessary time to apply those tools to their work processes, either individually or as part of a continuous improvement team.

## TOOLS FOR CONTINUOUS IMPROVEMENT

There are many methods and sources of tools that can be used in applying continuous improvement and, in general, no one is particularly better than the other. What needs to be done is to establish the method and select the tools that best fit each particular company and teach those tools to all employees. The primary reason for this is so that all employees are talking the same language and using the same methodology in addressing improvement opportunities.

One method is a 12-step process that involves the application of the tools to actual work processes an employee brings to the class. In this approach, employees are placed up into teams of two to four individuals. These teams then select a work process to work on during the formalized training sessions. There need to be guidelines furnished to ensure that the project chosen is a viable one—a project for which all of the tools being taught can be applied.

The students then receive four sessions of four hours each in learning and applying the tools for continuous improvement. These four sessions are shown in Figure 20-1. The actual tools and techniques taught are listed in Chapter 19.

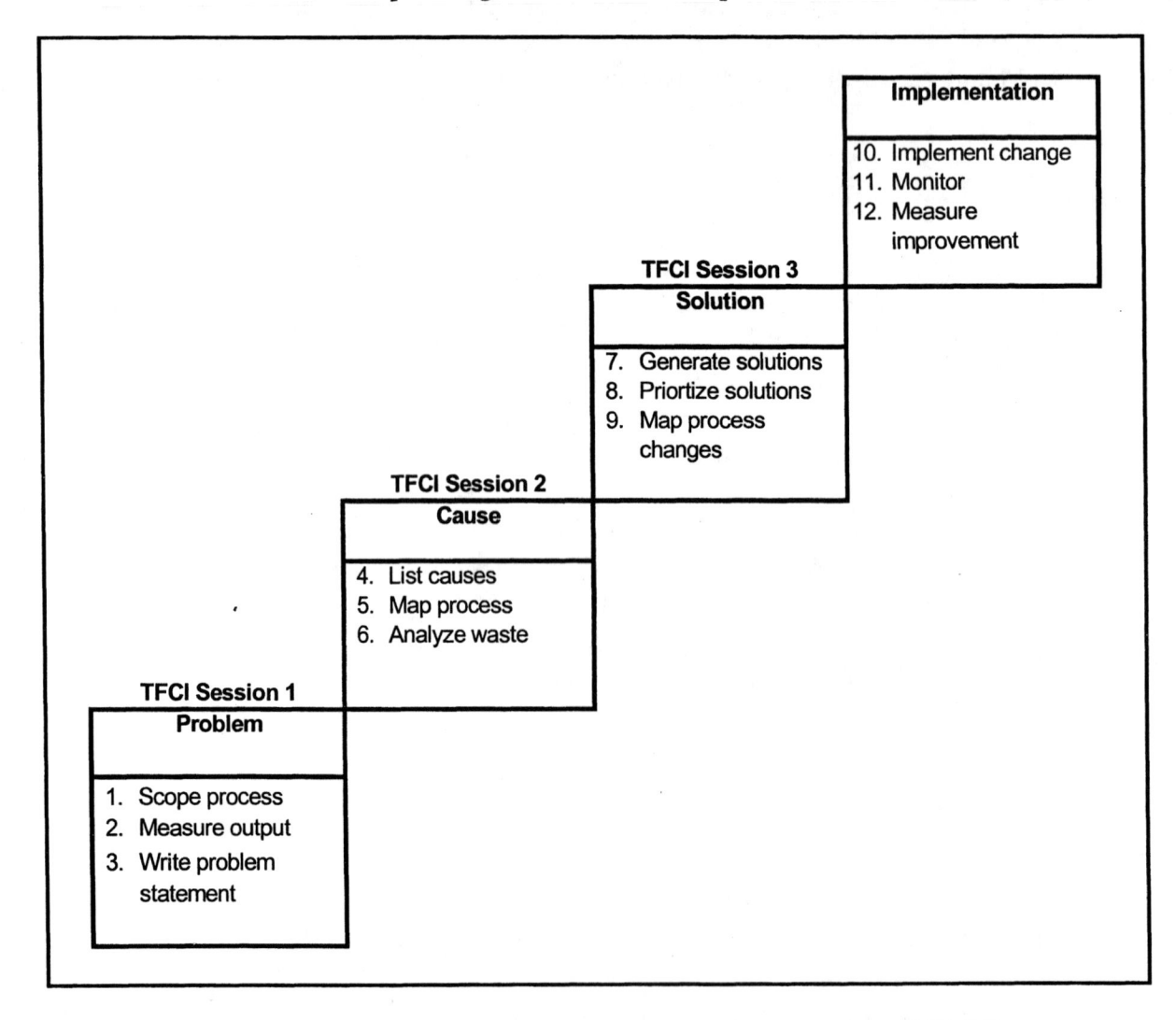

**Implementation**

10. Implement change
11. Monitor
12. Measure improvement

**TFCI Session 3**
**Solution**

7. Generate solutions
8. Priortize solutions
9. Map process changes

**TFCI Session 2**
**Cause**

4. List causes
5. Map process
6. Analyze waste

**TFCI Session 1**
**Problem**

1. Scope process
2. Measure output
3. Write problem statement

**Figure 20-1. Tools for Continuous Improvement (TFCI)—Process Improvement Model**

Some of the basic project improvement tools taught during these sessions include:

Session 1: Work Process Chart
    Run Chart
    Histogram

Session 2: Cause-Effect Diagram—Causes
    Process Map of existing process
    Pareto Chart of causes

Session 3: Cause-Effect Diagram—Solutions
    Process Map of revised process incorporating solutions
    Matrix chart prioritizing solutions

Session 4: PERT Chart
    Project Cost-Benefit Chart
    Gantt Chart

Figure 20-5 shows the tools that are included in each session.

One of the key tools that should be included in any continuous improvement program is that of process mapping.

## Process Mapping

If one defines quality as "the way we do our work," then mapping is the term used for diagramming of "how we do our work."

There are two types of mapping: that which is associated with processes and that which is associated with the office wherein or from which the process is conducted. Process mapping is very precise and simply documents, in a diagram format, the written words that describe how one does his or her work. Office mapping utilizes the same tools as process mapping but is approached differently.

Mapping may be done in several levels, beginning at Level 1, which is simply the name of the overall process. Examples would include corrective and preventive action, contract review, document control, logging, filing, getting dressed, etc. Level 2 includes the steps that make up the Level 1 process, presented in the sequence in which they occur. Level 3 selects any one of the Level 2 steps and breaks it up into individual steps from which it is made, presented in the sequence in which they occur. Level 4 and further levels do the same as the Level 3 approach. In general, one does not map below Level 5.

**The Purpose of Process Mapping** is to present, in a visible format, all of the process steps for the process being mapped. The end result of doing so allows one to easily see the redundant steps and the non-value added steps, giving a clearer picture of opportunities and ways to improve the process. Process mapping is also a way of documenting the process in a user-friendly format. Analysis of such mapping includes the number of process steps, the cycle time of each step, and of the overall process and the duplication of process steps. Duplication of work within each step is easily seen through the Level 3 mapping of the chosen Level 2 process step (reference Figure 20-2).

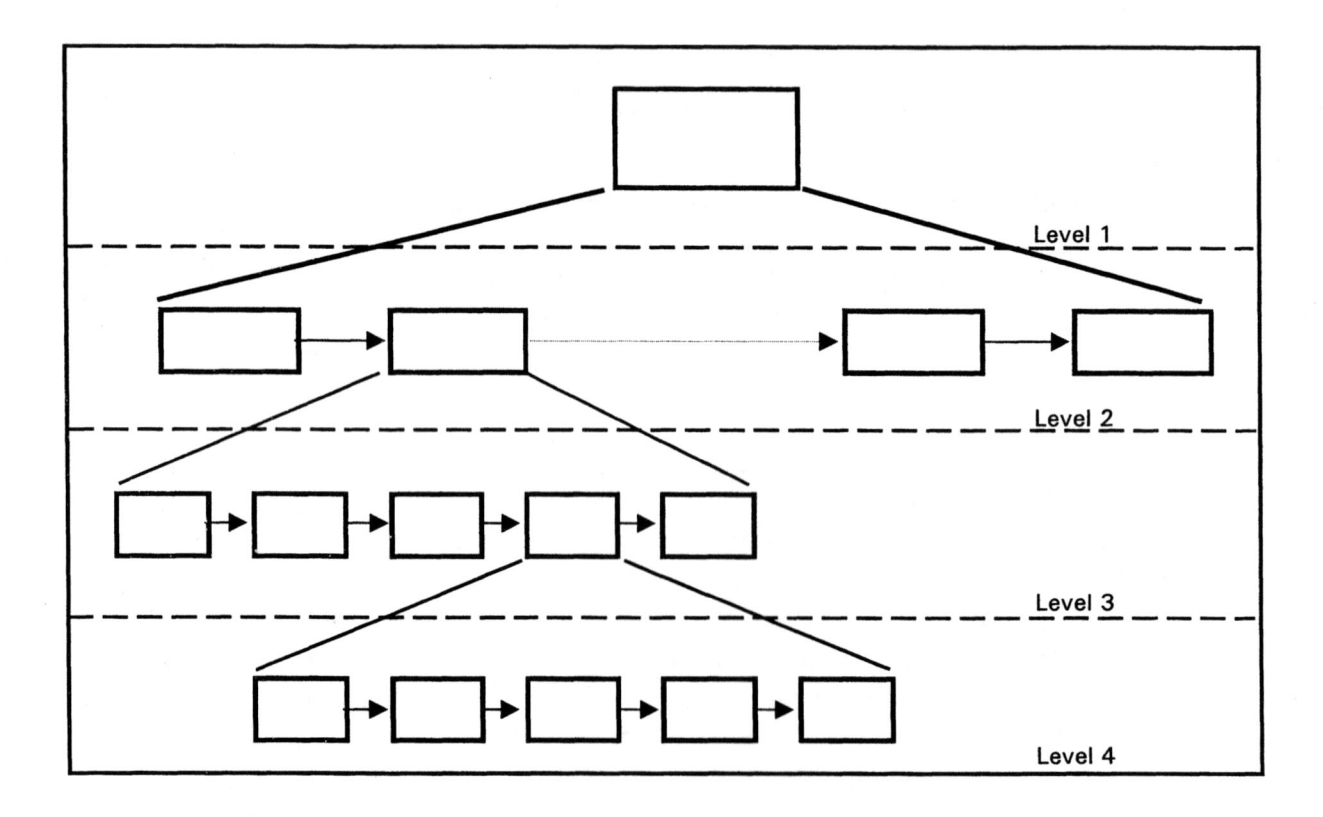

**Figure 20-2. Process and Office Mapping**

**The Purpose of Office Mapping** is to identify opportunities for improvement within the office through the analysis of the existing work within that office and then the generation of suggestions for possible improvement to that work. This is accomplished through the preparation of process maps incorporating the identified improvements. The office process map will be no different in format than the process map.

**The Approach to Process and Office Mapping** is to have the personnel who perform the process to work as a team to build the map. This is accomplished by using "Post-It" notes to construct the map, as shown in Figure 20-3. Following the mapping effort, the team identifies the opportunities associated with the process, identifies any idea that may surface relative to a better way to accomplish the process, and then proceeds to make a new process map that incorporates these improvements. These identified improvements may include the elimination of process steps, the reduction of cycle time, the elimination of logging, photocopying, and duplicating files. Always in a mapping effort, a Cost-Benefits Analysis must be done relative to the proposed changes in order to cost justify making the changes. The cost analysis must include the cost of implementation (training, documentation, equipment, etc.).

After the process map is completed, it is generally converted into a *flow diagram*. So doing allows for a better presentation for future use in training, analysis, documentation within procedures, and/or work instruction, etc. Figure 20-3 shows a portion of a process map using "Post-it" notes. Figure 20-4 shows that process in the format of a flow diagram.

It is not necessary to show the map in the style as shown in Figure 20-3. One can show only those steps in the specific level being mapped. In addition, all process steps should be shown, including the wait steps and move steps associated with the item flowing through the process. These steps are not shown in the referenced figure. Typically, incoming letters wait in the in-box until picked up, as would the incoming faxes.

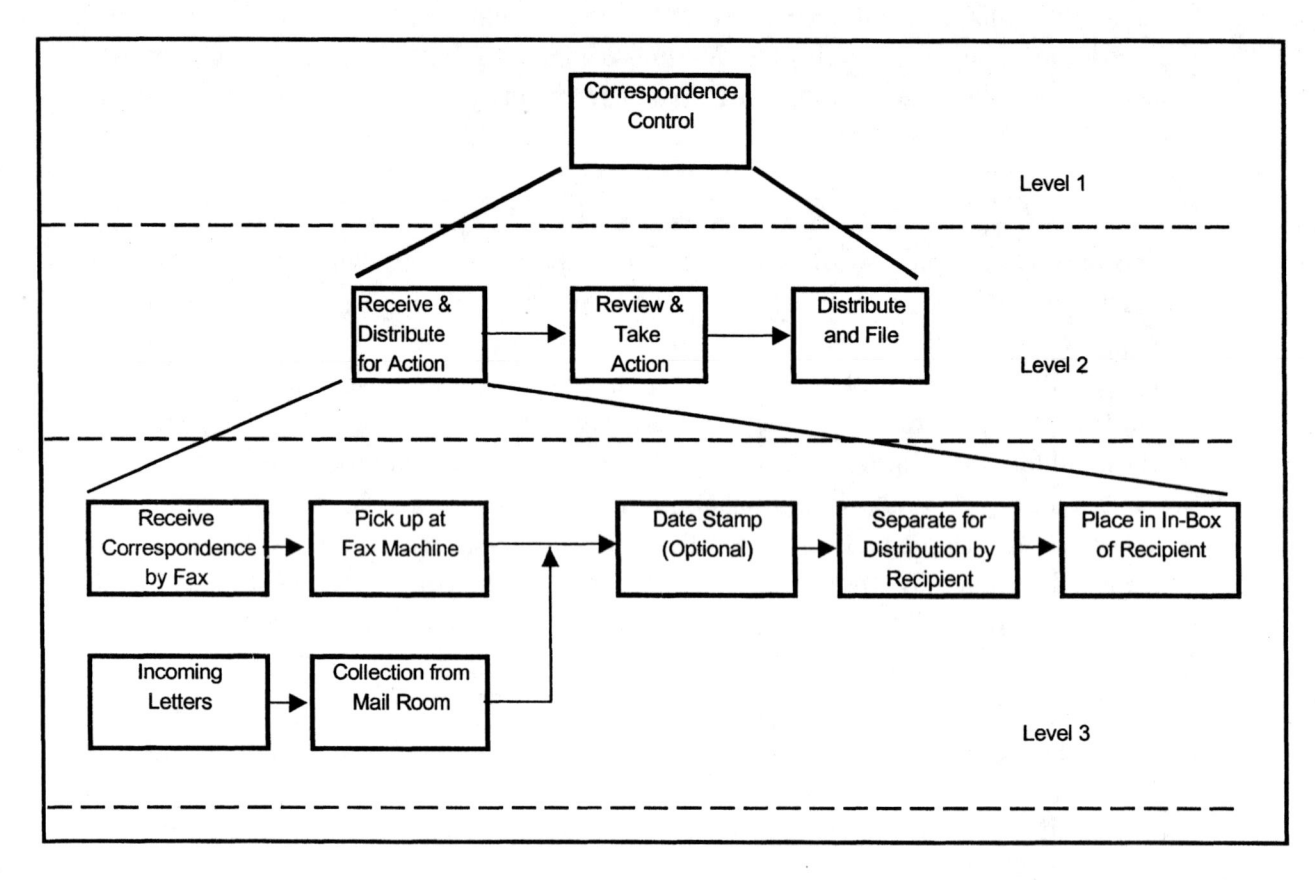

246 / *Implementing an ISO 9000-Based Quality System*

**Figure 20-3. Process Map—Correspondence Control**

## Correspondence Control Process

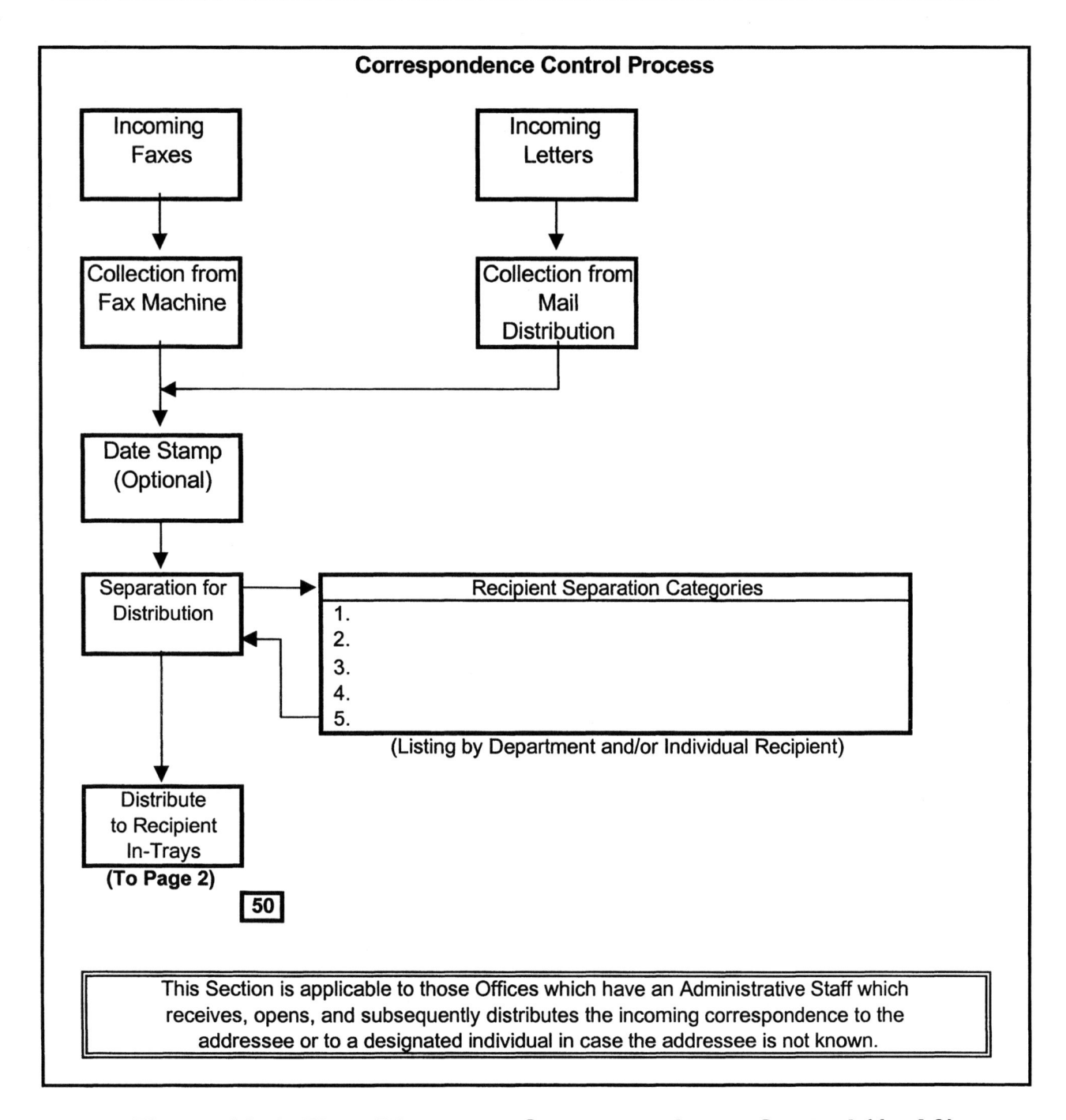

```
Incoming Faxes              Incoming Letters
    ↓                            ↓
Collection from            Collection from
Fax Machine                Mail Distribution
    ↓ ←————————————————————————┘
Date Stamp
(Optional)
    ↓
Separation for  ——→  Recipient Separation Categories
Distribution         1.
         ←———        2.
    ↓                3.
                     4.
                     5.
                    (Listing by Department and/or Individual Recipient)
Distribute
to Recipient
In-Trays
(To Page 2)
   [50]
```

This Section is applicable to those Offices which have an Administrative Staff which receives, opens, and subsequently distributes the incoming correspondence to the addressee or to a designated individual in case the addressee is not known.

**Figure 20-4. Flow Diagram—Correspondence Control (1 of 3)**

248 / Implementing an ISO 9000-Based Quality System

**Correspondence Control Process**

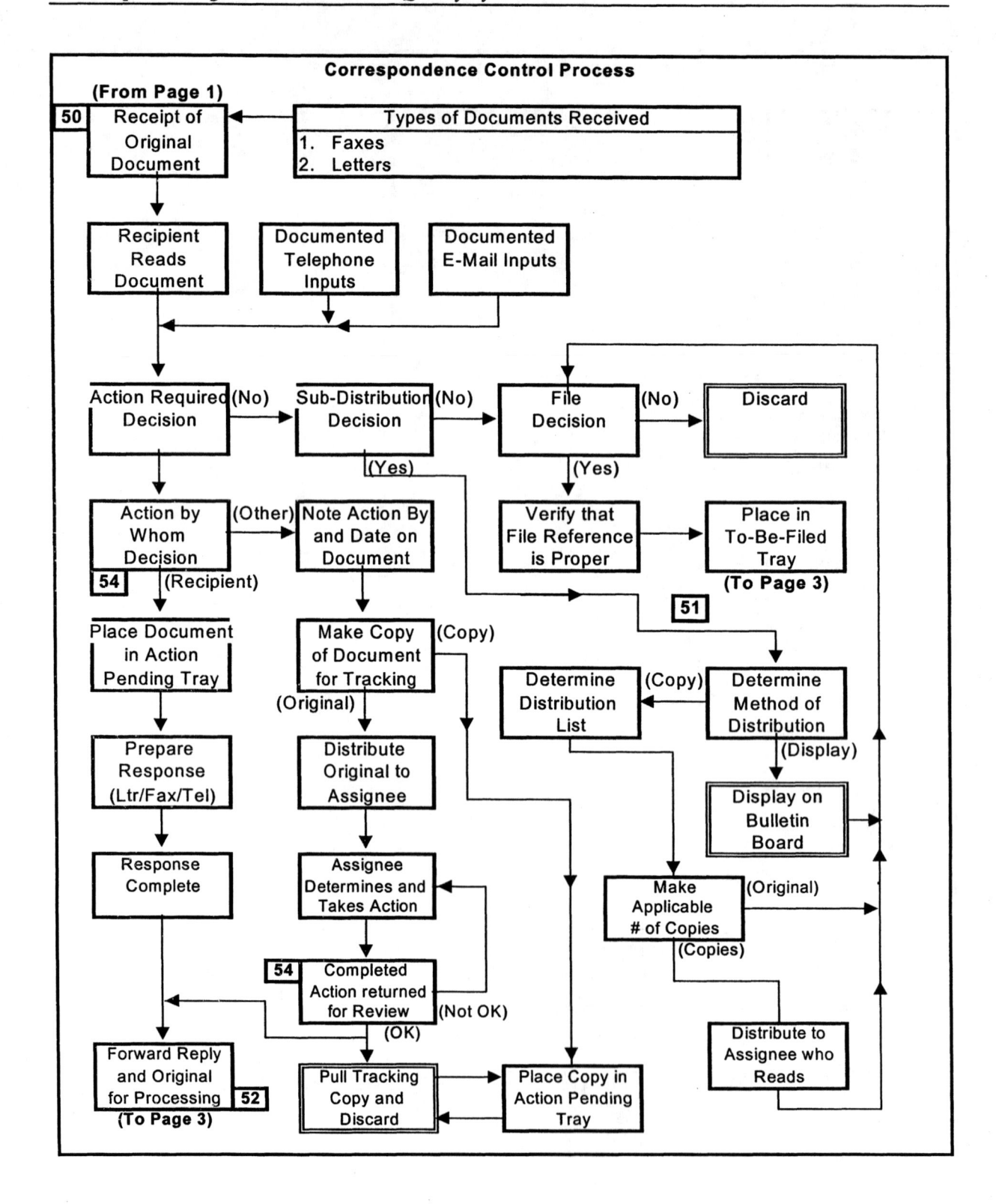

(From Page 1)

**50** Receipt of Original Document ← Types of Documents Received
1. Faxes
2. Letters

↓

Recipient Reads Document ← Documented Telephone Inputs, Documented E-Mail Inputs

↓

Action Required Decision —(No)→ Sub-Distribution Decision —(No)→ File Decision —(No)→ Discard

(Yes) ↓ (below Sub-Distribution)
(Yes) ↓ (below File Decision) → Verify that File Reference is Proper → Place in To-Be-Filed Tray (To Page 3)

Action by Whom Decision **54** —(Other)→ Note Action By and Date on Document

(Recipient) ↓

Place Document in Action Pending Tray

↓

Prepare Response (Ltr/Fax/Tel)

↓

Response Complete

↓

Forward Reply and Original for Processing **52** (To Page 3)

Make Copy of Document for Tracking —(Copy)→ 
(Original) ↓

Distribute Original to Assignee

↓

Assignee Determines and Takes Action

↓

**54** Completed Action returned for Review —(Not OK)→ (back to Assignee)
(OK) ↓

Pull Tracking Copy and Discard ← Place Copy in Action Pending Tray

**51** → Determine Method of Distribution —(Copy)→ Determine Distribution List
(Display) ↓

Display on Bulletin Board

Make Applicable # of Copies —(Original)→
(Copies) ↓

Distribute to Assignee who Reads

## Correspondence Control Process

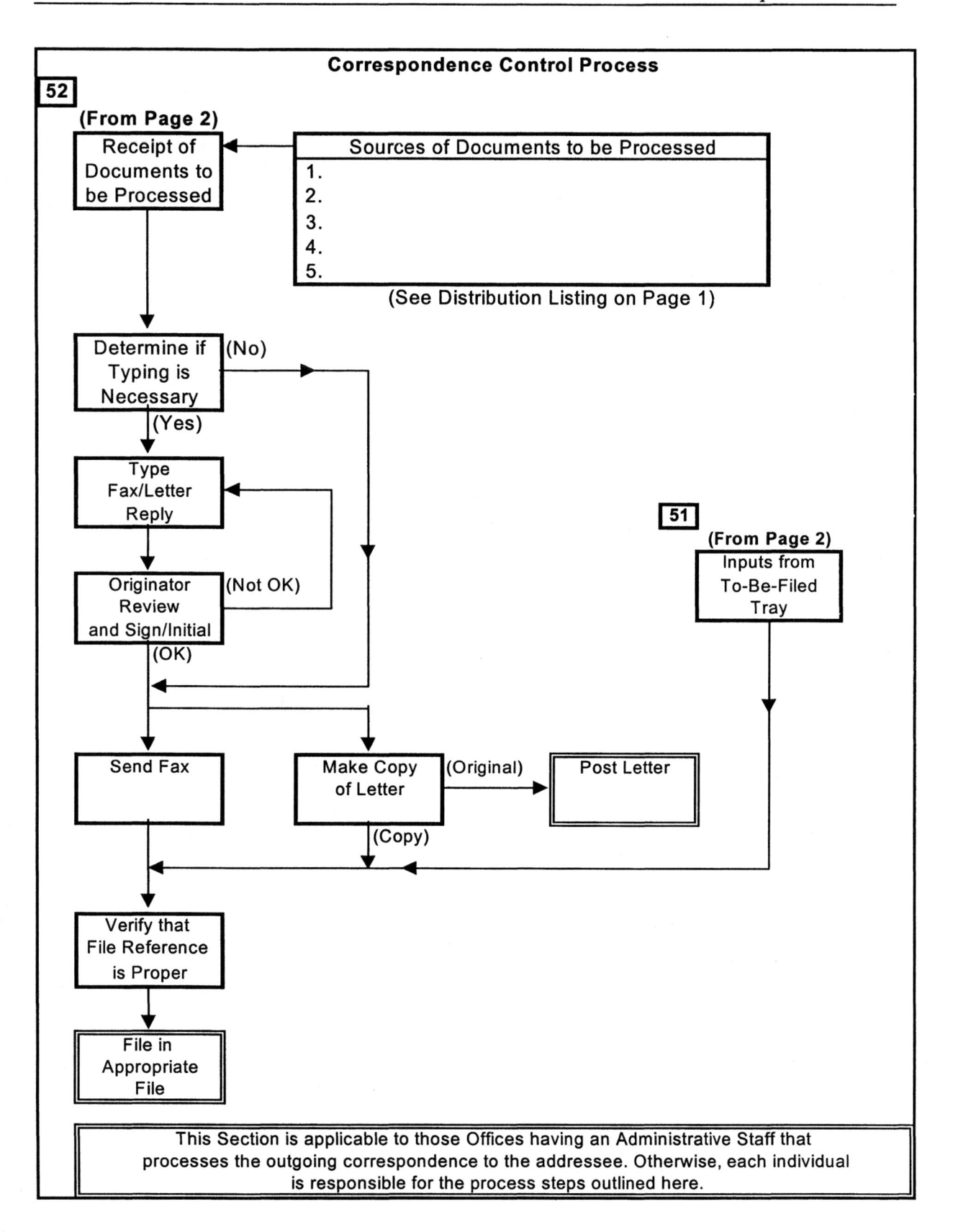

**52** (From Page 2)

- Receipt of Documents to be Processed ← Sources of Documents to be Processed
  1.
  2.
  3.
  4.
  5.
  (See Distribution Listing on Page 1)

- Determine if Typing is Necessary
  - (No) → (to Make Copy of Letter)
  - (Yes) ↓
- Type Fax/Letter Reply
- Originator Review and Sign/Initial
  - (Not OK) → back to Type Fax/Letter Reply
  - (OK) ↓
- Send Fax
- Make Copy of Letter
  - (Original) → Post Letter
  - (Copy) ↓

**51** (From Page 2)
- Inputs from To-Be-Filed Tray

- Verify that File Reference is Proper
- File in Appropriate File

This Section is applicable to those Offices having an Administrative Staff that processes the outgoing correspondence to the addressee. Otherwise, each individual is responsible for the process steps outlined here.

## Office Mapping

The approach to Office Mapping varies from that of Process Mapping and therefore is expanded here to allow for a better understanding. The Office Mapping is accomplished utilizing the same tools and techniques as Process Mapping and involves a majority of the staff members in the mapped office. The integral parts of the Office Mapping process include:

1. The identification of all of the processes occurring within each function of the office. Remember that a process is "a series of actions that produce a result," or "the work we do to convert process inputs to process outputs." From this listing will come those processes to be analyzed using the Office Mapping techniques.
2. The estimation of the types and percent of time spent in doing the work done within each function of the office. The breakdown is for each category of employee, such as Administrative Assistant, Engineer, Office Supervisor, etc.
3. The listing of all logs and databases maintained by each function within the office
4. The listing of all file types kept and maintained within the office

The work processes initially chosen for mapping are determined by the relative contribution to the types and percent of work performed of that process, the larger the contribution being the more likely mapping prospect. In addition, the contribution of the process towards non-value added work within the office itself is considered in the process selection.

**The Deployment of Office Mapping** is then accomplished by spending time with the personnel associated with the chosen processes to be mapped, allowing them to map the chosen process as it currently is performed, including all process steps and who accomplishes them. If logs or databases are kept, then each data field is listed. If copies are made, then the process path for each copy must be shown until it is either filed, destroyed, or ends its journey through the process.

The viewpoint in the mapping effort must be from that of the item going though the process (that which is happening to the item) and not from the viewpoint of who is performing the process. In other words, if a FAX is waiting in an in box, that is a process step from the viewpoint of the FAX, even though no work is being performed at that time on the FAX.

After the mapping of the current process steps for the process chosen, the participants hold a brainstorming session to list the current problems, issues, and barriers being experienced with the process. In addition, the participants list "challenge" goals for the new or revised process map, which is to be generated. These "challenge" goals might include such items as:

- Eliminate the making of photocopies.
- Eliminate duplicate files.
- Eliminate all logging or, as a minimum, reduce data fields associated with logging.
- Eliminate duplicate process steps.
- Eliminate duplicate processes.

The chosen process is then re-mapped utilizing the existing process map, the identified problems, issues and barriers, and the listed goals, beginning with a fresh piece of paper rather than modifying the existing process map.

After mapping, each identified problem, issue, and barrier is "bounced" against the new process to see if it was eliminated or reduced. This may cause further adjustments to the re-mapped process map. In like manner, the listed goals are "bounced" against the re-mapped process.

A "sanity check" should be performed on the re-mapped process to determine if the changes make sense from a number of different viewpoints. In addition, as stated earlier, a Cost-Benefits Analysis must be done for the re-mapped process, comparing the revised versus the current processes, This Cost-Benefits Analysis must be based on the respective process maps and must be coupled with a plan of implementation.

During the design of the re-mapped process, measurement points should be selected that will best determine the "health" of the process, so that the process can be accurately monitored, with the idea of continuous improvement in mind. Remember, if it is not measured, it is not managed and you cannot have quality without measurements. All processes can be measured.

Finally, one may want to convert the process map into a flow diagram format to better display and use in the future.

A resulting comprehensive report should be prepared containing an overall summary and the documentation associated with the mapping effort in the form of analysis and flow diagrams, if convenient.

Generally, management participates in the process and approval is gained on the revisions to the processes on-the-spot, with a corresponding plan for implementation prepared prior to the completion of the effort.

Each office staff member receives, through the application of the tools and techniques applied to a process in which they are personally involved, the training and motivation to proceed to map other processes in a team environment. The key for so doing, however, is to ensure the employees be allowed the time and given the encouragement to do so.

One of the end results is learning to question, asking questions like, "Why are we doing this?" "What are the requirements?" "Who is requiring this, and why?" "Is there a better, simpler way of doing it?" and, finally, "What is the nature of the communication between internal supplier and internal customer?"

## ENVIRONMENT FOR CONTINUOUS IMPROVEMENT

A Quality System requires adherence to the procedures and work instructions that each department has laid down. The concept of Continuous Improvement involves challenging those procedures, and everything that is done and the manner in which it is done, to constantly evaluate if there are better ways, smarter ways, more efficient ways to operate.

Over the past ten years, the majority of companies in the U.S., and many others globally, have been striving to improve the quality of their products and services. A few have found the key to real improvement. But many have only a certificate of compliance to show for their efforts. They have confused the introduction of a system with the need to develop a management philosophy.

Those companies that have experienced real benefit are the ones that have instilled a culture of continuous improvement throughout their organization. The challenge for all is to understand and to encourage such a culture.

One of the first steps is to establish a workplace environment that will not just allow, but which will stimulate employees to suggest innovative ideas that could improve the way in which we operate.

According to Frank Iarossi, Chairman of the American Bureau of Shipping,

*Our challenge is to create a workplace environment that encourages employee participation, teamwork, leadership, and innovation. All of this should be focused on fostering continuous improvement and appropriate decisionmaking at all levels of the organization. The challenge facing every ABS employee is to constantly ask themselves how they can do the jobs assigned to them more efficiently and more productively, and to then develop a broad consensus in support to the proposed change.*

This continuous improvement environment is an *informal* one. The formal procedures are contained in the Quality System. Continuous improvement requires that everyone continue to question what we do and how we do it, challenging every aspect of our operations.

Frank Iarossi further states that

*The major responsibility for fostering this new environment rests with managers at all levels who, in the new culture, must be prepared to not only encourage and support improvement suggestions from their subordinates, but to implement them.*

He is right on target!

When this culture takes hold, one will be able to say, "We have found that we have simplified the way that we work, we have become more innovative in the way that tasks are approached, and we have enhanced the quality of the entire work process."

Each employee holds the key to success. Every employee should know more about his or her individual work processes than anyone else. Everyone should have ideas for improving and simplifying these processes. The key to making these improvements happen is to encourage ideas to surface, to listen to the questions that are raised, and to respond to the challenges that are posed, without creating an environment of fear or of failure of rejection. Good ideas must be allowed to build momentum and achieve a broad consensus.

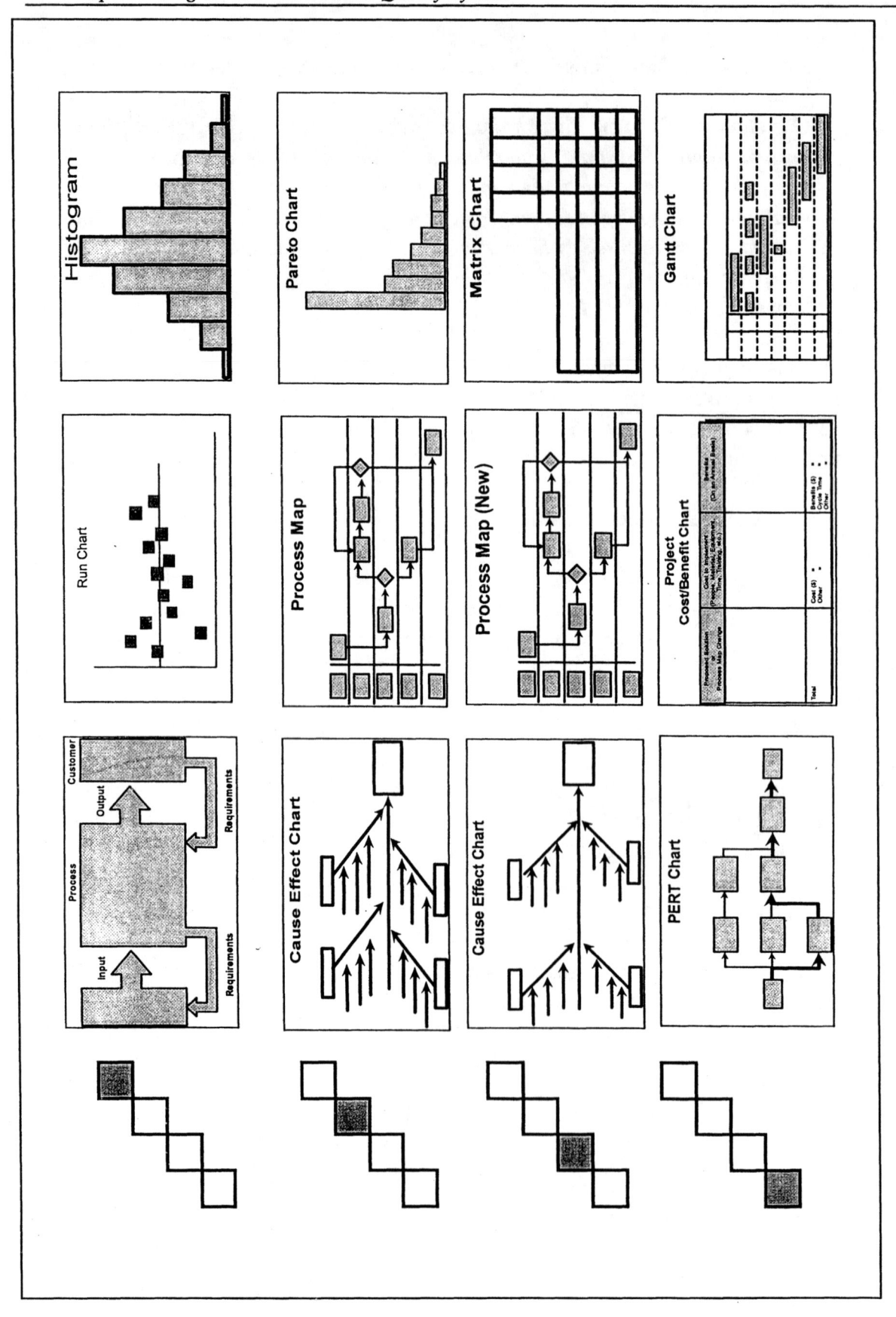

254 / Implementing an ISO 9000-Based Quality System

Figure 20-5. TFCI Project Tools

There is always the chance that, even though an idea may seem sensible to the person proposing it, it cannot be adopted for other reasons. Such a response should never be considered a failure or reason to lose face or, most importantly, to feel that any future suggestions will be rejected in the same way. It should never be considered a reason to stop participating in the process.

It can be difficult to make the time in a busy day to think through a work process and come up with a better method. But, by making time, and improving the way in which you do your job, you will be creating more time to think in the future. It is important that everyone resolves to take those risks, to make the time, and to have the courage to try to effect improvement.

If we do, then our jobs should be more enjoyable, less frustrating, and more fun. By supporting and encouraging each other in a positive manner, blame will take a back seat. Instead, we will be able to learn from our mistakes and from others' points of view. We will be able to exert some control over our professional lives, and over the future success of the company for which we work.

## HOW TO BE A PART OF CONTINUOUS IMPROVEMENT

- Develop a work environment that encourages continuous improvement.
- Identify those areas that are causing difficulty.
- Talk with each other and support each other in the search for better ways of doing things.
- Speak out when you have ideas or questions.
- Take the time to figure out why things aren't working as well as they should, rather than just complaining about the problems.
- Brainstorm the problem with your team.
- Identify and eliminate unnecessary "non-value" added steps from the way that work is done.
- Eliminate doing the same job twice (in part or in whole) because it was not done right the first time.
- Narrow alternatives down to the best solution.
- Develop consensus among those of your work mates who would be affected by a proposed change. Then the best, and most workable solution, is more likely to be developed and accepted.
- Carefully implement the agreed solution after informing all affected parties.

- Measure the impact of the new or revised way of doing things to determine if the change has really been for the better.
- Start the process all over again.

## Conclusion

**THERE IS NO FINISH LINE!**

# Chapter 21

# CASE STUDY: AMERICAN BUREAU OF SHIPPING (ABS)[1]

## The Mission of ABS

*We, the employees of the American Bureau of Shipping, seek to serve the public interest as well as the needs of our clients by promoting the security of life, property and the natural environment primarily through the development and verification of standards for the design, construction and operational maintenance of marine related facilities.*

## The Mission of ABS Group of Companies

*The mission of ABS Group of Companies is to assist its clients to improve the safety of their operations, to enhance the quality of their services, and to minimize the environmental impact of their activities.*

*The ABS Group of Companies pursue this mission by offering integrated services related to awareness, evaluation, training, implementation, verification and certification.*

*In fulfilling our vision of this mission:*
*We seek to be the foremost marine classification society in the world.*
*We seek to be the world's leader in the development of marine technology.*
*We encourage similar aspirations on the part of our affiliated companies in keeping with their respective missions.*

## Background

ABS was founded in 1862 as a not-for-profit self-regulatory agency of the marine industry to promote the safety of life and property at sea. Since that time it has performed this function through a procedure known as ship classification, a procedure which

---

[1] Includes the American Bureau of Shipping, its wholly owned subsidiary, ABS Group of Companies, and the operating subsidiaries of the ABS Group of Companies.

determines the structural and mechanical fitness of ships and other marine structures for their intended service.

The classification work of ABS involves two fundamental aspects. One is development of ABS Rules—the process by which standards for the design, construction and operational maintenance are established and updated. The other is the administration of ABS Rules—the process of analyzing designs and surveying new building structures for conformance to the Rules as well as surveying vessels in service to ensure maintenance in accordance with the Rules.

While the focus of ABS on ship classification has remained undiminished since its inception, the knowledge, experience, and resources of ABS have continuously progressed. More recently ABS Group of Companies was established as a wholly-owned, taxable subsidiary dedicated to diversifying the activities of ABS by rendering, to industrial clients throughout the world, integrated services aimed at improving safety, enhancing quality, and promoting environmental protection.

ABS continues to forge an identification with two all-important words—Safety & Quality—with Safety defining what we do and Quality defining how we do it.

## The ABS Journey—Overview

The ABS Journey to Excellence began in the spring of 1990, when ABS initiated a major strategic plan aimed at positioning ABS as a global enterprise providing a wide variety of maritime and industrial verification services. As explained by ABS Chairman, Frank J. Iarossi, "This strategic plan—called ABS 2000—is most importantly a renewal of our purpose, our principles, our values, and our dedication to providing a faithful balance of interests leading to the highest level of safety practical for the circumstances."

While the elements of ABS 2000 included a number of particular technical, administrative, and managerial objectives, a central objective running through all of the others is:

*an emphasis on quality and quality management in all aspects of ABS activities in order to totally integrate quality in all functions and to become a model of quality management for other companies to follow.*

Consistent with this goal, ABS made a commitment in 1991 to establish and implement a Total Quality Management Process. This commitment soon turned into a journey which expanded beyond Total Quality Management. It is a process of continuous improvement, which has no finish line and is called the "ABS Journey to Excellence."

The approach taken by ABS in its Journey to Excellence is one that aligns the activities of all employees and all management systems and processes within the organization with the *common focus on customer satisfaction through continuous improvement of all activities, goods, and services.* (Customer means a person or group, internal or external to the organization, to whom a service is provided.)

## Foundation of the ABS Journey to Excellence

In order to effect continuous improvement at an accelerated rate, ABS had first to establish a solid foundation on which to launch the journey. This involved the writing down of what we do (procedures and process instructions), doing what we write down (what we did anyway), and having visible evidence that we have done it (check sheets)—the essentials of an ISO 9001-based Quality System. Added to this is the establishment of an effective Corrective and Preventive Action System and an outstanding Internal Audit Program to ensure that we do what we wrote down.

From this foundation one need only close the loop by identifying opportunities for improving how we do our work and changing that which is written to reflect such. Of course training plays a big part in this overall process as well. The focus in the following text will be specific to the ISO 9001 effort of ABS, which forms the foundation for the Journey to Excellence, the lessons learned, and the successes gained.

The Journey to Excellence by the ABS organization worldwide is being accomplished in four concurrent phases.

**Phase 1** is the implementation of Process Management, which includes the installation of a Quality System based on the International Association of Classification Societies (IACS-QSCS) and the International Organization for Standardization (ISO) 9001-1994 standards. Phase 1 involved the following ten-step plan of action.

1. Senior management education and commitment
2. Quality awareness for all employees
3. Quality foundations—ISO 9001/IACS
4. Establishment of operating procedures/process instructions
5. Education and training of all employees
6. Establishment of a communication and recognition system
7. Installation of a corrective and preventive action system

8. Setting of goals
9. Establishment of metrics worldwide
10. Continued improvement and simplification of all ABS work processes

During 1992 this phase of the ABS Journey to Excellence the Quality System was installed and was completed in December of 1994 as evidenced by the receipt of both the IACS-QSCS and the ISO 9001-1994 global certificates.

ABS's ISO 9001 Certification was unique in several respects:

- The first Classification Society to achieve certification to the ISO 9001 (1994) Standard
- Single, global certificate for 95 offices in over 60 countries on six continents
- Certification includes all ABS support functions—Information Management Systems, Human Resources, Finance and Administrative functions, as well as all Technical and Operational functions
- One hundred percent (100%) of the ABS offices worldwide are assessed every three years on a continuous basis

In addition:

- All ABS affiliates also attained Single Certificate ISO 9001 (1994) certification for their worldwide operations

Certification to this worldwide standard documents that ABS has in place the policies, practices, and procedures throughout the total company to provide ship classification, statutory, and related services in compliance with the ISO Model. It is also indicative of the worldwide consistency, integrity, and quality of the ABS services offered.

Certification of the ABS Global Quality System has been undertaken by SGS International Certification Services, Inc. (SGS-ICS), under accreditation to RvA and RAB. The initial assessment took place over a three-month period during September through October 1994, totaling 89 assessment days and 37 offices worldwide.

Where does one go from here relative to an ISO Certified Quality System itself and outside of its part in the overall journey? ABS, in conjunction with its registrar, has instituted a new approach to the ISO surveillance audits, one of looking at only 12 of the major offices each year and relying on a "visitless" audit of the remaining 83 offices. This very cost-effective approach is based on the strength of the ABS internal audits, the effectiveness of the Corrective and Preventive Action System, and analysis of the five (5) surveillance audits by the registrar. In other words, the focus is on the true certification and verification of the ABS Quality System and not a duplication of the Quality System functions by the Registrar. In addition, a "continuous surveillance" process has been implemented which forgoes the need for a renewal audit every 3-year cycle.

The ISO 9000-based Quality System Implementation Process involved the following steps:

- Senior management commitment
- Establishing the organization's quality structure
- Selection of the appropriate ISO standard
- Perform an internal high level self-assessment
- Prepare a Quality System Implementation Plan
- Establish the organization's character:
    - Values and Principals
    - Code-of-Ethics
    - Mission Statement
    - Quality Policy
    - Organization's Quality Goals and Objectives
- Prepare the Quality System Manual
- Prepare the Common Quality System Procedures
    - Document Control
    - Storage and Retention of Controlled Documents
    - Corrective and Preventive Action
    - Internal Quality Audits
    - Operating Procedure Development
    - Work Instructions Development
    - Numbering and Indexing
    - Management Reviews
    - Nonconformance Reporting
    - Purchasing and Supplier Control
    - Contract Review
    - Service Statusing
    - Statistical Techniques
    - Confidentiality
    - Subcontracted Personnel
    - Training and Development
- Define, list, and group the Primary Work Processes
- Determine the training and knowledge requirements for each work process

- Make writing assignments with a go-by and instructions for each procedure/work instruction
- Prepare a company-wide job title matrix
- Prepare a Position Description Manual
- Prepare an Organizational Chart Manual
- Prepare a Delegation of Authority Manual
- Provide training for all employees relative to the Quality System as defined
- Implement the Quality System
- Follow-up with frequent internal audits and management reviews

The lessons learned before, during and after the implementation, are many and varied, many of which are company and culture specific.

Key success ingredients:

- Senior Level Management unanimous commitment, which is continuously demonstrated
- Detailed and thorough planning (if you fail to plan, you plan to fail)
- The establishment of a Senior Management Quality Steering Committee who meet regularly and review the plan progress and steps, making adjustments as necessary
- Good communications with employees as to the progress, what is to come, etc.
- Employee involvement from the very beginning, during, and after implementation
- Fast response in removing barriers discovered during the implementation process, including those related to specific personnel and specific processes
- Management must "walk the talk" as they will be tested by employees who will follow more of what management does rather than what management says to do.
- Keep everything very simple. The tendency is to exceed the requirements rather than meet them and there is a cost for so doing that is negative in the implementation phase. Simply write down what is done, do what is written down and provide visible evidence that you have done it and then establish a means of continuous improvement, which involves all employees, customers, and suppliers.
- Quickly eliminate programs that don't work or have out lived their value.
- Keep the vision always in front of yourself and everyone else too.

Key Lesson Learned:

- Forced implementation generates a backlash reaction from employees.

- If there is a history of management programs that did not meet the advertisements, then employees may look on the effort as "just another program" that will go away if we just ignore it and/or if we go through the motions of compliance.
- Employees accept the quality system requirements as an add-on to what they are currently doing rather than integrating it into "just the way we do our work," thereby feeling it is just more non-value added work for them. Time is the cure for this.
- There will be some dissenters who will be an undercover counter influence to the implementation effort.
- There will be some dissenters who will be very vocal.
- There will be those who cannot handle the controls associated with the Quality System.
- Don't start the process unless management is ready to support it because there is no turning back once the critical employee mass is reached.
- Base decisions on data but keep in the forefront perception, which becomes one's reality.
- Metrics are important in that "what gets measured gets done" and "you can't manage what you don't measure."

# REFERENCES

Camp, Robert C. *Benchmarking: The Search for Industry Best Practices That Lead to Superior Performance.* Milwaukee, WI: Quality Press, 1989.

Crosby, Philip B. *Quality Is Free.* New York: McGraw Hill, 1979.

Eicher, L. D. *Quality Management in the 90s: The ISO Phenomena.* Quality Forum, Vol. 10, No. 2, 1992.

Gale, Bradley T., and Robert Chapman Wood, *Managing Customer Value: Creating Quality and Service That Customers Can See.* Free Press, 1994.

*Malcolm Baldrige National Quality Award. 1998 Criteria for Performance Excellence.*

Rudy, Keith L. *Management Innovations, An Interpretation of ISO 9000.* A Presentation on ISO 9000 at the Fourth Annual Spring Accounting Expo, Houston, TX, 1993.

*Total Quality, An Executive's Guide for the 1990s.* The Ernst and Young Quality Improvement Consulting Group, Dow Jones-Irwin/Apics Series in Production Management, 1990.

# ABOUT THE AUTHOR

**Raymond J. Murphy** is the Director of Quality for the American Bureau of Shipping. He is a seasoned continuous improvement process leader and practitioner with hands-on experience in planning/implementing management systems and processes in challenging environments; orchestrating/sustaining process improvement through the involvement of people; strategic planning; managing all phases of operations including Engineering, Research and Development, Manufacturing, Quality Assurance, Project Management, Material Control, Engineering Support, Document Control, and Technical Publications. He directed the establishment of Total Quality Improvement Processes in several international organizations/industries engaged in technical services/consulting; planning and analysis; and process and utility. He served in several global, technical organizations as engineer, manager, senior executive, and consultant. He is a skilled facilitator and communicator with the ability to identify and resolve complex problems using a wide range of tools and techniques. He is known for his reputation as a process improvement pioneer and leader who works effectively with all levels of people and "walks the talk." This combination of Mr. Murphy's background uniquely qualifies him in the subject of this book.

Mr. Murphy served as a Malcolm Baldrige National Quality Award Examiner for three years and has received the Instrument Society of America's Excellence in Documentation Award. He is married with three daughters and resides in Conroe, Texas.

# GOVERNMENT INSTITUTES MINI-CATALOG

| PC # | ENVIRONMENTAL TITLES | Pub Date | Price |
|---|---|---|---|
| 585 | Book of Lists for Regulated Hazardous Substances, 8th Edition | 1997 | $79 |
| 4088 | CFR Chemical Lists on CD ROM, 1997 Edition | 1997 | $125 |
| 4089 | Chemical Data for Workplace Sampling & Analysis, Single User | 1997 | $125 |
| 512 | Clean Water Handbook, 2nd Edition | 1996 | $89 |
| 581 | EH&S Auditing Made Easy | 1997 | $79 |
| 587 | E H & S CFR Training Requirements, 3rd Edition | 1997 | $89 |
| 4082 | EMMI-Envl Monitoring Methods Index for Windows-Network | 1997 | $537 |
| 4082 | EMMI-Envl Monitoring Methods Index for Windows-Single User | 1997 | $179 |
| 525 | Environmental Audits, 7th Edition | 1996 | $79 |
| 548 | Environmental Engineering and Science: An Introduction | 1997 | $79 |
| 578 | Environmental Guide to the Internet, 3rd Edition | 1997 | $59 |
| 560 | Environmental Law Handbook, 14th Edition | 1997 | $79 |
| 353 | Environmental Regulatory Glossary, 6th Edition | 1993 | $79 |
| 625 | Environmental Statutes, 1998 Edition | 1998 | $69 |
| 4098 | Environmental Statutes Book/Disk Package, 1998 Edition | 1997 | $208 |
| 4994 | Environmental Statutes on Disk for Windows-Network | 1997 | $405 |
| 4994 | Environmental Statutes on Disk for Windows-Single User | 1997 | $139 |
| 570 | Environmentalism at the Crossroads | 1995 | $39 |
| 536 | ESAs Made Easy | 1996 | $59 |
| 515 | Industrial Environmental Management: A Practical Approach | 1996 | $79 |
| 4078 | IRIS Database-Network | 1997 | $1,485 |
| 4078 | IRIS Database-Single User | 1997 | $495 |
| 510 | ISO 14000: Understanding Environmental Standards | 1996 | $69 |
| 551 | ISO 14001: An Executive Repoert | 1996 | $55 |
| 518 | Lead Regulation Handbook | 1996 | $79 |
| 478 | Principles of EH&S Management | 1995 | $69 |
| 554 | Property Rights: Understanding Government Takings | 1997 | $79 |
| 582 | Recycling & Waste Mgmt Guide to the Internet | 1997 | $49 |
| 603 | Superfund Manual, 6th Edition | 1997 | $115 |
| 566 | TSCA Handbook, 3rd Edition | 1997 | $95 |
| 534 | Wetland Mitigation: Mitigation Banking and Other Strategies | 1997 | $75 |

| PC # | SAFETY AND HEALTH TITLES | Pub Date | Price |
|---|---|---|---|
| 547 | Construction Safety Handbook | 1996 | $79 |
| 553 | Cumulative Trauma Disorders | 1997 | $59 |
| 559 | Forklift Safety | 1997 | $65 |
| 539 | Fundamentals of Occupational Safety & Health | 1996 | $49 |
| 535 | Making Sense of OSHA Compliance | 1997 | $59 |
| 563 | Managing Change for Safety and Health Professionals | 1997 | $59 |
| 589 | Managing Fatigue in Transportation, *ATA Conference* | 1997 | $75 |
| 4086 | OSHA Technical Manual, Electronic Edition | 1997 | $99 |
| 598 | Project Mgmt for E H & S Professionals | 1997 | $59 |
| 552 | Safety & Health in Agriculture, Forestry and Fisheries | 1997 | $125 |
| 613 | Safety & Health on the Internet, 2nd Edition | 1996 | $49 |
| 597 | Safety Is A People Business | 1997 | $49 |
| 463 | Safety Made Easy | 1995 | $49 |
| 590 | Your Company Safety and Health Manual | 1997 | $79 |

Electronic Product available on CD-ROM or Floppy Disk

**PLEASE CALL OUR CUSTOMER SERVICE DEPARTMENT AT (301) 921-2323 FOR A FREE PUBLICATIONS CATALOG.**

## Government Institutes

4 Research Place, Suite 200 • Rockville, MD 20850-3226
Tel. (301) 921-2323 • FAX (301) 921-0264
E mail: giinfo@govinst.com • Internet: http://www.govinst.com

# GOVERNMENT INSTITUTES ORDER FORM

4 Research Place, Suite 200 • Rockville, MD 20850-3226 • Tel (301) 921-2323 • Fax (301) 921-0264
Internet: *http://www.govinst.com* • E-mail: *giinfo@govinst.com*

## 3 EASY WAYS TO ORDER

**1. Phone:** **(301) 921-2323**
Have your credit card ready when you call.

**2. Fax:** **(301) 921-0264**
Fax this completed order form with your company purchase order or credit card information.

**3. Mail:** **Government Institutes**
4 Research Place, Suite 200
Rockville, MD 20850-3226
USA
Mail this completed order form with a check, company purchase order, or credit card information.

## PAYMENT OPTIONS

❏ **Check** (*payable to Government Institutes in US dollars*)

❏ **Purchase Order** (this order form must be attached to your company P.O. Note: All International orders must be pre-paid.)

❏ **Credit Card**  ❏ VISA   ❏ MasterCard   ❏ American Express

Exp. ___/___

Credit Card No. _____

Signature _____
Government Institutes' Federal I.D.# is 52-0994196

## CUSTOMER INFORMATION

**Ship To:** (Please attach your Purchase Order)

Name: _____

GI Account# (*7 digits on mailing label*): _____

Company/Institution: _____

Address: _____
(please supply street address for UPS shipping)

City: _____ State/Province: _____

Zip/Postal Code: _____ Country: _____

Tel: ( ) _____

Fax: ( ) _____

E-mail Address: _____

**Bill To:** (if different than ship to address)

Name: _____

Title/Position: _____

Company/Institution: _____

Address: _____
(please supply street address for UPS shipping)

City: _____ State/Province: _____

Zip/Postal Code: _____ Country: _____

Tel: ( ) _____

Fax: ( ) _____

E-mail Address: _____

| Qty. | Product Code | Title | Price |
|---|---|---|---|
|  |  |  |  |
|  |  |  |  |
|  |  |  |  |
|  |  |  |  |
|  |  |  |  |
|  |  |  |  |
|  |  |  |  |

Subtotal _____
MD Residents add 5% Sales Tax _____
Shipping and Handling (see box below) _____
**Total Payment Enclosed** _____

❏ **New Edition No Obligation Standing Order Program**
Please enroll me in this program for the products I have ordered. Government Institutes will notify me of new editions by sending me an invoice. I understand that there is no obligation to purchase the product. This invoice is simply my reminder that a new edition has been released.

### 15 DAY MONEY-BACK GUARANTEE
If you're not completely satisfied with any product, return it undamaged within 15 days for a full and immediate refund on the price of the product.

**Within U.S:**
1-4 products: $6/product
5 or more: $3/product

**Outside U.S:**
Add $15 for each item (Airmail)
Add $10 for each item (Surface)

**SOURCE CODE: BP01**

Government Institutes • 4 Research Place, Suite 200 • Rockville, MD 20850
Internet: http://www.govinst.com • E-mail: giinfo@govinst.com